T0281034

Lecture Notes in Computer Science   **14700**

Founding Editors

Gerhard Goos
Juris Hartmanis

The series Lecture Notes in Computer Science (LNCS), including its subseries Lecture Notes in Artificial Intelligence (LNAI) and Lecture Notes in Bioinformatics (LNBI), has established itself as a medium for the publication of new developments in computer science and information technology research, teaching, and education.

LNCS enjoys close cooperation with the computer science R & D community, the series counts many renowned academics among its volume editors and paper authors, and collaborates with prestigious societies. Its mission is to serve this international community by providing an invaluable service, mainly focused on the publication of conference and workshop proceedings and postproceedings. LNCS commenced publication in 1973.

Pei-Luen Patrick Rau
Editor

Cross-Cultural Design

16th International Conference, CCD 2024
Held as Part of the 26th HCI International Conference, HCII 2024
Washington, DC, USA, June 29 – July 4, 2024
Proceedings, Part II

 Springer

Editor
Pei-Luen Patrick Rau
Tsinghua University
Beijing, China

ISSN 0302-9743   ISSN 1611-3349 (electronic)
Lecture Notes in Computer Science
ISBN 978-3-031-60900-8   ISBN 978-3-031-60901-5 (eBook)
https://doi.org/10.1007/978-3-031-60901-5

This Springer imprint is published by the registered company Springer Nature Switzerland AG
The registered company address is: Gewerbestrasse 11, 6330 Cham, Switzerland

If disposing of this product, please recycle the paper.

Foreword

This year we celebrate 40 years since the establishment of the HCI International (HCII) Conference, which has been a hub for presenting groundbreaking research and novel ideas and collaboration for people from all over the world.

The HCII conference was founded in 1984 by Prof. Gavriel Salvendy (Purdue University, USA, Tsinghua University, P.R. China, and University of Central Florida, USA) and the first event of the series, "1st USA-Japan Conference on Human-Computer Interaction", was held in Honolulu, Hawaii, USA, 18–20 August. Since then, HCI International is held jointly with several Thematic Areas and Affiliated Conferences, with each one under the auspices of a distinguished international Program Board and under one management and one registration. Twenty-six HCI International Conferences have been organized so far (every two years until 2013, and annually thereafter).

Over the years, this conference has served as a platform for scholars, researchers, industry experts and students to exchange ideas, connect, and address challenges in the ever-evolving HCI field. Throughout these 40 years, the conference has evolved itself, adapting to new technologies and emerging trends, while staying committed to its core mission of advancing knowledge and driving change.

As we celebrate this milestone anniversary, we reflect on the contributions of its founding members and appreciate the commitment of its current and past Affiliated Conference Program Board Chairs and members. We are also thankful to all past conference attendees who have shaped this community into what it is today.

The 26th International Conference on Human-Computer Interaction, HCI International 2024 (HCII 2024), was held as a 'hybrid' event at the Washington Hilton Hotel, Washington, DC, USA, during 29 June – 4 July 2024. It incorporated the 21 thematic areas and affiliated conferences listed below.

A total of 5108 individuals from academia, research institutes, industry, and government agencies from 85 countries submitted contributions, and 1271 papers and 309 posters were included in the volumes of the proceedings that were published just before the start of the conference, these are listed below. The contributions thoroughly cover the entire field of human-computer interaction, addressing major advances in knowledge and effective use of computers in a variety of application areas. These papers provide academics, researchers, engineers, scientists, practitioners and students with state-of-the-art information on the most recent advances in HCI.

The HCI International (HCII) conference also offers the option of presenting 'Late Breaking Work', and this applies both for papers and posters, with corresponding volumes of proceedings that will be published after the conference. Full papers will be included in the 'HCII 2024 - Late Breaking Papers' volumes of the proceedings to be published in the Springer LNCS series, while 'Poster Extended Abstracts' will be included as short research papers in the 'HCII 2024 - Late Breaking Posters' volumes to be published in the Springer CCIS series.

I would like to thank the Program Board Chairs and the members of the Program Boards of all thematic areas and affiliated conferences for their contribution towards the high scientific quality and overall success of the HCI International 2024 conference. Their manifold support in terms of paper reviewing (single-blind review process, with a minimum of two reviews per submission), session organization and their willingness to act as goodwill ambassadors for the conference is most highly appreciated.

This conference would not have been possible without the continuous and unwavering support and advice of Gavriel Salvendy, founder, General Chair Emeritus, and Scientific Advisor. For his outstanding efforts, I would like to express my sincere appreciation to Abbas Moallem, Communications Chair and Editor of HCI International News.

July 2024   Constantine Stephanidis

HCI International 2024 Thematic Areas and Affiliated Conferences

- HCI: Human-Computer Interaction Thematic Area
- HIMI: Human Interface and the Management of Information Thematic Area
- EPCE: 21st International Conference on Engineering Psychology and Cognitive Ergonomics
- AC: 18th International Conference on Augmented Cognition
- UAHCI: 18th International Conference on Universal Access in Human-Computer Interaction
- CCD: 16th International Conference on Cross-Cultural Design
- SCSM: 16th International Conference on Social Computing and Social Media
- VAMR: 16th International Conference on Virtual, Augmented and Mixed Reality
- DHM: 15th International Conference on Digital Human Modeling & Applications in Health, Safety, Ergonomics & Risk Management
- DUXU: 13th International Conference on Design, User Experience and Usability
- C&C: 12th International Conference on Culture and Computing
- DAPI: 12th International Conference on Distributed, Ambient and Pervasive Interactions
- HCIBGO: 11th International Conference on HCI in Business, Government and Organizations
- LCT: 11th International Conference on Learning and Collaboration Technologies
- ITAP: 10th International Conference on Human Aspects of IT for the Aged Population
- AIS: 6th International Conference on Adaptive Instructional Systems
- HCI-CPT: 6th International Conference on HCI for Cybersecurity, Privacy and Trust
- HCI-Games: 6th International Conference on HCI in Games
- MobiTAS: 6th International Conference on HCI in Mobility, Transport and Automotive Systems
- AI-HCI: 5th International Conference on Artificial Intelligence in HCI
- MOBILE: 5th International Conference on Human-Centered Design, Operation and Evaluation of Mobile Communications

List of Conference Proceedings Volumes Appearing Before the Conference

1. LNCS 14684, Human-Computer Interaction: Part I, edited by Masaaki Kurosu and Ayako Hashizume
2. LNCS 14685, Human-Computer Interaction: Part II, edited by Masaaki Kurosu and Ayako Hashizume
3. LNCS 14686, Human-Computer Interaction: Part III, edited by Masaaki Kurosu and Ayako Hashizume
4. LNCS 14687, Human-Computer Interaction: Part IV, edited by Masaaki Kurosu and Ayako Hashizume
5. LNCS 14688, Human-Computer Interaction: Part V, edited by Masaaki Kurosu and Ayako Hashizume
6. LNCS 14689, Human Interface and the Management of Information: Part I, edited by Hirohiko Mori and Yumi Asahi
7. LNCS 14690, Human Interface and the Management of Information: Part II, edited by Hirohiko Mori and Yumi Asahi
8. LNCS 14691, Human Interface and the Management of Information: Part III, edited by Hirohiko Mori and Yumi Asahi
9. LNAI 14692, Engineering Psychology and Cognitive Ergonomics: Part I, edited by Don Harris and Wen-Chin Li
10. LNAI 14693, Engineering Psychology and Cognitive Ergonomics: Part II, edited by Don Harris and Wen-Chin Li
11. LNAI 14694, Augmented Cognition, Part I, edited by Dylan D. Schmorrow and Cali M. Fidopiastis
12. LNAI 14695, Augmented Cognition, Part II, edited by Dylan D. Schmorrow and Cali M. Fidopiastis
13. LNCS 14696, Universal Access in Human-Computer Interaction: Part I, edited by Margherita Antona and Constantine Stephanidis
14. LNCS 14697, Universal Access in Human-Computer Interaction: Part II, edited by Margherita Antona and Constantine Stephanidis
15. LNCS 14698, Universal Access in Human-Computer Interaction: Part III, edited by Margherita Antona and Constantine Stephanidis
16. LNCS 14699, Cross-Cultural Design: Part I, edited by Pei-Luen Patrick Rau
17. LNCS 14700, Cross-Cultural Design: Part II, edited by Pei-Luen Patrick Rau
18. LNCS 14701, Cross-Cultural Design: Part III, edited by Pei-Luen Patrick Rau
19. LNCS 14702, Cross-Cultural Design: Part IV, edited by Pei-Luen Patrick Rau
20. LNCS 14703, Social Computing and Social Media: Part I, edited by Adela Coman and Simona Vasilache
21. LNCS 14704, Social Computing and Social Media: Part II, edited by Adela Coman and Simona Vasilache
22. LNCS 14705, Social Computing and Social Media: Part III, edited by Adela Coman and Simona Vasilache

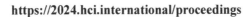

https://2024.hci.international/proceedings

Preface

The increasing internationalization and globalization of communication, business and industry is leading to a wide cultural diversification of individuals and groups of users who access information, services and products. If interactive systems are to be usable, useful and appealing to such a wide range of users, culture becomes an important HCI issue. Therefore, HCI practitioners and designers face the challenges of designing across different cultures, and need to elaborate and adopt design approaches which take into account cultural models, factors, expectations and preferences, and allow development of cross-cultural user experiences that accommodate global users.

The 16th Cross-Cultural Design (CCD) Conference, an affiliated conference of the HCI International Conference, encouraged the submission of papers from academics, researchers, industry and professionals, on a broad range of theoretical and applied issues related to Cross-Cultural Design and its applications.

A considerable number of papers were accepted to this year's CCD conference addressing diverse topics, which spanned a wide variety of domains. A notable theme addressed by several contributions was that of user experience and product design from a cross-cultural point of view, offering insights into design, user interaction, and evaluation across different domains and how cultural contexts shape user preferences, expectations, and behaviors. Furthermore, a considerable number of papers explore how individuals perceive, attend to, and process information within cultural contexts. Furthermore, the impact of culture across different application domains is addressed, examining technologies for communication, cultural heritage, and digital transformation and bringing together cutting-edge research, innovative practices, and insightful studies. Finally, the influence of culture on emerging technologies is a prominent theme, with contributions discussing extended reality, aviation and transportation, as well as artificial intelligence, addressing a multitude of aspects such as narrative design, interaction design, evaluation of user experience and performance, artificial empathy, and ethical aspects.

Four volumes of the HCII 2024 proceedings are dedicated to this year's edition of the CCD conference:

- Part I addresses topics related to Cross-Cultural Design and User Experience, and Cross-Cultural Product Design;
- Part II addresses topics related to Cross-Cultural Communication and Interaction, and Cultural Perception, Attention and Information Processing;
- Part III addresses topics related to Cross-Cultural Tangible and Intangible Heritage and Cross-Cultural Digital Transformation;
- Part IV addresses topics related to Cross-Cultural Extended Reality, Cross-Cultural Design in Aviation and Transportation, and Artificial Intelligence from a Cross-Cultural Perspective.

The papers in these volumes were accepted for publication after a minimum of two single-blind reviews from the members of the CCD Program Board or, in some cases, from members of the Program Boards of other affiliated conferences. I would like to thank all of them for their invaluable contribution, support and efforts.

July 2024   Pei-Luen Patrick Rau

16th International Conference on Cross-Cultural Design (CCD2024)

The full list with the Program Board Chairs and the members of the Program Boards of all thematic areas and affiliated conferences of HCII 2024 is available online at:

http://www.hci.international/board-members-2024.php

HCI International 2025 Conference

The 27th International Conference on Human-Computer Interaction, HCI International 2025, will be held jointly with the affiliated conferences at the Swedish Exhibition & Congress Centre and Gothia Towers Hotel, Gothenburg, Sweden, June 22–27, 2025. It will cover a broad spectrum of themes related to Human-Computer Interaction, including theoretical issues, methods, tools, processes, and case studies in HCI design, as well as novel interaction techniques, interfaces, and applications. The proceedings will be published by Springer. More information will become available on the conference website: https://2025.hci.international/.

General Chair
Prof. Constantine Stephanidis
University of Crete and ICS-FORTH
Heraklion, Crete, Greece
Email: general_chair@2025.hci.international

https://2025.hci.international/

Contents – Part II

Cultural Perception, Attention and Information Processing

Cross-Cultural Communication
and Interaction

Construction and Evaluation of Digital Experience Evaluation Index System in the Communication Industry

Xuefang Chai[(⊠)] and Qiaohui Jiang

Research Institute of China Telecom Corporation Ltd., Guangzhou 510630, China
chaixf@chinatelecom.cn

Abstract. Based on the key aspects of the whole journey between users and telecom operators, the article builds a digital experience evaluation system for telecom operators that covers the whole journey, all the touchpoints, and takes into account both user-side experience and enterprise-side operation practice. It analyzes the overall level of digital experience of users in the communication industry at this stage, the differences in population and geographical through quantitative assessment; explores the reasons for the low level of digital experience in the communication industry through qualitative mining, and puts forward suggestions for improving digital experience in phases. The results show that: the overall level of digital experience in China's communications industry is not high, and user satisfaction is relatively low, indicating that the current digital experience is far from meeting users' expectations; there are obvious differences in the importance of various indicators and the perception of digital experience among different generations and geographic regions; the level of digital experience implementation shows a regional differentiation feature of first tier cities > third/fourth tier cities > second tier cities.

Keywords: Digital experience · Experience evaluation · Experience management

1 Introduction

The advent of the digital economy has accelerated the digital transformation of all areas of society. National strategies such as "Made in China 2025" and "Digital China" have opened up a new space for Internet applications, actively promoting the digital transformation of communications carriers. The three major basic communications carriers have also invested heavily in 5G, computing power networks, and technological innovation to formulate transformation strategies.

At the level of communications operators, digital transformation is essentially the transformation and reengineering of the operation mechanism, breaking the fragmented operation system, promoting the integration of applications and data, and forming an operation mechanism for capacity sharing. At the level of ordinary users, users should be able to enjoy the dividends brought by the digital transformation of operators, and be able to use digital products and experience digitalized services. Therefore, the digital experience demand and perception evaluation of ordinary users is an important way to identify the deficiencies in the digital transformation process of operators and promote their continuous optimization.

Although there are many evaluation models of user experience or digital experience in the industry, there are fewer models that can be applied to the evaluation of digital experience of users of telecommunication operators; in particular, there is a lack of models that can reflect the overall perception from the perspective of user experience and the digital operation practice of operators. This paper focuses on both user-side and enterprise-side perspectives, and innovatively constructs a two-sided evaluation system for operators' digital user experience, so that the user-side experience indexes can be directed inward to the enterprise-side operation practice. This will help telecom operators to analyze the reasons at the enterprise operation level according to the evaluation results, so as to continuously improve and optimize the digital experience of the subscriber side.

2   Concept Definition and Research Foundations

2.1   Definition of Digital Experience Concept

Since the epidemic, the digital transformation of the service industry has brought great changes to the way the public handles business/services, and to a large extent has pulled up the user's experience perception and experience expectations of the service. So what exactly is digital experience? Ordinary users, the industry and operators, with different standpoints and perspectives, their understanding is not entirely consistent.

The Digital Experience Through the Eyes of Ordinary Users. User research found that the vast majority of users understand digitalization is relatively fragmented, staying in the relatively superficial and can be felt in some aspects. Focused on the following keywords: convenience, high speed and efficiency, intelligence, digitalization, informatization, technologization, online and so on. These keywords can be summarized into three categories: effect, mode and impression. The effect category is reflected in the improvement of experience, such as convenience, high speed and efficiency; the way category emphasizes such as digitalization, informatization, and online; and the impression category is such as intelligentization and technologization.

Industry's Perceptions of Digital Experience. Some of the industry's leading consulting/research organizations view digital experience in terms of the digital transformation of an organization. The Boston Consulting Group, for example, sees digital as the use of emerging technologies to facilitate a digital customer experience that delivers personalized service, emphasizes customer engagement, and hope to build long-term relationships with customers; and pursues business innovation on top of that. McKinsey sees digitalization as creating value in new areas of the business world, creating value in the processes that execute the customer experience vision, and building foundational capabilities to support the entire structure. According to Ernst & Young, digitalization is built, planned and implemented in five areas: business strategy, incubation and innovation, experience transformation, operations, and risk management.

What Companies Know About Digital Experiences. A typical example is the ROADS user digital experience features proposed by Huawei, which include five categories: Real-time, On-demand, All-online, DIY, and Social. Real-time refers to sufficient bandwidth and zero waiting; On-demand refers to the fact that users can handle all kinds of services they need as they wish; All online means that everything is always online, devices are always online, and business is always online; DIY refers to the fact that users defining their own services, applications, and network requirements; Socialization, as the name suggests, means that users will use social networks for sharing. Comprehensive user perspective, industry and enterprise three different roles on the basic understanding of digital experience, this paper defines digital experience from two aspects: the realization of the way, the experience effect. That is, the enterprise through the digital channel, with the help of digital technology means, in the interaction between the user and the enterprise, to bring the user more convenient and efficient, efficient, intelligent and personalized experience perception.

2.2   The Industry Research Base for Digital Experience Evaluation

From the viewpoint of practice in the industry, most of the current experience evaluation models in the industry are product-focused, and can be categorized into three types according to the scope of their evaluation: experience evaluation focusing on the use/operation of the product, experience evaluation based on the customer's cognition and use cycle, and overall evaluation of the product competitiveness in combination with the market and operation; each of which has a number of representative experience evaluation models (see Table 1 for details). The only digital experience model is the aforementioned Huawei ROADS Internet user experience standard, but its universal character makes it impossible to apply it wholesale to the digital experience evaluation of communication carriers. As a result, it can be said that a systematic digital experience evaluation model for the communications industry, starting from the overall operation of the enterprise and focusing on the customer, has not yet been formed.

In view of the above, it is necessary to build a set of assessment system that can reflect the overall digital experience perception of users and communication service characteristics, so as to indirectly reflect the level of operators' digital operation through users' subjective perception. Only in this way can the assessment system cover the key nodes of user-operator interactions and completely reflect the current status of operators' digital operations; for some relatively poor experience indicators, the reasons can also be analyzed and explored from the enterprise side; thus ultimately achieving the purpose of driving operators' digital transformation practices and promoting the improvement of users' digital experience through the assessment of digital experience.

Table 1. Industry representative experience evaluation models

	Model name	Assessment of indicators	Main features
Focus on experience evaluation of product use/operation	Ali: UES model	Ease of use, consistency, satisfaction, task efficiency, performance	Focus on evaluating the user's experience while using the product
	Kaufmann's mental model	User mind: pleasantness, ease of understanding, ease of use, task efficiency; User Attitude: Satisfaction, Fees, Recommendation, Loyalty	Measuring product experience in terms of both user mind and user attitude
	Model name	Assessment of indicators	Main features
Focus on experience evaluation of product use/operation	Google: HEART model	Pleasure, engagement, acceptance, retention, task completion	A user-centered evaluation system with metrics that point to what the product is trying to accomplish
Experience evaluation with a focus on customer perceptions and usage cycles	Baidu: Five Degree Model	Attractiveness, Completion, Satisfaction, Loyalty, Referrals	A product experience evaluation system that combines present and future, attitude and behavior based on user perception and user life cycle
Overall assessment of product competitiveness in relation to market and operations	China Mobile: "AND" index	Market categories: user size, user quality; Experience categories: functionality, interface, latency, power consumption; Operational categories: content, channels, marketing, tariffs, services; Word-of-mouth category: positive feedback, satisfaction, recommendations	Starting from specific products, product competitiveness is measured comprehensively from four aspects: market performance, product experience, enterprise operation, and user reputation
	Huawei ROADS model	Real-time, On-demand, All-online, DIY and Social	Internet user experience standards, focusing on the user's digital experience, and relatively complete

3   Research Design

3.1   Sample Selection and Data Sources

This paper adopts a combination of qualitative in-depth interviews and quantitative research to conduct the study; qualitative in-depth interviews to understand the subjective opinions of users and correct the assessment indicators, and quantitative research to understand the level of digital experience. The evaluation samples cover users of China Mobile, China Telecom, and China Unicom to reflect the overall digital experience perception of users in the communications industry. The total number of successful evaluation samples is 3858, including 39 qualitative samples and 3819 quantitative samples.

3.2   Basic Principles of Modeling

Throughout the User-Operator Journey and Its Key Links. The user's digital experience is not just an experience at a certain point or a certain moment, but a full journey experience from knowing the information, consultation, to the actual processing, after-sales maintenance and service. The evaluation system needs to be applied throughout the key aspects of the journey.

Covering All Channels and All Touch Points. Single-touchpoint, single-channel experience is only a part of user's experience perception; from the perspective of experience, $1 + 1$ is not necessarily greater than 2. The overall experience of all-channel, all-touchpoints and all-chain ultimately affects the user's experience evaluation. Different channels online and offline, artificial and intelligent contacts have different characteristics, and evaluation indexes should reflect their differences.

Two Sides of the Same Coin, Balancing User and Enterprise Sides. That is, user-side experience metrics should be able to point inward to enterprise-side operational practices. The indicator system should not only reflect the overall perception from the perspective of user experience, but also reflect the enterprise's digital operation practice. This is conducive to operators analyzing the causes of the enterprise's operational level based on the assessment results and making continuous improvements.

3.3   Model Building

Firstly, the whole journey of user-operator interaction is divided into three phases: understanding and consultation, service handling, daily use and after-sales service; the key scenarios in each phase are used to set up secondary indicators, which are subdivided into tertiary indicators as appropriate. Based on the digital features and attributes reflected by the secondary and tertiary indicators, they are then integrated into five primary dimensions according to the model building principles.

Tier 1 Indicators and What They Mean. T The first-level indicator system includes five dimensions, specifically: Personalized, Real-time, Available, Consistency, and Self-service. It is abbreviated as PRACS model (the same below) by taking its initials.

Personalized. Identify the user's identity, anticipate the user's needs, and recommend products or services relevant to the user's usage or browsing behavior; push relevant product/service information according to the user's preferred channel and time.

Real-Time. Users can quickly (or in the desired time) to get the service or product-related notification, feedback, response, etc., timely activation of services or products.

Available. Subscribers can conveniently obtain the content/products/services they need through various channels and touchpoints of the operator, including: channels available, information available, products available, services available, etc.

Consistency. Refers to cross-channel synergy and consistency, specifically including: product information consistency, preferential/policy consistency, service consistency, process consistency and so on.

Self-Service. Users do not need to go through manual counters to realize independent processing of services/products, independent experience, as well as obtaining product instruction guidelines, remote service support, and so on.

PRACS Model Three-Tier Indicator System. The PRACS model for digital experience assessment consists of a three-tier indicator system: five first-level dimensions, 14 s-level indicators, and 23 third-level indicators. Please refer to Table 2 for details.

3.4 Evaluation Methodology

Scoring Calculation Method. The indicators modeled in this paper are all positive indicators. For the above 23 level 3 indicators, the evaluation scores of "degree of realization", "importance" and "satisfaction" of each indicator are obtained by direct evaluation of users. The overall scores for the 14 level 2 indicators and 5 level 1 dimensions and their calculation process are as follows:

Step1. Based on the user direct evaluation of the three-level indicators, use the extreme difference standard method for percentage conversion to obtain the evaluation score of the experience perception of the three-level indicators.

Step2. The third-level indicators are aggregated to the second-level indicators, and the second-level indicators are aggregated to the first-level dimensions, both of which are processed by the averaging method, so as to obtain the evaluation scores of the second-level indicators and the first-level dimensions of the experience perception, respectively.

Step3. A weighted average method is adopted to weight the five indicators of the first level dimension to obtain the overall score of digital experience in the communications industry in terms of degree of realization, satisfaction, and importance.

Descriptive Statistical Tests. In order to test the accuracy and reliability of the evaluation statistical results, this paper tests the standard deviation and coefficient of variation of the final evaluation scores of the degree of realization, satisfaction and importance. The test results show that the evaluation statistical results of this paper are accurate and reliable. The specific results are shown in Table 3.

Table 2. PRACS model three-tier indicator system and its meaning

The first dimension	Secondary indicators	Tertiary indicators	Meaning of the indicator
Personalized	Personalization of information delivery	Preferred time period and frequency	Push information at user convenient times and frequency according to user habits
		Preferred channels	Push information with user-preferred channels, such as app alerts, WeChat official account, SMS, phone calls, etc
		Preferred way of presenting information	Presenting business promotional information in a user-friendly way (graphic, video, etc.)
	Personalization of business recommendation	Personalization of business recommendation	Recommendation of services based on subscriber's usage of packages, traffic, etc
Real-time	Real-time message alerts	bill reminders in real time	Sending reminders based on when users pay their bills
		Use reminders in real time	Send timely reminders based on subscriber package/traffic usage
		Contrac texpiration reminders in real time	Send timely renewal reminders based on the expiration of the user's contract
	Real time effectiveness of products	Real time effectiveness of products	When the user opens the service, the product can take effect in a timely manner and be used normally
	Real-time feedback on processing progress	Real-time feedback on processing progress	Real-time feedback on progress according to the handling of user services
The first dimension	Secondary indicators	Tertiary indicators	Meaning of the indicator
Available	Information availability	Information is available	Subscribers can obtain information about the services and products through commonly used channels

(continued)

Table 2. (*continued*)

The first dimension	Secondary indicators	Tertiary indicators	Meaning of the indicator
	Channel service availability	Human customer service is available	Artificial customer service can quickly access, accurately identify and solve all the user's problems, and provide consultation guidance for problems that cannot be solved
		Intelligent customer service is available	Online Intelligent Customer Service is responsive, accurately recognizing issues and transferring to human service or IVR (push-button menu service) when necessary
		Offline staffing services are available	Can easily contact nearby business hall personnel, area customer managers/installation and maintenance engineers, etc
Consistency	Information consistency	Information consistency	Consistency of product information and policy/offer information displayed across the operator's channels
	Process Consistency	Process Consistency	Operators are consistent in handling process sessions and documents used in each session across channels
	Consistency of all-touchpoint experience	Orders/work orders can be viewed	Orders/work orders in any of the operator's channels can be viewed in other channels
		Synchronized order/work order updates	Synchronized update of subscriber's order/work order process across all channels of operator
	One point handling	One point handling	No need to repeat previous communications or inquiries when switching between operator channels
	Limited disturbance	Limited disturbance	After any channel/personnel of the operator reaches the subscriber, no other channel/personnel will bother them anymore

(*continued*)

Table 2. (*continued*)

The first dimension	Secondary indicators	Tertiary indicators	Meaning of the indicator
Self-service	Self-service experience	Self-service experience	Subscribers can self-serve all services on the operator's various channels
	Self Service	Remote expert support	Operators provide remote business expert support for complex services such as Broadband/Smart Home
		video tutorial	Operators provide video tutorials on user self-service operations (including installation, trouble-shooting, repair, etc.)

Table 3. Descriptive statistics of the results of the composite score

	degree of realization	satisfaction	importance
average value	72.90	72.34	76.49
(statistics) standard deviation	11.94	12.29	11.32
coefficient of variation	0.16	0.17	0.15

4 Analysis of Evaluation Results

4.1 Summary of Overall Conclusions

Overall Situation Analysis of the First Level Dimensions. According to the PRACS assessment model of operators' digital experience, based on the aforementioned analytical methods for processing and analyzing the measurement data of indicators at all levels, the evaluation of the overall degree of realization of digital experience in the whole industry is obtained to be 73 points; the user's overall satisfaction with the current state of realization is 72 points, which is relatively low, indicating that the digital experience at the current stage is far from meeting the user's expectations.

Combined with the degree of realization, satisfaction, and importance, the real-time dimension is the most important to users, and operators have relatively the highest level of digital experience in this dimension, thus users are most satisfied with the real-time dimension. The two dimensions with high importance and low realization and satisfaction are self-service and consistency, with deviations of 7.5% and 6.4% for importance and satisfaction, respectively. See Table 4 for details of the ratings for each level of dimension.

Overall Situation Analysis of Secondary Indicators. The secondary indicators also show a low degree of realization and satisfaction of the indicators valued by users. The

Table 4. Degree of realization, importance, and satisfaction rating of the first level dimension of digital experience

	personalized	Real-time	available	consistency	self-service
Level of realization	73.98	75.72	72.5	72.63	71.26
significance	75.6	77.95	75.65	76.83	76.51
satisfaction	73.41	75.06	72.15	72.24	71.15

top three indicators most valued by users are "Real-time effectiveness of products, Limited disturbance, and Real-time feedback on processing progress"; With the exception of "real-time effectiveness of products", which has a high level of realization and satisfaction, "limited disturbance" has a low level both on realization and satisfaction. This shows that operators have maintained their traditional service advantages, but there is still much space for improvement in terms of new user experience needs in the new environment, such as self-service experience, quick response but keeping a suitable distance from the disturbance-free status. It is also because operators disturb users too often that users are not concerned about the indicators related to information push. See Fig. 1 for the evaluation of each secondary indicator.

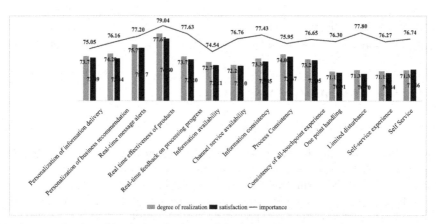

Fig. 1. Overall rating of level of realization, satisfaction and importance of secondary indicators

4.2 Comparative Analysis of Different Generations of Users

In terms of the specific age of generation division, we draw on the age division standards of Baby Boomers, Generation X, Millennials, Generation Z and Alpha Generation, which are commonly used in the industry; and we also refer to the characteristics of the birth years and values of different groups of people in the 60s, 70s, 80s and 90s in China. Before 1965, abbreviated as "retirement generation"; 1966–1975, the "Traditional Generation";

1976–1985, the "backbone Generation"; 1986–1995, the "Young Generation"; 1986–1995, the "Young Generation"; 1996–2005, referred to as the "New Generation"; 2006 and beyond, referred to as the "Student Generation".

The results of the data analysis show that there is a clear difference in the perception of the experience across generations. In terms of the level of realization, both in terms of primary dimensions and secondary indicators, the digital experience of carriers is already relatively high for the elderly of the retirement generation and the Young Generation of the 1986–1995 age group, while the new generation of the Post-95s, who have grown up in a networked environment, perceive the level of digital realization of carriers to be low. In terms of satisfaction, the younger generation of the post-1985 age group is tolerant, while the new generation of the post-1995 age group is picky. In terms of satisfaction ratings for each level one dimension, the younger generation is the highest, while the new generation group is the lowest. In terms of secondary indicators, the new generation is most dissatisfied with the three indicators of "one point handling, limited disturbance and self-service experience".

There are also significant differences in the importance evaluation of the primary dimension among different generations. With the post-85 young generation placing the highest importance on "real-time" and the lowest on "personalization", thus placing the highest importance on "real-time effectiveness of products" and " limited disturbance"; the traditional generation placing the highest importance on "personalization" and the lowest on "available"; and the student generation placing the highest importance on "self-service" over the other dimensions, The traditional generation values "personalization" and considers "available" to be the least important, while the student generation considers "self-service" to be more important than other dimensions, and therefore values "self-service experience, consistency of experience across all touchpoints" as the most important dimension. The traditional generation emphasizes "personalization" and considers "available" to be the least important.

4.3 Comparative Analysis of Users in Different Geographic Regions

Taking into account the political status, economic strength, city size, regional radiation power, and population size of the sample's geographic area, the geographic area is divided into three tiers: first-tier cities, second-tier cities, and third/fourth-tier cities. Overall, certain geographical differences are shown; users in Tier 1 cities value digital experience more and have higher actual experience levels than users in Tier 2 and Tier 3/4 cities; Tier 2 cities have the lowest level of satisfaction with digital experience.

First tier city users have a significantly higher awareness of the importance of digital experiences compared to other regions, while second tier cities and third/fourth tier cities have similar awareness of the importance. Specifically, users in Tier 1 cities particularly value "real-time", with an importance rating of 81.52, while "personalization" is the least important, with a rating of 77.42. On the contrary, users in Tier 3/4 cities are most interested in personalization-related indicators, while users in Tier 2 cities are more interested in channel service-related indicators, such as "channel service availability, consistency of all-touchpoint experience, and one point handling".

Looking at the degree of realization, users in Tier 1 cities rated the highest on most indicators, while users in Tier 2 cities rated the lowest, and users in Tier 3/4 cities rated in the middle (See Fig. 2 for details).

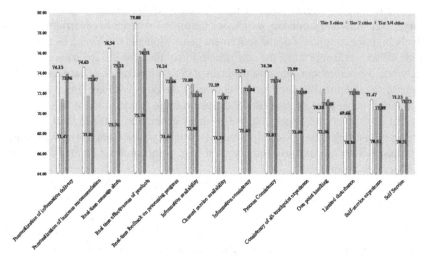

Fig. 2. Scores on the degree of realization of secondary indicators for users in different regions

The regional differences in satisfaction evaluation are also significant for the degree of achievement of various indicators. Users in Tier 1 cities are particularly dissatisfied with "Limited disturbance", with a score of 69.22, while they are more satisfied with "real-time effectiveness of products", with a score of 78.41. Users in Tier 2 cities are less satisfied with most of the indicators. Users in Tier 3/4 cities have relatively few indicators with low satisfaction ratings.

5   Analysis of Causes and Recommendations

Communication operators are in the critical climbing stage of digital transformation. Finding out the reasons from the perspective of users' digital experience, corresponding analysis of operators' current deficiencies in digital operation, and proposing corresponding enhancement suggestions will not only enable ordinary users to enjoy the benefits of digital transformation, but also help operators' digital transformation to proceed smoothly.

5.1   Analysis of the Reasons for the Current State of the Digital Experience

According to the PRACS model, subscribers do not rate the digital experience of operators highly, with the evaluation scores of the first level dimensions being relatively close and not reaching 80, mainly due to the existence of some prominent experience pain points in all five dimensions of the digital experience.

Personalization. At present, operators neither choose the appropriate push channels according to user preferences nor choose the right timing when contacting customers; instead, they bombard customers through various different channels such as SMS, outbound calls, business hall personnel, WeChat Enterprise Account, etc., and users feel disturbed; at the same time, they complain that the recommended products are not what they need. This shows that operators still need to be strengthened in identifying customer needs and making more accurate personalized recommendations.

Real-time. There are two outstanding issues: first, at present, operators basically do not have proactive response measures to provide real-time feedback on customers' online behavior; in particular, when the online process is interrupted for reasons such as unsuccessful submission of information, unlike large e-commerce platforms, there are personnel to follow up in a timely manner, which can easily lead to the loss of business opportunities. Secondly, the lack of timeliness of bill reminders is common, often sending reminders of this month's bill only after the customer has already paid the bill.

Available. Including Information accessibility and channel service accessibility; the outstanding problems in these two aspects are as follows: some of the more complex services (such as broadband), because it involves resources, professionalism and ability and other factors, can only be handled through offline channels, which is still a pain point for customers; the complexity of the business process for online handling and the problem of real-name authentication always being unsuccessful still exists; the professionalism and problem-solving ability of online customer service is insufficient. At the same time, the problem of insufficient keyword recognition accuracy of intelligent customer service is also more prominent.

Consistency. Lack of collaboration between different channels makes it impossible to achieve a completely consistent service experience. Currently, the main problems include: the interaction of customers in different channels cannot be shared between channels, resulting in the need for customers to repeat the explanation of the situation when switching to different channels; customer's orders/work orders in different channels cannot be cross-channel query; channel policies/discounts are inconsistent, resulting in the customer will be in more than one channel to consult the understanding of the channels, not only to increase the cost of the channel, but also the possibility of missing business opportunities.

Self-service. The self-service experience and remote support currently provided by operators is far from enough. On the one hand, for services like Smart Home, which involves the installation of terminals and equipment, there are basically no graphic or video guidelines for self-service installation, self-service checking and repairing of faults; on the other hand, the remote expert service support is not systematized and normalized; in addition, some services that require offline experience, the experience points are set up in fewer places and the conditions for experiencing in the halls of the existing experience points are limited.

5.2 Suggestions for Enhancement Digital Experience

The overall enhancement of digital experience is a systematic project, which is the external manifestation of the effectiveness of operators' digital transformation on the subscriber side. Thus, based on the research and analysis, combined with the long-term understanding of the operation of the communications industry, we put forward suggestions for operators' digital experience enhancement at both the near-term and long-term levels.

Focusing on "Areas of High Importance and Low Satisfaction" in the Near Future, and Making Breakthroughs to Fill the Shortcomings as Soon as Possible. Although the overall evaluation of operators' digital experience is not high, it is still possible to prioritize the improvement of digital experience through two-dimensional matrix analysis by combining users' importance and satisfaction ratings of each indicator.

Recently, the focus should be on experience indicators that fall into areas with high importance and low satisfaction, such as second-level indicators of consistency and self-service dimensions, and the channel service accessibility indicators, etc. Key breakthroughs should be made, prioritizing the improvement of their experience and filling in the gaps as soon as possible (Fig. 3).

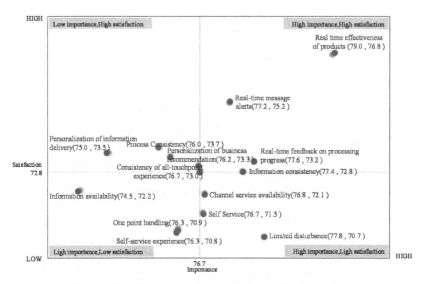

Fig. 3. Digital Experience Level 2 Indicator Matrix Analysis

Establishing a Professional Collaborative Digital Operation System with Shared Capabilities and Collaborative Capabilities in the Long Term. From the analysis of the previous reasons, a large part of the reason for the low level of digital experience perception lies in the fact that the existing organizational structure and its operating mechanism have not successfully achieved digital transformation. Operators are still business-centered chain-like vertical shaft operation system, which causes serious data fragmentation of various professional lines, data and channel capabilities are difficult to share, and ultimately transmitted to the end of the user, resulting in poor user digital experience.

Therefore, in order to fundamentally improve the digital experience of users, it is necessary in the long run to face and examine the current situation and problems that cause the poor digital experience of users from the perspective of the operation mechanism. This requires a customer-centered, professional and collaborative digital operation system that builds a ring of shared capabilities. That is to say, it is necessary to build a digital operation system with channel collaboration as the mechanism, capacity sharing as the basis, data value chain system as the guarantee, customer-centered, capacity sharing and all-channel synergy. Only in this way can we comprehensively and systematically solve the pain points of users' digital experience in different dimensions, and ultimately improve the digital experience level of the entire communications industry.

References

1. Chen, H.: Huawei Multinational Business Case Study, Tomorrow's Style (2016)
2. Editorial Board of Intelligent Buildings, Wireless Life Unlimited Excitement - 2015 Summit on the Construction and Operation of Wireless Networks in Venues and Buildings Held in Beijing (2015)
3. Chai, X.: How can operators enhance the digital experience?. China Telecom Industry (2022)
4. Shih, L.-W.: SPSS19.0 Statistical Analysis from Beginner to Master. Tsinghua University Press, Beijing (2013)
5. Yao, Q.: Customer Management. Enterprise Management Press, Hebei (2021)
6. Xing, S.: Data Empowerment. Electronic Industry Press, Beijing (2021)
7. Zhang, D., Liu, X.: Analysis and reflection on the development of digital transformation of channels. Commun. Enterp. Manage. (3) (2021)
8. Zhang, Z., Zhao, X.: Development trend and prospect of operators' digital intelligence. Commun. Enterp. Manage. (2) (2021)
9. Chen, H., Wu, Z.: An empirical test of the relationship between digitization and market competitiveness of state-owned enterprises. Stat. Decis. Making (23) (2022)
10. Zhao, H., Wang, W.: Construction and empirical measurement of digital business environment evaluation index system. Stat. Decis. Making (23) (2022)
11. Liu, L.: Learning from Huawei's Digital Transformation Experience (Next), Baidu Baike, 5 (2020)
12. Forrester: Orchestrate Customer Journeys To Drive Engagement, Improve Loyalty To Deliver Business Growth. FORRESTER.COM
13. Deloitte: Delivering Superior Customer Experience in China. deloitte.com/cn
14. Salesforce Research, Connected Subscriber Report, Industry Research: Communications and Media (2017)
15. Salesforce Research: State of the Connected Customer (2021)
16. Omdia: Smart Home Broadband Service Provider Tracker 2020: Analysis (2020)
17. WARC: The experience renaissance: How experience will drive growth for APAC organisations. warc.cn (2021)
18. WARC, Vodafone: Digitalization Journey of Vodafone's Online Sales. warc.cn (2021)

Understanding How Virtual 360-Degree Videos Generate Behavioral Intention to Visit Projected Destinations

Shih-Heng Chen[1,2,3] and Andrei O. J. Kwok[4(✉)] ⓘ

[1] Faculty of Tourism, University of Girona, Girona, Spain
[2] Faculty of Humanities, University of Southern Denmark, Odense, Denmark
[3] School of Economics and Business, University of Ljubljana, Ljubljana, Slovenia
[4] Department of Management, School of Business, Monash University Malaysia, Bandar Sunway, Selangor, Malaysia
andrei.kwok@monash.edu

Abstract. Existing virtual reality (VR) tourism research tends to emphasize VR headsets due to a higher level of immersion. However, there is a lack of discussion over the latent impact that virtual 360-degree videos as a basic form of virtual technology can exert as a more cost effective and accessible marketing instrument. This study explores the factors influencing consumers' behavioral intention to visit a destination after viewing a destination projected virtually on a 360-degree video. Virtual 360-degree video can offer omnidirectional clips to viewers. This non-headset technology has the potential to build a destination image and induce an intention to visit in its audience. This study surveys 201 participants to examine the influence of storytelling, authenticity, informativeness, telepresence, immersion, and joy on the behavioral intention to visit a projected destination, as an extension of the hedonic-motivation system adoption model (HMSAM). The findings offer insights into the associations among the different latent variables, and whether telepresence, immersion, and joy induce direct and positive effects on behavioral intention to travel. The findings contribute to the theoretical literature and have implications for tourism practitioners who are considering adopting virtual 360-degree videos as marketing instruments for a competitive advantage.

Keywords: 360-degree videos · virtual reality · virtual tourist experiences · hedonic-motivation system adoption model (HMSAM) · behavioral intentions · destination marketing

1 Introduction

The proliferation of virtual technologies has transformed the tourism industry, as tourists can easily explore a distant destination with a local guide while sitting at home. Such travel experiences can occur through a live-streamed walking tour hosted by Airbnb or Amazon, a prerecorded virtual 360-degree video shot by a destination marketing organization (DMO) [1], or an immersive and interactive excursion experienced through an

P.-L. P. Rau (Ed.): HCII 2024, LNCS 14700, pp. 18–36, 2024.
https://doi.org/10.1007/978-3-031-60901-5_2

Oculus, HTC VIVE or a Samsung Gear VR headset. To date, tourism practitioners from different subcategories have begun rolling out and testing their strategies. For example, DMOs from the United Kingdom, the United States, Thailand, and other countries have put significant efforts into creating promotional videos using omnidirectional cameras [2, 3]; airports [4] and hotel groups [5] have also adopted this approach as a marketing tool. As a result, destination marketers can provide an engaging experience that was not possible before the proliferation of virtual reality (VR) [6].

Virtual 360-degree videos are considered an application sitting on the boundary between traditional 2D displays and the latest VR headsets. Compared to VR headsets, the non-headset virtual 360-degree video is a significantly less expensive, less sophisticated and more accessible technology that can be used on a variety of devices (e.g., smartphones and computers) and that still offers an immersive user experience that can enhance the perceived image of a destination and thus prompt the intention to travel [7]. The use of such omnidirectional clips is likely a step toward the future purchase of more advanced VR headsets [8]. Both destination marketers and travelers first discovered the benefits of the narrative and cinematic potential of virtual 360-degree videos as an effective marketing tool when YouTube and Facebook initiated their services in 2015 [3].

Surprisingly, however, virtual 360-degree videos have not received the same level of attention as the more popular VR headsets. Within the virtual technology research field, comparatively more effort has been focused on understanding the theories and practices involving VR headsets [9]. Furthermore, despite rising interest in VR tourism among scholars, there remains a lack of academic discourse regarding the use of hedonic motivation systems in travel-related contexts [10]. The factors that drive individuals to adopt virtual 360-degree videos for hedonic purposes have been understudied, and the conceptual frameworks designed to develop deeper understanding have been underapplied to this virtual technology from an academic perspective. As such, the efficacy of virtual 360-degree videos in stimulating the behavioral intention to travel among viewers remains unclear. The research question is as follows: How can virtual 360-degree videos stimulate the behavioral intention to travel among viewers?

To address this gap, we aim to take a closer look at how this less prominent technology can contribute to tourism. Specifically, the research aims are to uncover the latent potential of virtual 360-degree videos for destination marketing, by examining the hedonic motivation system adoption model and its positive effects on travel intention in the context of omnidirectional film viewing. This study contributes to a new model that integrates theories across several fields. The dimensions of this model include the hedonic-motivation system adoption model (HMSAM), flow theory, and destination image digital storytelling.

2 Theoretical Background and Hypothesis Development

Hedonic motivations in information systems were initially studied in the context of online gaming and virtual worlds [11]. As virtual technologies have been increasingly adopted for various purposes in the travel sector, Huang et al. [12] claimed that the technology acceptance model (TAM) encompassing hedonic constructs applies to VR tourism. Several researchers have tried to better understand the behavioral intentions of VR users in the travel context using these models [10, 12–14]. Nevertheless, the meticulous examination of the TAM in various fields has identified hedonic-motivation systems as the primary issue to be addressed in information systems research [11]. Although VR-related applications are becoming more common, there are few user acceptance studies about VR practices [15]. Regarding travel, the research concerning consumer behavior in VR tourism, particularly those using HMSAM, is limited theoretically and requires more deliberation by future researchers [10, 16]. Considering that the literature about TAM and HMSAM primarily involves the latest immersive experiences supported by VR headsets, this study takes a different path. We select the comparatively less discussed virtual 360-degree videos as a research subject.

According to Huang et al. [14], destination marketers can exploit the power of computer-generated three-dimensional environments to reach potential travelers by providing virtual experiences that contain rich destination information. From a tourism practitioner's perspective, the use of virtual technologies to either offer innovative travel products or conduct promotional campaigns is highly relevant. The main reason for this lies in the essence of appliances such as video games, social media platforms, and VR. Unlike utilitarian-motivation system (UMS) users, hedonic system users are more concerned about the experience obtained through the system [11]. More importantly, such experiences can generate significant immersion and loyalty [17] and evoke strong emotions that can affect behavioral changes [18]. Additionally, empirical research has revealed that virtual technologies hold the potential to stimulate consumer purchase intentions [19–21] and the conceptual models tested were found to be pertinent to virtual travel contexts [12, 22]. On the premise that virtual 360-degree videos can be regarded as part of the VR family through the adoption of a broader definition [2, 8, 23], this study combines the previous theories and findings of VR studies to propose a new model based on Kim and Hall's [10] HMSAM framework to specifically explore this revolutionary video format. This new model examines several variables/constructs, along with their associated hypotheses, which are presented and discussed in the following subsection.

2.1 Storytelling and Immersion

Storytelling in VR is defined as bringing the viewer into a recreated scenario as the narrative unfolds [24]. Watching a virtual 360-degree video is akin to watching a film but enables a more immersive cinematic experience; hence, the narrative can trigger user engagement and personal and emotional connection, engendering an immersive experience [25]. As Pressgrove & Bowman [26] argued, storytelling and narratives cannot be overlooked because they are decisive sources that facilitate the feeling of being in a (mediated) story. Although the VR headset itself might be capable of increasing the feeling of being in a (mediated) place, this does not necessarily predict the behavioral intentions of virtual experience providers. A similar perspective was also demonstrated by Bindman et al. [27], who found that engaging and compelling content and narrative techniques are more significant determinants than the platform used. Likewise, in terms of provoking prosocial attitudes and a willingness to help, Ma [28] found that the platform used in immersive virtual environments is not necessarily more effective than traditional media platforms. These findings further indicate that storytelling is key to mentally engaging users in constructed narratives and can result in specific intentions as designed by the content providers. With the rising trend of using virtual experiences to generate or strengthen particular behavioral intentions, it is pivotal for developers and content creators to consider how to incorporate effective storytelling in their productions. Thus, we propose the following hypothesis:

H_1: *The storytelling of virtual 360-degree videos directly and positively impacts immersion.*

2.2 Authenticity and Telepresence

The term "authenticity" can be seen as an objective (criteria-based evaluation) and constructive (subject to the viewer's interpretation) measure [36]. Tourists seek authentic travel experiences because they prefer tangible products and can consume destinations with all their senses [29]. Although virtual travel activities are not ideal substitutes for physical visits [29], recently developed virtual technologies can serve as a better medium for digital exploration and have more powerful simulation functions than conventional technologies. Scholars across different disciplines have identified the importance of authenticity that arises from its strong relationship with telepresence. For example, in a survey about a theme park, Waysdorf and Reijnders [30] demonstrated that visitors genuinely experience a sense of being there (telepresence) when the simulation of the thematic atmosphere is regarded as authentic. In addition, decent and authentic graphics in the virtual world, supported by well-planned spatial and emotional content, can enhance users' perceived telepresence [31]. Therefore, we hypothesize the following:

H_2: *The authenticity of virtual 360-degree videos directly and positively impacts telepresence.*

2.3 Authenticity and Immersion

Currently, frameworks meant to assess the role of authenticity in virtual technologies are still inadequate [32]. Nevertheless, some research findings regarding authenticity and immersion in other academic spheres might provide theoretical guidance. Immersion is defined as "the objective level of sensory fidelity a VR system provides" [33]. Waysdorf and Reijnders [30] found that authentic sensations such as tastes, smells, sounds, and motions are crucial elements of an immersive experience. In addition, a delicately structured simulation of specific environments can form a feeling of immersion [34]. In a study on the psychological process that is stimulated by immersive technologies, Pressgrove and Bowman [26] underlined that when viewers consider displays on the screen to be authentic stories, they find it easier to visualize the activities described, thus triggering an emotional response. This can be explained as a kind of visual experience. In addition, although computer-generated environments (at present) optimize the user's experience with decent optical and auditory effects, genuine and precise representations of real-world objects are likely to enhance a user's involvement in the virtual environment [35]. As a result, we hypothesize the following:

H_3: *The authenticity of virtual 360-degree videos directly and positively impacts immersion.*

2.4 Authenticity and Joy

Joy can be used to specify the perceived enjoyment derived from using a virtual 360-degree video as distinct from any other consequence in the performance arising from its use [11]. According to Huang et al. [14], the similarity of touristic destinations, landscapes, or cultural ambiance in virtual travel experiences positively correlates to users' perception of joyfulness. In a study on visitor experiences with theme parks, Waysdorf and Reijnders [30] showed that attractions that skillfully integrate relevant, authentic narration more easily engage visitors and result in higher levels of enjoyment. Therefore, we offer the following hypothesis:

H_4: *The authenticity of virtual 360-degree videos directly and positively impacts joy.*

2.5 Informativeness and Immersion

While the main foundation of this study is the HMSAM, which is a theoretical structure focused on understanding intrinsic motivations, the variable "informativeness" is included in this study's proposed model. Although the construct may seem utilitarian and thus out of place, informativeness is a crucial dimension of novel virtual technologies. According to Guttentag [36], providing supplemental product information facilitates VR's commercial success in marketing implementations. This makes informativeness inevitable because travelers can feel anxiety about unfamiliar destinations during the previsit phase [37]. For tourism marketers, informativeness is a principal issue. Drawing from the role of informativeness in emerging virtual technologies such as augmented reality (AR) wearables [38], we hypothesize the following:

H_5: *The informativeness of virtual 360-degree videos has a direct and positive impact on immersion.*

2.6 Telepresence and Behavioral Intention to Visit

Telepresence, which is the sense of being present in the simulated scene, has been identified as a crucial variable in virtual tourism studies. This sense of presence is one feature that differentiates virtual technologies from conventional communication media. Sukoco and Wu [39] referred to the condition as the sensation of being "transported" elsewhere by cutting-edge technology, while Steuer [40] expressed it as a feeling of being present in an environment through the use of a means of communication. Currently, this fascinating characteristic allows users to experience remote sites and enables effective marketing strategies. Fiore et al. [41] showed that telepresence directly affects the willingness to purchase in the online retailing world. Algharabat [19] shared a similar finding in the same context, but the impact was indirect in that study. In tourism, manipulating the sense of "being there" via web-mediated environments leads to a positive destination image [7]. Based on the above findings, we offer the following hypothesis:

H_6: *Telepresence generated from virtual 360-degree videos directly and positively impacts the behavioral intention to visit.*

2.7   Immersion and Behavioral Intention to Visit

The term "immersion" used in this study is often expressed as "flow state" in other studies e.g., [11, 42]. According to Novak et al. [42], regardless of the choice of words used to describe it, immersion refers to a condition that occurs when consumers are so intensely focused on a navigation experience that they become mentally disconnected from proximity to the physical world. Based on Csikszentmihalyi's [43] definition, this mental condition can also be understood as the state of complete involvement that people can feel when experiencing certain events. While there are divergent interpretations of the word, the concept has been treated as an indispensable part of hedonic-motivation system (HMS) discourses. Scholars in the virtual tourism field are already aware of the significance of the immersion/flow state. From a tourism promotion perspective, virtual devices are powerful marketing instruments because even though there are multiple types providing various levels of immersion, all can positively impact a traveler's motivation to visit [2]. Huang et al. [12] also concluded that the flow state could strongly influence VR users' behavioral intentions to travel. Thus, in conjunction with earlier research that showed a strong correlation between immersion and consumer intention, we hypothesize the following:

H_7: *Immersion generated from virtual 360-degree videos directly and positively impacts the behavioral intention to visit.*

2.8   Joy and Behavioral Intention to Visit

Joy, as defined earlier, plays a vital role in intrinsic motivation studies. Since the theoretical foundation of this study is based on HMSAM, joy is predefined as one of the three factors for evaluating the latent effects on the behavioral intention to visit. In the virtual technology sphere, existing research has confirmed the remarkable role of joy in enhancing specific motivations. For example, after evaluating the newly suggested HMSAM, Lowry et al. [11] found that joy is more effective than usefulness in enticing behavioral intention. Additionally, in the tourism context, joy is also a reflection of enjoyment and the main reason for the use of virtual products and platforms [14]. Disztinger et al. [13] showed that in the use of VR for travel planning, the intention to use such technology is significantly correlated with how much enjoyment the users experience in its use. In general, joy is often included in discussions about hedonic-motivation systems because hedonic-oriented systems need to be delightful [11]. Given that several scholars have categorized virtual leisure products as hedonic-motivation systems [10, 11, 44], we hypothesize the following:

H_8: *Joy generated from virtual 360-degree videos directly and positively impacts the behavioral intention to visit.*

In brief, we constructed the proposed research model by combining the revised Kim and Hall's [10] HMSAM model with the "three pillars of the virtual" as coined by Mütterlein [45]. Our model employs commonly adopted variables such as telepresence, immersion, and joy to characterize the virtual essence of the technology. The variable "behavioral intention," which is commonly studied in TAM, has been slightly modified to "behavioral intention to visit" to highlight the fact that this framework is suggested for examining a phenomenon in the tourism industry. In addition, we introduce variables such as storytelling, authenticity, and informativeness into the virtual reality tourism framework. Building on virtual 360-degree videos as a type of HMS, these three constructs are added because they have been found to have positive effects on other factors in the tourism literature. Storytelling is suggested because it has been identified as a decisive facilitator of a high degree of immersion [26]. Authenticity has been found to have positive effects on telepresence [30, 31], immersion [34, 35], and joy [14]. Finally, informativeness is proposed as part of the model, although it is mainly considered to be a construct in utilitarian motivation systems (UMSs). In the end, eight hypotheses that represent the latent correlations among seven variables are proposed for testing (refer to Fig. 1).

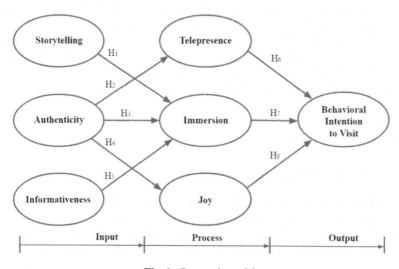

Fig. 1. Research model

3 Materials and Method

3.1 Research Method

A survey was conducted based on a nonprobability sampling of 201 participants recruited online from June 28 to August 28, 2021, during COVID-19 mobility restrictions, as this allowed researchers to enable much broader participation. The research was undertaken according to the ethical principles of the National and European Union regulations and the handling of individual information followed the European Union General Data Protection Regulation (GDPR) guidelines. The University of Girona, Spain provided the ethics clearance. The survey specifically targeted respondents who understand how virtual 360 videos work and the type of immersive experience that these films offer or who have even had prior experience with them through any kind of digital device. At the start of the survey, the definition of virtual 360-degree videos and some typical applications of this type of technology were explained to the respondents as follows:

"As technology progresses, compared with traditional 2D videos, these virtual 360-degree videos today allow us to enjoy more immersive views and navigate the virtual world through various digital devices (smartphones, tablets, and laptops, etc.). In the travel industry, we see many adoptions of virtual 360-degree videos, such as 360-degree virtual city walking tours, the option to explore hotel rooms before booking them, virtual museum tours, and the use of drones equipped with 360-degree cameras to shoot promotion videos."

The participants were asked to answer all the survey questions by recalling their previous experiences watching virtual 360-degree videos. Nevertheless, to avoid misunderstandings about this type of technology, links to four YouTube videos were provided so that participants who were unclear about the technology could seek clarification to complete the survey. The sample virtual 360-degree videos presented the following travel destinations: Longshan Temple (Taiwan) (https://www.youtube.com/watch?v=9S1QKPf_vAo), Underwater National Park (the United States) (https://www.youtube.com/watch?v=v64KOxKVLVg), Paris (France) (https://www.youtube.com/watch?v=EkshFcLESPU), and Victoria Falls (Zimbabwe and Zambia) (https://www.youtube.com/watch?v=WsMjBMxpUTc). The above travel destinations were selected due to their domestic and international popularity and their relatability to target participants. The method of sampling videos is similar to Jung and Hwang's [46] study. These four different types of destinations were presented to appeal to different individual preferences. Participants were allowed to freely use any digital device (smartphones, tablets, or laptops, etc.) to complete the survey through simulated practical reality. As a precaution, since the method of interacting with the videos, i.e., navigation, depended significantly on which device was used, instructions were provided to assist participants while navigating through the sample videos: "To see the views of different directions, you only have to move around your device (if you are watching on a smartphone or tablet, open the YouTube App); just click the arrow keys on the screen or hit the 'W', 'S', 'A' and 'D' keys on your keyboard (if you are watching on a laptop or desktop computer)." This ensured that participants checking the samples would know how to interact with and experience the virtual 360-degree videos and could focus on their related past experiences.

Table 1 shows the measurement instrument used (construct, items and cronbach's alpha).

3.2 Descriptive Statistics

During the study, 201 valid surveys were collected from respondents in 25 countries in Asia, Europe, the Americas, and Africa. More than two-thirds of the respondents were female (69.7%). Most participants were aged between 18 and 30 (86.1%). The second-largest group of respondents was aged between 31 and 40 (11.4%). Respondents older than 40 represented less than 2.5% of the sample. Regarding educational background, 43% of the respondents had a postgraduate degree or higher, while nearly all of the remaining respondents (55%) had an undergraduate degree. Almost three-fourths of the respondents (73.6%) were from Taiwan. The remaining respondents were from 24 countries in Asia (e.g., Vietnam, Thailand, Myanmar), Europe (e.g., Spain, Slovenia, Denmark), the Americas (e.g., Canada, Mexico, Nicaragua), and Africa (Kenya).

Table 1. Measurement Instrument.

Construct	Items	Cronbach's alpha
Storytelling (adapted from Zhang et al. [31]	While watching the story presented in the virtual 360-degree videos, I NEVER forgot that I was watching a video introducing travel destinations	.70
	While watching the story presented in the virtual 360-degree videos, the story-generated world was more real or present for me compared to the "real world" around me	
	I believe that the virtual world constructed by the virtual 360-degree videos is able to generate emotions	
	The virtual world constructed by the virtual 360-degree videos made me feel emotions (anxiety, sadness, happiness, etc.)	
	I felt excited after watching the virtual 360-degree videos	
	I would not get bored while experiencing the virtual world constructed by the virtual 360-degree videos	
Authenticity (adapted from Zhang et al. [31]	I could feel the bodily sensations (wind, heat, cold, etc.) at the destination presented in the virtual 360-degree videos	.81
	The visual aspects of the environment (vision) in the virtual 360-degree videos engaged me	
	The auditory aspects of the environment (hearing) in the virtual 360-degree videos engaged me	
	What I experienced in the virtual world constructed by the virtual 360-degree videos was consistent with other travel experiences in the real world	
	My sense of objects moving through space in the virtual 360-degree videos was fascinating	

(*continued*)

Table 1. (*continued*)

Construct	Items	Cronbach's alpha
	My sense of moving around inside the virtual environment in the virtual 360-degree videos was fascinating	
Informativeness (adapted from Kim & Hall [10]	I gained knowledge from watching the virtual 360-degree videos	.84
	Watching the virtual 360-degree videos is useful to collect information	
	Watching the virtual 360-degree videos is beneficial	
Telepresence (adapted from Zhang et al. [31]	When I was watching the virtual 360-degree videos, I had the sense of "being at the travel destination."	.68
	When I was watching the virtual 360-degree videos, I felt like I was traveling at the presented travel destination, and I almost forgot about the world outside	
	I felt that I could have reached into the virtual world and grasped an object in the virtual 360-degree videos	
	I felt disoriented or confused in the virtual environment constructed by the virtual 360-degree videos	
Immersion (adapted from Kim & Hall [10]	When I was watching the virtual 360-degree videos, I felt totally captivated	.81
	When I was watching the virtual 360-degree videos, time seemed to pass very quickly	
	When I was watching the virtual 360-degree videos, I forgot all my concerns	
	Watching the virtual 360-degree videos often made me forget where I am	
Joy (adapted from Kim & Hall [10]	Watching the virtual 360-degree videos is enjoyable for me	.93

(*continued*)

Table 1. (*continued*)

Construct	Items	Cronbach's alpha
	Watching the virtual 360-degree videos is pleasurable for me	
	Watching the virtual 360-degree videos is fun for me	
	Watching the virtual 360-degree videos keeps me happy	
Behavioral Intention to Visit (adapted from Kim & Hall [10]	In the future, I will visit the travel destinations presented in the virtual 360-degree videos	.78

4   Results

Structural equation modeling (SEM) was performed using SPSS and AMOS (version 27). Some of the research results were unexpected. Before the final phase of data analysis, several tests, including Cronbach's alpha test (>.7) for internal consistency and a multicollinearity test (with inner VIF values > .25 and < 3) (Table 2), were conducted to ensure the reliability of the proposed model and construct set.

Table 2. Multicollinearity test for inner VIF value.

Hypothesis	Input Variable	Output Variable	Inner VIF Value
H_1	Storytelling	Immersion	2.18
H_2	Authenticity	Telepresence	2.63
H_3	Authenticity	Immersion	2.64
H_4	Authenticity	Joy	2.66
H_5	Informativeness	Immersion	1.34
H_6	Telepresence	Behavioral Intention to Visit	1.94
H_7	Immersion	Behavioral Intention to Visit	2.92
H_8	Joy	Behavioral Intention to Visit	2.35

Eventually, three constructs (two for storytelling and one for telepresence) were dropped from the model because they showed factor loadings that were below the minimum threshold. Twenty-seven items were retained for further analysis. In the end, the statistical computation demonstrated that the four dependent constructs (telepresence, immersion, joy, and behavioral intention to visit) showed large R-squared (R^2) values (.75, .85, .60, and .39, respectively), indicating that the model is reliable. Figure 2 shows the relationships among the variables. The results demonstrate significance in the relationships between authenticity and telepresence ($\gamma = .89, p < .001$), immersion ($\gamma = .89$,

$p < .001$) and joy ($\gamma = .89, p < .001$). In addition, positive associations were observed between storytelling and immersion ($\gamma = .18, p < .05$), telepresence and behavioral intention to visit ($\gamma = .52, p < .01$), and joy and behavioral intention to visit ($\gamma = .33, p < .01$). Contrary to initial expectations, however, informativeness had a negative direct effect on immersion ($\gamma = -.21, p < .001$). Surprisingly, the relationship between immersion and behavioral intention to visit was not significant ($\gamma = -.31, p = .0051$).

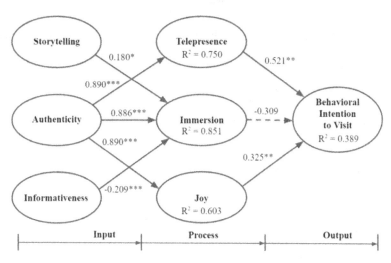

Fig. 2. SEM results of the proposed research model (*$P < 0.05$; **$p < 0.01$; ***$p < 0.001$)

The results of all the hypothesis tests are displayed in Table 3 (below). In total, six out of eight of the study hypotheses are supported. The only two exceptions are Hypotheses H5 and H7. The former hypothesis is rejected since the final correlation coefficient value between informativeness and immersion is negative. In contrast, the latter is rejected because the p value is greater than the statistical benchmark for confirmation of its validity.

Based on the explanatory amounts of variance in the model, this research model provides a solid framework for understanding user experiences with virtual 360-degree videos. Hypotheses H2, H3, and H4 are supported since they show a significant, strong, and positive association with authenticity. At the same time, Hypotheses H1, H6, and H8 are also supported, although the degree of the relationships between variables is not as clear. All of these findings, however, provide a reference for future scholars attempting to examine the implementation of virtual 360-degree videos in the tourism sector.

Table 3. Hypotheses test results.

Hypothesis	Statement	Result	Statistics
H_1	Storytelling of virtual 360-degree videos has a direct and positive impact on immersion	Supported	$\gamma = .18$; $p = .016$
H_2	Authenticity of virtual 360-degree videos has a direct and positive impact on telepresence	Supported	$\gamma = .89$; $p < .001$
H_3	Authenticity of virtual 360-degree videos has a direct and positive impact on immersion	Supported	$\gamma = .89$; $p < .001$
H_4	Authenticity of virtual 360-degree videos has a direct and positive impact on joy	Supported	$\gamma = .89$; $p < .001$
H_5	Informativeness of virtual 360-degree videos has a direct and positive impact on immersion	Not supported	$\gamma = -.22$; $p < .001$
H_6	Telepresence generated from virtual 360-degree videos has a direct and positive impact on behavioral intention to visit	Supported	$\gamma = .52$; $p = .001$
H_7	Immersion generated from virtual 360-degree videos has a direct and positive impact on behavioral intention to visit	Not supported	$\gamma = -.31$; $p = .051$
H_8	Joy generated from virtual 360-degree videos has a direct and positive impact on behavioral intention to visit	Supported	$\gamma = .32$; $p = .001$

5   Discussion

This section discusses the study's findings and offers theoretical and practical implications for both tourism scholars and tourism practitioners.

5.1   Theoretical Implications

This study contributes to integrating a revised framework of Kim and Hall's [10] HMSAM utilizing Mütterlein's [45] three pillars of VR. Hence, it can be seen as an early exploration of the relatively less studied technological medium from the HMSAM perspective. More importantly, this study calls for more attention to be given to the emerging genre of spherical videos, and several findings have generated invaluable insights.

First, the positive impact that storytelling can induce on immersion indicates that cutting-edge technology does not inherently guarantee a satisfactory customer experience. Our findings identified a positive but somewhat weaker relationship between storytelling and immersion ($p < 0.05$), supporting H1. However, this finding is still in line with our initial expectation based on studies that argued that engaging narratives are more important for a fully immersive experience than the type of advanced virtual device used [26, 28]. It is possible that presently, more effort has been put into constructing immersive 3D environments rather than developing enchanting stories [31]. Hence, in a similar way as in-game storytelling captivates video gamers [47], tourism researchers need to consider how narratives can fascinate viewers.

Next, authenticity exerts a significant influence on telepresence, immersion and joy both directly and positively (p < .001), supporting H2, H3 and H4, respectively. This evidence shows that authenticity is associated with the subjective and perceived destination image [48, 49], which is considered a significant attribute in the travel decision-making process [50, 51]. From the theoretical point of view, the strong and positive effect of authenticity on telepresence, immersion, and joy indicates that in virtual tourism, simply borrowing existing models, such as TAM, HMS, UMS, or HMSAM, from similar studies may not be a good practice. Since these models are not structured to evaluate human-computer interactions in a tourism context, latent variables that exist only in virtual tourism may be overlooked. Thus, we recommend that tourism scholars incorporate this construct in their models when assessing user perceptions in future virtual tourism studies.

In another contradiction to one of our hypotheses, H5, we find that informativeness negatively affects a respondent's degree of immersion. Informativeness demonstrated a negative (but significant) influence on perceived immersion, indicating that viewers did not perceive the informativeness of the videos as an element that promotes hedonic experience [44]. Rather, viewers might associate informativeness with utility since virtual technologies offer users more detailed information than conventional communication instruments [36]. It is possible that viewers do not expect and are not looking for practical information while watching virtual 360 videos. In other words, the viewers of virtual clips could be stimulated by intrinsic motivations rather than goal-oriented tasks [11]. We recommend further studies to better understand the role of informativeness in virtual technologies [38]. Future researchers aiming to incorporate this factor into their frameworks are encouraged to be aware of the fundamental differences between HMS and UMS. We also recommend a model that distinguishes between goal-oriented travelers in a pretravel phase and those who are casually browsing videos for leisure purposes.

Meanwhile, the moderate positive association between telepresence and behavioral intention to visit, as well as that between joy and behavioral intention to visit, aligns with previous findings. Both H6 and H8 are supported. Hence, researchers undertaking future VR-related studies should consider including these two factors in their research and examine whether their results are consistent with previous research.

Last and interestingly, no statistical significance is observed between immersion and behavioral intention to visit. Furthermore, a negative correlation is observed. A probable explanation for the aforementioned unexpected finding is that virtual 360-degree videos do offer a quality of experience that is inferior to more technically advanced VR headsets, so survey participants did not think the provided sample clips were engaging enough. Such debate can also be found in the discussions among consumers and relevant professionals, where some people claim that these spherical clips are not sufficiently exquisite to be considered real VR [8]. Nevertheless, the fact that H7 is not supported in this research implies that the virtual 360 videos may not be immersive enough. Future studies from other scholars will be needed to further verify the latent impact that immersion exerts on the intention to travel. Thus, this finding has brought up two questions for the seemingly unchallengeable assumptions regarding immersion: Should immersion be the incontrovertible priority in virtual experience design? Moreover, from a tourism marketing perspective, does immersion necessarily motivate travelers to visit?

5.2 Practical Implications

Drawing from the discussion on theoretical implications, we further expound on the findings of this empirical research to provide practical suggestions for destination marketers and manufacturers of virtual technologies and devices. The findings of this research on the variable "authenticity" show that travelers look forward to authentic experiences. However, DMOs or travel agencies must consider that previous research has found a substantial difference between different market segments regarding what constitutes "authentic" destinations or activities [52]. Moreover, differences in how residents and foreign tourists interpret the same city can vary significantly. As a result, tourism marketers should conduct robust market research to understand and define their target audience and the elements of the attractions that they perceive to be authentic so that they can subsequently design specific and more effective marketing content.

Travel service providers should consider the findings around the element of storytelling. From the real-world success stories of Disneyland/Disneyworld and the Wizarding World of Harry Potter, we can see that enchanting storylines and storybook vibes are sufficient even without virtual technologies to engage visitors in a fantasy world. The Harry Potter theme park has achieved this by integrating the story background and physical separation [30]. Disney theme parks gained popularity by presenting vivid simulations of landscapes and incorporating brand images to win customer loyalty [53]. As such, tourism marketers who wish to achieve success must design and present narratives that fascinate their target audience. Otherwise, visitors who are not involved in the settings will be mere passive recipients of messages rather than passionate consumers of the presented storyline [47].

Finally, one of the most surprising results of this study is that immersion is not significantly related to behavioral intention to visit. This should be meaningful to tourism practitioners, as previous research on virtual technologies has commonly found that immersion positively affects behavioral intention. This difference in results can provide tourism practitioners with an opportunity to reflect on a question that was raised by Sussmann and Vanhegan [54] related to virtual tourism experiences: Is virtual tourism a replacement for, or a complement to, conventional travel activities? Although surrogate travel experiences can be eye-catching and exciting, can they substitute for the need to travel physically? This question may provide future opportunities for testing by both researchers and industry professionals.

6 Conclusion

This study aimed to answer two research questions associated with virtual 360-degree tourism videos: what are the associations among the different latent variables, and do telepresence, immersion, and joy induce direct and positive effects on behavioral intention to travel? While most of the existing virtual tourism literature has focused on the virtual experiences provided by technically advanced HMSs, this study proposes a new framework to address the less discussed technology of virtual 360-degree videos. By incorporating previous theories such as HMSAM, flow theory, the three pillars, and travel marketing concepts such as destination image and digital storytelling to evaluate user perceptions in a VR environment, this research finds that virtual 360-degree videos are relevant to destination marketing. A variety of real-world tourism industry practices were reviewed to ensure that this research is not just an academic matter for scholars but rather a work that offers insightful material and consideration for tourism practitioners.

This study's empirical findings provide meaningful implications for the tourism research field. While six of the eight hypotheses offered are aligned with the results of earlier research, two were not. Authenticity is an element with great potential to encourage travel intentions since it significantly influences telepresence, immersion, and joy. Although in classic tourism research, authenticity has been found to have a profound impact on building a perceived destination image or providing satisfaction, the inclusion of authenticity as a variable in VR tourism models is still uncommon. The finding of authenticity's influence over other variables may encourage authors of future tourism studies to incorporate authenticity in their models and initiate further discussion over its role in tourism industry practices.

Meanwhile, storytelling was found to positively impact immersion. Telepresence and joy were found to stimulate travel intention. This implies that tourism industry players who wish to adopt virtual 360-degree videos as a means of stimulating intention to travel must also include narration to appeal to their chosen market segment(s). Contrary to initial expectations, however, this study also found that informativeness deters immersion and that immersion is not necessarily a determinant of travel intention. Possible explanations for these results are that most viewers of the omnidirectional video clips presented perceived the videos as HMS rather than UMS. This may have resulted in respondents perceiving the rich information provided in the videos as irrelevant. Nevertheless, other respondents may have fulfilled their travel needs by engaging in these virtual experiences, leading to a reduced intention to travel. This study's results show that many research opportunities in the virtual tourism field are still waiting to be explored by adventurous scholars. We encourage scholars to use our framework to conduct further research.

In summary, this study sheds light on the use of virtual 360-degree videos in tourism. With increasing interest in using emerging virtual technologies in the dynamic field of tourism, destination marketing will evolve in the future. More novel products or practices using omnidirectional video experiences can be expected. Researchers will need to constantly update their theories and models to keep up with developments in cutting-edge virtual applications. This study provides information for more people, especially tourism practitioners, to discuss and better understand this novel technology and the competitive advantage it can offer them and their industries.

References

1. Alegro, T., Turnšek, M., Špindler, T., Petek, V.: Introducing Amazon explore: a digital giant's exploration of the virtual tourism experiences. J. Tourism Futures (2023)
2. Gibson, A., O'Rawe, M.: Virtual reality as a travel promotional tool: insights from a consumer travel fair. In: Jung, T., tom Dieck, M. (eds.) Augmented Reality and Virtual Reality. Progress in IS. Springer, Cham (2018). https://doi.org/10.1007/978-3-319-64027-3_7
3. Peltier, D.: Tourism boards still aren't sold on 360-degree destination videos. Skift. (2017). https://skift.com/2017/04/07/360-degree-destination-videos-are-still-experiments-for-many-tourism-boards/
4. Kelling, C., Väätäjä, H., Kauhanen, O.: Impact of device, context of use, and content on viewing experience of 360-degree tourism video. In: Proceedings of the 16th International Conference on Mobile and Ubiquitous Multimedia, pp. 211–222 (2017)
5. Ting, D.: Hilton launches a new video ad campaign to push direct bookings. Skift (2016). https://skift.com/2016/04/26/hilton-launches-a-new-video-ad-campaign-to-push-direct-bookings/
6. Kwok, A.O.J., Koh, S.G.M.: COVID-19 and extended reality (XR). Curr. Issues Tour. **24**(14), 1935–1940 (2021)
7. Hyun, M.Y., O'Keefe, R.M.: Virtual destination image: testing a telepresence model. J. Bus. Res. **65**(1), 29–35 (2012)
8. Stuart, H.: The debate about whether 360 video is VR- and why it doesn't matter. VR 360. (2016). https://www.virtualreality-news.net/news/2016/sep/14/debate-about-whether-360-video-vr-and-why-it-doesnt-matter/
9. Pestek, A., Sarvan, M.: Virtual reality and modern tourism. J. Tourism Futures **7**(2), 245–250 (2020)
10. Kim, M.J., Hall, C.M.: A hedonic motivation model in virtual reality tourism: comparing visitors and non-visitors. Int. J. Inf. Manage. **46**, 236–249 (2019)
11. Lowry, P.B., Gaskin, J.E., Twyman, N.W., Hammer, B., Roberts, T.L.: Taking "fun and games" seriously: proposing the hedonic-motivation system adoption model (HMSAM). J. Assoc. Inf. Syst. **14**(11), 617–671 (2013)
12. Huang, Y.C., Backman, S.J., Backman, K.F., Moore, D.: Exploring user acceptance of 3D virtual worlds in travel and tourism marketing. Tour. Manage. **36**, 490–501 (2013)
13. Disztinger, P., Schlögl, S., Groth, A.: Technology acceptance of virtual reality for travel planning. In: Schegg, R., Stangl, B. (eds.) Information and communication technologies in tourism 2017, pp. 255–268. Springer, Cham (2017). https://doi.org/10.1007/978-3-319-51168-9_19
14. Huang, Y.C., Backman, K.F., Backman, S.J., Chang, L.L.: Exploring the implications of virtual reality technology in tourism marketing: an integrated research framework. Int. J. Tour. Res. **18**(2), 116–128 (2016)
15. Sagnier, C., Loup-Escande, E., Lourdeaux, D., Thouvenin, I., Valléry, G.: User acceptance of virtual reality: an extended technology acceptance model. Int. J. Hum. Comput. Interact. **36**(11), 993–1007 (2020)
16. Yung, R., Khoo-Lattimore, C.: New realities: a systematic literature review on virtual reality and augmented reality in tourism research. Curr. Issues Tour. **22**(17), 2056–2081 (2019)
17. Jegers, K.: Pervasive game flow: understanding player enjoyment in pervasive gaming. Comp. Entertainment (CIE) **5**(1), 9-es (2007)
18. Csikszentmihalyi, M.: Flow: The Psychology of Optimal Experience. Harper and Row (1990)
19. Algharabat, R.S.: The role of telepresence and user engagement in co-creation value and purchase intention: online retail context. J. Internet Commer. **17**(1), 1–25 (2018)

20. Kang, H.J., Shin, J.H., Ponto, K.: How 3D virtual reality stores can shape consumer purchase decisions: the roles of informativeness and playfulness. J. Interact. Market. **49**, 70–85 (2020)
21. Li, H., Daugherty, T., Biocca, F.: Impact of 3-D advertising on product knowledge, brand attitude, and purchase intention: the mediating role of presence. J. Advert. **31**(3), 43–57 (2002)
22. Kim, M.J., Lee, C.K., Bonn, M.: Obtaining a better understanding about travel-related purchase intentions among senior users of mobile social network sites. Int. J. Inf. Manage. **37**(5), 484–494 (2017)
23. Wiltshier, P., Clarke, A.: Virtual cultural tourism: six pillars of VCT using co-creation, value exchange and exchange value. Tour. Hosp. Res. **17**(4), 372–383 (2017)
24. Shin, D.: Empathy and embodied experience in virtual environment: to what extent can virtual reality stimulate empathy and embodied experience? Comput. Human. Behav. **78**, 64–73 (2018)
25. Marasco, A.: Beyond virtual cultural tourism: history-living experiences with cinematic virtual reality. Tourism Heritage J. **2**, 1–16 (2020)
26. Pressgrove, G., Bowman, N.D.: From immersion to intention? Exploring advances in prosocial storytelling. J. Philanthropy Mark, **26**(2), e1689 (2021)
27. Bindman, S.W., Castaneda, L.M., Scanlon, M., Cechony, A.: Am I a bunny? The impact of high and low immersion platforms and viewers' perceptions of role on presence, narrative engagement, and empathy during an animated 360 video. In: Proceedings of the 2018 CHI Conference on Human Factors in Computing Systems, pp. 1–11 (2018)
28. Ma, Z.: Effects of immersive stories on prosocial attitudes and willingness to help: testing psychological mechanisms. Media Psychol. **23**(6), 865–890 (2020)
29. Mura, P., Tavakoli, R., Sharif, S.P.: 'Authentic but not too much': exploring perceptions of authenticity of virtual tourism. Inf, Technol. Tourism **17**(2), 145–159 (2017)
30. Waysdorf, A., Reijnders, S.: Immersion, authenticity and the theme park as social space: experiencing the wizarding world of Harry Potter. Int. J. Cult. Stud. **21**(2), 173–188 (2018)
31. Zhang, C., Perkis, A., Arndt, S.: Spatial immersion versus emotional immersion, which is more immersive? In: 2017 Ninth International Conference on Quality of Multimedia Experience (QoMEX), pp. 1–6. IEEE (2017)
32. Kronqvist, A., Jokinen, J., Rousi, R.: Evaluating the authenticity of virtual environments: comparison of three devices. Adv. Human Comp. Interact. **2016**, 1–14 (2016)
33. Slater, M.: A note on presence terminology. Presence Connect **3**(3), 1–5 (2003)
34. Darley, A.: Visual Digital Culture: Surface Play and Spectacle in New Media Genres. Routledge (2002)
35. Reiners, T., et al.: Authentic, immersive, and emotional experience in virtual learning environments: the fear of dying as an important learning experience in a simulation. Transformative, innovative and engaging. In: Proceedings of the 23rd Annual Teaching Learning Forum, 30–31 January 2014. The University of Western Australia, Perth (2014)
36. Guttentag, D.A.: Virtual reality: applications and implications for tourism. Tour. Manage. **31**(5), 637–651 (2010)
37. Lee, O., Oh, J.E.: The impact of virtual reality functions of a hotel website on travel anxiety. Cyberpsychol. Behav. **10**(4), 584–586 (2007)
38. Holdack, E., Lurie-Stoyanov, K., Fromme, H.F.: The role of perceived enjoyment and perceived informativeness in assessing the acceptance of AR wearables. J. Retail. Consum. Serv. **65**, 102259 (2020)
39. Sukoco, B.M., Wu, W.Y.: The effects of advergames on consumer telepresence and attitudes: a comparison of products with search and experience attributes. Expert Syst. Appl. **38**(6), 7396–7406 (2011)
40. Steuer, J.: Defining virtual reality: dimensions determining telepresence. J. Commun. **42**(4), 73–93 (1992)

41. Fiore, A.M., Kim, J., Lee, H.H.: Effect of image interactivity technology on consumer responses toward the online retailer. J. Interact. Market. **19**(3), 38–53 (2005)
42. Novak, T.P., Hoffman, D.L., Yung, Y.F.: Measuring the customer experience in online environments: a structural modeling approach. Market. Sci. **19**(1), 22–42 (2000)
43. Csikszentmihalyi, M.: Beyond Boredom and Anxiety. Jossey-Bass, San Francisco (1975)
44. van der Heijden, H.: User acceptance of hedonic information systems. MIS Q. **28**, 695–704 (2004)
45. Mütterlein, J.: The three pillars of virtual reality? Investigating the roles of immersion, presence, and interactivity. In: Proceedings of the 51st Hawaii International Conference on System Sciences, pp. 1407–1415 (2018)
46. Jung, H., Hwang, J.: The information characteristics of YouTube tourism content and their impacts on user satisfaction and intention to visit and share information: the moderating role of word-of-mouth information acceptance. Asia Pac. J. Tourism Res. **28**(2), 143–156 (2023)
47. Bormann, D., Greitemeyer, T.: Immersed in virtual worlds and minds: effects of in-game storytelling on immersion, need satisfaction, and affective theory of mind. Soc. Psychol. Personal. Sci. **6**(6), 646–652 (2015)
48. Jiang, Y., Ramkissoon, H., Mavondo, F.T., Feng, S.: Authenticity: the link between destination image and place attachment. J. Hosp. Market. Manage. **26**(2), 105–124 (2017)
49. Lu, L., Chi, C.G., Liu, Y.: Authenticity, involvement, and image: evaluating tourist experiences at historic districts. Tour. Manage. **50**, 85–96 (2015)
50. Chen, C.F., Tsai, D.: How destination image and evaluative factors affect behavioral intentions? Tour. Manag. **28**(4), 1115–1122 (2007)
51. Echtner, C.M., Ritchie, J.B.: The meaning and measurement of destination image. J. Tourism Stud. **2**(2), 2–12 (1991)
52. Sedmak, G., Mihalič, T.: Authenticity in mature seaside resorts. Ann. Tour. Res. **35**(4), 1007–1031 (2008)
53. Mitrasinovic, M.: Total Landscape, Theme Parks, Public Space. Routledge (2016)
54. Sussmann, S., Vanhegan, H.: Virtual reality and the tourism product: Substitution or complement? In: Proceedings of the European conference on information systems, p. 117 (2000)

The Human-Computer Dynamic Structural Analysis of Interactive Installations

Yun-Ju Chen[1] and Tsuei-Ju Hsieh[2]([✉])

[1] National Taipei University of Business, 321, Section 1, Jinan Road, Taipei 100, Taiwan
[2] National Tsing Hua University, 101, Section 2, Kuangfu Road, Hsinchu 300, Taiwan
Taiwanhsiehtj@mx.nthu.edu.tw

Abstract. This study employed Don Ihde's Human-Technology Relations Theory as its methodological framework within the context of the Phenomenology of Technology. It also incorporated relevant concepts from Phenomenology and Hermeneutics Theory to establish the research context. The primary focus of this research was the exploration of creativity and discourse in the realm of new media art, with a particular emphasis on the role of perception and physical engagement. The thesis underscores the necessity for four distinct human-computer dynamic structures and provides an analysis of these structures in the context of interactive installations. The primary goal of this study, which also serves as its principal contribution, is to offer new media artists valuable insights into the design of interactive installations, encompassing interactive processes and the creative structures of dynamic systems.

Keywords: Interactive Installations · New Media Art · Dynamic Structures

1 Introduction

This study explores the "Human-Technology" relationship in new media interactive installations, focusing on the relationship between technology and human experience and culture and investigating a specific dynamic structure in the relationship between humans and technology, people and the world. It attempts to start from a perspective of technological phenomenology, takes new media art interactive installations as the primary analysis object, and explains its development context. In addition to analyzing and exploring the meaning of dynamic structure relationships derived from new media interactive installations, the study also examines the technology and perception linkages displayed in new media interactive installations. This study examines the development process and historical significance of the dynamic structure between humans and technology in new media art interactive installations. The study uses new media artworks as research texts. The method is based on Don Ihde's phenomenology of technology, emphasizing the dynamic structure relationship between humans and technology in new media art interactive installations, with a further analysis of relevant phenomenology and hermeneutic theories.

P.-L. P. Rau (Ed.): HCII 2024, LNCS 14700, pp. 37–46, 2024.
https://doi.org/10.1007/978-3-031-60901-5_3

Interactive installations are one of the forms of expression in New Media Art, which invites the audience to interact with the artwork interactively, changing the artwork's structure and the audience's physical sensory experience. "New Media Art" has had many different names since the 1970s. With the development of computer technology, art that was applied to emerging computer media was called Computer Art, later replaced by Multimedia Art with multiple sensory stimulations and Net Art with hypertext links (from the 1960s to the 90s). Nowadays, New Media Art and Digital Art are interchangeable concepts that have become a huge umbrella, encompassing all forms of emerging art creation [1]. Today, New Media Art deals with the invisible, transforming systems and interactivity, an art that emerges from multiple interactive processes in the electronic space. Roy Ascott [2] defines five characteristics of this type of new media art: (1) Connectivity: of the part to part, person to person, mind to mind; (2) Immersion: into the whole, and the dissolution thereby of subject and ground; (3) Interaction: as the very form of art, such that art as the behavior of forms has become art as a form of behavior; (4) Transformation: perpetual flux of image, surface, and identity; (5) Emergence: the perpetual coming into being of meaning, matter, and mind. These five characteristics of "connectivity," "immersion," "interaction," "transformation," and "emergence" will serve as the cornerstone for the research of the dynamic structure between humans and technology in interactive new media art installations.

In general, new media interactive works emphasize the collaboration between the viewer and data, structure, interface, systems, and new forms through technology. Therefore, establishing interactive works has become essential for developing new media art. This study aims to analyze the thinking and transformation in the creation of new media art through the relationship theory between "human-technology" and the characteristics of new media art creation and to view new media artworks through the perspectives of creators and researchers. The dynamic structure that expands under the "human-technology" relationship in interactive works will be analyzed and classified. The human-computer dynamic structure that interactive works possess will be summarized, which can more comprehensively discuss the perspectives of creators and researchers. In exploring the issues of "perception" and "body activity," this study provides new media art creators with a technological phenomenology perspective to conceptualize the dynamic structure system and creative path in interactive works.

2   Human-Technology Relationship

The main focus of the "human-technology" relationship theory is on how people form relationships with technology through their bodily experiences or by using technology to interact with the environment. Four characteristics are analyzed and deduced from the mutual experiences between people and technological products, instruments, and other forms of technology. This perspective, which analyzes the relationship between human perceptual and bodily activities and technology, is similar to that of new media art, which uses various new media and technologies as means of creating interactive environments and devices that invite participation. The artworks are changed by the participants' bodily actions and behaviors, and the relationship between the artworks and the participants evolves accordingly. In the late 21st century, new media art has become a field that aims to integrate technology and art, with both forms and media being essential components of the integration. Therefore, this study will delve deeper into the four relationships in the "human-technology" relationship phenomenology, analyzing how people from different perceptual experiences through technology intermediation and how different technologies have different impacts on perceptual and bodily experiences, using new media art as an example.

2.1 Embodiment Relations

Don Idhe described the "Embodiment relations" as "(I - Technology) → World" using the formula of intentionality formula. This relationship can be expressed as humans and technology merging to intend the world. Technology, in essence, transforms our perception and in this relationship, technology acts as a mediator between humanity and the world, expanding human perception and allowing people to experience the world through technology. People's experiences are changed by technology's in-between and people and technology merge into one entity. In the process of creating new media interactive installations, the participation of human beings becomes one of the crucial elements. By creating dynamic situational worlds through technological intermediaries, new media artists expand the perception of the participants, extending their senses. Participants experience the dynamic situational world through the interactive installations. Through technological intermediation, "human (participants) and technology products (new media interactive installations) can co-shape or co-constitute the subjective and objective world in any situation [3]. "We take the technologies into our experience in a particular way by way of perceiving through such technologies and through the reflexive transformation of our perceptual and body senses [4]."

2.2 Hermeneutic Relations

Embodiment relations are the extension of the human body, while hermeneutic relations are the extension of human language. According to Don Ihde, "In hermeneutic relations, the technology is not so much experienced-through as experienced-with. The perceptual act directed toward the technology is a specialized interpretive act [5]". The hermeneutic relations can be expressed by the intentional formula: "I → (Technology - World)". This relationship can be understood as the world presented in the technological text that the person intends. Technology is an extension of human language - a form of "reading" that involves interpreting technology in a technical context and revealing some aspect of the world to the human interpreter. This kind of interpretation requires a special mode of behavior and perception that is similar to "reading," in which the text affects our bodies in a particular way. For example, on a very hot day, you use your smartphone to check the temperature outside and find out it's 39 degrees Celsius. You know it's boiling outside, but you don't feel the heat indoors. However, if you step outside, you will personally experience the scorching heat of 39 degrees. This kind of interpretation that allows you to know that it's hot outside has a sense of immediacy, and it points to the represented object in a special way. This means that the relationship between numbers/data and the things they represent is the key to visualizing numbers/data and fully analyzing and interpreting them. Computers can convert numbers into different visual graphics and colors, but you must establish the connection between numbers/data and the real world, that is, pointing to the things and world they represent through numbers/data.

2.3 Alterity Relations

The concept of Alterity Relations exists beyond the relations of embodiment and hermeneutics. Alterity Relations refer to the situation where technology becomes an independent entity in use, becoming an "other." Automated machinery is a representative of this relationship, characterized by its ability to make decisions and function autonomously. The intentional formula used by Don Ihde is expressed as "I → Technology - (- World)". This relationship can be expressed as the relationship between a person and technology, where technology becomes an "other" or "quasi-other" in relation to me, and the world becomes the context and background. These devices seem to operate automatically, and their appearance or behavior, full of vitality, resembles some kind of animal, creature, or human, making them fascinating and more closely resembling quasi-life. A very important manifestation of its alterity relation is the personification perspective, that is, artificial intelligence and machine learning. The focus of new media interactive installation creation is on the dynamic structure between the body and technology, making its creation directly or indirectly generate potential similar to the human body.

2.4 Background Relations

With Background Relations, "this phenomenological survey turns from attending to technologies in the foreground to those which remain in the background or become a kind of near-technological environment itself. [4]" In the background relation, Don Ihde did not provide a specific intentional formula, but it is commonly described by researchers as "I - (- Technology) → World". This relationship can be expressed as technology receding into the background of the human-world relationship, with humans intending the world within the context of technology as a backer The background relation is at work when technology is operating but not drawing attention to itself work. However, it is still shaping people and their surrounding environment. It also refers to the fact that we cannot live without technology in our daily lives. Technological products have become an essential part of our daily lives, and as technology products gradually recede into the background, the world returns to the foreground position of focus. Technology has infiltrated daily life and merged with the living environment and landscape. Public art installations featuring lighting have become part of the street view, seemingly receding to the background as an unobtrusive element of everyday experience and an integral part of the current environment and residents' emotions. Technology has become part of our bodily perception, and we bracketing bracket out our awareness of it. In other words, the existence of technology has become a background element of our living space or environment.

3   Human-Computer Dynamic Structure Relationship

In the interactive process of new media installation, interaction is not only a driving behavior of sense but also a necessary process and way to construct the entire dynamic system [6]. Technology is an essential structure in new media art creation. New media artists transform programming languages and data into interactive installations in the form of modules and structures. In other words, a human-computer dynamic structure is generated as an automatic algorithmic interactive system through programming languages, data, or new technologies. This interactive system itself is a human-computer dynamic structure, and by inviting viewers to engage in interactive behavior, they become the providers, co-constructors, or decision-makers of the meaning of the interactive system. In such an open, non-static, and non-fixed dynamic structure, constantly interacting and adding new elements, the dynamic structure becomes an important structure of the interactive installation work, and the viewer and the work co-shape or co-constitute the dynamic structure system. In other words, this human-computer dynamic structure focuses on how to co-shape the specific dynamic world (objectivity) and the specific participants (subjectivity) in the dynamic world created by the interactive device work [7]. This human-computer dynamic structure can be seen as a method and basic framework for experimental phenomena of the relationship between humans and technology. The dynamic world created by the interactive device work is a dynamic system jointly constructed by participants and the work itself. In this case, the structure relationship of "Viewer/Participant (Human) - Interactive Installation (Technology) - Dynamic System (World)" in interactive installation is studied (see Fig. 1), to provide an analysis of the four types of human-computer dynamic structure in interactive dynamic processes, which will be further explained below.

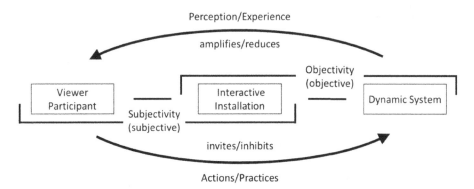

Fig. 1. "Human – Technology - World" Structure in Interactive Installation.

3.1   Dynamic Passive Structure

This type of interactive installation is a dynamic and continuous environment created by artists through program calculations, mechanical devices, or virtual technology simulations. The viewing experience is similar to watching a movie in that once a movie is completed, it can only be played according to the original narrative structure and cannot be changed in real time. However, with the rise of artificial intelligence, the fixed narrative structure can be broken, and the closed image can be transformed into an open, random, and variable narrative structure. Although artificial intelligence technology can convert the fixed image structure into a randomly generated one, viewers still do not have control over the content and elements of the work through interactive behavior. Viewers participate in the dynamic world the artist creates through observation, generating connections and interpretations of the work through each viewing. Therefore, in the "Dynamic Passive Structure" (see Fig. 2), new media artists create interactive installations that establish a situational atmosphere. The system of this work is dynamically flowing with the environment and time through program calculations, mechanical devices, or virtual technology simulations. In this passive structure, viewers do not have control and cannot drive or modify any content in the interactive installation. However, through the virtual dynamic world created by the artist, viewers' participation in their thoughts extends the "passive" construction of subtle emotional connections and imagination in the process of body perception, creating a unique sensory experience through viewing.

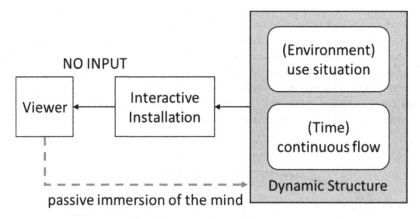

Fig. 2. Dynamic Passive Structure.

3.2 Dynamic Interactive Structure

The completion of an interactive installation artwork requires the viewer to participate in some form of action or behavior for the artwork concept to be operational and executed. The interactive process transforms the viewer into a participant who collaboratively creates the interactive experience through their engagement. This shift from passive observer to active participant involves the participant's interaction behavior being guided into the interactive installation artwork. This type of human-computer dynamic structure is called a "dynamic interactive structure," where the viewer must become a participant to enter the dynamic structure and engage in dialogue with the artwork. This structure refers to the participant's behavior linking with the computer/machine, with their mutual interaction being conveyed through programming and execution messages, transforming behavior into commands and descriptions, allowing for dynamic processes that can be controlled and automatically run. In essence, within the "dynamic interactive structure" (see Fig. 3), the artist creates a feedback loop system that responds in real time, establishing a relationship between the participant and the interactive installation artwork through communication within the dynamic system of the artwork. The participant's engagement behavior through physical activity, such as using hands, limbs, or objects, drives the artwork and changes its content, making the participant a part of the interactive installation artwork as a whole.

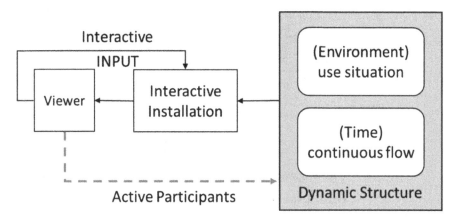

Fig. 3. Dynamic Interactive Structure.

3.3 Dynamic Interactive Crossing Structure

So far, interactive installations discussed are considered a dynamic system that undergoes further changes with the introduction of interaction. The viewer's role has evolved from being a mere spectator to an active participant. As the content of the work is rewritten with each iteration, the overall meaning of the piece is also constantly rewritten. Whether through programming or as contained within the work, the work gradually moves towards a mathematical description of images or shapes through algorithmic computation. "Through appropriate algorithmic manipulation, media becomes programmable. [8]" The result is a dynamic system that is more open, two-way, and nonlinear in structure, creating a continuous, dynamic, and open appearance of the work that generates real-time changes and unpredictable dynamic patterns and forms based on differences in participants, time points, and elements. This type of human-computer dynamic structure is called a "dynamic interactive crossing structure" (see Fig. 4). In this structure, artists not only create a system that can respond and provide feedback in real time but also emphasize programming coding, detection and recognition, procedures, and logical systems and focus on the interaction between participants' physical activities, message transmission, actions, responses, and feedback. They attach great importance to the interdependence and co-construction between the elements provided by the participants and the overall dynamic system. They use computer computation to modify, simulate, and reproduce participants' data, deriving an interactive structure with real-time changes in unpredictable and varied forms. The emphasis of this dynamic interactive crossing structure lies in the participation and interaction of participants, which is considered part of the work's element. This element's concept is an important part of the work, and if it is removed from the work, not only does it lose its completeness, but it also loses its spirit and meaning.

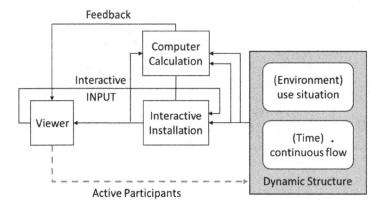

Fig. 4. Dynamic Interactive Crossing Structure.

3.4 Dynamic Intelligence Structure

With the development of artificial intelligence, robots have become more human-like, and computer technology provides a field for interaction between humans and artificial intelligence, involving the integration of symbiosis, thinking, imagination, and creativity. From an artistic perspective, this can transform social and cultural diversity and produce rich interpretations and definitions in science, art, and philosophy. In short, artificial intelligence responds to humans' desire for something beyond the deep psyche, that is, to achieve a non-material, spiritual, intelligent system beyond the body and mind and beyond the limitations of time and space. This intelligence system, achieved through artificial intelligence and learning systems, is called the "dynamic intelligence structure". This structure has a system that can transform behavior and cognitive abilities and covers the procedures and architecture of biological evolution, a form of the artificial intelligence system. This system structure has an open-mindedness based on the ideas of information, feedback, and learning, which influences the decisions and behaviors of subsequent machine development. In the "dynamic intelligence structure" (see Fig. 5), the artist constructs a system with machine learning, which provides a way to input elements into the work. This input method comes not only from images, videos, sounds, texts, and data on the Internet but also from elements that may come from the present participants. Through each audience participation, each computer calculation, each machine learning, and each feedback, a dynamic artwork form that is endlessly algorithmically generated is collectively formed.

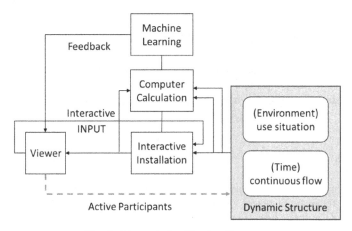

Fig. 5. Dynamic Intelligence Structure.

4 Conclusion

This study summarizes four human-computer dynamic structures of new media interactive installations: "Dynamic Passive Structure," "Dynamic Interactive Structure," "Dynamic Interactive Crossing Structure," and "Dynamic Intelligence Structure." These structures represent the modes of human-computer interaction and provide a foundation for creating unique dynamic structures in new media interactive installations.

The researchers argue that digital technology is a medium for new media artists to transform programming languages and data into interactive devices that are logical, modular, and structured. By translating information transmission, bodily activity, and memory into programming code, coding language becomes another form of perception and body activity within dynamic systems. The dynamic system aggregates people's perception and body activity and becomes an element of interactive installation works. Random and algorithmic logic processes invite participants to interact with the work and become providers, co-constructors, or decision-makers of the dynamic system meaning. In this open, non-static, and non-fixed dynamic structure, participants continuously interact and immerse themselves, adding new elements that become important dynamic structure content. The data content of people's perception and body activity is transformed and emerges as a dynamic structural element that participants and artworks co-create.

New media art interactive installation works combine images, devices, and space to create different perception pathways for participants, immersing them in dynamic situations. The work is transformed into a field of communication through participant and work interaction, creating a dynamic structural relationship. This study only examines the dynamic structural relationship of new media art interactive installation works that use computer technology, programming, mechanical devices, or virtual technology. With the development of digital technology, the media form and dynamic system of new media art interactive installations are becoming increasingly diverse and complex. However, due to the research focus and length limitations, not all interactive installations suit the "four dynamic structures" classification. This is a research limitation, and future research directions can explore more interactive procedures and dynamic system structure aspects of interactive installations. It is hoped that new media researchers and creative practitioners can further consider the deconstruction of the human-machine dynamic system of new media interactive installations, reflecting on the potential of technological dynamic aesthetics and expanding the contemporary meaning of new media interactive installation art through a comprehensive understanding of technology and its applications.

References

1. Paul, C.: Digital Art, 3rd edn. Thames & Hudson Ltd, London (2015)
2. Ascott, R.: Telematic Embrace: Visionary Theories of Art, Technology, and Consciousness. University of California Press, London (2003)
3. Rosenberger, R., Verbeek, P.P.: A field guide to postphenomenology. In: Postphenomenological Investigations: Essays on Human-Technology Relations. Lexington Books, USA (2015)
4. Ihde, D.: Technology and The Lifeworld: From Garden to Earth. Indiana University Press, USA (1990)
5. Ihde, D.: Instrumental Realism: The Interface between Philosophy of Science and Philosophy of Technology. Indiana University Press, Bloominton (1991)
6. Chen, Y.J.: The study of human-computer dynamic structure relationship in new media interactive installations. Artistica TNNUA NO. **24**, 105–127 (2022)
7. Chen, Y.J.: Structural analysis of interactive installation in new media art. Arts Rev. No. **42**, 1–39 (2022)
8. Manovich, L.: The Language of New Media. MIT Press, Cambridge (2001)

The Study of Cross-Cultural Differences in Online Visual Merchandising of Imagery Fluency and Pleasure Between Eastern and Western Consumers

Xiu-Qi Hung[(⊠)] [iD] and Tseng-Ping Chiu

National Cheng Kung University, No. 1, University Road, Tainan City 701, Taiwan
{p36114050,mattchiu}@gs.ncku.edu.tw

Abstract. In online stores, consumers rely on "sight" to evaluate products. Higher fluency of product pictorial presentation increases consumer preferences. The cultural context also affects customers' behavior, Eastern consumers tend to focus on the relationship between the subject and the context more than Western consumers. This study investigates how product display in different fluency influences cross-cultural consumers' cognition and attention and the Eye-tracker is applied to record participants' eye movement. The result demonstrates that while the product images present with semantically matched text and simpler context, the consumers can perceive information in a shorter time. Furthermore, compared to Western consumers, Eastern consumers pay more attention to product images and are stimulated by mismatched image-text contexts, which increase their imagination.

Keywords: Online Visual Merchandising · Fluency · Pleasure · Cultural Context · Eye-tracking

1 Introduction

The e-commercial market is growing. When shopping online, Consumers rely on "sight" to evaluate products (Kahn, 2017; Park et al., 2008). Through online visual merchandising (OVM) the online store can showcase product features vividly, highlighting unique advantages to arouse consumer interest and encourage purchase decisions (Kumar and Yinliang, 2013).

Improving the fluency of OVM can create a user-friendly online store. High fluency enhances consumer satisfaction and also provides a better shopping experience (Chrobot, 2014; Szymanski and Hise, 2000). Complexity is one of the factors that affect fluency. Higher complexity would decrease fluency. However, moderate complexity created the highest preference (Wu et al., 2016).

Cultural context affects consumers' preferences and visual perception. People have habitual cognitive ways and form perception bias (Norman, 1976). In the Eastern cultural context, people tend to think holistically and focus on the relationship between the

P.-L. P. Rau (Ed.): HCII 2024, LNCS 14700, pp. 47–61, 2024.
https://doi.org/10.1007/978-3-031-60901-5_4

subject and the context; Western cultures tend to analytical thinking style, focusing on the subject and ignoring the context (Masuda and Nisbett, 2001). For customers, stimuli that conform to the bias will produce higher fluency and create a hedonic experience (Kisielius and Sternthal, 1984).

An interesting and informative online store design can keep consumers engaged (Jakhar et al., 2020). The study aims to investigate the impact of fluency and complexity on consumers' perception of product pictorial presentation. Utilizes eye tracking as an objective tool to analyze consumers' eye movements and considers the variations in cognitive preferences between Eastern and Western cultural contexts. The results will suggest an effective online product visual display strategy for Eastern and Western consumers and offer recommendations for future e-commerce platform design.

2 Literature Review

2.1 Online Visual Merchandising

E-commerce Market. Non-store retailing is a marketing method in which retailers sell products and provide services to consumers without physical stores (Hirschman, 1980; Rosenberg and Hirschman, 1980). Among non-store retailing, electronic retailing has garnered considerable attention owing to its potential for growth (Doherty and Ellis-Chadwick, 2010). According to the U.S. Department of Commerce statistics, electronic retail sales in the United States reached a historical high of $1.03 trillion in 2022 (Conley, 2023). The sales of electronic retailing continue to rise and reach 14.7% in the second quarter of 2023 (Commerce, 2023). Forecasts predict that electronic retailing in the United States will reach $1.6 trillion by 2028. On a global scale, Amazon, based in the United States, is the largest e-commerce platform, receiving a significant number of visits, with a browsing number reaching 3.2 billion per month in 2022. The largest e-commerce market is in Asia, with sales reaching $1.7 trillion in 2022 (Gelder, 2023). The number of global electronic retailers is estimated to be between 12 to 24 million and continues to increase (Shepherd, 2023), offering consumers a wider range of shopping options. In online stores, customers can effortlessly navigate between different stores with just a click. Therefore, online stores must find ways to keep customers engaged and encourage them to revisit (Chen et al., 2010; Jakhar et al., 2020; Kahn, 2017).

Online Store Visual Communication. Due to the lack of physical experience, the appeal of an online store mostly depends on its visual communication. When shopping online, consumers rely on visual cues to evaluate products (Kahn, 2017; Park et al., 2008). The design and environment of an online store can evoke both positive and negative emotions in consumers, therefore influencing their attitudes, purchase intentions, and behavior within the store (Wu, 2014).

The vividness and interactivity of product displays are important design features that impact online visual marketing (Shih, 1998). Vividness refers to the richness of the information conveyed to users through mediums such as the environment. A vivid online store can capture users' attention and stimulate their imagination. Interactivity refers to the extent to which users can participate in modifying the product or environment (Steuer et al., 1995). For example, allowing consumers to change the product background, viewing angles or distances, and customizing product features. Interacting with virtual products helps generate ideas on how to use the product, and increases consumers' willingness to purchase.

Vividness and interactivity both impact consumers' online shopping experiences from the quality of information conveyed to the consumer and the way consumers interact with the product (Kumar and Yinliang, 2013). Previous research indicated that consumers prefer online stores that offer more engaging and interesting information (Jakhar et al., 2020). When websites provide detailed product descriptions and visually appealing elements, it fosters trust in the website and encourages consumers to revisit it (Hubert et al., 2018). Therefore, how e-retailers provide consumers with accurate information and an enjoyable online shopping experience is essential.

Fig. 1. Dimensions of online visual merchandising.

Online Visual Merchandising. Online visual merchandising (OVM) is a marketing technique that showcases the unique advantages of products by vividly displaying their features, thereby stimulating consumer interest and prompting purchase decisions (Kumar and Yinliang, 2013). It is widely used to create attractive shopping environments and retain consumers. OVM can create excellent product displays and visually appealing online store, enhancing consumers' perception of product quality and encouraging them to keep engaging, providing the hedonic value of shopping online (Friedrich et al., 2019; Jiang et al., 2016; Vieira et al., 2018).

Jakhar (2020) categorized the previous OVM literature and proposed four dimensions of online visual merchandising with 16 sub-items defined. The four dimensions include (see Fig. 1):

1. Pictorial Presentation: The display techniques used when showcasing individual products.
2. Product Information: Information beyond product images, including descriptions, sizes, styles, colors, and customer reviews, can help consumers make purchasing decisions.
3. Customization: Online retailers meet customers' personalized product demands, providing better interaction for virtual stores, and thereby enhancing consumers' emotional experiences.
4. Webstore Environment: The atmosphere and sensory characteristics within a store, which, though not directly related to product display or sales, can influence the shopping experience by altering consumers' perceptions and emotions.

Jakhar's study also blends fuzzy numbers and the Analytical Hierarchy Process to create a fuzzy evaluation model prioritizing the relative weights of visual merchandising dimensions in OVM and found that "Pictorial Presentation" is the most significant factor affecting OVM.

2.2 Imagery Fluency

Visual Perception and Bias. Visual perception constructs consumers' cognition and emotions, influencing their attitude, memory, and behavior toward websites (Krishna, 2012). Perception is defined as an active interpretive process that includes intention and attention, therefore generating expectations for the viewer (Bettman, 1979). This process may lead to the formation of biases and influence consumer choices (Norman, 1976; Wu et al., 2019). Elder and Krishna (2012) experimented to demonstrate the impact of perception bias on consumers. The study used mirrored product images and found that for right-handed individuals, a cup with the handle on the right side elicited smoother mental simulations and higher purchase intention. Previous research has also indicated that perceptual fluency has a positive effect on stimuli (Reber et al., 1998), making positive stimuli more positive and negative stimuli more negative (Kisielius and Sternthal, 1984).

Fluency. Processing fluency refers to the ease with which people process new information (Schwarz, 2004), and is highly related to perception. Fluency affects viewers' metacognitive experiences (Reber et al., 2004), and impacts various aspects including text comprehension, the connection between advertising content and brands, the presentation of artworks and the enjoyment of exhibitions, first impressions of products, and emotions and decision-making on online shopping websites.

Visual stimuli provide consumers with the imagination of the products (Alter and Oppenheimer, 2009). The more vivid the visual display of a product, the more fluently viewers can imagine the related products and services. High fluency also brings pleasurable experiences to customers and creates positive aesthetic evaluations (Reber et al., 2004).

Schwarz (2004) distinguished processing fluency into two dimensions, Perceptual Fluency and Conceptual Fluency (Fig. 2). Perceptual Fluency refers to the speed and accuracy of recognizing the physical characteristics of stimuli, which belongs to low-level information processing processes (Jacoby et al., 1989). The contrast between the subject and background in an image, the clarity of the stimuli, the duration of stimulus presentation, or the degree of prior exposure to stimuli can all affect perceptual fluency. Conceptual Fluency refers to the speed and accuracy of recognizing the meaning and semantics of stimuli, which belongs to high-level information processing processes (Whittlesea, 1993). The predictability of semantics, the consistency between context and stimuli, and the appropriateness of categorization can all affect conceptual fluency.

Both perceptual fluency and conceptual fluency have a positive effect on pleasure. If consumers find the information in product images easy to recognize and understand, they are more likely to have positive feelings toward the product.

Complexity and Fluency. Previous research has suggested a close relationship between fluency and complexity. According to Miceli (2014), visual complexity refers to the

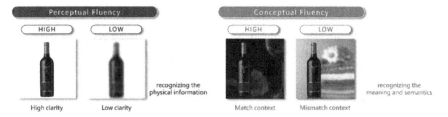

Fig. 2. Perceptual Fluency and Conceptual Fluency.

diversity of visual information and its impact on consumer shopping pleasure. Complexity is related to the speed of contrasting and identifying information. Visual complexity decreases both perceptual and conceptual fluency. When a product pictorial presentation contains more textual information, the visual complexity will increase. Therefore, consumers need more effort in identifying each piece of information and understanding its meaning.

Contextual Information and Fluency. The background information of a product display can impact its fluency. The context of the background image might interfere with the mental image. Previous research suggests that background information might enhance complexity and reduce fluency (Maier and Dost, 2018b; Reber et al., 2004; Wu et al., 2016). Moreover, compared to a white background, a contextual background has a lower contrast between the product and the environment, making the product less obvious. Contextual backgrounds carry semantic meaning (Scott and Vargas, 2007) and can enhance fluency and assist customers in understanding the stimulus. Maier and Dost, (2018b) discovered that with an appropriate contextual background, viewers can perceive the content of an image clearly and form a mental image of the product. Conversely, if the visual stimulus is challenging to perceive (e.g., low clarity) or goes against expectations (e.g., paired with an uncommon usage scenario), the customers may find it hard to generate mental imagery and affect preferences also purchase intentions to the product.

Text in the picture captures viewers' attention. The font type, size, and amount of text would impact text display. Pieters and Wedel (2004) utilized eye-tracking technology and found that text garnered the most additional attention compared to brands and images. When perceiving text, viewers require more focused attention and more fixations to comprehend the message, resulting in slower and more effort to perception.

Additionally, excessively complex images can lead to visual overload (Mazzoni et al., 2014), making it challenging for consumers to locate and process product information. Wu et al. (2016) discovered that sellers in Chinese online stores tend to include promotional activities, product features, and service information in product display images and found that the inclusion of text in the images increased visual complexity and decreased both perceptual and conceptual fluency.

2.3 Cross-Cultural Differences

Humans play a role in shaping culture, and in turn, culture has a profound impact on humans. Culture arises from the diverse characteristics found within human communities, such as place of residence, social class, gender, race, ethnicity, and so on. These cultural distinctions influence how ideas are shared and practiced among members of society, shaping individuals' experiences and behaviors, and also contributing to cross-cultural differences. Additionally, culture establishes common perspectives on meaning and defines important aspects of society and individual well-being. As a result, it significantly influences the development of personality traits, shapes personal beliefs and motivations, and affects perceptions, understanding, and evaluations of various things.

According to Hall (1976), cultures can be categorized as high-context and low-context based on the level of context involved. Eastern cultures, in general, are considered high context, as they excel in conveying implications in messages. On the other hand, Western cultures are typically seen as low context, as they prefer direct and explicit message expressions.

Holistic Thought Versus Analytic Thought. Masuda and Nisbett (2001) and his team have also demonstrated differences in cognition and perception between East Asians and Westerners. Western civilization originated in Greek citizens and tended to be analytic thought, showing a tendency to focus on main objects. On the other hand, traditional Chinese cultures such as Taoism and Confucianism emphasize the relationship between subject and environment, influencing East Asians' inclination towards holistic thinking.

The team conducted a visual cognition study (Fig. 3), inviting participants from Japan and the United States to view a picture depicting a water scene and asked them to recall and describe what they saw in the image. The results showed that Japanese participants were better at providing descriptions related to subject-background relationships. In the recall test, Japanese participants provided more "background information," such as water grass, frogs, and small fish in the background, while American participants tended to prioritize recalling the brightly colored big fish in the scene. The experiment also showed that Japanese individuals are highly sensitive to context and are willing to sacrifice emphasis on the subject to highlight background information. Furthermore, they were more accurate than Americans in identifying repeated subject-background combinations, demonstrating their high-context and holistic thinking, which emphasizes contextual relationships.

As to aesthetics, another experiment asked participants from East and West to take four portrait photographs of the model that were most aesthetically pleasing to them. The result shows that Americans mainly focused on capturing the upper body of the person, while Japanese participants included the surrounding scene and environmental information, showcasing the Eastern preference for a background-oriented style, whereas Westerners focused on the subject (Masuda et al., 2008).

Fig. 3. Cross-cultural differences in visual perception.

3 Hypotheses

"Sight" creates consumers' first impression of online stores (Kahn, 2017; Park et al., 2008), while high fluency generates positive consumer experiences (Maier and Dost, 2018a, 2018b; Reber et al., 2004; Wu et al., 2016), cultural backgrounds contribute to the differences in visual perception and preferences between Eastern and Western consumers (Masuda et al., 2008; Masuda and Nisbett, 2001). This study explores consumers' visual perception, aiming to understand the eye movements and reaction speeds of Eastern and Western consumers when viewing images with different conceptual and perceptual fluency. An eye tracker will be used as an objective physiological measurement tool. In this experiment, the complexity of the product image will be the factor to control the perceptual fluency and the concept fluency will be controlled by determining whether the textual semantics match the product content. The following hypotheses are proposed:

Hypothesis 1: Fluency.

- H1-1: When the product picture is presented with higher fluency, the customers will react faster.
- H1-2: When the product picture is presented with less complexity, the customers will react faster.

Hypothesis 2: Cultural Context and Fluency.

- H2-1: Due to the holistic thinking tendency, Eastern customers can better recognize the relationship between subject and environment compared to Western individuals.

Hypothesis 3: Cultural Context and Attention.

- H3-1: Due to the holistic thinking tendency, Eastern customers may tend to prioritize image information more than Western individuals.

Hypothesis 4: Pleasure and Fluency.

- H4-1: Fluency has an impact on pleasure. When fluency is high, the participants experience a greater sense of pleasure.

4 Experiment

In this study, participants will be shown a series of 48 product images displayed on a computer screen. Each image consists of a black-and-white outline of the product along with a noun object text. Participants will be required to answer two questions based on the image content, their response time and eye movement will be collected by an eye tracker to measure fluency.

The study is a within-subjects design, using 2 (perceptual fluency: simple/complex images) × 2 (conceptual fluency: image-text consistent/inconsistent) factor. Participants from both Eastern and Western cultures will be invited to examine how different cultural contexts affect attention and pleasure.

4.1 Method

Participants. In this experiment, a total of 24 participants from Eastern Asia, all from Taiwan, and 12 participants from Western countries such as Austria, the United States, and Germany, were included. All the participants with ages ranging from 20 to 30 years old. It was a requirement for all participants to have good eye health and not wear magnifying contact lenses or colored contact lenses, to ensure the eye tracker captured eye data accurately.

Materials. A total of 12 product types were gathered from the e-commerce platforms (Amazon, Shopee), each type having 4 distinct styles. The 48 product images were selected as the material of this study. By using Adobe Illustrator, an image editing software, each product was transformed into a black-and-white outline. This involved removing colors and any branding information to ensure color and brand preferences would not affect the experimental outcomes.

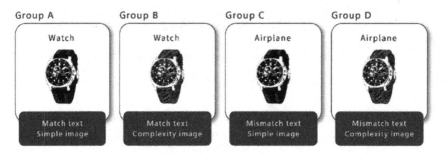

Fig. 4. Sample of Materials.

Each product was made into 4 kinds of materials and distributed into four timelines (see Fig. 4). Each participant will only see one timeline. The dependent variables for the material are designed as follows:

Perceptual Fluency: The study increases the complexity by adding brush textures to the product images, as the material of low perceptual fluency.

Conceptual Fluency: This study created a text list that includes the product names corresponding to the 12 sample product types (e.g. "headphone" for headphone images). Another list consists of 48 object words that are unrelated to the product samples (e.g., rhino, clown). These words are presented with the product image, while the image and word are semantically matched, the material is in high conceptual fluency, mismatched means low on the other hand.

The experiment was carried out with participants from both Eastern and Western cultures. Separate versions were created in Chinese and English. The control variables for the material design include:

1. All the backgrounds are blank.
2. The position and size of the product images and text are controlled.
3. The image resolution is 1920 × 1920 pixels.

Procedure. This experiment is conducted with the following steps.

Instruction: The researchers will provide a detailed explanation of the experimental procedure, including precautions and methods to ensure the confidentiality of personal data.

Eye Tracker Calibration. The participant will sit in front of the computer screen at 40–70 cm, maintaining a comfortable viewing position. This study utilizes the Tobii Pro Nano eye tracker device, which is installed at the bottom of the computer screen. Before the experiment, the eye tracker will be calibrated to minimize external interference and let the participant familiarize with the viewing position.

Visual Perception Experiment. A total of 48 images of materials will be presented randomly. The participant needs to answer as soon as possible whether the product image in each material is consistent with the accompanying text content. The "F" key on the keyboard should be pressed for "consistent" whereas the "J" key pressed for "inconsistent". Once an answer is provided, the subsequent question will automatically appear. The study will record the participant's responses and response times for further analysis of fluency.

Subjective Emotional Experiment. Following the presentation of each product material, the participant will be asked to answer whether the presentation method stimulated their imagination. The "F" key should be pressed for "Yes" and the "J" key press means "No". Upon responding, the next materials will play automatically. This question serves as a measure of the participant's emotional response.

Semi-structured Interview. Once all the materials have been presented, the participant will be presented with a list of all the materials and asked if there were any samples that they found confusing or difficult to answer. To deeper understand consumer perception and conception development.

4.2 Results and Discussion

Manipulation Check. According to the results of the visual perception experiment, the participants' responses will be encoded, and their answers will be determined if they are correct. To ensure the control of semantic matching is valid, data from the experiment will exclude materials with an accuracy below 50% to ensure participants identify the semantic of sample images and text correctly.

Fluency. In H1-1, this study hypothesized that a fluent presentation style can reduce participants' reaction time. The experimental results supported this hypothesis (F (3,330) = 5.92, p < 0.05). Compared to the inconsistent condition (M = 1.56, SD = 1.01), both Eastern and Western participants had shorter response times in the condition that the images and text content were consistent (M = 1.35, SD = 0.51) (Fig. 5).

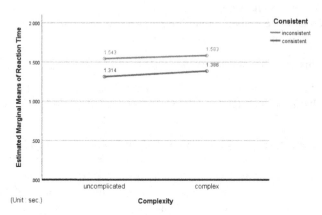

Fig. 5. Estimated Marginal Means of Reaction Time.

Regarding H1-2, this study supposes that the complexity of images also affects the participants' response time. However, the data did not show a significant result (F(3,330) = 0.41, p = 0.52 > 0.05). Therefore, this study further analyzed the participants' total fixation duration on the product images in the materials and found a significant effect (F(1,332) = 4.98, p < 0.05). This indicates that compared to simple images (M = 0.696, SD = 0.252), participants spend more time viewing complex images (M = 0.803, SD = 0.564). This result suggests that the complexity of product images affects the participants' perceptual fluency, as they take longer to recognize complex images. However, the overall reaction time was not significantly affected. It is speculated that increasing the difficulty of recognizing samples can strengthen the impact of complexity on visual perception.

Cultural Context and Fluency. In hypothesis 2, the study discusses the relationship between cultural context and fluency, it is speculated that due to people from Eastern cultures tend to think holistically, they might understand the relationship between the subject and the environment quickly compared to participants from Western cultures. The results of the experiment confirm this hypothesis, showing a significant impact of cultural context on response time (F(7,326) = 7.026, p < 0.05). Eastern participants (M = 1.357, SD = 0.846) made judgments faster compared to Western participants (M = 1.591, SD = 0.726).

Cultural Context and Visual Perception. H3 assumes that since Easterners are inclined to holistic thinking, they might pay more attention to image information compared to Westerners. The study divides the experimental material into two AOIs (Areas of Interest), namely product images (Image) and textual information (Text) (see Fig. 6), and analyzes the participants' total fixation duration in each AOIs.

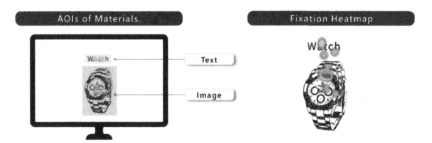

Fig. 6. Areas of Interest

The cultural context significantly affects the Total Fixation Duration on AOIs ($F(3,668) = 17.367$, $p < 0.05$), with an interaction effect between cultural background and AOI attributes ($F(3,668) = 20.04$, $p < 0.05$) (Fig. 7). Overall, images attract participants' attention more than text ($F(3,668) = 227.96$, $p < 0.05$), and there is no difference between Eastern and Western participants in the total fixation time on the text. However, cultural background has a significant impact on the attention to images while Eastern participants (M = 0.847, SD = 0.479) have a longer fixation time compared to Western participants (M = 0.617, SD = 0.338). The result indicates that image information can attract more attention from Eastern participants than Western individuals.

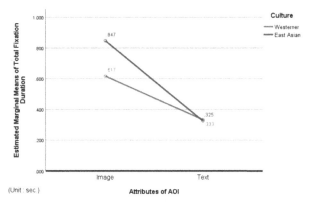

Fig. 7. Cross-cultural attention in each AOI.

Pleasure and Fluency. Imagination is one of pleasure. In this study, the researcher asked participants if they could generate imagination through the displays in the experimental samples to assess whether they could derive pleasure from the online product displays.

The results show a significant impact of culture on imagination ($F(7,326) = 45.471$, $p < 0.05$). Eastern individuals (M = 0.448, SD = 0.213) are more prone to generating imagination compared to Western individuals (M = 0.281, SD = 0.269) (Fig. 8). However, the influence of complexity on imagination is not significant ($F(7,326) = 0.011$, $p = 0.915 > 0.05$).

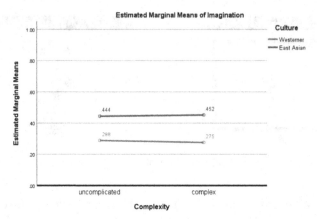

Fig. 8. Cross-cultural imagination of complexity.

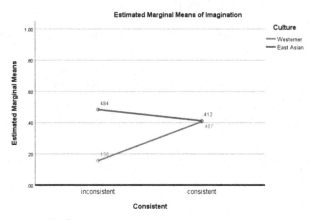

Fig. 9. Cross-cultural imagination of consistent.

In terms of consistency, culture shows an interactive effect ($F(7,326) = 42.638$, p < 0.05) (Fig. 9). When text and image semantics are consistent, there is no difference in imagination scores between Eastern and Western participants. However, when the pictures are paired with mismatched text, Eastern participants rate their imagination significantly higher than Western participants. Interestingly, for Eastern participants, the mismatched presentation of images and text is more likely to stimulate their imagination, while Western participants tend to give higher imagination scores with matched images and text.

5   General Discussion

The enhancement of fluency improves the pleasure of consumers in online stores. Therefore, this study investigates the influence of fluency on consumers' visual perception to comprehend how the online visual presentation of products can generate a positive user experience. It also explores the variations in behavior and preferences between Eastern and Western consumers to develop online product display techniques that cater to cross-cultural customers.

This study examines the consistency of image-text semantics in product display as a factor affecting conceptual fluency, and the complexity of images as a factor of perceptual fluency. The eye tracker is used as an objective tool to assess consumers' eye dynamics, and a questionnaire is used to understand consumers' subjective emotional experiences.

In terms of fluency, this study proves through experiments that the combination of text and images has an impact on the reaction time of participants. When the text and images are semantically consistent, participants can respond more quickly. Although the complexity of the images does not affect the response time of participants, the eye-tracking data reveals that participants spend more time viewing complex product images compared to simple ones. The result reveals that when the product is present in the online store, display with semantically matched texts and utilizing simpler images can let consumers identify the product more fluently.

As to culture, participants from the East tend to react faster than those from the West. This result may be related to Masuda's (2001) theory of culture, which suggests that individuals from the East are inclined towards holistic thinking and therefore excel in perceiving the relationship between the subject and its background.

Associate to attention, product images catch more attention than text in each situation. However, while taking culture into concern, Eastern participants spend significantly more time looking at images compared to Western participants, indicating that images are more attractive to Eastern individuals. Suggest that the design of product displays in online stores can enhance the use of images to make their store more attractive, especially for the Easterners.

The study also considers the pleasure of online shopping. By using imagination as an indicator of pleasure, the result shows significant differences in imagination between Easterners and Westerners. While products are presented in matched context text and images, the imagination scores of both East and West were almost the same. However, for Eastern consumers, mismatched text and images can stimulate their imagination, whereas Western consumers showed higher imagination when the text and images matched. This result does not align with the assumption that high fluency leads to high pleasure. Future research could explore other indicators of pleasure, such as excitement, amusement, and thrill, to understand whether the presentation of product images in online stores, along with slightly inconsistent text descriptions, can attract the interest and attention of Eastern consumers.

References

Alter, A.L., Oppenheimer, D.M.: Uniting the tribes of fluency to form a metacognitive nation. Pers. Soc. Psychol. Rev. **13**(3), 219–235 (2009)

Bettman, J.R.: An information processing theory of consumer choice (1979)

Chen, Y.-H., Hsu, I.C., Lin, C.-C.: Website attributes that increase consumer purchase intention: a conjoint analysis. J. Bus. Res. **63**(9), 1007–1014 (2010). https://doi.org/10.1016/j.jbusres.2009.01.023

Chrobot, N.: The role of processing fluency in online consumer behavior: evaluating fluency by tracking eye movements. Paper presented at the Proceedings of the Symposium on Eye Tracking Research and Applications, Safety Harbor, Florida (2014). https://doi.org/10.1145/2578153.2583037

Commerce, U. S. D. o.: Quarterly Retail E-Commerce Sales (2023). https://www.census.gov/retail/ecommerce.html

Conley, P.: US ecommerce in 2022 tops $1 trillion for first time (2023). https://www.digitalcommerce360.com/article/us-ecommerce-sales/

Doherty, N.F., Ellis-Chadwick, F.: Internet retailing: the past, the present and the future. Int. J. Retail. Distrib. Manag. **38**(11/12), 943–965 (2010)

Elder, R.S., Krishna, A.: The "visual depiction effect" in advertising: facilitating embodied mental simulation through product orientation. J. Consum. Res. **38**(6), 988–1003 (2012)

Friedrich, T., Schlauderer, S., Overhage, S.: The impact of social commerce feature richness on website stickiness through cognitive and affective factors: an experimental study. Electron. Commer. Res. Appl. **36**, 100861 (2019)

Gelder, K.V.: Total retail e-commerce revenue worldwide in 2022, by region (2023). https://www.statista.com/forecasts/1117851/worldwide-e-commerce-revenue-by-region

Hall, E.T.: Beyond Culture: Anchor (1976)

Hirschman, E.C.: Innovativeness, novelty seeking, and consumer creativity. J. Consum. Res. **7**(3), 283–295 (1980)

Hubert, M., Hubert, M., Linzmajer, M., Riedl, R., Kenning, P.: Trust me if you can–neurophysiological insights on the influence of consumer impulsiveness on trustworthiness evaluations in online settings. Eur. J. Mark. **52**(1/2), 118–146 (2018)

Jacoby, L.L., Kelley, C.M., Dywan, J.: Memory attributions. Varieties of memory and consciousness: essays in honour of Endel Tulving, pp. 391–422 (1989)

Jakhar, R., Verma, D., Rathore, A.P.S., Kumar, D.: Prioritization of dimensions of visual merchandising for apparel retailers using FAHP. Benchmark. Int. J. **27**(10), 2759–2784 (2020). https://doi.org/10.1108/BIJ-11-2019-0497

Jiang, Z., Wang, W., Tan, B.C.Y., Yu, J.: The determinants and impacts of aesthetics in users' first interaction with websites. J. Manag. Inf. Syst. **33**(1), 229–259 (2016)

Kahn, B.E.: Using visual design to improve customer perceptions of online assortments. J. Retail. **93**(1), 29–42 (2017). https://doi.org/10.1016/j.jretai.2016.11.004

Kisielius, J., Sternthal, B.: Detecting and explaining vividness effects in attitudinal judgments. J. Mark. Res. **21**(1), 54–64 (1984)

Krishna, A.: An integrative review of sensory marketing: engaging the senses to affect perception, judgment and behavior. J. Consum. Psychol. **22**(3), 332–351 (2012). https://doi.org/10.1016/j.jcps.2011.08.003

Kumar, A., Yinliang, T.: Value of IT in online visual merchandising: a randomized experiment to estimate the value of online product video. SSRN Electron. J. (2013). https://doi.org/10.2139/ssrn.2235033

Maier, E., Dost, F.: Fluent contextual image backgrounds enhance mental imagery and evaluations of experience products. J. Retail. Consum. Serv. **45**, 207–220 (2018). https://doi.org/10.1016/j.jretconser.2018.09.006

Maier, E., Dost, F.: The positive effect of contextual image backgrounds on fluency and liking. J. Retail. Consum. Serv. **40**, 109–116 (2018). https://doi.org/10.1016/j.jretconser.2017.09.003

Masuda, T., Gonzalez, R., Kwan, L., Nisbett, R.E.: Culture and aesthetic preference: comparing the attention to context of East Asians and Americans. Pers. Soc. Psychol. Bull. **34**(9), 1260–1275 (2008). https://doi.org/10.1177/0146167208320555

Masuda, T., Nisbett, R.E.: Attending holistically versus analytically: comparing the context sensitivity of Japanese and Americans. J. Pers. Soc. Psychol. **81**(5), 922–934 (2001). https://doi.org/10.1037//0022-3514.81.5.922

Mazzoni, G., Vannucci, M., Batool, I.: Manipulating cues in involuntary autobiographical memory: verbal cues are more effective than pictorial cues. Mem. Cogn. **42**, 1076–1085 (2014)

Miceli, G.N., Scopelliti, I., Raimondo, M.A., Donato, C.: Breaking through complexity: visual and conceptual dimensions in logo evaluation across exposures. Psychol. Mark. **31**(10), 886–899 (2014)

Norman, D.A.: Memory and attention: an introduction to human information processing (1976)

Park, J., Stoel, L., Lennon, S.J.: Cognitive, affective and conative responses to visual simulation: the effects of rotation in online product presentation. J. Consum. Behav. Int. Res. Rev. **7**(1), 72–87 (2008)

Pieters, R., Wedel, M.: Attention capture and transfer in advertising: brand, pictorial, and text-size effects. J. Mark. **68**(2), 36–50 (2004)

Reber, R., Schwarz, N., Winkielman, P.: Processing fluency and aesthetic pleasure: Is beauty in the perceiver's processing experience? Pers. Soc. Psychol. Rev. **8**(4), 364–382 (2004)

Reber, R., Winkielman, P., Schwarz, N.: Effects of perceptual fluency on affective judgments. Psychol. Sci. **9**(1), 45–48 (1998). https://doi.org/10.1111/1467-9280.00008

Rosenberg, L.J., Hirschman, E.C.: Retailing without stores. Harv. Bus. Rev. **58**(4), 103–112 (1980)

Schwarz, N.: Metacognitive experiences in consumer judgment and decision making. J. Consum. Psychol. **14**(4), 332–348 (2004)

Scott, L.M., Vargas, P.: Writing with pictures: toward a unifying theory of consumer response to images. J. Consum. Res. **34**(3), 341–356 (2007)

Shepherd, J.: 21 Essential eCommerce Statistics You Need to Know in 2023 (2023). https://thesocialshepherd.com/blog/ecommerce-statistics#there-are-between-12-and-24-million-online-stores

Shih, C.F.: Conceptualizing consumer experiences in cyberspace. Eur. J. Mark. **32**(7/8), 655–663 (1998)

Steuer, J., Biocca, F., Levy, M.R.: Defining virtual reality: dimensions determining telepresence. Commun. Age Virtual Real. **33**, 37–39 (1995)

Szymanski, D.M., Hise, R.T.: E-satisfaction: an initial examination. J. Retail. **76**(3), 309–322 (2000). https://doi.org/10.1016/S0022-4359(00)00035-X

Vieira, V., Santini, F.O., Araujo, C.F.: A meta-analytic review of hedonic and utilitarian shopping values. J. Consum. Mark. **35**(4), 426–437 (2018)

Whittlesea, B.W.A.: Illusions of familiarity. J. Exp. Psychol. Learn. Mem. Cogn. **19**(6), 1235 (1993)

Wu, F., Swait, J., Chen, Y.: Feature-based attributes and the roles of consumers' perception bias and inference in choice. Int. J. Res. Mark. **36**(2), 325–340 (2019). https://doi.org/10.1016/j.ijresmar.2018.12.003

Wu, J.: Consumer response to online visual merchandising cues: a case study of forever 21 (2014)

Wu, K., Vassileva, J., Zhao, Y., Noorian, Z., Waldner, W., Adaji, I.: Complexity or simplicity? Designing product pictures for advertising in online marketplaces. J. Retail. Consum. Serv. **28**, 17–27 (2016). https://doi.org/10.1016/j.jretconser.2015.08.009

IPSD-EM Experience Evaluation System for Internet of Things Solution

Xiaolei Li[1], Manhai Li[2(✉)], Yu Liu[1], Lixin Feng[1], and Zexin Du[2]

[1] China Mobile 5G Internet of Things Open Laboratory, Chongqing 400000, China
lixiaolei@cmiot.chinamobile.com
[2] Chongqing University of Posts and Telecommunications, Chongqing 400065, China
limh@cqupt.edu.cn

Abstract. The Internet of Things service is a complex solution that requires consideration of both business complexity and deployment flexibility, as well as powerful functionality and ease of use. It requires a comprehensive experience evaluation system throughout the entire process. This article proposes an IPSD-EM experience evaluation system by summarizing multiple practical cases. This evaluation system covers multiple aspects of Internet of Things solution, including software experience, hardware experience, service experience, etc. It summarizes user experience in terms of indicator system, implementation methods, discrimination standards, scoring criteria, and composition of evaluators. Finally, we have established a practical, replicable, and quantifiable universal product and service experience evaluation method based on the characteristics of Internet of Things solution. This method is applicable to the experience evaluation of the vast majority of Internet of Things solutions, helping enterprises achieve innovation in Internet of Things products and services by identifying weak points in the product and service experience.

Keywords: Internet of Things · IoT · Service Design · Experience Evaluation

1 Background

1.1 Internet of Things

The Internet of Things, abbreviated as IoT, refers to the communication network that extends and extends the connection between users to items based on the traditional Internet, and realizes the information exchange between things and things and people [1]. The Internet of Things products refer to the products that connect different devices to the Internet through the Internet of Things technology, and realize data exchange and intelligent control through the integration of sensors, devices, networks and computer software technologies.

The service targets of Internet of Things are extremely wide, including various customer types such as individuals, enterprises, and governments. Among them, the Internet of Things products for government and enterprise customers often appear in the form

P.-L. P. Rau (Ed.): HCII 2024, LNCS 14700, pp. 62–74, 2024.
https://doi.org/10.1007/978-3-031-60901-5_5

of a complete set of solutions. The Internet of Things solution is an innovative and comprehensive technology application mode, which can help enterprises to improve production efficiency, reduce operating costs, improve service quality, and achieve sustainable development. A perfect and well experienced Internet of Things solution should not only need to pay attention to specific function bearing products, but also pay attention to the demand analysis, solution output, delivery and implementation, installation and maintenance, service support and other whole process experience.

1.2   Internet of Things Solutions

With the continuous progress of technology and the continuous expansion of application scenarios, various Internet of Things solutions emerge in an endless stream, and they cover more and more application scenarios. With the increasing maturity of the Internet of Things industry, it serves more and more types of customers, and the competition is becoming more and more fierce. At present, the user experience re-search on the Internet of Things solutions has been widely concerned and valued by more and more Internet of Things enterprises and research institutions. The user experience research of Internet of Things products has become one of the important directions to enhance the competitiveness of enterprises. It can help enterprises improve product quality and user experience, promote product development and improvement, and increase the commercial value of products. In order to gain advantages in the competitive market, Internet of Things products need to constantly optimize the user experience and present higher quality IoT products for all kinds of users.

The Internet of Things service is a complex solution that requires consideration of both business complexity and deployment flexibility, as well as powerful functionality and ease of use. It requires a comprehensive experience evaluation system throughout the entire process. Therefore, it is necessary to establish an end-to-end and full process experience evaluation system based on the experience evaluation practice of IoT products. We named it the IPSD-EM model, which is the *IoT Platform-Service-Devices Experience Measure.*

2   Building the IPSD-EM Experience Evaluation System

The IPSD-EM model refers to a set of general Internet of Things experience evaluation models built based on the composition and characteristics of the Internet of Things solutions. The model aims to cover the dimensions of "hardware quality, software experience, pre-sale service, in-sale service, after-sales service, and competitive product benchmarking", to find product experience problems from the perspective of customers and promote product innovation and optimization iteration.

Through the evaluation of the IPSD-EM model, the "product experience index" can be used to quantify the whole process experience of the Internet of Things products. Its specific application can involve the demand analysis, planning and design, research and development and testing, release, trial commercial or commercial, post-operation evaluation, and exit and other links of the Internet of Things products. It aims to help enterprises embed experience index requirements and control points in key links, for process control, self-inspection and inspection, and to continuously monitor, track and improve products in the operation process [2].

2.1 The Service of IoT Solution

The process of IoT solution is relatively long, involving multiple roles, and has the characteristics of having related derivative needs, dedicated personnel responsible for procurement within the company, long overall purchase delivery time, and a large number of people affecting purchase results. Due to the poor experience in any aspect, it is possible to interrupt the entire business process. Therefore, the service experience of IoT solutions is particularly important[3]. It is necessary to serve multiple stakeholders within the enterprise, such as demanders, users, purchasers, and management.

Three Processes of IoT Service. The whole process of common IoT service generally include pre-sales, in sales, and after-sales processes. It is necessary to evaluate the service perception experience of the product sales throughout the entire process, It involves accuracy of service feedback results, effectiveness of solutions, timeliness of responses, standardization of behavior, and convenience of channels [4] (Fig. 1).

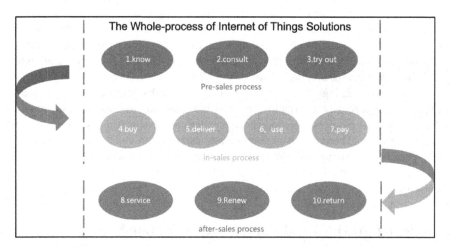

Fig. 1. Three processes of Internet of Things service

- Pre-sales process mainly covers service timeliness, service professionalism and service specification from the aspects of business consultation, resource exploration, plan formulation, contract signing and other aspects [5].
- In-sales process mainly covers signing opening, deployment installation, product use, settlement account dimensions for the service of the contract signing time, business opening time, business delivery installation time, site personnel service specification, deliverables and acceptance process specification.
- After-sales process mainly covers complaint troubleshooting, change subscribe dimensions of after-sales service channel selection convenience, accuracy of reply,

consulting answer professional degree, problem solving effectiveness, response timeliness, business change success rate to evaluate after-sales service experience.

The experience evaluation of in sales services aims to ensure the efficiency and good experience of in sales services. It is worth mentioning that the design of its experience evaluation indicators should be based on the principle of in sales service applicable to the vast majority of B-end products, and the weight ratio of the indicators can be flexibly adjusted according to the differences between different products.

Three Experience Levels of IoT Service. Service related issues can be classified based on two dimensions: user experience perception and whether user inquiries have been resolved. If the hit rate of the key points in the response to a consulting question is over 80%, then the problem is considered resolved; If the hit rate of the key points is less than 80%, or there is a contradiction between the content before and after, then the problem is judged as unresolved. The specific level classification is as follows.

- High level: The lack of some service capabilities has a great impact on user perception, such as no service channel introduction or service channel unavailable, and the lack of important links of the service process, such as wireless ordering.
- Medium level: It has a certain impact on user perception, and is easy to lead to complaints of user dissatisfaction and complaints, such as business opening, subscription and change is not implemented according to the promised time limit, complaint handling timeout, etc.
- Low level: It has little impact on user perception, which belongs to the defects in service details, and can be optimized and improved, such as non-standard service, lack of necessary reminders, lack of professional ability of service personnel, not uniform dress, etc.

Through user satisfaction surveys and customer follow-up, the China Mobile 5G Internet of Things Open Laboratory Product Evaluation Center, in combination with enterprise management requirements such as the "China Mobile Service Quality Standard Management Measures" and the "Customer Perceived Service Quality Standard System Construction White Paper (2022 Edition)", has divided the timeliness standards of pre-sales, in sales, and after-sales service indicators for IoT solutions into three levels: "gold, silver, and copper", The response time of service indicators is defined as the time interval between the two closest communication nodes between service personnel and customers during the service process. It is applicable to indicators such as service response time, business activation time, and complaint feedback time. Specific reference suggestions are as follows.

- Gold service: If the customer's needs can be feedback or resolved within 4 h, then the customer feels better about the service experience.
- Silver service: If the customer's needs can be feedback or resolved within 8 h, then the service experience is still acceptable.
- Bronze medal service: If the customer's needs are not responded to and feedback is not received after 24 h, then the user's perceived experience is relatively poor, which

may lead to adverse situations such as escalating complaints and potential customer loss.

The experience issues of two representatives in the pre-sales, in sales, and after-sales processes of the Internet of Things mall are divided into three experience levels, as shown in the following Fig. 2.

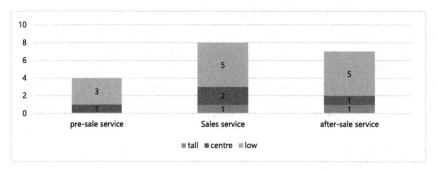

Fig. 2. Three experience levels of IoT service

2.2 The Usability Evaluation of IoT Solution

The usability evaluation of IoT solution refers to a comprehensive experience evaluation from the dimensions of functionality, performance, reliability, security, etc., identifying product experience issues, outputting problem lists and evaluation reports, providing optimization suggestions, and following up on corrective actions.

Functionality Dimension. The following aspects can be referred to in the usability test.

- Functional completeness: It mainly evaluates whether the functions provided by the product can meet the needs of users, and tests whether the functional process of the product is reasonable.
- Functional effectiveness: Evaluates whether the functions provided by the product are available and whether the results achieved are meeting the results expected by the user.
- Platform compatibility: Compatibility with mainstream models and mainstream browsers in the market, and test the compatibility performance of products under different platforms, different browsers and different operating systems.

Functional problems can be divided into 5 levels, as shown below:

- Level 1: It has a great impact on user perception, such as product crash, crash, unresponsive, restart, forced shutdown more than 3 times in a day, product program cannot be installed normally, user data is damaged and restored, the main function of the product is completely lost or wrong, etc.

- Level 2: It has great influence on user perception, such as loss or instability of critical functional parts, which occasionally occurs more than 10 times a day, or influence the realization of other main functions. Generally, the main product process cannot be carried out, and the functions and services provided are obviously affected; the program causes security risks of user client or browser.
- Level 3: It has a certain influence on user perception, which does not affect the implementation of other secondary function. Main function is not stable, which occasionally occurs more than 5 times a day, program performance inconsistent with demand documents or user expectations, interface confusion affect understanding, affect user part function use compatibility problems.
- Level 4: It has little impact on user perception, such as secondary function errors or content, function affect user understanding and operation, unstable main function, which occasionally occurs more than 3 times a day, and compatibility problems that do not affect the normal use of users.
- Level 5: It has little impact on user perception, not affecting the function, and belongs to the functional details.

The usability of a certain software product has been tested, and the number of functional usability issues is shown in the following Fig. 3.

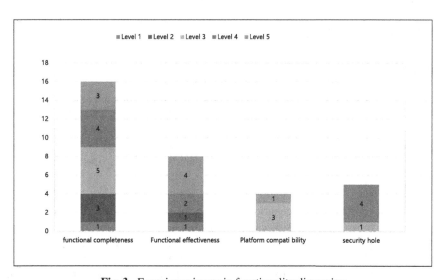

Fig. 3. Experience issues in functionality dimension

Performance Dimension. Performance test is to evaluate the use fluency experience of the tested products through specific methods and tools, and test the operation response time, task success rate, pressure performance, operation resource occupation and other indicators [6]. The experience evaluation of IoT services can be tested from dimensions such as latency, stability, and interface performance to ensure that the performance of production systems can meet user needs. The following are several aspects that can be referenced when conducting performance testing.

- Time delay: Evaluating the users 'timeliness perception during the use of the product, test the users' button response, page jump, list load, network connectivity and other delays during the use of the product, including login delay, network delay, startup speed, operation feedback time, etc.
- Stability: Evaluating user stability perception in the use of products, generally measured by task success rate.
- Stress test: Testing whether the average response time, transaction success rate, and throughput meet the standard when the system receives large concurrent transaction requests.
- Resource usage: Testing the quantity and type of resources used by the product to perform its functions, and evaluate the requirements for customer configuration, such as bandwidth, memory, CPU, disk usage, etc. [7].

Through forms such as questionnaire survey, telephone follow-up, customer interviews, and focus groups, covering the analysis and summary of 1293 real user surveys, and referring to standards such as ISO 25023 2016 Systems and Software Quality Requirements and Evaluation and GB/T25000.10-2016 Software Product Quality Model, the China Mobile 5G Internet of Things Open Laboratory Product Evaluation Center proposed the "239" principle for software interaction response time, This principle applies to indicators such as page redirection, button clicks, and page loading. Specific reference suggestions are as follows:

- Challenge value: From the level of user perception, if the interactive feedback time is less than 2 s, then the experience perception is better.
- Standard value: When the software interaction wait time is 3 s, the user experience is good and acceptable.
- Limit value: When the user waits for more than 9 s after the operation, the user perception experience is worse.

In some special business scenarios, if the above standards cannot be met due to various objective reasons, it is suggested to conduct targeted optimization in software interaction design and improve user experience through interface design optimization and other ways. For example, if the waiting time of a smart charging pile exceeds 10 s, no matter how to optimize the process, network and hardware, it cannot be reduced to the standard value in 3 s, the interactive design such as interesting waiting animation or intuitive display task progress bar can be added to the waiting interface of the user after scanning the code to improve the user's experience perception. The page loading and button response performance of the key pages and important operation steps of a certain IoT mall product were tested, and the number of experience problems found during the test is shown in the following Fig. 4.

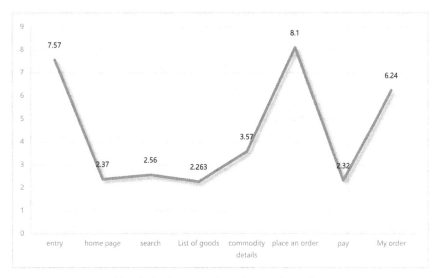

Fig. 4. Performance data of a certain product

Reliability Dimension. The experience evaluation of reliability dimension refers to a comprehensive experience evaluation of the appearance, anti-drop, dust-proof, water-proof, button life, battery life, and power consumption of IoT products. Evaluate whether the product can maintain normal operation and achieve expected performance under specific conditions and environments, to ensure reliable terminal quality and good experience of the product, identify weak points of the product, and develop corresponding rectification and promotion strategies.

The hardware quality evaluation case of a certain product is shown in Fig. 5.

Security Dimension. According to the *GB/T 30279–2020 Guidelines for Classification and Grading of Network Security Vulnerabilities in Information Security Technology*, the degree of harm of security vulnerabilities can be divided into four levels from low to high, namely low risk, medium risk, high risk, and super risk, based on their exploitability, environmental factors, and degree of impact [8]. Therefore, in the security dimension of experience evaluation, it is divided into four levels, namely level 4, level 3, level 2, and level 1.

3 Application of the IPSD-EM Experience Evaluation System

3.1 Scoring Criteria for Different Kinds of Indicators

There are five scoring criteria for different indicators, as follows.

- Scoring criteria for service indicators: The maximum score for each functionality indicator is 100 points. The deduction points vary for different levels of problems. The higher the level of the problem, the more points will be deducted. The deduction points for high, medium, and low levels are 5, 3, and 1 respectively. Stop after deduction.

First indicator	Secondary indicator	Third indicator	result
Appearance	Easy to operate	Overall appearance perception	pass
		Camera viewing angle	pass
		Docking buttons are easy to operate	pass
Reliable and durable	Anti-fall test	Anti-fall test	pass
	environmental test	Camera heating performance	pass
		Camera lag	pass
		Camera for video quality	pass
		Camera night vision quality	pass
		Camera temperature adaptability	pass
		Camera humidity adaptability	pass
		Real-time intercom sensitivity	fail
		High temperature stress test	pass
		Low temperature stress test	pass
		Humid heat test	pass
		Dust test	pass
		waterproof test	pass
	Key-press test	Key-press life test	pass
	Endurance test	Endurance test	fail

Fig. 5. Reliability evaluation of a certain product

After obtaining the rating for this indicator, it will be included in the total score of the product experience index according to the established weight.

- Scoring criteria for functionality indicators: The maximum score for each functionality indicator is 100 points. The deduction points vary for different levels of problems. The higher the level of the problem, the more points will be deducted. From level 1 to level 5, the deduction points will be 15, 10, 5, 3, and 1 in order. Stop after deduction.
- Scoring criteria for performance indicators: The maximum score for each security indicator is 100 points. Each indicator is set with three standard lines: challenge value (A), achievement value (B), and triple achievement value (C). According to actual testing requirements, collect several test values and calculate the average value as the test result. If the actual test average reaches the challenge value A, it can earn 100 points. If it reaches the standard value B, it can earn 60 points. If it reaches three times the standard value C, it can only earn 0 points. According to the scoring rules, a linear score is obtained. Assuming R is the test result, if $R \geq A$, then $S = 100$; If $A \leq R \leq B$, then $S = 60 + 40 * (R-A)/(B-A)$; If $R \leq C$, then $S = 0$.
- Scoring criteria for reliability indicators: The maximum score for each security indicator is 100 points. The reliability index adopts a one vote veto system. If the test result passes, 100 points will be given, and if the test result does not pass, 0 points will be given. There is no intermediate score.

- Scoring criteria for security indicators: The maximum score for each security indicator is 100 points. If one extremely dangerous or high-risk vulnerability is found, 20 points will be deducted; If one medium risk vulnerability is found, 10 points will be deducted; If one low-risk vulnerability is found, 5 points will be deducted; If the total number of vulnerabilities exceeds 5, an additional 20 points will be deducted, and the deduction will be terminated.

After obtaining the rating for this indicator, it will be included in the total score of the product experience index according to the established weight.

3.2 Experience Evaluation Data Presentation

After passing the IPSD-EM model evaluation, the user experience index score can be calculated after completing the evaluation, and can be summed according to the scores and weights of each evaluation index [9].

After completing the product experience evaluation and quantitative calculation, the evaluation results can be visually displayed through icons, clearly showing the shortcomings and problems of the product in terms of experience. The results of evaluating a certain product through the IPSD-EM model are shown in Fig. 6.

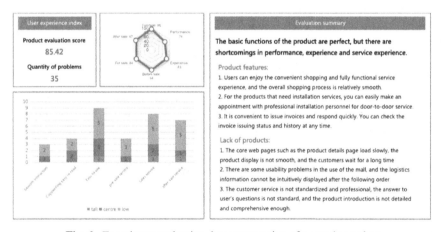

Fig. 6. Experience evaluation data presentation of a certain product

3.3 Experience Evaluation Benchmarking Analysis

Benchmarking analysis of IoT solutions refers to comparing and analyzing the solutions of competitors with their own solutions, understanding the differences and advantages and disadvantages of both parties. The experience evaluation benchmarking analysis of IoT solutions mainly focus on the three dimensions of platform usage, terminal quality, and service experience, in order to discover the optimization and improvement directions of the products. Specific indicators can be compared by selecting corresponding secondary indicators from the previous description based on the purpose of benchmark-ing analysis, and the proportion of indicator weights can be flexibly adjusted according to different benchmarking purposes. The results of a certain public network intercom product's competitors are detailed in Fig. 7.

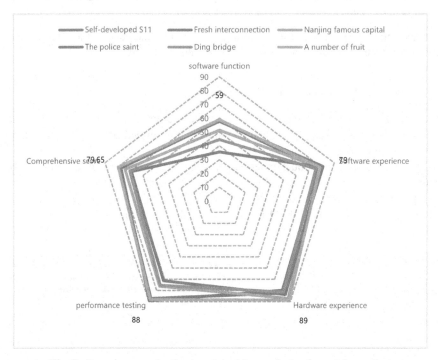

Fig. 7. Experience evaluation benchmarking analysis of a certain product

Product use evaluation mainly from the perspective of customers, covering "practical function, use smooth, safe, good experience" four aspects, according to the characteristics of the product key evaluation of product software "function, performance, compatibility, user experience", guarantee software function complete and effective [10], and ensure that no obvious problems and compatible with the mainstream operating system and browser, etc. The index setting is based on the vast majority of software products, and the weight ratio can be flexibly adjusted according to the characteristics and attribute differences between products.

The IPSD-EM model quantifies the degree of usability, ease of use, and ease of use of IoT products and services based on a unified standard, starting from the entire process experience. This model can cover the entire product lifecycle for user experience evaluation from two aspects: product quality management and product business process. The specific application of this model is shown in Fig. 8.

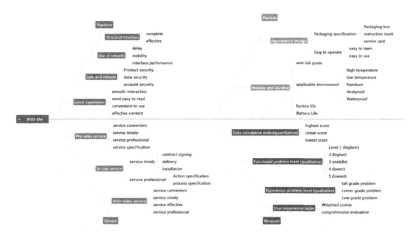

Fig. 8. Basic framework of the IPSD-EM model

4 Conclusion

Based on the large number of product evaluation experience of China Mobile 5G Internet of Things open laboratory, this paper extracts the IPSD-EM model through the combination of theoretical research and evaluation practice. The experience evaluation model adopts the modular design idea, and can be continuously adjusted and optimized according to the evaluation practice experience, technology development, business model change, etc. It has the following characteristics:

- Strong versatility: IPSD-EM model combines the characteristics of the Internet of Things products, and selects the universal evaluation dimension and the first and second level indicators as the core framework, which is suitable for the experience evaluation of the vast majority of IoT products.
- Strong expansibility: For the differentiation of different types of products, personalized three-level indicators can be expanded and set based on the guidance and scoring principles of the core framework of IPSD-EM model, starting from product characteristics, to meet specific evaluation needs.
- Strong flexibility: IPSD-EM model adopts a modular design, where each evaluation module can independently conduct testing or flexibly select multiple modules for combination based on the evaluation purpose. Then, through the weighted scoring rules of multiple evaluation modules, they are organically combined into a whole, outputting a quantifiable product experience index.
- Strong applicability: Based on the characteristics of the product lifecycle, this model can evolve into evaluation types such as "R&D acceptance evaluation, trial commercial evaluation, commercial evaluation, and full process experience evaluation" through modular free combination, serving key links in the product lifecycle. Quality and experience indicators are embedded in key control points for R&D process control, self-inspection, product innovation, and optimization.

References

1. Guo, B.: Research and realization of RFID security certification technology in the Internet of Things, Jiangsu University of Science and Technology (2013)
2. Gu, Q.: A new software process improvement implementation model based on CMMI, Qingdao University of Technology (2010)
3. Xue, H., Wu, J., Wang, S.: Thinking on intelligent home system under the background of artificial intelligence and Internet of Things. Netw. Secur. Technol. Appl. **12**, 154–155 (2019)
4. Liu, J.: Master dissertation on logistics service quality evaluation research based on online reviews, Nanjing University of Aeronautics and Astronautics (2019)
5. Du, C.: A Master's dissertation of customer satisfaction management optimization research, Hebei University of Science and Technology (2019)
6. Liu, W., Tan, K., Ding, C.: Android optimization of the performance test tool Emmagee. Electron. Test. **17**, 81–83 (2016). https://doi.org/10.16520/j.cnki.1000-8519.2016.17.037
7. Wu, H., Dai, D., Fu, Q., Chen, J., Lu, W.: Combination method of reinforcement learning and generative adversarial network. Comput. Eng. Appl. **10**, 36–44 (2019)
8. Li, L., Hao, Y.: Information security vulnerability related standards introduction. Inf. Secur. China **07**, 68–72 (2016)
9. He, X.: Product user recognition evaluation based on user data. In: User Friendly 2014 and UXPA China the 11th User Experience Industry Annual Conference Proceedings, pp. 7–9. ZTE Corporation Limited (2014)
10. Yue, X.: Master dissertation of "Kangbashi Smart Tourism" APP based on Android, InnerMongolia (2017)

Addressing Cross-Cultural Design Challenges in Social Media Platforms: A Human-Computer Interaction Perspective

Lanjie Li[(✉)] [iD]

School of Arts and Communication, China Jiliang University, Hangzhou, China
690709915@qq.com

Abstract. With the global popularity of social media, people are increasingly relying on social media platforms for their daily information sharing and social interactions. However, due to the differences in people's values, habits and behaviours across cultures, the experience of using social media varies across cultural groups, which poses a challenge for cross-cultural design. To address this issue, this study aims to explore a culturally sensitive human-computer interaction (HCI) approach to promote the effective use of social media platforms globally. Through in-depth understanding of the usage habits and behavioural patterns of users from different cultures, the findings of the study include specific methodological and quantitative analyses to provide an effective design methodology that promotes social media platforms that can be successfully applied in cross-cultural environments and improves the user experience and usability of social media platforms in different cultural contexts. Thus, the usability of social media platforms can be increased and the user experience of users around the world can be improved.

Keywords: Cross-cultural design · Cultural sensitivity ·
Human-computer interaction (HCI) · social media platforms · user
experience

1 Introduction

1.1 Background and Challenges

As the diversity of social media users increases, it's important to recognize the new challenges designers face in meeting user needs. The term social media, also known as social networking, originates from the e-book "What is Social Media", published in 2007 by American academic Anthony Mayfield. Mayfield's e-book titled "What is Social Media" was published in 2007. According to him, social media is an umbrella term for a range of online media that are participatory, open, communicative, conversational, collaborative and networked, that enable anyone to create and distribute content [2], and whose main feature is the "socialization" of content production and consumption [1]. Social media is no longer

© The Author(s), under exclusive license to Springer Nature Switzerland AG 2024
P.-L. P. Rau (Ed.): HCII 2024, LNCS 14700, pp. 75–88, 2024.
https://doi.org/10.1007/978-3-031-60901-5_6

just a tool to transmit information, but a platform for cultural exchange and many symbioses. Therefore, we need to fully understand the unique needs of different cultures on social media so that the platforms we develop can bridge cultural differences by respecting and incorporating the characteristics of different cultures.

Cultural sensitivity is an understanding and appreciation of different cultures, their traditions, languages, customs and beliefs [3]. In language services, cultural sensitivity is not limited to language competence; respecting and recognizing cultural differences is also important; for example, particular attention should be paid to cultural sensitivity in the following four areas

- Understanding the intercultural context
- Raising cultural awareness to avoid offensive language
- Intellectual handling of culturally sensitive information to gain credibility.
- Overcoming cultural differences.

When it comes to cultural sensitivity in communication, cultural nuances and taboos can hinder inclusive communication. When it comes to cultural sensitivity, conflicts arise for the following reasons:

- Differences in cultural background
- Different forms of non-verbal communication
- Differences in the choice of words
- Consideration of time differences
- cultural taboos
- sensitive topics
- body language and gestures [4–6].

Against this background, this study takes into account Dr Milton Bennett's model (Fig. 1) for fostering intercultural sensitivity to better integrate global multiculturalism into social media platforms to enhance the user experience and

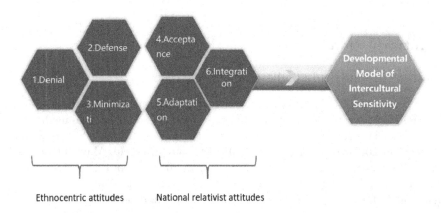

Fig. 1. Developmental Model of Intercultural Sensitivity(DMIS)

to develop a culturally sensitive approach to human-computer interaction (HCI). It aims to provide designers with a set of practical tools and strategies to facilitate global cultural communication and interaction through an approach Through extensive research on the complexities of different cultural perspectives, we hope to provide sound theoretical underpinnings and practical guidance for addressing cross-cultural design challenges in global social media platforms.

1.2 Purpose and Significance of the Study

With the widespread use of social media platforms around the world, we are faced with a major challenge: how can social media platforms actually build bridges between different cultures? This is not only a technical question, but also a global problem that affects many fields such as culture, psychology and sociology. The aim of this study is to explore ways in which cross-cultural design problems of social media platforms can be addressed from the perspective of human-computer interaction. The goal is to enable natural, simple and effective interactions so that users can have a better experience when using computer systems. The goal is to enable natural, simple and effective interactions so that users can have a better experience when using IT systems. The challenge is therefore to bring the functionality of social media closer to users' expectations while focusing on innovative design techniques to meet the needs of users from different cultural backgrounds. Through an in-depth study of social media usage habits in different cultural environments, we seek to go beyond traditional design and propose a culturally sensitive design methodology so that social media platforms can better serve users from around the world.

2   Related Works

With the dawn of the digital age, social media platforms have gained unprecedented popularity worldwide. In Europe and the US, the first Facebook and Twitter dominate, along with the modern Instagram and TikTok, while in the Asia-Pacific region, WeChat, Xiaohongshu and Bilibill take centre stage. Social media has become an integral part of people's daily lives. Globally, the number of social media users has increased dramatically (as shown by public data on WeChat users in recent years) (Fig. 2), including not only individual users but also various forms of organizations such as companies and government agencies.

This global trend towards social media has changed the way people access information and express their views, creating a huge virtual social network across the world. The popularity of social media is no longer confined to developed countries, but is gradually spreading to developing countries and isolated regions. This trend has led to a globalization of information and a blending of cultures, which poses a number of challenges for intercultural communication [7,11,19].

Of particular concern is the fact that social media is no longer just a platform for disseminating text and images; the introduction of multimedia forms such as

Fig. 2. Statistical analysis of the number of monthly active WeChat user accounts

video, live streaming and virtual reality has transformed the social media platform into a three-dimensional, interactive space. This diversity not only enhances the user experience, but also enriches the forms of cultural expression in social media.

In a way, the popularity of social media platforms has brought different cultures around the world closer together, but it has also raised a pressing issue - namely how the interface and functionality of a global social media platform can be designed to cater for users from different cultural backgrounds. The globalization of social media platforms has led designers to better understand and respect the unique needs of different cultures so that platforms are not only global, but also inclusive.

3   Methodology

3.1   Exploring the Functions of Social Media Platforms

With the development of the internet and social media, the use of social media platforms has become more diverse. Today, a typical social media user can be active on several different platforms at the same time. These online social media platforms have a wide variety of functions due to their unique starting position, different development directions and ever-changing user needs. Previous research has focused on user behaviour when interacting with one or more features of a single social media platform, but less on a comprehensive study of the relationship between social media platform features and user behaviour and a holistic view of the features of different social media platforms [19–22].

On social networking platforms, user behaviour depends on a combination of factors. Although users can utilize different features of the platform individually or in combination with each other, it all depends on the architecture or processes developed by designers and developers based on the ideas and technological foundations of Web 2.0 [12]. The generation of content on social media platforms is so closely linked to the actions of users that it cannot be generated and exist independently of their participation. Therefore, when studying user behaviour on social media, the existence of functional modules on social media platform pages cannot be ignored. These modules influence the actions and behaviour of users to a considerable extent and should be included in the study. A deeper understanding and investigation of the functionality of social media platforms is necessary to address cross-cultural design challenges. This study will provide a comprehensive and in-depth investigation of the functionality of social media platforms through the following steps:

In the area of classifying or categorizing user participation behaviour on social media platforms, Yang Zhenliang's work classified user participation behaviour on these platforms into the three most common forms of online participation - audience participation, expressive participation and broadcast participation - based on user behaviour, usage purposes and performance on these platforms [13]. On the other hand, Yu Jianye et al. examined the "group function" combined with WeChat characteristics, classified user participation behaviour on social media platforms and developed two indicators, namely message response and message sharing, focusing on the participation behaviour of WeChat users in WeChat groups. Although these studies classify user participation behaviour on social media platforms, they are limited by the traditional research method, making it difficult to fully disclose the overall user participation behaviour on social media platforms. In addition, these studies did not consider the similarity of social networking platforms in creating platforms based on Web 2.0 development and the similarity of user engagement behaviour [14]. To better understand user behaviour on social networking platforms, more innovative research methods are needed to identify the nature and commonalities of this behaviour. For this reason, we will clearly define and categorize the main functions of social media platforms. These include functions such as information sharing, social interaction, content creation and privacy settings. By clearly categorizing the functions, we will be able to better understand the needs and expectations of social media users.

Having identified the features of social media, we will examine the different needs of users from different cultures in relation to these features. Through extensive user surveys and participatory design techniques, we will gather cross-cultural perspectives on social networking features and explore their specific preferences and needs in terms of information sharing and social interaction.

Firstly, a user questionnaire is designed that covers multiple cultural contexts. When designing the questionnaire, the specific needs of different cultures are taken into account, it is ensured that the wording and content of the questions are correctly understood in the different cultural contexts, and cultural differences such as language, values, social habits, etc. are taken into account to ensure the validity of the questionnaire. Secondly, social media users with different cultural backgrounds were randomly selected to ensure the representativeness and diversity of the sample. In selecting the sample, care was taken to ensure the completeness and reliability of the data by paying particular attention to the size and characteristics of each cultural group. In addition, user responses were collected both online and in face-to-face interviews. The data analysis focuses on the attitudes, frequency of use and satisfaction of users from different cultures with the functions of social networks. The quantitative analysis serves to determine the significance and validity of the data [16].

Based on the above in-depth analysis of the needs of culturally diverse users, a set of functional solutions for social media based on multimodal roles [15]with cultural sensitivity will be developed so that social media platforms can fully meet the specific needs of culturally diverse users on a global scale and thus improve the cultural adaptability of the platforms.

Interface design enhances the user's cultural experience by incorporating elements that resonate culturally, such as the use of symbols, colours and images that correspond to different cultural habits and values [17]. For example, in the login interface, the account form selection was designed to match the common use of social media in all cultures to help users log into the interface more quickly; and more elements representing emotions from different cultures were added to the emoticons in social media to help users feel closer and better understood when communicating with each other Fig. 3.

Fig. 3. Movie ticket folder interface display in Europe, America and Asia-Pacific region, for example, Europe and America are inclined to cool colours, diffuse wind design, with left and right sliding interface, the overall interface is simple and generous; Asia-Pacific region is inclined to warm colours, the interface display is up and down sliding, and the page is compact.

Another focus is innovative multilingual support, and we will provide users with multilingual support features. In addition to traditional translation services, culturally sensitive language processing technologies will be explored to enable more accurate and culturally appropriate translation of messages. Users will be able to choose the language they are most familiar with, making the social media platform truly global in terms of language coverage Fig. 4.

Fig. 4. Interface design of the login page in the case of a film app with different language options

In order to meet the individual cultural needs of users, the introduction of user-defined functionality in the interface was utilized to allow users to personalize the platform according to their cultural preferences. This flexibility will make it easier for users to adapt to the platform and increase user satisfaction Fig. 5.

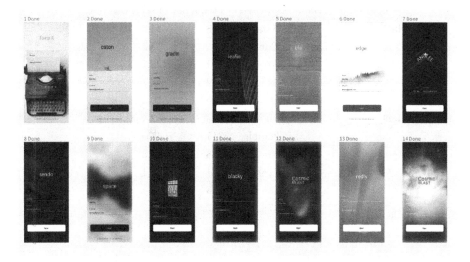

Fig. 5. Custom Interface Functions

At the same time, a mechanism for evaluating and updating the cultural adaptation of social media has been established to ensure the practical effectiveness of design solutions. By regularly monitoring user feedback, social interaction data and cultural trends on social media platforms, designs are continuously optimized to ensure that social media platforms remain culturally sensitive for users around the world. The aim of these design solutions is to provide users with a more personalized and intimate social media experience that takes into account and understands different cultural contexts and to become a digital space that promotes cultural exchange and understanding on a global scale.

3.2   Survey on Social Media Usage Needs in Multicultural Contexts

In order to gain a deeper understanding of social media usage habits in a multicultural context, this study will use a multi-level survey method to obtain more comprehensive and in-depth data. Quantitative research methods are used in this study, and questionnaires are also used for research data collection. One of the main reasons for choosing the quantitative method is that its data are authentic and reliable and aim to be more generalisable. In social science research, the questionnaire is the most commonly used data collection tool. In addition, the questionnaire in this study uses closed-ended questions to obtain relevant information in the most reliable and valid way. The source of data for the study uses raw data, i.e., data obtained from the questionnaire instrument [18]. The following are the details of our survey data (as an example of international students from different countries in our university):

Table 1. Basic information about the sample (n = 444)

Demographic variables	Options	Frequency	Percentage (%)
Nations	Asian	198	44.5
	Europe	68	15.3
	Africa	101	22.7
	Americas	32	7.2
	Oceania	45	10.1
Genders	Male	233	52.4
	Female	211	47.5
Age	18~20	68	15.3
	21~23	231	52.1
	24~26	113	25.4
	27~29	32	7.2

A total of 444 respondents participated in this study, and the basic information is shown in Table 1. The findings show that 44.5 per cent of the respondents

Table 2. Reliability statistics of formal questionnaires

Dimension	Cronbach's Alpha	Item count
Aggregation	0.869	18
Integration of cultural symbols	0.753	3
Multi-language support	0.794	3
User-defined features	0.904	3
Information Sharing Requirements	0.808	3
Social interaction preferences	0.823	3
Platform experience	0.767	3

were Asian, 15.3 per cent European, and 22.7 per cent, 7.2 per cent and 10.1 per cent from Africa, the Americas and Oceania respectively. In terms of gender, 52.4 per cent of the respondents were male and 47.5 per cent were female, which is basically equal for the sake of data fairness. In addition, most of the respondents who participated in the survey were 21–23 years old college students, accounting for 52.1%.

Table 2 shows the results of the formal questionnaire reliability analysis. The overall reliability coefficient of the questionnaire, Cronbach's Alpha, is 0.869, and the Cronbach's Alpha of each dimension of the questionnaire is greater than 0.70, and the Cronbach's Alpha of more than 50% of the dimensions is greater than 0.80. The results show that the questionnaire has a good internal consistency and a high degree of reliability between the various scales of the questionnaire, and that the data of the overall study are reliable. The results show that the scales of the questionnaire have good internal consistency and high reliability.

Table 3. KMO and Bartlett's test of the formal questionnaire

KMO Sample Suitability Quantity		0.836
Bartlett Sphericity Test	Approximate chi-square	4343.766
	(Number of) degrees of freedom	156
	Significance	0

The results of the validity analysis of the formal questionnaire are shown in Tables 3, 4. In the process of validity testing of the questionnaire, factor analysis was used. The overall validity KMO value of the questionnaire was 0.836, and the KMO values of all dimensions of the questionnaire were greater than 0.60, and the KMO values of 50% of the dimensions were greater than or equal to 0.70. The results showed that the correlation between the variables of the

Table 4. KMO for each dimension of the formal questionnaire

Dimension	KMO value
Integration of cultural symbols	0.678
Multi-language support	0.643
User-defined features	0.726
Information Sharing Requirements	0.702
Social interaction preferences	0.700
Platform experience	0.657

dimensions of the questionnaire was better, and it was suitable for factor analysis. In addition, the significance probability of the chi-square statistic value of Barlet's test of sphericity Sig.$=0<0.05$ indicates that the validity of the results of the questionnaire is good (Table 5).

Table 5. Statistical analysis of dimension scores

Analysis term	Labels	Dimension 1 score	Dimension 2 score
Q7	YES	0.354	−0.014
	NO	−0.354	0.014
Q8	Local language	0.451	0.708
	English	−0.384	−0.604
Q9	Developing cultural globalism	0.073	0.355
	Understanding different cultures	0.995	−0.615
	Achieving pluralism	−0.889	0.635
	Other	0.080	−0.430
Q10	YES	−0.483	0.244
	NO	0.483	−0.244
Q11	Personalized themes	−0.099	0.103
	Custom Function Buttons	0.103	−0.107
Q12	Adaptation of usage habits	1.030	0.334
	Increase media usage	−0.400	−0.906
	Conformity to personal aesthetics	0.443	0.701

In this study, the correlation between a total of six items such as Q7 was investigated, and thus multiple correspondence analysis was used for the study. The dimension score is the specific value of the coordinates of each category item on each dimension, which represents the distance and position of each point in space and reflects the relationship between the points (as shown in Fig. 6). According to the corresponding figure, the dimensions of "personal aesthetics" and "local language" are more important in the use of social media, and the user group cares more about their personal feelings and usage habits. In the era of big data, recommending suitable products according to user profile groups can retain users and keep them active.

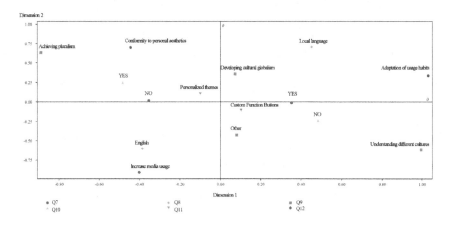

Fig. 6. Dimension 1 and dimension 2 correspondence charts

Through this multi-layered approach, we hope to gain a comprehensive under-standing of the needs and behaviors of social media users in a multicultural con-text, in order to better guide our design process. This will help ensure that social media platforms are better adapted to users from different cultures around the world and improve the cultural adaptability of the user experience.

4 Results

4.1 Results of the Multicultural Survey Analysis

The in-depth analysis of the multicultural survey data provided us with a lot of information to better understand the habits, perspectives and needs of social media users in different cultures. In this study, we focused on several key aspects, the main findings of which are summarized below:

First, we found significant differences between cultures in terms of social media usage habits. Some cultures are more family and group orientated and tend to share family life and social activities on social media, while other cul-tures are more individualistic and prefer to emphasize personal achievements and independent opinions. This difference is particularly noticeable in users' desires for features on social media platforms.

Secondly, social media plays an important role in sharing culture. The survey data shows that in some cultures, social media is widely used as a platform for sharing traditional culture, customs and values. Users are more inclined to share culturally relevant content on social media to preserve and pass on their cultural identity, giving social media platforms the opportunity to become more involved in cultural transmission.

In addition, we found significant differences in users' attitudes towards privacy and security between cultures. Members of some cultures are more privacy-conscious and demand higher privacy settings on social media platforms, while members of other cultures are more willing to share more information to enhance social interaction. Therefore, social media platforms have strategies in place to further differentiate themselves in terms of privacy settings.

Finally, the analyses conducted in this study show the profound influence of culture on users' preferences for social media content. Some cultures favour visual and graphic content, while other cultures are more text-heavy and expressive. Therefore, social media platforms need to take cultural differences into account when presenting content and recommendation algorithms.

Overall, in-depth analyses of multicultural surveys provide a better understanding of the diversity of global users and offer practical advice and suggestions to improve the cultural adaptation of social media platforms. The findings strongly support a methodology for design and functional implementation so that social media platforms can better serve users from diverse cultural backgrounds around the world.

4.2 Analyzing the Results

After an in-depth analysis of the results of the multicultural survey and the functional implementation of the social media platforms, an in-depth evaluation of the research results was carried out. The following is an evaluation of the research findings and related points:

First, the main finding of this study is the successful innovation of social media platform functionality through the implementation of a culturally sensitive HMI design methodology that achieved significant benefits. The implementation of a new user interface, multilingual support and culturally sensitive recommendation algorithms enables the social media platform to better adapt to the needs of global multiculturalism. This result is not only of practical value, but also sets a new direction for the development of the social networking industry on a global scale.

Secondly, the analysis of multicultural surveys provides a better understanding of the habits and behaviors of social media users in different cultural contexts. It provides valuable cultural insights for the future development and global expansion of social media platforms and is an important reference for industry professionals to better understand and serve global users.

In addition, the integrated use of design methods and the implementation of the functionality of social networking platforms have received positive feedback from users. The effectiveness of methods such as participatory design, integration of cultural patterns and cross-cultural testing have been validated in practice. This is an example of a successful experiment for future HMI design and a recommendation for cross-cultural design research in other areas.

While a number of notable results were achieved, we also recognize that the cultural adaptation of social media platforms remains a dynamic process. Future research and development should continuously focus on the changing needs and emerging trends of users from different cultures in order to further optimize design methods and functional implementations. This requires close collaboration with users on the one hand and constant innovation through the use of new technologies and data analysis tools on the other.

After analyzing the results obtained, we are convinced that this study provides useful theoretical support and practical experience for the general development of social networking platforms. We hope that this study will serve as a reliable guide for industry professionals to promote social media platforms to better adapt to multiculturalism on a global scale.

5   Conclusion

In this study, we have successfully explored the cross-cultural design challenges of social media platforms on a global scale and proposed a culturally sensitive human-machine interaction (HMI) approach to facilitate the effective use of social media platforms. The study begins with a comprehensive review and analysis of social media usage habits in different cultural contexts from the perspective of users with different cultural backgrounds, which provides an empirical basis for the study. Based on this, a comprehensive graphical user interface design methodology including cultural factor analysis, user participatory design and cross-cultural user testing is proposed and developed to address the cultural adaptability of social media platforms. To test the reliability of the design methodology and to ensure the validity of the questionnaire, the reliability of the questionnaire was analyzed using Cronbach's alpha criterion. The results of the study show that a culturally sensitive design approach can significantly improve the user experience and usability of social media platforms by respecting and meeting the specific needs of users from different cultural backgrounds. The importance of this study is that it provides useful guidelines and insights for the design and development of global social media platforms and promotes cross-cultural integration and exchange. In the future, this research should be extended to other digital platforms and expand the theoretical framework of culturally responsive design to adapt it to changes in the global digital environment. Through further collaboration, practice and technological innovation, the cultural responsiveness of global social media platforms can be further enhanced to facilitate more useful and meaningful intercultural communication in global social media.

References

1. Lin, X., Xu, S., Qi, W.: A review of social media development and research. Res. Librarianship **14**, 13–16 (2016). https://doi.org/10.15941/j.cnki.issn1001-0424.2016.14.002
2. Mayfield, A.: What is Social Media (2008)
3. Foronda, C.L.: A concept analysis of cultural sensitivity. J. Transcult. Nurs. **19**(3), 207–212 (2008)
4. Lutz, S.A.: Cultural sensitivity: Importance, competencies, and public relations implications (2017)
5. Bennett, M.J., Hammer, M.: A developmental model of intercultural sensitivity. In: The International Encyclopedia of Intercultural Communication, vol. 1, no. 10 (2017)
6. Chen, G.-M.: A review of the concept of intercultural sensitivity (1997)
7. Russo, A.: Transformations in cultural communication: social media, cultural exchange, and creative connections. Curator Museum J. **54**(3), 327–346 (2011)
8. Marcus, A., Gould, E.W.: Cultural dimensions and global web user-interface design: What? So what? Now what. In: Proceedings of the 6th Conference on Human Factors and the Web, vol. 19 (2000)
9. Hofstede, G.: Cultural dimensions in management and planning. Asia Pacific J. Manag. **1**, 81–99 (1984)
10. Yeo, A.W., Ferguson, R.B.: Towards a culture-aware HCI curriculum. In: Proceedings of the 25th BCS Conference on Human-Computer Interaction, pp. 423–428 (2011)
11. Wang, X.: A comparative study of the terms international competence, globalisation competence and intercultural competence. Comparative Educ. Res. **39**(04), 23–30 (2017). https://doi.org/10.20013/j.cnki.ice.2017.04.003
12. Yue, S., Wei, H.: Behavioural spectrum and behavioural hierarchy model construction for user engagement on social media platforms. Library Intell. Work **66**(09), 40–52 (2022). https://doi.org/10.13266/j.issn.0252-3116.2022.09.005
13. Yang, Z.: Analysis of netizen participation behaviour and public management response in online public crisis events. J. Humanit. **05**, 162–168 (2012). https://doi.org/10.15895/j.cnki.rwzz.2012.05.021
14. Yu, J.Y., et al.: Evolutionary analysis of social network users' information sharing behaviours based on social evolution game. Electron. J. **46**(01), 223–229 (2018)
15. Wang, J., Sidi, Yu, Y.: Multimodal cross-decoupling for sample less learning method. J. Natl. Univ. Defence Technol. **46**(01), 12–21 (2024)
16. Yi-Yi, Z., Sai-Yu, H.: How to use questionnaire method in survey research. Fujian Educat. **36**, 26–29 (2023)
17. Qian, W.: Research on the role analysis and application of visual elements in UI interface design. Tiangong. **20**, 48–50 (2023)
18. Zhang, T., Li, P., Pang, S.: A quantitative study of college students' motivation for leisure use of WeChat group users. News Knowl. **09**, 13–22+93 (2023)
19. Rogers, Y.: New theoretical approaches for HCI. Ann. Rev. Inf. Sci. Technol. **38**(1), 87–143 (2004)
20. Adams, A., Lunt, P., Cairns, P.: A qualititative approach to HCI research, pp. 138–157 (2008)
21. Soloway, E., Guzdial, M., Hay, K.E.: Learner-centered design: the challenge for HCI in the 21st century. Interactions **1**(2), 36–48 (1994)
22. Bourges-Waldegg, P., Scrivener, S.A.R.: Meaning, the central issue in cross-cultural HCI design. Interact Comput. **9**(3), 287–309 (1998)

Comparative Case Studies: Cross-cultural Communication Strategies of the Digital Platforms of Global Trade Fairs

Wenhua Li and Ziqi Ye[(✉)]

Guangzhou Academy of Fine Arts, No. 168, Waihuan West Road, Panyu District, Guangzhou, China
42417290@qq.com

Abstract. Trade fairs are adopting digital platforms and services to enhance global participation. However, effective cross-cultural communication remains a challenge. This study analyzed digitalization approaches of 6 major trade fairs across North America, Europe, and Asia through a comparative case study methodology. Data was collected from secondary sources and interviews with organizers. Findings reveal key differences in cultural communication priorities - fairs in Asia emphasize language support and relationship building in their digital offerings, while Western fairs focus more on quick information exchange. Providing culturally sensitive communication platforms is thus still an emerging practice. A notable finding is that Asian trade fairs take a more relational approach compared to the transactional tendencies of Western counterparts. A key recommendation is for fair organizers to offer cultural awareness training and develop online platforms with multilanguage functionality in order to properly engage diverse global audiences. The paper discusses current digitalization trends in the trade fair industry and provides insights into formulating culturally appropriate communication strategies that connect effectively across cultures. It offers both theoretical and practical implications for global business.

Keywords: Digital Platform · Trade Fair · Cross-cultural Communication · Interaction Design

1 Introduction

In an increasingly intertwined global economy, trade shows and exhibitions are crucial hubs for cultivating international business networks. Annual fairs are dedicated periods where major stakeholders - exhibitors, buyers, sponsors, and visitors – physically converge to enable vital face-to-face business interactions around product launches, deals, partnerships, and knowledge exchange. As epicenters of commerce that draw participants worldwide, trade shows have long realized the necessity for intercultural engagement.

However, the spread of digital technologies and recent impetus towards virtual events is significantly transforming trade show strategies across regions. Online platforms,

P.-L. P. Rau (Ed.): HCII 2024, LNCS 14700, pp. 89–98, 2024.
https://doi.org/10.1007/978-3-031-60901-5_7

video conferencing tools, and innovative virtual environments now allow fairs to mirror real-world networking at a global scale. Global participation is expanding through reduced barriers related to travel, time, and costs. Yet these emerging digital tools also introduce nuanced challenges around designing culturally inclusive online experiences to fully leverage global connectivity. As trade fairs evolve into thriving blended ecosystems combining physical and virtual elements, this crucial need for cross-cultural communication assumes centerstage.

This paper closely examines this intersection of the digital evolution in trade fair industry and consequent cultural considerations through a comparative case study analysis. It takes a cross-regional perspective analyzing patterns, commonalities and differences in digital engagement strategies adopted across six high-profile fairs in North America, Europe, Middle East and Asia. Using Hofstede's established cultural dimensions framework, it also evaluates if and how cultural variables may influence online platform design choices by these fairs to cater to diverse target audiences. Key goals of this research are two-fold:

To trace wider digital transformation trajectories, tools and global participation goals within the trade fair ecosystem based on secondary data and industry reports;

To examine differences around cross-cultural communication challenges and cultural design sensitivity in the digital offerings of selected case study fairs based on first-hand interviews with organizers.

By analyzing these dual perspectives, this study derives recommendations for fair organizers worldwide who seek to drive digital innovation while respecting cultural contexts. It provides practical insights into crafting inclusive communication strategies that effectively engage global audiences, thereby enabling trade fairs to fulfill their crucial role as international business platforms.

On a broader level, this research contributes to academic theory at the intersection of virtual communication, cross-cultural business and trade show management. As digitalization permeates across industries, there is growing scholarly emphasis on taking an intercultural lens for technologies aimed at global audiences in order to prevent cultural disconnectedness or exclusion. However, such culturally centered perspectives remain relatively scarce around virtual communication design within the specific trade fair context, though its multi-stakeholder global orientation warrants attention. Therefore, by underscoring cultural considerations in virtual trade fair participation, this paper enriches understanding of how to nurture digital platforms as springboards for global business rather than inadvertent barriers.

2 Literature Review

2.1 Digital Transformation in Trade Fair Industry

The trade fair and exhibition industry has undergone significant digital disruption and innovation over the past decade as organizers adopt virtual and hybrid models to complement conventional in-person events [1]. Three broad evolutionary phases of this digital transformation journey are identified. The first phase focused on basic web presence and digital supplementary channels like emails and electronic brochures to provide online information access to attendees, exhibitors and organizers in the 1990s and early 2000s.

This supplemented physical fairs by enabling basic pre-event and post-event communications. The second phase from the mid-2000s involved automation of key processes to increase efficiency, reduce costs and improve experiences. Digital tools were adopted for visitor registration, payments, surveying, data tracking, and post-event follow-ups. Email marketing became more sophisticated. This improved organizers' ability to profile attendees, personalize communication, and nurture relationships. The current phase exhibits rapid innovation in virtual environments, artificial intelligence, augmented/virtual reality, integrated systems, and omnichannel experiences to create digital-physical hybrid models for trade fair participation. Immersive online platforms are being adopted to showcase exhibitor profiles, products, conduct meetings, and live stream keynotes and conferences. Mobile apps provide real-time notifications, navigation and networking.

According to UFI, over 90% of trade fair organizers globally now offer online business matchmaking platforms and meeting scheduling tools to enable meaningful pre-fair connections between attendees [1]. Sophisticated data analytics provides visitor profiling for personalized content and experiences onsite.

Such virtual engagement solutions significantly expand the reach and participation in events at lower costs for attendees who need not incur travel and accommodation expenses. It generates additional revenue streams for organizers through year-round online platforms, worldwide access and new exhibitor categories [2]. During disruptions like the COVID pandemic, digital channels helped maintain business continuity and engagement.

However, Kirchgeorg explains that traditional organizations have shown reluctance to abandon physical experiences entirely for virtual events [3]. Change resistance and lack of digital skills among some stakeholder groups persists. Smaller fairs are also challenged by the substantial investments required in advanced technologies, platforms, devices and digitally skilled talent.

While virtual attendance amplifies reach, the lack of in-person interactions can negatively impact lead conversions and relationship development compared to physical fairs [1]. Data privacy, system integration complexity and measuring return on digital investments remain areas requiring resolution [2].

In summary, while digital innovation is rapidly transforming the trade fair industry, it is an evolution involving gradual adoption of emerging technologies based on user readiness. Thoughtful change management and continuous improvement of digital capabilities are vital for organizers to provide digitally-enabled experiential value [3].

2.2 Cross-cultural Communication Considerations

As trade fairs bring together participants from diverse cultural backgrounds, effectively designing communication and engagement platforms requires cross-cultural sensitivity [4]. Cultural values and dimensions profoundly influence behaviors, expectations and preferences of attendees from different regions. Hofstede established influential cultural dimensions that explain cross-national variations - individualism versus collectivism, power distance, uncertainty avoidance, masculinity versus femininity, and long-term versus short-term orientation [5].

In individualistic societies, the focus is on self-interest and autonomy. Collectivist cultures prioritize group interests and shared objectives [5]. Communication styles and decisions differ accordingly. Collectivist Asian cultures tend to be more indirect and relationship-focused compared to direct approaches in individualistic Western cultures.

Power distance refers to the acceptance of inequality and hierarchies. In high power distance societies like China, communications are more deferential to authority. Low power distance Nordic cultures prefer more participative, informal exchanges.

Uncertainty avoidance measures risk tolerance. Cultures high on this dimension favor structured interactions, formalities and detailed planning to minimize ambiguity. Masculine cultures emphasize achievements, competition and results. Feminine cultures value cooperation, empathy and quality of life.

Long-term orientation considers the time horizon of relationships and decisions. Asian cultures score high on long-term orientation with a focus on persistence, prudence and tradition. The West exhibits more short-term orientation.

These cultural dimensions profoundly shape participant expectations, etiquette, relationship-building priorities, and communication styles at global trade fairs. As Rothlauf explains, Swiss attendees prefer quick, direct exchanges to get factual information while Chinese participants expect more indirect, ceremonial conversations focused on establishing rapport [6].

Hofstede's high power distance dimension is visible in the formal communications and protocols favoured in Asian and German fairs [6]. Uncertainty avoidance drives the emphasis on structure, planning and authority in Chinese culture contrasted against risk-taking in American culture.

Thus, trade fair organizers must sensitively balance messaging tones, relationship-building time, participant interactions, content styles and engagement platforms to align with the cultural dimensions of target markets.

With virtual engagement gaining prominence, designing culturally appropriate digital communication and experiences is equally crucial for global trade fairs. For instance, collaborative tools that allow document co-creation align well with collectivist cultures while efficient messaging platforms suit individualistic ones. Virtual reality tours can minimize uncertainty for risk-averse cultures. Avatars and agents could be designed to display culturally suitable tone, formality and etiquette. Providing relevant language translations and interfaces is also vital. Visual aesthetics and colors that appeal to local cultural sensibilities require consideration [6]. Thus, Hofstede's established cultural dimensions theory provides a valuable framework for trade fair organizers to assess target markets and sensitize communication designs for cross-cultural relevance.

However, balancing cultural alignment with global integration remains an ongoing challenge. A customized local approach can fragment experiences while standardized messaging overlooks cultural nuances. Developing "glocal" strategies that balance localization and globalization is advised by many researchers. This requires continually evaluating user data and feedback to improve communication designs. Intercultural training for event staff is also recommended to avoid misunderstandings [4]. As virtual engagement increases, creating culturally hybrid digitally-enabled experiences emerges as a key priority for global trade fair success.

3   Research Methodology

This study adopts a comparative case study approach to analyze the digitalization and cross-cultural communication strategies adopted by leading trade fairs worldwide. Case study method allows an in-depth investigation of real-world contemporary events and provides insights into complex issues [7]. The comparative design enables identifying common patterns and differences across multiple cases based on selected parameters [8].

Six major international trade fairs were purposively selected as cases to provide diversity across geographies, industries, and digital advancement:

- Hannover Messe (Germany) - Industrial technology
- CES (USA) - Consumer electronics
- Mobile World Congress (Spain) - Telecommunications
- GITEX (UAE) - Information technology
- Auto Expo (India) - Automotive
- Canton Fair (China) - General merchandise

The fairs cover key regions of Europe, North America, Middle East, Asia and major emerging markets like China and India. Both B2B and B2C events are included. They also represent industries at varying levels of digital transformation, allowing for rich insights.

The cases are compared on the following key parameters: type and scale of digital platforms adopted; online exhibitor profiles and engagement tools; use of virtual/augmented reality, live streaming and conferencing, mobile apps and networking features, multilingual and cultural sensitivity, website content and accessibility.

Secondary data is gathered from the official websites, annual reports, visitor statistics and other digital assets of each fair. Primary data is collected through interviews with the digital marketing and communication teams of the respective fair organizers. The interviews focus on understanding their digital and cross-cultural communication strategies and challenges.

4   Findings and Discussions

4.1   Overview of Digitalization Approaches

The comparative analysis revealed diverse digitalization strategies adopted by the six global trade fairs:

Hannover Messe has an extensive online exhibitor profile system that includes detailed product brochures, videos, and messaging options. Visitors can schedule meetings prior to the event via the website. The app offers augmented reality navigation, live chats with exhibitors, and real-time notifications.

CES provides both exhibitor profiles and a separate online showroom to showcase new product launches. Their app has built-in AI to provide personalized recommendations to attendees. CES offers live streaming of keynotes and conferences as well as virtual reality experiences of exhibitor booths for online visitors.

Mobile World Congress facilitates business matching and meeting scheduling through the website. The app includes maps, alerts, bookmarks and networking features. 5G connected cameras provide live streaming of activities across venues. VR demonstrations of new mobile technologies are also showcased.

GITEX has relatively basic online exhibitor listings but offers an AI-powered business matching platform. Their mobile app provides real-time navigation, information, and networking options. The Shift X conference is live streamed on their website and social media.

Auto Expo has recently launched visitor registration and exhibitor profile creation systems on their website. Their app offers basic information and navigation. Conferences are recorded and uploaded after the event for online visitors. Options for live streaming or virtual exhibition booths are currently limited.

Canton Fair has end-to-end integrated systems for online exhibitor management, product showcases, meeting scheduling and live chat. The website and app provide multilingual support in 9 languages. Video conferences with exhibitors in real-time are enabled through the 'Cloud Canton Fair' platform.

4.2 Commonalities and Differences Among Platforms

The analysis revealed some common patterns as well as key differences in the digital platforms and features adopted across the global trade fairs.

All six fairs implemented online exhibitor profiles and product listings on their websites to enable attendees to access information prior to the physical events, aligning with Rinallo et al.'s phase of supplementary web presence. However, the depth of data provided in these digital profiles varied [2].

Four out of six fairs offered mobile apps for attendees. While the apps uniformly facilitated navigation, alerts and basic networking during the fairs, they differed significantly in the extent of personalization, use of emerging technologies like artificial intelligence and virtual reality, and overall sophistication.

Business matchmaking and meeting scheduling functionalities were made available through the websites by most fairs, reflecting the growing industry practice highlighted by UFI [1]. However, Canton Fair and Mobile World Congress stood out for implementing more advanced, integrated systems for automated matchmaking.

Live streaming of keynote sessions and conferences was prevalent across four fairs but not utilized by Auto Expo and GITEX, despite its potential for broader virtual attendee engagement as argued by Rothlauf [6].

Notable strategic differences emerged between Western and Asian fairs' digital focus. Canton Fair offered the most comprehensive suite of integrated online showrooms, video conferencing, and multilingual platforms aligned with relationship-focused collectivist cultures [5]. Whereas fairs in mature Western markets prioritized advanced technologies like artificial intelligence and virtual reality for efficient, personalized experiences per the tenets of individualistic cultures [6].

4.3 Cross-cultural Communication Differences

The cross-cultural communication variations were analyzed through the lens of Hofstede's cultural dimensions theory [5]. Significant differences were observed between the Western trade fairs situated in individualistic, low-context cultures like the United States and Northern Europe versus Asian fairs embedded within collectivist, high-context environments.

Trade fairs catering to Eastern and Southern regions emphasized building relationships, ceremonial engagement protocols, and indirect communication patterns. For instance, the Canton Fair and Mobile World Congress integrated video conferencing, interpreters, meeting coordinators, and extensive relationship-building time. This aligns with collectivist cultures that prioritize group interests over individuals [5].

In contrast, Western fairs like CES and Hannover Messe reflected individualistic cultural preferences for direct, concise, transactional communication focused on content over relationships. The contrasting communication styles correlate with the distinctions between high-context communication rich in symbolism versus low-context explicit styles as analyzed by Hall [9].

Hofstede's power distance dimension was visible in the hierarchical, formal communications adopted in German and Chinese fairs. High uncertainty avoidance cultures drove the emphasis on rituals, structured interactions and authority in Asia. GITEX incorporated Arabic language, social media and community engagement highlighting Middle East's contextual communication.

The emphasis on aesthetics and symbolic imagery in Asian fairs relates to their long-term orientation [5]. Masculine cultures at Western fairs prioritized efficiency, results and quick information access over elaborate ceremonial exchanges. Thus Hofstede's framework provides valuable insights into cross-cultural communication variations at global trade fairs.

4.4 Effective Practices for Online Engagement

The comparative analysis revealed a range of effective practices implemented by leading trade fairs worldwide to facilitate online visitor and exhibitor engagement on their digital platforms.

Several fairs offered robust online matchmaking and meeting scheduling tools to enable meaningful pre-fair connections between attendees [2]. For instance, Mobile World Congress facilitated business matching through AI algorithms while Canton Fair provided interpreters and coordinators to support relationship building between international exhibitors and buyers.

Fairs that adopted emerging technologies like augmented and virtual reality provided distinctive digital experiences. For example, CES offered virtual reality previews of exhibitor booths and products while Hannover Messe used augmented reality for navigation and information access.

Multilingual support across online platforms and mobile apps, exemplified extensively at Canton Fair, helped overcome language barriers highlighted as key considerations for global business contexts by Lauring and Selmer [4]. Providing relevant cultural translations and etiquette guidance to international visitors was another effective engagement practice.

Several fairs live-streamed keynotes, conferences and new product launches to engage remote audiences, consistent with Rothlauf's recommendations on expanding exhibitor reach and visitor knowledge-sharing globally through virtual events [6].

In summary, personalized matching services, interactive digital experiences, multilingual content, and live streaming expanded online participation while exhibiting cultural sensitivity at global trade fairs.

4.5 Key Considerations for Communication Design

Creating culturally inclusive experiences for diverse trade fair audiences represents an intricate challenge with multifaceted dimensions for organizers to address sensitively.

Incorporating extensive language support emerges as an obvious yet critical starting point. Provision of multilingual translations and real-time interpreters, as exemplified by the Canton Fair, aids relationship building aligned to the richer contextual preferences of collectivist Asian cultures contrasted against Western transactional efficiency priorities [5, 10]. However, nuanced linguistic fluency alone is insufficient if underlying messaging styles remain incongruent across cultures. Adapting informational, promotional, and relational content themes to align with audience preferences is vital for resonance [6]. For instance, feminine cultures may resent aggressive hard-selling approaches. Images and examples used should reflect local environments rather than seeming alien or irrelevant, thus straining engagement.

Beyond language and content, the actual online and onsite platforms enabling participation equally warrant careful localization. Factors like navigation flows, visual layouts, interface aesthetics, symbolic elements, colors, and typography should appeal to cultural sensibilities in target geographies [5, 9]. Keeping platforms versatile for personalization and iteration allows incorporating user feedback for continuous improvement rather than a one-time adaptation, as advised by change management models.

While complete localization remains impractical, some standardization for efficiency and global consistency is logical. Finding the strategy equilibrium between customized and shared elements is recommended by glocalization theory proponents [13], enabled by insights from analytics and staff intercultural training. Additional exploratory frameworks like dialogic communication [14] or cultural intelligence models [15] can reveal innovations in engaging diverse trade fair audiences both online and onsite.

In summary, creating inclusive global trade fair experiences spans multifaceted complexities around customized language provision, culturally adaptable content, versatile interactive platforms, change responsiveness, and balanced glocalization. Further academia-industry research leveraging qualitative inquiries like discourse analysis and quantitative data analytics can provide continuous advances.

5   Conclusions

This comparative case study analysis of digital transformation and cross-cultural communication strategies in global trade fairs provides valuable insights into an increasingly vital intersection for industry policymakers and academic researchers alike. The trade fair ecosystem is undoubtedly experiencing profound technology-led disruption, mirrored across sectors from media and retail to hospitality, education and beyond [11]. However, an overemphasis on digital innovation risks alienating diverse cultural audiences through standardized one-size-fits-all platforms. This analysis soundly highlights why a nuanced, human-centric approach balancing business transformation objectives with end-user inclusivity across cultures is prudent yet complex for organizers [4, 6]. The findings revealed common adoption of basic online functionalities for information and networking access, indicating trade fairs are still aligning with early supplementary and process enhancement stages of technology assimilation [2]. This gradual evolution is understandable considering the cultural diversity, change resistance, and infrastructure limitations persisting across emerging markets and traditionalist stakeholder groups [3]. Canton Fair and CES also provide illuminating examples of more mature digital business model innovation harnessing advanced technologies for value creation rather than just cost efficiencies. Their pioneering experiments with integrated video conferencing, AI-driven personalization and virtual reality hint at the expansive frontiers still ahead for the industry if user readiness and cultural alignment can keep pace with technological capabilities [5].

Regional variations in digital strategy priorities proved significant through the comparative analysis using established cultural dimensions theory [5]. The predominance of relationship-focused, customized and contextual communication in Asian fairs contrasted starkly against efficient, concise information exchanges at Western fairs. Thus, while shared online platforms aid global accessibility, localized experiences anchored in cultural insights drive meaningful participation as supported by scholars [4, 6]. Achieving this strategy balance remains an ongoing challenge warranting continued examination.

The hybrid model is rising as the dominant paradigm, potentially delivering the 'best of both worlds' by synergizing virtual scalability and in-person interactions. Yet the formula for crafting optimal blends is far from standardized. Creating integrated omnichannel experiences that align physical showrooms, interactive conferences, online meeting schedulers, mobile apps, streaming content and immersive technologies requires continual customization based on value perceptions across target cultures [10]. Therefore, follow-up studies surveying user attitudes and technology readiness are warranted to validate, generalize and extend the exploratory cultural patterns identified here. Larger multi-year analyses may reveal maturity trajectories for the hybrid model across regions and sectors. Investigating optimal combinations of physical, digital and hybrid elements to create bespoke experiential value for diverse trade fair stakeholders is imperative as the next research frontier [2].

For industry organizers seeking digital transformation, this analysis recommends an insights-driven roadmap centered on cultural inclusion. Launching multiple localized pilot initiatives allows testing innovations on willing user segments before evaluating scalability [3]. Staff training is crucial to avoid cultural disconnectedness or misunderstandings in increasingly blended engagement mediums [4]. However, balancing standardization for cost efficiency with regional adaptation remains a persisting tightrope walk. Ongoing monitoring of diverse visitor segments through feedback loops, user data and analytics allows course corrections in communication designs [10]. But organizational cultures also require maturation to accept failures during digital experimentation journeys in complex global environments. Progress may seem patchy rather than linear. Thus, by underscoring cultural sensitivity as a pivotal priority while harnessing digital disruption, this study contributes timely perspectives for both scholars and practitioners steering the global trade fair industry towards an integrated, inclusive world business ecosystem. But it also triggers imperative new questions on participant-centric experiential optimization making way for the research avenues ahead at the crossroads of culture and technology.

Acknowledgements. The authors would like to acknowledge Philosophy and Social Sciences Fund in Guangdong Province (GD22CYS17), Educational Science Planning Project (Higher Education Special) in Guangdong Province (2022GXJK230), Educational Science Planning Project (Higher Education Special) in Guangdong Province (2023GXJK343) for research support.

References

1. UFI: Trade Fair Industry Re-opening: Challenges and Opportunities (2021). https://www.ufi.org/wp-content/uploads/2022/01/UFI_trade_fair_industry_reopening_report_2021.pdf. Accessed 10 Jan 2024
2. Rinallo, D., Borghini, S., Golfetto, F.: Exploring visitor experiences at trade shows. J. Bus. Ind. Mark. **31**(4), 553–562 (2016)
3. Kirchgeorg, M., Jung, K., Klante, O.: The future of trade shows: insights from a scenario analysis. J. Bus. Ind. Mark. **25**(4), 301–312 (2010)
4. Lauring, J., Selmer, J.: Multicultural organizations: common language and group cohesiveness. Int. J. Cross Cult. Manag. **10**(3), 267–284 (2010)
5. Hofstede, G.: Culture's Consequences: Comparing Values, Behaviors. Sage Publications Institutions and Organizations across Nations, Thousand Oaks (2001)
6. Rothlauf, J.: A Global View on Intercultural Management: Challenges in a Globalized World. Walter de Gruyter GmbH & Co KG, Berlin (2014)
7. Yin, R.K.: Case Study Research: Design and Methods, 6th edn. Sage Publications, Thousand Oaks (2018)
8. Goodrick, D.: Comparative Case Studies: Methodological Briefs-Impact Evaluation No. 9. UNICEF-IRC (2014). https://www.unicef-irc.org/publications/pdf/brief_9_comparativeca sestudies_eng.pdf. Accessed 10 Jan 2024
9. Hall, E.T.: Beyond Culture. Anchor Books, Palatine (1976)
10. Bond, M.H., Hwang, K.K.: The social psychology of Chinese people. In: Bond, M.H. (ed.) The Psychology of the Chinese People, pp. 213–266. Oxford University Press, Oxford (1986)
11. Rogers, E.M.: Diffusion of Innovations. Free Press, New York (1995)
12. Daft, R.L., Lengel, R.H.: Organizational information requirements, media richness and structural design. Manag. Sci. **32**(5), 554–571 (1986)
13. Robertson, R.: Globalisation or glocalisation? J. Int. Commun. **1**(1), 33–52 (1994)
14. Kent, M.L., Taylor, M.: Toward a dialogic theory of public relations. Publ. Relat. Rev. **28**(1), 21–37 (2002)
15. Earley, P.C.: Redefining interactions across cultures and organizations: moving forward with cultural intelligence. Res. Organ. Behav. **24**, 271–299 (2002)

Exploring User Engagement with Smartwatch Health Services: A Comparative Study Between Taiwan and Singapore

Chih-Chang Lin[1], Fang-Wu Tung[2]([✉]), and Chien-Hsiung Chen[1]

[1] National Taiwan University of Science and Technology, No. 43, Keelung Road, Section 4, Da'an District, Taipei City 106335, Taiwan (R.O.C.)
[2] National Tsing Hua University, 101, Section 2, Kuang-Fu Road, Hsinchu 300044, Taiwan (R.O.C.)
fwtung@mx.nthu.edu.tw

Abstract. This study explores the differences in health attitudes, the roles of smartwatches, their Perceived Persuasiveness, Satisfaction, and Continuance Intention between respondents from Singapore (N = 139) and Taiwan(n = 140) using smartwatch technologies. Through the collection of survey data, we conducted independent samples t-tests to analyze the variance in respondents' attitudes and intentions towards smartwatch usage. It highlights significant regional differences in the adoption and usage of wearable technology. In Singapore, users exhibit a more pronounced engagement with health-oriented behaviors and a stronger emphasis on healthy lifestyles compared to their Taiwanese counterparts. This suggests a higher accessibility to health resources and a greater emphasis on health in Singapore. Smartwatches are primarily viewed as practical tools that enhance productivity and efficiency, with a secondary role as health and fitness coaches. Despite subtle differences in perceived persuasiveness, overall satisfaction levels with smartwatch technology were comparable between the two regions. However, Singaporean users showed a greater intention to continue using smartwatches, possibly reflecting a more vibrant health and fitness culture and higher technological engagement. These findings underscore the influence of cultural and regional factors on technology acceptance and highlight the need for tailored public health strategies and technology marketing approaches that consider the unique cultural and social dynamics of each market.

Keywords: Smartwatch · Health attitude · Perceived Persuasiveness · Satisfaction · Continuance Intention

1 Introduction

Smartwatches have transitioned from mere timekeepers to vital health and communication devices, integrating into our daily lives [1]. With the advancement of technology, wearable devices such as smartwatches are playing an increasingly significant role in personal health management [2]. These devices provide monitor health indicators such

P.-L. P. Rau (Ed.): HCII 2024, LNCS 14700, pp. 99–114, 2024.
https://doi.org/10.1007/978-3-031-60901-5_8

as heart rate, step count, and sleep quality [3], and push health recommendations through apps, helping users better understand their health status and achieve better health management outcomes [4]. However, consumers from different cultural backgrounds may have different levels of acceptance and usage habits regarding smartwatches in health management, and these differences may be influenced by attitudes towards health. This study aims to explore, in the different cultural contexts of Singapore and Taiwan, users' attitudes towards health and how they perceive the role of smartwatches in promoting health. By comparing the phenomena and correlations of perceived persuasiveness, satisfaction, and continuance Intention among smartwatch users in these two Asian regions, this study hopes to achieve the following objectives:

1. Compare with the relationship and differences between health attitudes and smartwatch usage among users in Singapore and Taiwan.
2. Investigate the perceptions of Singaporean and Taiwanese users towards the health services system provided by smartwatches and the role these functions play in daily health management.
3. Conduct a thorough analysis of the variances in perceived persuasiveness, user satisfaction, and the inclination towards continued use of smartwatches between the consumer bases in Singapore and Taiwan.

This exploration aims to unravel the impact of cultural distinctions on these aspects, providing insights into the broader implications of cultural context on technology adoption and sustained engagement. Through this exploratory study, the objective is to unearth valuable insights for the product design and market strategy of smartwatches, aiming to cater to the needs of consumers from diverse cultural backgrounds. Furthermore, the findings will enhance our understanding of the application of persuasive technology and theories of continued use across different cultural contexts, offering a reference for future research in related fields.

2 Literature Review

2.1 Health Attitudes

Health attitudes play a pivotal role in shaping individuals' overall well-being, encompassing behaviors and attitudes towards regular exercise, balanced diet maintenance, seeking health assistance, and willingness to modify unhealthy habits [5]. The establishment of a regular exercise routine is fundamental, as numerous studies have highlighted its significance in enhancing both physical and mental health. Regular physical activity is associated with improved cardiovascular function, muscle strength, emotional stability, and self-regulation, underscoring the importance of adhering to a consistent exercise regimen for health improvement [6, 7]. Furthermore, the maintenance of a balanced diet is crucial in the prevention of chronic diseases and the promotion of overall health [8]. Research indicates that a balanced diet supports weight management and reduces the risk of various chronic conditions, including cardiovascular diseases and diabetes, emphasizing the need for individuals to adopt and maintain healthy dietary practices [9]. Aside from engaging in physical activity and maintaining a healthy diet, actively pursuing support, and accessing information concerning both physical and mental well-being is crucial for improving individual health outcomes [10]. This involves consulting health professionals, participating in health programs, and engaging with health-related information, which collectively empower individuals with the knowledge to identify and address health issues proactively [11]. Moreover, the willingness to undergo regular health check-ups and alter unhealthy habits constitutes a critical aspect of a positive health attitude [12]. Regular health screenings facilitate the early detection of potential health problems, allowing for timely interventions. Simultaneously, the readiness to change detrimental habits, such as smoking cessation and reducing alcohol consumption, plays a vital role in diminishing illness risks and elevating the quality of life [13]. These comprehensive approaches to health behavior and attitudes highlight the multi-faceted nature of health maintenance and the importance of integrated efforts in achieving optimal health outcomes.

2.2   The Role of Smartwatches in Health

Smartwatches are increasingly recognized as indispensable tools for health tracking and monitoring. These devices, equipped with advanced sensors and algorithms, track and monitor a variety of health indicators, including physical activity, heart rate, and sleep patterns, providing users with insights into their health status and progress towards fitness goals [14]. With technological advancements, improvements in accuracy and reliability of smartwatches are overcoming the limitations of early sensor technology, making them effective companions for health management. Furthermore, the virtual coaching functions of smartwatches actively engage users in their health and fitness journeys [15]. By offering personalized exercise recommendations, tracking progress, and providing motivational feedback tailored to users' fitness levels and preferences, these devices highlight their potential as effective virtual coaches [16]. In addition to health monitoring and personalized fitness guidance, smartwatches also serve as comprehensive health management tools, offering features such as medication reminders, emergency alerts [17], and continuous health data monitoring. These features are particularly beneficial for individuals with chronic conditions, providing a layer of safety and convenience in daily health management tasks. Moreover, integrated entertainment features, such as music playback and games [18], not only increase user satisfaction and engagement but also contribute to a more enjoyable and sustainable user experience, encouraging continuous use and adherence to health and fitness monitoring routines. This underscores the multifaceted value of smartwatches in modern life.

2.3   User Experiences and Continuance with Smartwatches

Perceived Persuasiveness. Perceived persuasiveness (PP) is the user's subjective impression of the capability of smartwatches to influence health behavior changes [26]. This concept is vital in the design of smartwatches' health services, such as step and heart rate monitoring, and evaluates if these features can effectively encourage users towards healthier lifestyles [21, 22]. Real-time feedback from these devices plays a crucial role in motivating users to improve their habits [23]. Enhancing user experience with personalized features improves the technology's persuasiveness [24], which is essential in health-related apps as it affects user adherence to recommendations and continued use of the technology [25]. Designers must focus on interface and interaction methods to maximize smartwatches' persuasive potential.

Satisfaction: User satisfaction (STC) is a critical determinant of Continuance Intention (CI) for smartwatches, influencing whether users will keep using their devices [27]. Satisfaction, driven by the product's performance, design, and price, boosts use frequency and brand loyalty [28]. Emotional responses and health features also affect satisfaction levels, potentially impacting the continued use of smartwatches [29]. Manufacturers must focus on user feedback to refine smartwatch offerings and enhance user satisfaction.

Continuance Intention. Continuance Intention (CI) in smartwatch use is users' willingness to persist in using the device, shaped by their satisfaction, perceived value, and habits [2]. Control variables like age, gender, frequency of use, health attitudes, and roles influence CI, as younger users might be more tech-savvy and gender can dictate health feature priorities [2, 31]. CI is complex, intertwining psychological, behavioral, and demographic factors [32], crucial for enhancing smartwatch design and marketing strategies.

3 Methodology

This study aims to explore the relationship between health attitudes, role perceptions, perceived persuasiveness, satisfaction, and continuous usage intention among smartwatch users in Singapore and Taiwan. By comparing users from two different cultural backgrounds, the study seeks to reveal how cultural differences affect the acceptance and usage behavior of smartwatches.

Research Method. A cross-cultural study design, combining quantitative and qualitative mixed methods for data collection, is employed. Specific methods include online survey questionnaires and street interviews with random questionnaire distribution, to gain a comprehensive and in-depth understanding of user experiences and views.

Sample and Data Collection. The target population for this study comprises current smartwatch users in Singapore and Taiwan, encompassing individuals of all genders aged 18 and above, without restrictions based on professional backgrounds. A total of 391 questionnaires were collected, out of which 279 Table 1 Singapore N = 139 and Taiwan Table 2 N = 140 were deemed valid. Validity criteria included completeness, consistency, and verification of authenticity. Data collection methods employed include an online survey conducted through the SurveyMonkey platform, with promotion through social media and professional forums to ensure wide dissemination. Additionally, street questionnaire surveys and interviews were conducted in selected public areas such as shopping malls, university campuses, and parks, utilizing random sampling techniques to gather more diverse and in-depth data.

Questionnaire Design. The questionnaire meticulously gathers basic demographic details of participants, such as age, gender, nationality, alongside their smartwatch usage patterns, encapsulating frequency and duration of use, as well as preferred features. It

Table 1. Demographics of respondents of Singapore

Singapore Statistics	Count	Percentage
Gender		
Male	97	69.78%
Female	42	30.22%
Age		
18–24	24	17.27%
25–34	5	3.60%
35–44	28	20.14%
45–54	52	37.41%
55–64	20	14.39%
65+	10	7.19%
Using Time		
Less than half a year	18	12.95%
Half a year to a year	27	19.42%
One to two years	78	56.12%
Over three years	16	11.51%
Role		
Tool	77	55.40%
Coach	25	17.99%
Mento	3	2.16%
Companion:	5	3.60%
Administrator	29	20.86%

Table 2. Demographics of respondents of Taiwan

Taiwan Statistics N = 140	Count	Percentage
Gender		
Male	93	66.43%
Female	47	33.57%
Age Group		
18–24	5	3.57%
25–34	32	22.86%
35–44	52	37.14%

(*continued*)

Table 2. (*continued*)

Taiwan Statistics N = 140	Count	Percentage
45–54	40	28.57%
55–64	8	5.71%
65+	3	2.14%
Using Time		
Less than half a year	3	2.14%
Half a year to a year	5	3.57%
One to two years	79	56.43%
Over three years	53	37.86%
Role		
Tool	85	60.71%
Coach	22	15.71%
Mentor	4	2.86%
Companion	7	5.00%
Administrator	22	15.71%

further probes into participants' perceptions of smartwatches' roles in their daily lives, spanning from tools and coaches to mentors, companions, managers, and even toys. In Scale Design Table 4, we meticulously developed four scales aimed at quantifying health attitudes, perceived persuasiveness, satisfaction levels, and the intention to continue using smartwatches. Each of these scales includes five items and utilizes a 7-point Likert scale for responses, ranging from "strongly disagree" to "strongly agree," facilitating nuanced evaluation. The formulation of these scales is informed by thorough literature review, ensuring each construct is accurately represented as per Table 3. To guarantee the questionnaire's clarity and precision, and to account for cultural nuances, it is crafted in both English and Traditional Chinese.

Data Analysis Techniques. In this study, we conducted independent samples t-tests using SPSS 25 to analyze the differences in Health Attitude, Perceived Persuasiveness, Satisfaction, and Continuance Intention among smartwatch users in Singapore and Taiwan. By calculating mean values, standard deviations, and p-values and t-values (two-tailed), we assessed the statistical significance of differences between the two national cohorts. The analysis was performed under the assumption of unequal variances, with a significance level set at $p < 0.05$ to determine statistical significance.

Moreover, Table 5 displays the reliability and validity metrics for the scale, encompassing four constructs: Health Attitude, Perceived Persuasiveness (PP), Satisfaction (STC), and Continuance Intention (CI). These metrics include factor loadings, Cronbach's alpha values greater than 0.7 (indicating internal consistency), Composite Reliability (CR) values above 0.7, and Average Variance Extracted (AVE) values exceeding 0.5. The data confirm that all constructs meet the generally accepted standards for

Table 3. Operational definition

Constructs	Definition	Ref.
Health Attitude	An individual's attitude and behavior towards health, including their values, beliefs, and active engagement in actions promoting health	[5]
Perceived Persuasiveness	Refers to the subjective assessment or judgment made by an individual regarding the effectiveness or strength of a message, argument, or communication in influencing their attitudes, beliefs, or behaviors	[20]
Satisfaction	Feeling pleased or content with a product, service, or experience based on personal expectations or desires	[31]
Continuance Intention	The intention or willingness to keep using a product, service, or engaging in a behavior over time	[2]

Table 4. Questionnaires

Constructs	Items
Health Attitude (HA) [5]	a. I have a regular exercise routine b. I pay attention to maintaining a balanced diet c. I proactively seek assistance when it comes to my physical and mental health d. I actively seek health information, such as reading articles or participating in courses e. I undergo regular health check-ups f. I think that I am willing to change unhealthy habits
Role [16]	a. Tool: Provides practical functions b. Coach: Offers exercise advice c. Mentor: Provides personalized advice d. Companion: Accompanies you through each day e. Administrator: Monitors health data f. Toy: Provides entertaining features g. Other
Perceived Persuasiveness (PP) [26]	a. The data display on the smartwatch helps me better understand my physical condition b. The notification feature on the smartwatch promptly alerts me to important health information c. Through self-monitoring data, I gain a better understanding of my physical condition, influencing me to adjust my lifestyle d. The goal-setting feature on the smartwatch motivates me to engage more actively in health activities e. Through gamification, earning reward badges encourages me to participate more actively in physical activities

(continued)

Table 4. (*continued*)

Constructs	Items
Satisfaction (STC) [33]	a. I am satisfied with the health data display provided by the smartwatch b. I believe that receiving important notifications on my smartwatch positively influences my lifestyle c. I feel dissatisfied with my smartwatch d. I believe that the accuracy of health data on my smartwatch meets my expectations e. Achieving goals on my smartwatch gives me a sense of accomplishment
Continuance Intention (CI) [31]	a. I am going to continue using my smartwatch b. I perceive my smartwatch as an integral part of my daily routine c. I am considering discontinuing using my smartwatch d. I will be using the health service system on my smartwatch in the future e. I find the fitness and exercise functionalities of my smart watch to be essential for my daily activities

Cronbach's alpha, CR, and AVE, demonstrating the scale's good internal consistency, composite reliability, and convergent validity.

Table 5. Reliability and Validity Table

Constructs	Factor loading	α	C.R	AVE
Health Attitude	0.880	0.932	0.947	0.747
	0.871			
	0.814			
	0.914			
	0.903			
Perceived Persuasiveness (PP)	0.877	0.909	0.938	0.738
	0.923			
	0.934			
	0.828			
	0.716			
Satisfaction (STC)	0.960	0.983	0.987	0.938
	0.970			
	0.964			

(*continued*)

Table 5. (*continued*)

Constructs	Factor loading	α	C.R	AVE
	0.986			
	0.963			
Continuance Intention (CI)	0.904	0.951	0.962	0.835
	0.928			
	0.912			
	0.912			
	0.914			

4   Results

Table 6 presents distinct differences in health behaviors between Singaporean and Taiwanese respondents, particularly in regular exercise routines. Singaporeans reported a higher mean score (5.81) versus Taiwanese respondents (3.49), marking a significant gap (2.320) with statistical significance (p < 0.001). This indicates a stronger inclination towards or more frequent engagement in regular exercise among Singaporeans. In terms of dietary habits, Singaporeans also scored higher on maintaining a balanced diet (5.64) compared to their Taiwanese counterparts (5.22), with this difference being statistically significant (p = 0.001), highlighting a more pronounced focus on dietary balance in Singapore. Additionally, Singaporeans showed higher proactivity in seeking health-related assistance (5.76 vs. 5.13), suggesting differences in cultural or social support systems, with a significant disparity (p < 0.001). While Singaporeans also lead in seeking health information and undergoing regular health check-ups, indicating greater health awareness and a proactive approach to preventive health measures, the study found no significant difference between the two groups in these domains (p = 0.954).

Table 7 indicates a preference for utilitarian roles, such as "Tool" and "Administrator," in both Singapore and Taiwan, with "Tool" being the most popular role in both countries, followed by "Administrator." The data indicates a significant gender disparity in the "Tool" role, with males outnumbering females in both regions, suggesting male dominance in certain industries or functions. Meanwhile, the gender distribution within the "Administrator" role shows relative balance in Singapore, but a male majority in Taiwan.

Besides, "Mentor" and "Companion" roles attract fewer individuals, hinting at these roles' lesser prominence or demand within the specific contexts of Singapore and Taiwan. This analysis highlights the intricate relationships between nationality, gender, and preferred roles, underlining the impact of gender on role selection across different cultural backgrounds and the varying prevalence of roles within society.

Regarding perceived persuasiveness, as detailed in Table 8, there are noticeable differences between the respondents from Singapore and Taiwan, especially concerning the item "Perceived Persuasiveness-b." Here, Singaporean respondents rated slightly higher

Table 6. Health Attitudes of Smartwatches Among Respondents

Health Attitude	Nation	Mean	Std. Deviation	t-value	p-value (2-tailed)
HA-a	Singapore Taiwan	5.81 3.49	0.982 0.502	24.871	<0.001
HA-b	Singapore Taiwan	5.64 5.22	1.014 0.997	3.478	0.001
HA-c	Singapore Taiwan	5.76 5.13	0.734 0.973	6.127	< 0.001
HA-d	Singapore Taiwan	5.68 5.34	1.051 0.829	2.943	0.004
HA-e	Singapore Taiwan	5.91 5.47	1.021 0.985	3.622	<0.001
HA-f	Singapore Taiwan	6.09 6.10	0.932 0.931	-0.058	0.954

Table 7. Nation, Gender, and Role Crosstabulation

Role	Gender	Singapore	Taiwan	Total
Tool	Male	58	55	113
	Female	19	30	49
	Total	77	85	162
Coach	Male	17	14	31
	Female	8	8	16
	Total	25	22	47
Mentor	Male	3	3	6
	Female	0	1	1
	Total	3	4	7
Companion	Male	4	5	9
	Female	1	2	3
	Total	5	7	12
Administrator	Male	15	16	31
	Female	14	6	20
	Total	29	22	51
Total	Male	97	93	190
	Female	42	47	89
	Grand Total	139	140	279

Table 8. Perceived Persuasiveness of Smartwatches Among Respondents

Perceived Persuasiveness	Nation	Mean	Std. Deviation	t-value	p-value (2 tailed)
PP-a	Singapore	5.60	0.535	1.926	0.055
	Taiwan	5.47	0.555		
PP-b	Singapore	5.63	0.592	2.144	0.033
	Taiwan	5.49	0.556		
PP-c	Singapore	5.60	0.634	1.863	0.064
	Taiwan	5.46	0.555		
PP-d	Singapore	5.46	0.581	1.340	0.181
	Taiwan	5.37	0.528		
PP-e	Singapore	5.27	0.635	0.325	0.745
	Taiwan	5.25	0.564		

than their Taiwanese counterparts (5.63 vs. 5.49), with this variance reaching statistical significance (p = 0.033). This outcome suggests that Singaporean respondents tend to assess perceived persuasiveness marginally higher. While other items also recorded higher average ratings from Singaporean respondents, these variations did not achieve statistical significance (p-values > 0.05). This indicates that, aside from the specific aspect of "Perceived Persuasiveness-b," there are no substantial differences in perceived persuasiveness between the two groups across other evaluated items.

Table 9. Satisfaction of Smartwatches Among Respondents

Satisfaction	Nation	Mean	Std. Deviation	t-value	p-value (2 tailed)
STC-a	Singapore	5.63	0.684	−0.222	0.824
	Taiwan	5.64	0.589		
STC-b	Singapore	5.69	0.721	0.607	0.544
	Taiwan	5.64	0.589		
STC-c	Singapore	5.55	0.724	−0.794	0.428
	Taiwan	5.61	0.531		
STC-d	Singapore	5.60	0.786	−0.300	0.764
	Taiwan	5.63	0.541		
STC-e	Singapore	5.67	0.706	0.632	0.528
	Taiwan	5.62	0.543		

Regarding satisfaction in Table 9, the average ratings for both respondent groups are closely aligned, with no statistically significant differences observed across all satisfaction variables (p-values > 0.05). This uniformity suggests that respondents from Singapore and Taiwan share comparable levels of satisfaction, indicating that the product, service, or concept examined maintains a consistent satisfaction level irrespective of cultural context. This consistency underscores the universal appeal and effectiveness of the offering, highlighting its capability to meet diverse user expectations across varied cultural backgrounds.

Table 10. Continuance Intention of Smartwatches Among Respondents

Continuance Intention	Nation	Mean	Std. Deviation	t-value	p-value (2 tailed)
CI-a	Singapore	6.36	0.67	5.293	<0.001
	Taiwan	5.96	0.598		
CI-b	Singapore	6.18	0.673	4.179	<0.001
	Taiwan	5.85	0.645		
CI-c	Singapore	6.23	0.618	6.547	<0.001
	Taiwan	5.76	0.570		
CI-d	Singapore	6.13	0.679	5.531	<0.001
	Taiwan	5.71	0.594		
CI-e	Singapore	6.10	0.695	3.52	0.001
	Taiwan	5.80	0.732		

According to Table 10 continuance intention, Singaporean respondents' average ratings were significantly higher than those of Taiwanese respondents across all items, with these differences being highly significant statistically (p-values less than 0.001). This shows that Singaporean respondents have a much higher intention to continue using the product or service compared to Taiwanese respondents. This could reflect cultural differences, market acceptance, or differences in satisfaction with the product/service. Overall, the results for perceived persuasiveness and satisfaction show a consistent experience among respondents from both countries, with most item differences being insignificant, except for one item in perceived persuasiveness. However, in terms of continuance intention, Singaporean respondents significantly outscored Taiwanese respondents, which might indicate higher loyalty or satisfaction among Singaporean respondents, or a greater willingness to accept and continue using these products services.

5   Discussion

5.1   Health Attitude

The comparative analysis between Singaporean and Taiwanese respondents highlights significant differences in health behaviors, such as regular exercise, proactive health assistance seeking, and routine health check-ups, with Singaporeans displaying higher engagement. These disparities may stem from Singapore's robust promotion of a healthy lifestyle through extensive public health initiatives, including those by the Health Promotion Board [33]. Meanwhile, the similarity in changing unhealthy habits between the two groups underscores the global challenge of modifying entrenched lifestyle behaviors. These findings emphasize the importance of customizing public health strategies to the distinct cultural and social contexts of different populations. It points to the need for personalized health communication strategies to effectively meet the diverse needs of various communities. Future research should explore the socio-psychological and environmental factors affecting health behavior change, aiming to identify key elements that either facilitate or impede such changes.

5.2 The Roles of Smartwatches

The most significant role identified by respondents from both Singapore and Taiwan is that of a Tool, with 113 males and 49 females viewing smartwatches primarily as functional devices. This highlights a general recognition of smartwatches as devices that boost productivity and efficiency, likely attributed to their capacity to streamline communication, manage tasks, and swiftly access information. Additionally, the role of a Coach, which focuses on health and fitness guidance, receives substantial attention, though to a lesser degree. This mirrors the increasing trend of leveraging technology for personal health management, portraying smartwatches as personal trainers that monitor physical activities, suggest workouts, and track health metrics. Intriguingly, the roles of Mentor, Companion, and Administrator are less emphasized, suggesting these facets may not be the primary drivers for smartwatch adoption in these regions. This could imply that while smartwatches are appreciated for their practical utility and health-centric features, their potential as educational tools, means of social connection, or organizational aids might not have been fully tapped or promoted.

5.3 Perceived Persuasiveness

The findings indicate a nuanced landscape of perceived persuasiveness, with PP-b (Singapore: 5.63, Taiwan: 5.49) showing a statistically significant difference ($t = 2.144$, $p = 0.033$), suggesting that certain features or benefits of smartwatches are more persuasive in Singapore than in Taiwan. However, the marginal differences in PP-a and PP-c, along with the lack of statistical significance in PP-d and PP-e, imply that the overall persuasiveness of smartwatches does not drastically differ between the two regions. This could be attributed to global similarities in technological trends and consumer expectations from wearable devices.

5.4 Satisfaction

The satisfaction scores reveal no significant differences between the two countries across all aspects, indicating a general contentment with smartwatch technology in both regions. This uniform satisfaction might reflect the global standards and quality of smartwatch features that cater well to consumer needs in diverse markets. The close mean scores suggest that regardless of geographical location, users have similar satisfaction levels, possibly due to comparable functionalities and user experiences offered by smartwatch brands internationally.

5.5 Continuance Intention

Continuance Intention presents a stark contrast, with all aspects (CI-a through CI-e) showing significant differences, indicating a stronger intention to continue using smartwatches among Singaporean respondents. This could suggest that Singaporeans, possibly due to a higher engagement with technology or more pronounced health and fitness culture, see more value in continuing the use of smartwatches. The significant t-values and low p-values (<0.001 for CI-a, CI-b, CI-c, and CI-d; 0.001 for CI-e) highlight a definitive intention among Singaporean users to incorporate smartwatches into their daily lives over the long term. These results underline the importance of cultural and regional factors in technology acceptance and usage. While the perceived persuasiveness and satisfaction with smartwatches do not significantly differ, the stark difference in continuance intention underscores the potential influence of societal norms, health consciousness, and technological integration within a region.

6 Conclusion

This study explores smartwatch usage attitudes and behaviors among Singaporean and Taiwanese respondents, highlighting cultural and regional impacts on technology acceptance. While continuance intention shows notable differences, with Singaporeans more inclined towards ongoing use, perceived persuasiveness and satisfaction levels remain consistent across both regions, indicating smartwatches' regional appeal. Gender and role perception variances provide insights for targeted marketing and product customization. The study underscores the importance of acknowledging cultural nuances in health attitudes for effective public health strategies. Emphasizing the need for technology products to resonate with diverse user preferences, future research should focus on cultural influences and the development of strategies to enhance smartwatch appeal worldwide.

Research Limitations: This study faces several limitations. First, the sample size and representativeness may restrict the diversity of smartwatch user perspectives in Singapore and Taiwan, impacting the results' generalizability. Second, despite efforts to compare these regions, the study might not fully capture the cultural differences' impact on smartwatch usage, overlooking factors like socioeconomic status and education level. Additionally, focusing solely on Singapore and Taiwan limits the findings' applicability to other regions with different cultures or healthcare systems. Lastly, interpreting results can be challenging due to cross-cultural differences, potentially affecting the accuracy of the observed differences between the two regions.

Acknowledgments. We sincerely thank all the participants who generously shared their time and insights in Singapore and Taiwan. Without their valuable contributions, this research would not have been possible. Additionally, this study was partially supported by the National Science and Technology Council of the Republic of China, under grant number NSTC 112-2410-H-007-101.

References

1. Bölen, M.C.: Exploring the determinants of users' continuance intention in smartwatches. Technol. Soc. **60**, 101209 (2020)
2. Chuah, S.H.W.: You inspire me and make my life better: Investigating a multiple sequential mediation model of smartwatch continuance intention. Telemat. Inform. **43**, 101245 (2019)
3. Cipriano, M., Costagliola, G., De Rosa, M., Fuccella, V., Shevchenko, S.: Recent advancements on smartwatches and smartbands in healthcare. In: Chen, Y.-W., Tanaka, S., Howlett, R.J., Jain, L.C. (eds.) Innovation in Medicine and Healthcare. SIST, vol. 242, pp. 117–127. Springer, Singapore (2021). https://doi.org/10.1007/978-981-16-3013-2_10
4. Dooley, E.E., Golaszewski, N.M., Bartholomew, J.B.: Estimating accuracy at exercise intensities: a comparative study of self-monitoring heart rate and physical activity wearable devices. JMIR mHealth uHealth **5**(3) (2017)
5. Dutta-Bergman, M.J.: Primary sources of health information: comparisons in the domain of health attitudes, health cognitions, and health behaviors. Health Commun. **16**, 273–288 (2004)
6. Haible, S., Volk, C., Demetriou, Y., Höner, O., Thiel, A., Sudeck, G.: Physical activity-related health competence, physical activity, and physical fitness: analysis of control competence for the self-directed exercise of adolescents. Int. J. Environ. Res. Publ. Health **17**(1), 39 (2020)
7. Kaushal, N., Rhodes, R.E., Meldrum, J.T., Spence, J.C.: The role of habit in different phases of exercise. Br. J. Health. Psychol. **22**(3), 429–448 (2017)
8. Adams, J.: Addressing socioeconomic inequalities in obesity: democratising access to resources for achieving and maintaining a healthy weight. PLoS Med. **17**(7), e1003243 (2020). https://doi.org/10.1371/journal.pmed.1003243
9. Bates, B., Collins, D., Cox, L., Nicholson, S., Page, P., Roberts, C., et al.: National Diet and Nutrition Survey Years 1 to 9 of the Rolling Programme (2008/2009–2016/2017): Time Trend and Income Analyses. Public Health England, London (2019)
10. Bangerter, L.R., Griffin, J., Harden, K., Rutten, L.J.: Health information–seeking behaviors of family caregivers: analysis of the health information national trends survey. JMIR Aging **2**(1), e11237 (2019)
11. Lambert, S.D., Loiselle, C.G.: Health information—seeking behavior. Qual. Health Res. **17**(8), 1006–1019 (2007)
12. Hajek, A., Bock, J.O., König, H.H.: The use of routine health check-ups and psychological factors—a neglected link. Evidence from a population-based study. J. Publ. Health **26**, 137–144 (2018)
13. Park, B.H., Lee, B.K., Ahn, J., Kim, N.S., Park, J., Kim, Y.: Association of participation in health check-ups with risk factors for cardiovascular diseases. J. Korean Med. Sci. **36**(3) (2021)
14. Siepmann, C., Kowalczuk, P.: Understanding continued smartwatch usage: the role of emotional as well as health and fitness factors. Electron. Mark. **31**, 795–809 (2021). https://doi.org/10.1007/s12525-021-00458-3
15. Martinato, M., et al.: Usability and accuracy of a smartwatch for the assessment of physical activity in the elderly population: observational study. JMIR mhealth uhealth **9**(5), e20966 (2021)
16. Lopez, G., Abe, S., Hashimoto, K., Yokokubo, A.: On-site personal sport skill improvement support using only a smartwatch. In: 2019 IEEE International Conference on Pervasive Computing and Communications Workshops (PerCom Workshops), pp. 158–164. IEEE, March 2019
17. Choi, J., Kim, S.: Is the smartwatch an IT product or a fashion product? A study on factors affecting the intention to use smartwatches. Comput. Hum. Behav. **63**, 777–786 (2016)

18. Fogg, B.J.: Persuasive Technology: Using Computers to Change What We Think and Do. Morgan Kaufmann, Burlington (2003)
19. Khakurel, J., Pöysä, S., Porras, J.: The use of wearable devices in the workplace - a systematic literature review. In: Gaggi, O., Manzoni, P., Palazzi, C., Bujari, A., Marquez-Barja, J.M. (eds.) GOODTECHS 2016. LNICSSITE, vol. 195, pp. 284–294. Springer, Cham (2017). https://doi.org/10.1007/978-3-319-61949-1_30
20. Kim, H., Song, M.: Personalized health recommendation system using machine learning algorithms on smartwatch data. IEEE Access **9**, 123456–123467 (2021)
21. Ramezani, R., Cao, M., Earthperson, A., Naeim, A.: Developing a smartwatch-based healthcare application: notes to consider. Sensors **23**(15), 6652 (2023)
22. Oyibo, K., Orji, R., Vassileva, J.: Investigation of the persuasiveness of social influence in persuasive technology and the effect of age and gender. In: Ppt@ persuasive, pp. 32–44, April 2017
23. Orji, R., Vassileva, J., Mandryk, R.L.: Modeling the efficacy of persuasive strategies for different gamer types in serious games for health. User Model. User-Adap. Inter. **24**, 453–498 (2014)
24. Beerlage-de Jong, N., Kip, H., Kelders, S.M.: Evaluation of the perceived persuasiveness questionnaire: user-centered card-sort study. J. Med. Internet Res. **22**(10), e20404 (2020)
25. Couchoud, C., et al.: Low incidence of SARS-CoV-2, risk factors of mortality and the course of illness in the French national cohort of dialysis patients. Kidney Int. **98**(6), 1519–1529 (2020)
26. Siepmann, C., Kowalczuk, P.: Understanding continued smartwatch usage: the role of emotional as well as health and fitness factors. Electron. Mark. **31**(4), 795–809 (2021)
27. Uzir, M.U.H., et al.: The effects of service quality, perceived value and trust in home delivery service personnel on customer satisfaction: evidence from a developing country. J. Retail. Consum. Serv. **63**, 102721 (2021)
28. Hong, J.C., Lin, P.H., Hsieh, P.C.: The effect of consumer innovativeness on perceived value and continuance intention to use smartwatch. Comput. Hum. Behav. **67**, 264–272 (2017)
29. Rekha, I.S., Timothy, P.S.: Understanding the antecedents to smart watch user's continuance intention. Int. J. Bus. **25**(4), 367–381 (2020)
30. De Wulf, K., Schillewaert, N., Muylle, S., Rangarajan, D.: The role of pleasure in web site success. Inf. Manag. **43**(4), 434–446 (2006)
31. Vinzi, V.E., Trinchera, L., Amato, S.: PLS path modeling: from foundations to recent developments and open issues for model assessment and improvement. In: Handbook of Partial Least Squares: Concepts, Methods and Applications, pp. 47–82 (2010)
32. Farrell, A.M., Rudd, J.M.: Factor analysis and discriminant validity: a brief review of some practical issues. In: Australia and New Zealand Marketing Academy Conference 2009. Anzmac (2009)
33. HPB Homepage. https://www.hpb.gov.sg. Accessed 16 Feb 2024
34. Sports Administration Homepage. https://www.sa.gov.tw. Accessed 16 Feb 2024

Research on the Design of Digital Interactive Medical Goggles with Integrated Modeling

Jingjing Mu[1,2,3](✉) and Olena Vasylieva[3]

[1] Nanjing College of Fine Arts and Design, Communication University of China, Beijing, China
2395893918@qq.com
[2] College of Design and Art, Shaanxi University of Science and Technology, Xian, China
[3] Kyiv National University of Technologies and Design, Kyiv, Ukraine

Abstract. Purpose Digital interactive medical goggles are designed to provide not only a diverse aesthetic experience for medical workers, but also a unique interactive experience. In view of the growing environment of medical device design, medical personnel's high demand for equipment applicability and aesthetics, this paper analyzes the current situation of medical goggle design and the use process of medical personnel, analyzes the current situation of medical goggle design and the use process of medical personnel, and conducts a systematic design and innovation research and design practice for medical protective goggles. **Methods** The five key factors of medical goggles in terms of shape, structure, color, function and material are established by entropy weight method, then the KANO model is used to identify the user requirements, the Quality Function Deployment (QFD) method is applied to transform the requirements into design parameters, and the problems in the design process are solved with the help of the TRIZ theory, and finally the systematic design innovation research and design practice is carried out. **Results** The user requirement items are constructed, the real needs of medical personnel for goggles at three levels of necessity, expectation and charm are screened out, and then transformed into quality characteristics and importance ranking, which are verified through experiments, and the aesthetics, safety and ease of use of the product are taken into consideration, and the product is placed in the "man-machine-environment", so that the user experience, function configuration and adaptability are improved. The user experience, function configuration and adaptability are improved. **Conclusion** The integrated application of KANO-QFD-TRIZ model proposes a new design scheme for medical goggles, which can provide a reference for the design of medical goggles in the future.

Keywords: KANO-QFD- TRIZ · Medical Goggle Design · Digital Interaction

1 Medical Goggles Status and Problem Analysis

From the existing literature, the current research on the design of goggles is relatively single form, this paper is a comprehensive method of assessment, through the KANO model to sort out the user needs in the use of medical goggles, the use of quality function deployment (QFD) method and TRIZ theory, combined with the user interviews on the

P.-L. P. Rau (Ed.): HCII 2024, LNCS 14700, pp. 115–128, 2024.
https://doi.org/10.1007/978-3-031-60901-5_9

market the overall situation of the existing medical goggles, the innovative design of medical goggles, emphasize the Human-computer interaction feedback effect, improve the comfort and safety of goggles, and improve the degree of lightweight.

2 Theoretical Foundations

2.1 Entropy Weight Method

Entropy weight method is a multi-criteria decision-making method based on the principle of information entropy, which can reduce the error caused by human factors, and obtain the weight value and evaluation results of each evaluation index scientifically and accurately. In decision-making problems, multiple evaluation criteria or indicators are often involved, and the importance weights of these criteria may be different. The entropy weighting method can help decision makers to consider the importance of these criteria and assign a corresponding weight to each criterion, which makes the decision-making results more reasonable and reliable.

2.2 Kano Model

Kano model is a quality management tool used to help enterprises understand and satisfy the hierarchy and characteristics of customer needs, by analyzing and classifying customer needs and satisfaction with the characteristics of the product or service, qualitative and quantitative way to classify and rank user needs, and provide the priority of the needs for product design and development [1].

2.3 QFD-TRIZ

Quality Function Deployment (QFD) is a multilevel deductive analysis method to satisfy the quality management system, and its core content is requirement transformation. This helps product development teams accurately translate user needs into design requirements and ensures that the product development process is aligned with user needs. Theoretical Innovation (TRIZ) is a systematic approach to innovation aimed at solving technical and engineering problems.TRIZ provides a set of tools and principles for analyzing problems and finding innovative solutions.

QFD-TRIZ is an innovation tool that combines the two approaches of Quality Function Deployment (QFD) and Theoretical Innovation (TRIZ). The combination of QFD-TRIZ combines the customer orientation and design transformation capabilities of QFD with the problem solving and innovation methods of TRIZ. The aim is to complement the strengths of QFD and TRIZ with each other to better solve problems in product development and innovation and understand user needs. By using QFD-TRIZ, product development teams can find more innovative and feasible design solutions while meeting user needs.

2.4 Design Process Under Entropy Weight Method-Kano-QFD-TRIZ Integration Model

In this study, the entropy weight method-Kano-QFD-TRIZ integrated model is used to construct an innovative design scheme, and the combination of the four can form the design process of medical protective goggles from researching and acquiring requirements to functional development. The entropy weight method is used to objectively assign weights to the demand indicators of medical goggles, the Kano model accurately describes the demand for medical goggles, and different demand attributes are classified to filter out the real demand for goggles from medical personnel at three levels of necessity, expectation, and charisma; the combination of the entropy weight method and the Kano model can be used to more scientifically and efficiently analyze the demand indicators of medical goggles. Using QFD theory to establish the correlation matrix between user requirements and design requirements, the running data of the Kano model can be transformed into design elements and quality characteristics, which can provide decision-making for product development and design. Then the TRIZ tool can be used to solve the problems between the characteristics of medical protective goggles and come up with innovative solutions for design.

3   Design Process

3.1 Technical Function Analysis of Medical Goggle Products

Observation Analysis and User Requirements.   By observing the overall situation of the existing medical goggles on the market, such as appearance, surface fogging treatment process, man-machine experience [2], etc., combined with user interviews, policy standards, literature and design specifications, etc., in-depth investigation of the functional technology of the existing goggles, wearing comfort and other practical situations. Taking this as a reference element, the collected user information is subject to data statistics and organization, and 46 statistical items of medical goggles user requirements are initially established [3], taking functional requirements as an example, and the specific contents are shown in Table 1.

In order to ensure the accuracy of the demand elements, 30 designers of related research directions and 20 experts were invited to evaluate and score the content of the above demand items according to the Likert five-level scale method, and the user needs were screened and categorized through the degree of agreement of professionals, and 25 demand items of 5 categories were finally identified (Table 2), and the affinity diagram method was used to establish the demand element set of the medical goggles, and the functional requirements were used as an example for the description of the specific content (Table 3).

Table 1. Statistics on user demand for medical goggles (functional requirements)

Demand information (observation content)	Requirements	Types
De-fogging function, can quickly eliminate the fog, to avoid the fog in use to affect the clarity of vision and work efficiency of health care workers [4]	defog	functional requirement
Contains an internal cleaning filter to block dust, particles, bacteria and other contaminants from entering the eye area	Clean filtration	
Real-time monitoring of fogging status, timely feedback warning information to remind the user to deal with, to maintain a clear field of view	Fogging Detection	
Avoid complementary colors to interfere with the observation and judgment of medical personnel for the color information of the work area, to ensure the visual accuracy in use and reduce visual fatigue	Avoid complementarycolor interference	
Removes moisture and heat from around the face in time to ensure eye safety, comfort and clarity of vision while wearing [9]	outgassing	
Breathable to ensure adequate oxygen supply to the face and reduce discomfort during use	air permeability	
It can sterilize and disinfect the goggles to prevent the growth and spread of bacteria, viruses and other pathogens on the goggles, and effectively protect the personal safety of health care workers	sterilization	
Easy to carry around, light weight, small size, will not take up too much space, reduce the workload	conveniently portable	

(*continued*)

Table 1. (*continued*)

Demand information (observation content)	Requirements	Types
Reduces static buildup on the surface of the goggles to avoid dust and other impurities from adhering to the lenses and maintains a high level of transmittance	Electrostatic properties	
Reduces the pressure and weight of goggles worn by healthcare workers and improves comfort while wearing them	depressurize	

3.2 Establishing and Defining User Requirements

Indicator Construction and Questionnaire Design. The questionnaire design of KANO model is centered on the 25 design elements screened above, the related issues of demand items, to further clarify the core needs of healthcare workers. The questionnaire design adopts the "positive and negative questions" model, and is divided into two scoring standards according to the degree of user satisfaction with the needs. (See Table 4 for details).

Based on the principle of proximity, the medical and nursing staff of hospitals in Nanjing, Jiangsu Province were selected as samples, with an average of 30–50 questionnaires per hospital, a total of 325 questionnaires were distributed, and 309 valid questionnaires were returned, with a validity rate of 95%.

Data Collection and Processing. The obtained data is based on the KANO model of medical goggles design of 25 demand elements for attribute percentage calculation, and then the percentage of the same demand attributes to sum up, to determine the number of each demand attribute, and analyze the positioning of the attributes to which it belongs. The KANO model of the evaluation results of the classification of the cross-reference table, A represents the charismatic attributes, M represents the necessary attributes, O represents the desired attributes, I represents the non-differentiated attributes, R represents the reversed attributes and Q stands for suspicious attribute [1].

Since medical goggles involve multiple demand attributes sorting and grading, it is necessary to calculate the Better-Worse coefficient value of each demand element separately, and its calculation formula is shown below:

Better = (A share + O share)/(A share + O share + M share + I share)
Worse = −1 ∗ (O share + M share)/(A share + O share + M share + I share)

The resulting positive and negative Better values calculated represent different levels of user satisfaction. Positive values close to 1 represent a strong influence of consumer satisfaction when the element is available, while negative values close to −1 represent a strong degree of consumer dissatisfaction when an element is not available. According

Table 2. Primary evaluation of the demand for medical goggles

Functionality categorization	number	Elements of demand	weights	Functionality categorization	number	Elements of demand	weights
modeling Z	Z1	Man-machine size	4.593	materialC	C1	Soft comfortable	4.8
	Z2	field of view	4.331		C2	lightweight	4.752
	Z3	Fitting Masks	3.976		C3	Safe & Healthy/Skin Friendly	4.593
	Z4	Simple hard-edged	3.675		C4	wear resistant	4.233
	...	...	...		C5	Environmentally friendly/recyclable	3.876
					C6	Adjustability of the elastic band	3.681
structureJ	J1	easy handling	4.463		C7	Lens Clarity	3.536
	J2	Easy disassemble	4.139		...	...	...
	J3	fully enclosed	3.728	functionG	G1	defog	4.461
	...	...	...		G2	Clean filtration	4.283
					G3	Fogging Detection	3.947
Colors	S1	sense of calm	4.228		G4	outgassing	3.832
	S2	Avoid complementary color interference	3.921		G5	air permeability	3.818
	S3	technology	3.743		G6	sterilization	3.625
	S4	A sense of quiet and purity	3.514		G7	wireless charging	3.563
	...	...	...		...	...	...

to the KANO model, a scatter plot of the Better-Worse coefficient values is plotted to clarify the order of importance of each demand element in the direction of product design.

Classification and Ranking of Requirement Categories. Relying on the above data analysis, take "Z1 man-machine size" as an example, from $0 > A > M > I > R(Q)$, so Z1 is the desired attribute, and so on, the 25 demand factors are positioned in 6 categories of attributes. According to the importance ranking of the demand elements in the diagram, the demand factors corresponding to I, R and Q attributes are sifted out, and finally 3 types of attributes are determined for the evaluation of the medical goggle design elements, Messential attributes, O expected attributes and A charismatic attribute, which contain a total of 15 factors.

Z4, C1, C2, C3 belong to the essential needs (M), which mainly include the four elements of "simplicity and rigidity", "softness and comfort", "lightness", and "safety and health/skin-friendliness", Z1, Z2, C6, C7, J2, and G2 belong to the expected requirements

Table 3. User demand level of medical goggles (functional requirements)

Firstly requirements	Secondary requirements	Specific description of requirements
G functional requirement	G1defog	Rapid de-aeration and fogging to maintain a clear field of vision
	G2Clean filtration	Blocking and filtering dust, particles, bacteria and other pollutants
	G3Fogging Detection	Real-time monitoring, timely feedback, warning alerts
	G4Avoid complementary color interference	Avoid complementary color interference, use green, blue, etc.
	G5outgassing	Timely removal of internal moisture, heat, etc.
	G6air permeability	Adequate oxygen supply to ensure eye safety
	G7sterilization	Prevent the growth and spread of pathogens such as bacteria and viruses

Table 4. Primary evaluation of the demand for medical goggles

problems	options				
If medical goggles have this element, do you think that	unnecessary	Not really	cannot be said	more necessary	Most necessary
If the medical goggles do not have this element, do you think that	non-acceptance	Not really	cannot be said	more acceptable	most acceptable

(O), which mainly include "human-machine dimension", "field of vision", "elasticity", Z1, Z2, C6, C7, J2, and G2 belong to the expected requirements (O), which mainly include six elements: "human body size", "field of view", "adjustability of elastic band", "lens clarity", "easy to disassemble", and "cleaning and filtration". Z3, C4, G3, G4, G5 are attractive requirements (A), which mainly include "fitting the mask", "wear-resistant and easy to drop", "fogging detection", "venting", "exhausting", "wear-resistant and easy to drop", "wear-resistant and easy to drop", "easy to remove", "easy to clean" and "clean filtration". "Fogging detection", "Exhaust treatment" and "Breathability" (see Fig. 1).

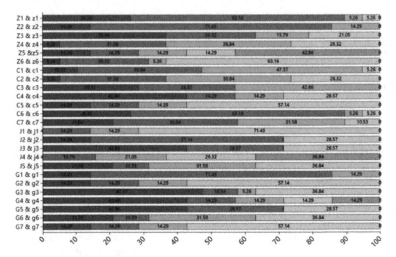

Fig. 1. Demand factor attributes of medical goggles.

3.3 Design Quality House Construction and Analysis

Design Feature Transformation. Constructing. QFD quality function development, clarifying design guidelines and strategies, and improving the accuracy and effectiveness of design. Among them, the construction of House of Quality model (HOQ) is the focus, through the development of the quality of the House of more intuitive and clear performance of the user expectations and technical needs of the specific needs of the correlation between the comprehensive weight indicators [5], the demand for the elements of the indicators into the importance of the weight formula, the formula is shown below, through the calculation of the designers more effective access to the design elements of the weight order, to achieve a more efficient design with a lower design cost. Design.

In the formula: Rij is the value of quality house relationship; Wi is the demand weight.

$$M_j = \sum_{i=1}^{j} R_{ij} W_i$$

Feature Analysis and Solution. A total of 15 demand factors of 3 types of attributes screened by KANO model are assigned twice to get the comprehensive demand weights, which are imported into the left wall of the House of Quality (HOQ); the House of Quality (HOQ) model is constructed by searching for 40 TRIZ innovation theories to find the ones that are suitable for the demand factors, which are imported into the ceiling of the House of Quality (HOQ) (Table 5). In the matrix diagram of the HOQ, ● is used to indicate strong relevance, ▲ is used to indicate medium relevance, and ○ is used to indicate weak relevance to score the medical goggle demand one-to-one with the innovation principle according to the relevance, in which ● is assigned a value of 5, ▲ is assigned a value of 3, and ○ is assigned a value of 1, and the blank of the intersecting rows and columns indicates no relevance. According to the correlation between the two of the integrated demand weights and the innovation principle, the symbols are filled in to score the correlation, and the correlation matrix is constructed, i.e., the house body of the HOQ. The importance weights of the design solutions are calculated and imported into the basement of the house of quality (HOQ). Since the selected TRIZ innovation principles are juxtaposed to each other and independent of each other, there is no correlation and there is no correlation matrix for the roof section.

Using QFD quality house method to calculate the weights of medical goggle product requirement characteristics, we get the importance and priority ranking of product characteristics, and the ranking results are as follows: pre-compensation principle (19.63) > feedback principle (10.55) > flexible shell/film principle (10.13) > separation principle (9.35) > separation principle (8.85) > unattained/overacting principle (8.65) > Nesting Principle (8.53) > Self-Service Principle (7.57) > Porous Material Principle (7.53) > Inert Environment Principle (6.44) > Changing Color Principle (2.78).

4   Specific Program Design

4.1   Design Description

Pre-compensation Principle. From the entropy weight method-Kano-QFD-TRIZ integrated research path, it is concluded that the innovation principle with the highest weight of demand characteristics in medical goggles is the pre-compensation principle. Pre-compensatory principle means taking precautions in advance before a problem occurs in order to prevent or minimize the danger. To prevent problems and injuries encountered while wearing goggles, the following solutions were derived from the precompensation principle:

First of all, in order to prevent the goggles from slipping off, we investigated the human body size in detail during the construction process of this product, and the head measurement data of Roger, Tilley, etc. show that the height of human head is 109–137 mm, and the width of human head is 130–184 mm. However, the general practice statistics of the human head in Asia, Europe, and the U.S.A. show that the height of human head is 112–147 mm, and the width of human head is 140–168 mm. 140–168 mm (2) According to the analysis of different human head measurements, it can be seen that women's head load-bearing force is significantly smaller than men's, and female healthcare workers produce more obvious strangulation marks when wearing protective goggles for a long time. Therefore, in the design of the elastic band, cotton, silicone and other related materials are added to ensure the safety and comfort of healthcare workers when wearing, and the head-mounted type is used to disperse the pressure on the way of wearing [6]. (3) The nosepiece of traditional medical goggles is made of hard material, which directly conveys the pressure to the skin when it is hit by external force. According to ergonomics, it is known that men and women have different nasal bone width and nose characteristics, in order to meet the user's needs and ensure that the medical protective goggles are comfortable and stable to wear, this product uses a soft material to fit the nosepiece to reduce the impact on the skin, and the 360° omni-directional fit also avoids the risk of a gap between the mask and the nosepiece. (4) In order to ensure the sealing to isolate the pollution and at the same time, consider the ventilation and filtration as well as the visual interference of water vapor, this product is designed with a combination of goggle-mask system, which is not only convenient to wear but also realizes the integration of functions. In the function of the PTC constant temperature heating principle [7], placed in the bottom of the mask on both sides of the micro-pressurized fan, in order to effectively help health care workers blowing away the fog at the same time to play a role in decompression, which is characterized by ① equipped with a demisting indicator ② uniform increase in the wind ③ will not shock the voltage ④ easy cleaning of filters and energy-saving ⑤ with a variable frequency wind speed size adjustment device, the user can adjust the wind speed according to the actual situation (see Fig. 2).

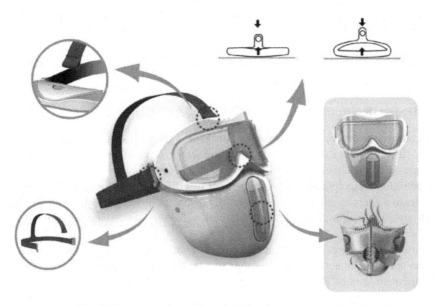

Fig. 2. Demonstration of the principle of pre-compensation.

Feedback Principle. Medical goggles in the demand characteristics of the second weight of the innovation principle is the principle of feedback, in the process of product design first consider the visual feedback that is the color treatment, first from the medical protective goggles itself, the product belongs to the medical supplies, the doctor because in the process of surgery eyes see always bright red blood, a long time, and occasionally transfer the line of sight to the companion's white coat, you will see the blood stains, so that the visual This will produce confusion and affect the surgical effect. The human eye in a long time to watch a color, the optic nerve is easy due to stimulation and fatigue, in order to reduce this fatigue, the optic nerve will be induced by a complementary color to do self-regulation. Medical goggles main color using green can eliminate the green illusion due to a long time to look at the red; Secondly, the user is more inclined to warm tones, can make the equipment feel warm and soft, reduce the sense of distance; Finally, starting from the medical goggles and the environment, the color and the environment should echo each other, harmony and unity. In the hospital such an environment, the most important thing is to create a pure and comfortable environment and operating experience. To sum up, we can combine the actual situation, give full consideration to the user's color perception image, and choose adjectives suitable for the user's perceived psychology for the color scheme design of medical protective eyewear, such as "safe, high quality, stable" [8] and so on. The color matching card is established from the mirror angle, user angle and environment angle for medical protection. Secondly, from the perspective of function indicator, add indicator in the main function module to increase the focus of visual interaction, and at the same time, every time you touch the buttons and switches and other interactive areas there are flashing lights, slight vibration or prompting music and so on as the interactive feedback, to avoid the fatigue process of medical personnel in the process of accidental contact or repeated operation, resulting in delays in the problem(see Fig. 3).

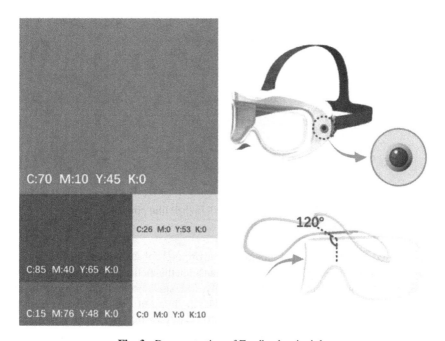

Fig. 3. Demonstration of Feedback principle.

Flexible Shell Film Principle. The innovative principle with the third highest weight in the design process is the flexible shell film principle, a method used for solving technical problems, which is particularly suitable for dealing with problems related to the structure of flexible shell films. The bendability and stretchability of flexible shell films are utilized to solve problems. By adjusting the shape, size, and thinness of the shell film, it is possible to change its performance and functionality, and increase the degree of light weighting. Product appearance and performance are inseparable from the choice of materials. Materials suitable for medical protective lenses are analyzed according to need. Medical protective lens lenses using transparent PC lenses, material general protective glasses using polyvinyl chloride (PVC), this design shell using vinyl, soft and lightweight and easy to bend, elastic band on the use of soft silicone and cotton products, the choice of materials, the entire design of the edge of the wrapped silicone pads filled with sponge pads internally as a way to better fit the skin, thereby reducing strangulation marks. Most of the modules of the product are designed with shell and membrane, leaving a large number of cavities for support and circulation, while the thin shell wall makes the product much lighter and reduces the fatigue loadofmedicalpersonnel (see Fig. 4).

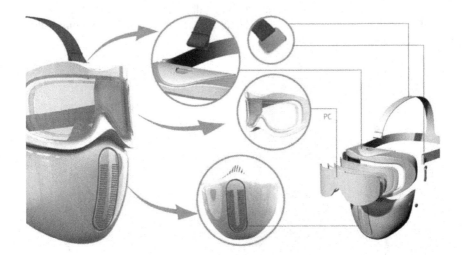

Fig. 4. Demonstration of Flexible shell film principle.

Others. Based on the principle of separation, the principle of segmentation, the principle of transition action and other TRIZ theory guidance, in the medical goggles also focus on human humidity comfort, increase the humidity drainage system in the design, the use of PTC thermostatic heating principle to regulate the humidity, see Fig. 5-12 Fig. 4-10. Summer, the human body in the humidity of 40%–80% of the environment is suitable for the winter season should be controlled at 30%–60%. Influenza is more frequent and lower air humidity is closely related. When the ambient air humidity is lower than 40%, dust, bacteria, etc. are easy to adhere to the mucous membrane, irritate the throat, triggering coughing, and at the same time easily induced bronchitis, asthma and other respiratory diseases. Too much humidity is also not conducive to health, people may feel nausea, loss of appetite, irritability, fatigue, dizziness and so on. Being in a humid and moldy environment for a long time also increases the risk of allergic diseases such as asthma and eczema.

Ordinary plastic medical goggles work for a long time making the interior foggy. There is a micro-pressurized bladeless fan with filter in this product, which not only removes the fog, but also filtersandcleansit (see Fig. 5).

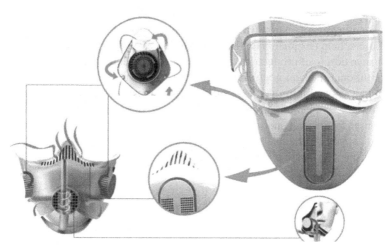

Fig. 5. Demonstration of others.

4.2 Design Evaluation

At the end of the design process needs to carry out usability evaluation of the design solution, the actual product will be issued to the user to carry out live experiments, the actual test of the user needs to meet the degree of satisfaction on the 15 demand points identified in the KANO extracted to form a questionnaire to evaluate the indicators, according to the user to wear the situation of the actual experience of the formation of the design of the feedback radar chart, the rating score for 0–5. For the 15 indicators, which the human-machine size For the 15 indicators, the ratings of man-machine size, obvious reminder light, adjustability of elastic band, de-fogging, avoiding interference of complementary colors, soft and comfortable, lightweight, safety and health/skin-friendliness are all above 4.5 points, except for the ease of dismantling, the ratings are all above 4 points, which shows that the overall satisfaction with the design has reached the standard, but the dismantling still needs to be improved.For the 15 indicators, the ratings of man-machine size, obvious reminder light, adjustability of elastic band, defogging, avoiding interference of complementary colors, soft and comfortable, lightweight, safety and health/skin-friendliness are all above 4.5 points, except for easy disassembly, the ratings are all above 4 points, which shows that the overall satisfaction with the design has already reached the standard, but there is still a need to improve the disassembling performance.

5 Conclusion

With the continuous improvement of product maturity, the iteration of medical products needs to follow a more meticulous and perfect design thinking model. This paper verifies the feasibility of the model in the innovation design of medical goggles based on the entropy weight method-Kano-QFD-TRIZ integrated research path, which provides certain theoretical guidance for the design of related products in the future. The path can be more comprehensive and systematic for innovation design, and the data analysis selects a combination of qualitative and quantitative aspects to reasonably locate the real needs of users, help designers find the best entry point, and provide a new direction for the innovative design of products to solve the pain points and improve user satisfaction. Unlike traditional medical goggles, this product is designed with a combined goggle-mask product system, improved man-machine parameters in the structure, and the use of PTC constant temperature heating, ventilation and defogging in the function, which improves user feedback. It not only solves the problems arising from the use of traditional medical goggles by healthcare workers, but also fills the market gap to a certain extent, forming a new case of optimized output.

References

1. Mu, J.J.: Design of medical protective goggles based on KANO modelling. Guangxi Normal University (2021)
2. Gong, R.E., Zeng, R.M., Li, C.H.: Problems and responses in the use of personal protective equipment in isolation wards for new crown pneumonia. Chin. J. Infect. Control **19**(04), 324–327 (2020)
3. Yin, D.P., Li, H.F., Zhang, S.B.: Survey on the effect of goggle use among medical staff in Wuhan Vulcan Mountain Hospital. Chin. J. Hosp. Infect. **30**(12), 787–1792 (2020)
4. Kong, F.J., Li, H.F.: Application effects of several anti-fogging methods in medical goggles in a new crown isolation ward. Chin. J. Infect. Control **19**(03), 274–276 (2020)
5. Li, W.K., Zhou, Y.D., Yang, Y.M.: Design of intelligent human security gate for high-speed rail station based on KJ-AHP-QFD. Hunan Packag. **38**(06), 137–142 (2023)
6. Ci, H.M., Zhang, X.Y., Wu, J.: Clinical effects of an improved general medical goggle. Intell. Health **8**(36), 120–123 (2022)
7. Wang, Y.X., Wang, H.L., Shi, J.W.: Research on heating and defogging technology of medical goggles based on indium tin oxide film. Nanjing Sci. Technol. J. **46**(01), 15–23 (2022)
8. Fang, K., Zhang, Y.Z., Xu, C.D., et al.: Optimization of injection molding process and improvement of defects of goggles based on Moldex3D. Plast. Ind. **49**(07), 61–65 (2021)
9. Yang, W.X., Chen, T.S., Wang, H.N.: Simulation of medical goggles to stop airborne transmission of viruses: computational fluid dynamics in ergonomics. Ergonomics **66**(3), 350–365 (2023)

Exploring the Impact of Emotional Valence in Advertisements and Compassion Fade on Donation Intention for War Victims

Alina Paniuta[1], Yi-Hsing Han[1(✉)], and Shih-Hsien Hsu[2]

[1] National Chengchi University, Taipei, Taiwan
paulhan@nccu.edu.tw
[2] National Taiwan University, Taipei, Taiwan

Abstract. In the context of the largest war of the twenty-first century in Ukraine, current research seeks to investigate the messaging strategies that will inspire individuals to donate to war victims. Prior research has explored the effectiveness of positive and negative appeals in charitable advertising [1–3]. Some studies suggest that negative appeals, invoking emotions such as sadness [4] and anger [5], may be more effective in motivating donations. However, the mixed findings of previous studies and the evolving modern media environment necessitate a closer examination, especially given the drastic changes in the pace and forms of non-profit communications over the past decade. Furthermore, the phenomenon of compassion fade, defined as the negative correlation between the willingness to help and the number of victims, adds a layer of complexity to understanding donor behavior. In this study, it was proposed that negatively framed appeals would elicit more favorable attitudes toward donation. Emotions of different valences, including sadness, anger, compassion, hope, and pride, were expected to play mediating roles in this process.

Contrary to the initial hypothesis, the results revealed that positive framing was more effective in fostering favorable attitudes and donation intentions. This study specifically addresses the role of hope, an emotion found to mediate this relationship. Another notable finding, the difference in donation amounts influenced by perceived need and victim's identifiability, adds a new dimension to the understanding of compassion fade phenomenon. The study provides valuable recommendations for charitable organizations, emphasizing the importance of positive messaging and the careful consideration of emotional appeals to effectively engage donors and support war victims.

Keywords: Charitable Advertising · Emotional Appeals · Hope · Compassion Fade · Ukrainian War

1 Introduction

1.1 Research Background

The current war in Ukraine, the largest continental conflict since World War II, presents a unique opportunity to expand academic literature on charity advertising directed towards war victims in the modern media landscape. In 2022, a group of six Ukrainian girls

P.-L. P. Rau (Ed.): HCII 2024, LNCS 14700, pp. 129–146, 2024.
https://doi.org/10.1007/978-3-031-60901-5_10

launched "Divchata Power" (translated as "Girls Power" in Ukrainian), a fundraising project. One of the authors was involved in promoting it on social media. The success speaks for itself: within a month, the project raised around USD$60,000 to aid Ukrainian women and children. However, upon restarting the project in March 2023, a year later, engagement and donation amounts significantly declined. While various factors like decreased media attention and general war fatigue may have contributed, the decrease in willingness to help observed with increasing victim numbers, known as "compassion fade," might be impacting the results.

Research has shown that a compassion fade can be closely linked to the identifiability of victims. Individuals are more inclined to donate to causes featuring single, identifiable victims rather than to those representing non-identifiable groups [6]. In light of this, a potential strategy for mitigating compassion fade in the 'Divchata Power' initiative could involve highlighting the stories of specific, identifiable war victims in the project's advertising campaign.

The inclusion of personal stories in charity advertising raises the question of optimal framing for engaging potential donors: positive or negative? Although meta-analyses suggest fear appeals can be effective [7], exposing audiences to graphic imagery of war victims raises ethical concerns. Conversely, Chang and Lee (2009) found images of happy beneficiaries evoked hope, prompting questions about its comparative efficacy [8]. While existing research on message framing in charity advertising (including valence manipulation) has yielded diverse and sometimes contradictory results, it often lacks specific focus on war victims. Additionally, while prior studies primarily employed static photo stimuli, today's social media landscape suggests short videos may be more effective in capturing attention and driving engagement.

1.2 Research Objectives

The debate surrounding the effectiveness of positive versus negative messaging in charity advertising has permeated various contexts and sectors [9]. Despite this extensive research, a critical gap remains in our understanding of its impact on donations to war victims, particularly within the dynamic landscape of modern social media. This study aims to address this gap by investigating the optimal framing for war-related charity advertising in today's social media environment.

Therefore, the first objective is to determine the impact of message valence (positive vs. negative) on attitudes towards donating to war victims, mediated by affect. This builds upon past research by specifically focusing on a war-related context and examining the emotional response as a potential mechanism underlying the message's impact [10]. The second objective is to examine the relationship between attitudes and donation intention. While previous studies may have focused solely on attitude shifts [11], this study moves beyond to assess the crucial transition to concrete action. The third purpose it to explore the mediating role of emotions evoked by different message framings in influencing donation behavior intention. This delves deeper into the psychological processes at play, understanding how emotions connect message framing to attitudes and donation behavior intention [12]. The fourth objective is to investigate the influence of compassion fade on both attitudes and donation intentions. Recognizing the potential decrease in empathy over time [13], this objective examines its impact on the effectiveness of charity messages and seeks potential strategies to overcome it.

This research will advance our understanding of how war-related charity advertising can be optimized for effectiveness in the modern social media context. By identifying the most impactful framing strategies, considering the mediating role of emotions, and addressing the challenge of compassion fade, this study can provide valuable insights for non-profit organizations seeking to effectively engage donors and support war victims. The current study proposes the following research questions. First, what message valence (positive or negative) is more effective in influencing attitudes towards donating to war victims, mediated by specific emotions (e.g., hope, empathy, sadness, anger)? Second, do attitudes affect donation behavior intention, and what factors might explain this transition? Third, how do emotions evoked by different message framings (e.g., fear, hope, compassion) mediate the influence of valence on donation behavior intention? Does compassion fade affect attitudes and donation intentions, and how can these effects be mitigated through message framing or other strategies?

2   Literature Review

2.1   Prospect Theory and Message Framing Effectiveness

Within the realm of charitable advertising, understanding the potential influence of message framing on donor behavior is crucial. Prospect Theory, proposed by Kahneman and Tversky (1979), offers a valuable framework for examining how perceived risk shapes decision-making processes based on framing (positive vs. negative). This theory posits that identical outcomes presented as gains or losses can significantly impact choices. Applying it to charity advertising, positive appeals highlight the beneficial outcomes for recipients (gains) if donations are made, whereas negative appeals emphasize the detrimental consequences (losses) of not donating. Prospect Theory suggests that the drive to avoid negative outcomes may motivate riskier decisions, encouraging donations in response to negative appeals [1]. Although previous studies suggested the potential impact of negative framing in promoting pro-social behaviors like donations and volunteering, it is important to consider the potential drawbacks and ethical implications of exploiting negative emotions for persuasion.

2.2   Theory of Planned Behavior and Donation Intentions

The Theory of Planned Behavior (TPB) by Ajzen (1991) offers another relevant framework for understanding donation intentions within the context of message framing. This theory proposes that behaviors are shaped by a combination of attitudes, subjective norms, and perceived behavioral control. Smith and McSweeney (2007) emphasized the critical role of intention as a key determinant of behavior, highlighting that actions are more likely when perceived as easy and within one's control. TPB has demonstrated strong predictive power across various behaviors, with research including meta-analyses by Armitage and Conner (2001) indicating that attitudes, subjective norms, and PBC account for approximately 40–50% of the variance in intentions and 30% in behavior

[14]. Considering the evidence supporting the effectiveness of negative framing in charity advertising and the interconnectedness of attitudes, intentions, and behaviors outlined in TPB, the following hypotheses were proposed:

Hypothesis 1: Participants exposed to the negatively-framed ad will exhibit more favorable attitudes toward donating money to war victims compared to those exposed to the positively-framed advertisement.
Hypothesis 2: The more favorable the attitudes toward donating money to war victims, the higher the intention to donate.

2.3   Emotions and Decision-Making in Charitable Giving

Modern psychological research heavily emphasizes the crucial role emotions play in shaping our decisions [15]. Keltner and Lerner (2000) propose that even seemingly deliberate choices are often driven by underlying emotions, with individuals subconsciously seeking to reduce negative emotions like guilt and enhance positive ones like pride or happiness [12]. This emotional cycle extends beyond the initial decision, as the chosen course of action can in turn trigger new emotions.

Appraisal Tendency Framework (ATF): Nuances of Emotional Influence. Seeking to refine existing decision-making theories through a focus on specific emotions, Lerner and Keltner (2000, 2001) introduced the Appraisal Tendency Framework (ATF) [12]. This framework links different emotional appraisals with specific decision outcomes. Key to the ATF is the notion that emotions, even those with similar valence (e.g., happiness and anger), can sometimes produce contrasting effects on decisions, while emotions with different valence (e.g., fear and anger) may exert similar influences. The ATF conceptualizes emotional influences on decisions as goal-oriented processes persisting until the underlying emotional concern is resolved. It posits that emotions can trigger cognitive biases, causing individuals to interpret new situations through the lens of the emotion's core appraisal dimensions. These appraisals effectively function as automatic filters shaping how we perceive future events [12].

One set of early studies informing the ATF development examined the differential impact of sadness and anger on causal reasoning [16]. While both emotions share negative valence, sadness is linked to perceptions of situational control, while anger is associated with personal control. The researchers theorized that these differing control perceptions could influence how individuals attribute responsibility for events. Their findings supported this hypothesis, demonstrating that incidental anger led to increased attributions of personal responsibility, whereas sadness prompted increased attributions to fate or external factors.

Negative Emotions and Charitable Giving. Negative emotions, often used in charity advertising, have been extensively studied due to their perceived effectiveness in capturing attention and influencing prosocial behavior. Key examples include sadness, anger, and compassion:

Sadness. Defined as a response to emotional distress or grief, sadness can trigger empathy and willingness to help [17]. Individuals exposed to sad expressions in charity appeals may experience compassion, leading to increased donation intentions [17].

Hypothesis 3a: Exposure to the negatively-framed advertisement will increase feelings of sadness compared to the positively-framed advertisement.

Anger. Triggered by perceived injustice or suffering, anger can motivate action and donations [4]. Anger directed towards specific perpetrators in fundraising messages might encourage action, provided it serves a restorative function [5].

Hypothesis 3b: Exposure to the negatively-framed advertisement will increase feelings of anger compared to the positively-framed advertisement.

Compassion. Encompassing both sensitivity and a desire to alleviate suffering, compassion has emerged as a potent motivator for prosocial behavior [18]. Positive correlations between compassion and donation intentions have been observed [19].

Hypothesis 3c: Exposure to the negatively-framed advertisement will increase feelings of compassion compared to the positively-framed advertisement.

Mediating Role of Emotions. Beyond understanding the independent effects of emotions, exploring their potential mediating role in influencing donation intentions is crucial. This section acknowledges the ongoing debate around mediating mechanisms and proposes hypotheses for further investigation:

Hypothesis 4a: The higher the level of experienced sadness, the more favorable attitudes toward donating money to war victims.
Hypothesis 4b: The higher the level of experienced anger, the more favorable attitudes toward donating money to war victims.
Hypothesis 4c: The higher the level of experienced compassion, the more favorable attitudes toward donating money to war victims.

Positive Emotions and Charitable Giving. While negative emotions often dominate war-related charity advertising, recent research highlights the potential of positive emotions to influence prosocial behavior. This section examines how hope and pride, specifically, may motivate individuals to donate to war victims.

Hope. Defined as the "yearning for better and believing the wished-for improvement is possible" [20], hope fosters optimism and the belief in positive change. In the context of war-related charity, hope-oriented messages can emphasize the potential for rebuilding lives, restoring peace, and creating a brighter future for affected communities. This optimistic outlook can encourage individuals to contribute, believing their donation empowers positive change and fosters a sense of agency. Studies show hope-evoking messages resonate in healthcare and environmental contexts [21], with similar potential to motivate charitable donations [22].

Hypothesis 5a: Exposure to the positively-framed advertisement that emphasizes hope will increase feelings of hope compared to the negatively-framed advertisement.
Hypothesis 6a: The higher the level of experienced hope, the more favorable attitudes toward donating money to war victims.

Pride. Characterized as a "sense of accomplishment, joy, or pleasure in something a person has accomplished and/or is capable of accomplishing" [23], pride arises from perceived personal responsibility for positive outcomes. Charity advertising can foster pride by highlighting the impact of individual contributions. Messages emphasizing how donations directly contribute to rebuilding efforts, providing aid to victims, or supporting long-term solutions can evoke a sense of ownership and personal responsibility. This, in turn, can motivate individuals to donate, driven by the desire to contribute meaningfully and make a positive difference [24]. Recent research delves into the nuanced effects of positive emotions on prosocial behavior, emphasizing their diverse impact beyond simply the opposite of negative emotions.

Hypothesis 5b: Exposure to the positively-framed advertisement that emphasizes the impact of individual contributions will increase feelings of pride compared to the negatively-framed advertisement.
Hypothesis 6b: The higher the level of experienced pride, the more favorable attitudes toward donating money to war victims.

2.4 Compassion Fade and Victim Identifiability in the Ukraine War

Compassion fade, a documented psychological phenomenon, describes the decrease in empathy and willingness to help as the number of victims in a crisis increases. In the context of the prolonged Ukraine war, with mounting casualties, this suggests that individuals may become less susceptible to emotional appeals for aid despite continued awareness of the situation. This study explores whether increasing victim identifiability through personalized stories or imagery can counteract this compassion fade and encourage sustained support for the Ukrainian people.

Compassion fade raises concerns for several reasons. Firstly, it contradicts conventional principles of valuing human life equally, regardless of numbers [25]. Secondly, it clashes with our expectations of helping others in need [26]. Finally, it implies that addressing major humanitarian and environmental crises like severe hunger or global warming might require tackling not just economic and political obstacles, but also psychological barriers [27].

Several possible explanations exist for compassion fade, encompassing emotional, cognitive, and motivational factors. One explanation is that individuals feel stronger empathy for a single victim compared to multiple victims, leading to a larger emotional response [28]. Smith, Faro, and Burson (2013) suggest it might partly stem from perceiving groups as less united, as understanding individual perspectives is easier than comprehending group viewpoints [29]. From a motivational standpoint, Cameron and Payne (2011) propose that anticipating requests to help many people, individuals proactively reduce their emotional responses to avoid feeling overwhelmed [30]. These various explanations, though not mutually exclusive, all contribute to understanding compassionate behavior.

Extensive research in the charity field links compassion fade to victim identifiability. Studies consistently show that identifiable victims evoke stronger emotional responses and attract larger charitable donations compared to non-identifiable or statistical victims. For example, Small, Loewenstein, and Slovic (2007) demonstrated increased donation propensity when individuals were presented with the story of a single, identifiable person in need compared to a group of unidentified individuals [28]. This effect is attributed to the emotional connection and specific empathy formed with an identifiable person, which is weaker when faced with abstract numbers or anonymous groups.

Kogut and Ritov (2005) further highlight the "identifiable victim effect," finding that people were more willing to help a single, identifiable child than an unidentified child or a group of children [31]. Jenni and Loewenstein (1997) explored the decreasing willingness to help as the number of victims increases [32]. Västfjäll, Peters, and Slovic (2014) built upon this, demonstrating that emotional responses to an identifiable victim decline when additional statistical lives are mentioned. Additionally, Genevsky, Västfjäll, Slovic, and Knutson (2013) used neuroimaging to show that identifiable victims elicit stronger affective responses in the brain compared to statistical victims [6].

These studies collectively reinforce the notion that appeals to help smaller, identifiable groups of people are more effective in eliciting compassion and encouraging donations than appeals for larger groups of non-identifiable or statistically represented victims. Based on these findings, this study will employ a two-pronged approach to operationalize compassion fade in terms of perceived need and victim identifiability. Therefore, the following hypotheses are proposed:

Hypothesis 7: The higher compassion fade, the lower the level of compassion experienced.
Hypothesis 8: The higher the compassion fade, the less favorable the attitudes towards donating to war victims.

3   Method

3.1   Experimental Design and Participants

To investigate the impacts of framing valence in charity advertisements and compassion fade on individuals' attitudes and intentions to donate, a 2×2 cross-sectional experiment was conducted. The positive versus negative framing manipulated advertisement valence. Positive advertisement aimed to evoke positive emotions by emphasizing the positive outcomes for war victims resulting from donations. Conversely, negative advertisement aimed to evoke negative emotions by highlighting the detrimental consequences for Ukrainian war victims if donations aren't made. Additionally, compassion fade was manipulated through general and specific conditions. While general advertisements appealed for assistance for Ukrainian children and mothers, specific advertisements requested support for a single, identifiable refugee family (the Shevchenko family).

On December 18th, 2023, 220 participants were recruited online through Amazon Mechanical Turk (MTurk). Random assignment divided them into four conditions: positive/general, positive/specific, negative/general, and negative/specific. Twenty-two participants failing an attention check were excluded, resulting in a final sample of 198 participants, all over 18 years old. Among these, 130 (66%) identified as male, and 68 (34%) identified as female. Additionally, 72% possessed a bachelor's degree, and 82% were employed full-time. 42% reported a monthly income within the USD$1000–3000 range (Table 1).

Table 1. Sample size of each condition ($N = 198$)

Frame Compassion Fade	Negative	Positive
General	47 (23.7%)	57 (28.8%)
Specific	51 (25.8%)	43 (21.7%)

An online experiment (Google Forms) recruited participants across four conditions. They completed five sections: introduction, watching a short video ad soliciting donations for Ukrainian war victims (resembling Divchata Power ads), answering questions about their emotions, evaluating the ad and donation intentions, and reporting demographics. Finally, they self-assessed their donation willingness.

3.2 Stimulus Materials

Four 50-s videos, one for each condition, served as study stimuli. They shared a similar structure but varied in script, visuals, and music to manipulate frame valence (positive/negative) and compassion fade (general/specific).

Positive Frame. Emphasized positive outcomes for victims ("hope, strength, better tomorrow") with an optimistic tone.

Negative Frame. Highlighted negative consequences of not donating ("lost families, homes, lives") with a negative tone.

Compassion fade was operationalized as perceived victim number and identifiability, adapted from Kogut & Ritov (2005) [31].

General Appeal. Requested assistance for children and mothers in Ukraine.

Specific Appeal. Introduced a single refugee family (the Shevchenko family) needing support.

Manipulation Checks. To ensure the effectiveness of independent variable manipulation and intended perception of the stimuli, the questionnaire included several checks:

Sentiment. Participants rated the video's overall tone on a 7-point scale (1 = Very Negative, 7 = Very Positive). Those who were in positive frame condition ($M = 5.51$, $SD = 1.04$) rate the sentiment more positively than those who were in negative frame condition ($M = 2.58$, $SD = 1.04$), $t(196) = -19.678$, $p < .001$.

Victim Number. Participants chose their perception of the number of Ukrainians requesting assistance (options: "One Family" to "More than five families"). Those who were in the general condition ($M = 2.26$, $SD = .50$) had a higher estimate of victim number than those who were in the specific condition ($M = 1.38$, $SD = .53$), $t(196) = 11.936$, $p < .001$).

Victim Identifiability. Participants selected how they perceived the victims presented (options: "A specific, identifiable family" or "General, non-specific war victims"). Those who were in the general condition ($M = 1.68$, $SD = .46$) had a stronger impression that they perceived general, non-specific var victims than those who were in the specific condition ($M = 1.08$, $SD = .28$), $t(196) = 10.76$, $p < .001$).

3.3 Measures

This study defines three dependent variables: attitudes and donation intentions towards donating money to war victims in Ukraine, and the amounts they would like to donate.

Attitudes are operationalized by gauging participants' level of agreement with three statements ($\alpha = .89$, $M = 3.36$, $SD = 1.02$): "I think people should help war victims in Ukraine," "I think helping war victims in Ukraine is important," and "I think war victims in Ukraine should receive support from others." These statements use a 5-point Likert scale ranging from "strongly disagree" to "strongly agree". *Donation intentions* ($\alpha = .88$, $M = 3.17$, $SD = 1.13$) are measured using three statements from Ranganathan and Henley (2008) on a 5-point Likert scale: "I am likely to donate to the war victims in Ukraine," "I'm definitely going to donate to the war victims in Ukraine," and "I will donate to the war victims in Ukraine next time." Additionally, participants indicate the amount of money they are willing to donate, ranging from U.S. $0–20 to $500–1,000 ($M = 3.42$, $SD = 1.20$).

This study hypothesizes five discrete emotions as mediators: three negative emotions (sadness, anger, compassion) and two positive emotions (hope, pride). Each emotion is operationalized as the average score of three synonymous adjectives participants rated on a 1–5 scale (very slightly or not at all to extremely) after exposure to the stimuli. The survey utilized was adapted from Rottenberg et al. (2007) [33] and has been employed in previous research (Lerner & Keltner, 2001).

- *Anger* ($\alpha = 0.83$, $M = 3.08$, $SD = 1.11$): anger, irritation, hostility.
- *Sadness* ($\alpha = .84$, $M = 3.18$, $SD = 1.15$): sadness, sorrow, distress.
- *Compassion* ($\alpha = .80$, $M = 3.97$, $SD = .86$): empathy, compassion, pity.
- *Hope* ($\alpha = 0.85$, $M = 3.36$, $SD = 1.14$): hope, optimism, faith.
- *Pride* ($\alpha = 0.81$, $M = 3.86$, $SD = .89$): pride, self-accomplishment, fulfillment.

4 Results

4.1 Effects of Frame Valence on Attitudes

To examine the effect of frame valence on attitudes towards donating to war victims (H1), an independent-samples t-test was conducted. Contrary to predictions (H1), participants exposed to the positive-framed advertisement ($M = 4.21$, $SD = .33$) displayed less favorable attitudes than those exposed to the negative-framed advertisement ($M = 2.49$, $SD = .38$), with a statistically significant difference ($t(196) = 33.32$, $p < .001$). Therefore, H1 regarding the positive impact of positive framing on donation attitudes was not supported.

4.2 Effects of Attitudes on Donation Intentions and Amounts

Controlling for demographic variables (age, gender, education, employment, and income), a hierarchical regression analysis revealed a strong positive effect of attitudes on donation intention ($b = .91, p < .001$), supporting H2. This suggests that individuals with more favorable attitudes towards donating to war victims reported a higher likelihood of actually donating. Furthermore, attitudes also demonstrated a strong positive effect on the amount participants were willing to donate ($b = .58, p < .001$). This indicates that participants with more favorable attitudes were also willing to donate larger amounts.

4.3 Frames' Effects on Emotions and Mediating Effects of Emotions on Attitudes and Donation Intention

Three parallel mediation analyses were conducted to investigate the effects of framing on emotions (anger, sadness, compassion, hope, and pride) and the mediating effects of these emotions on attitudes, donation intentions, and intended donation amounts. Table 2 shows that compared to the positively-framed advertisement, exposure to the negatively-framed advertisement increased feelings of anger and sadness, supporting Hypotheses H3a and H3b. However, H3c was not supported, as negativity did not increase compassion.

Furthermore, Table 2 indicates that frames did not indirectly influence attitudes towards donating to war victims through negative emotions (anger, sadness, and compassion) because these emotions did not affect donation attitudes. Therefore, Hypotheses H4a-H4c were not supported.

Regarding positive emotions, Table 2 demonstrates that the hope-emphasizing positively-framed advertisement increased feelings of hope compared to the negative framing, supporting Hypothesis H5a. However, as pride did not increase with positive framing, Hypothesis H5b was not supported.

Concerning the mediating effects of positive emotions, Table 2 reveals that framing indirectly affects donation attitudes through hope ($b = .18, 95\% C.I. [.01, .34]$). Pride did not exhibit this mediating effect because it did not impact donation attitudes. Therefore, Hypothesis H6a was supported, while H6b was not.

Table 2. Path Coefficients and Indirect Effects for Mediation Model on Attitudes

Path	Path Coefficients		Indirect Effects	
	b	p-value	Estimate	95% CI
Frame → Attitudes	.90***	<.001		
Frame → Anger	−.70***	<.001		
Frame → Sadness	−.71***	<.001		
Frame → Compassion	.08	=.21		
Frame → Hope	.83***	<.001		
Frame → Pride	.09	=.19		
Anger → Attitudes	.01	=.75		
Sadness → Attitudes	.07	=.07		
Compassion → Attitudes	−.05	=.06		
Hope → Attitudes	.10	<.05		
Pride → Attitudes	.00	=.92		
Frame → Anger → Attitudes			−.02	−.14, .10
Frame → Sadness → Attitudes			−.11	−.23, .01
Frame → Compassion → Attitudes			−.01	−.02, .00
Frame → Hope → Attitudes			.18*	.01, .34
Frame → Pride → Attitudes			.00	−.01, .01

Note. Frame was coded 1 as negative frame and 2 as positive frame. All the path coefficients were standardized estimate based on bias-corrected percentile bootstrapping method with 1,000 bootstrap samples. *** p < .001, ** p < .01, * p < .05

4.4 Effects of Compassion Fade

To test Hypothesis 7 (H7), an independent-samples t-test was conducted. The results indicated no significant difference between the specific compassion fade condition ($M = 4.01$, $SD = .71$) and the general compassion fade condition ($M = 3.93$, $SD = .74$) in terms of participants' reported level of compassion ($t(196) = .81, p = .41$). Therefore, H7 was not supported. Similarly, no significant difference was found between the specific compassion fade condition (M = 3.26, $SD = .93$) and the general compassion fade condition (M = 3.44, SD = .92) in terms of participants' attitudes towards donating to war victims ($t(196) = −1.38, p = .16$). Thus, Hypothesis 8 (H8) was also not supported.

4.5 Frames' Effects on Emotions and Mediating Effects of Emotions on Donation Intention and Intended Donation Amount

The current study further investigated the mediating effects of emotions on donation intentions and intended donation amounts. Notably, only hope was found to play a mediating role in determining the intended donation amount ($b = .34$, 95% *C.I.* [.04, .65]), as detailed in Tables 3 and 4.

Table 3. Path Coefficients and Indirect Effects for Mediation Model on Donation Intention

Path	Path Coefficients		Indirect Effects	
	b	p-value	Estimate	95% CI
Frame → Intention	.98***	<.001		
Frame → Anger	−.70***	<.001		
Frame → Sadness	−.71***	<.001		
Frame → Compassion	.08	=.21		
Frame → Hope	.83***	<.001		
Frame → Pride	.09	=.19		
Anger → Intention	.00	=.97		
Sadness → Intention	−.01	=.39		
Compassion → Intention	.00	=.95		
Hope → Intention	−.01	=.82		
Pride → Intention	−.01	=.39		
Frame → Anger → Intention			.00	−.06, .05
Frame → Sadness → Intention			.02	−.03, .08
Frame → Compassion → Intention			.00	−.00, .00
Frame → Hope → Intention			−.02	−.10, .05
Frame → Pride → Intention			.00	−.01, .00

Note. Frame was coded 1 as negative frame and 2 as positive frame. All the path coefficients were standardized estimate based on bias-corrected percentile bootstrapping method with 1,000 bootstrap samples. *** p < .001, ** p < .01, * p < .05

Table 4. Path Coefficients and Indirect Effects for Mediation Model on Intended Donation Amount

Path	Path Coefficients		Indirect Effects	
	b	p-value	Estimate	95% CI
Frame → Amount	.39***	< .001		
Frame → Anger	−.70***	<.001		
Frame → Sadness	−.71***	<.001		
Frame → Compassion	.08	=.21		
Frame → Hope	.83***	<.001		
Frame → Pride	.09	=.19		
Anger → Amount	.00	=.99		
Sadness → Amount	−.16	=.05		
Compassion → Amount	.02	=.62		
Hope → Amount	.20*	<.05		
Pride → Amount	−.07	=.17		
Frame → Anger → Amount			.00	−.22, .23
Frame → Sadness → Amount			.23	−.03, .46
Frame → Compassion → Amount			.00	−.00, .02
Frame → Hope → Amount			.34*	.04, .65
Frame → Pride → Amount			−.01	−.04, .01

Note. Frame was coded 1 as negative frame and 2 as positive frame. All the path coefficients were standardized estimate based on bias-corrected percentile bootstrapping method with 1,000 bootstrap samples. *** $p < .001$, ** $p < .01$, * $p < .05$

5   Discussion and Conclusion

The present study investigated how the valence of message framing (positive vs. negative) and compassion fade affect people's attitudes towards donating to war victims, their donation intentions, and the amounts they are willing to donate, while exploring the mediating role of five emotions. The results provide valuable insights for both academic research and practical application in charitable organizations.

5.1 Positive Framing Leads to Improved Attitudes and Higher Donation Intentions

Initially, Hypothesis 1 proposed that negative framing in charity advertisements would be more effective in fostering favorable attitudes towards donating, based on Prospect Theory. This theory suggests that individuals are more risk-averse and motivated to avoid losses than to achieve gains. The assumption was that highlighting the negative consequences of the war would lead to improved attitudes and motivate donations. However, the results did not support this hypothesis, finding that positive framing, emphasizing the beneficial outcomes and positive impact of donating, was more effective in eliciting favorable attitudes. This contradicts Prospect Theory in the context of charitable fundraising for war victims, suggesting that positive emotional appeals may be more effective than negative ones. Furthermore, the results revealed that participants exposed to positive framing not only displayed more favorable attitudes but also expressed significantly higher donation intentions and larger donation amounts compared to those in the negative framing group.

This finding challenges the previous finding that negative framing, focusing on losses and adverse outcomes, is more potent in eliciting donations. This finding opens up new avenues for research and strategy in charitable advertising, emphasizing the potential of positive emotional appeals. Theoretically, emotional contagion explains the effectiveness of positive framing [35]. This theory suggests that positive emotions evoked by the message "spread" to the audience, promoting favorable attitudes. This contradicts the well-documented negativity bias [36], where negative information typically holds more weight in decision-making. In the context of this study, empathy and the desire to help might overcome the usual dominance of negative information when facing the plight of war victims.

5.2 The Effects of Compassion Fade

The study explored compassion fade, defined by perceived need and victim identifiability, yielding surprising results. Contrary to predictions (H7 and H8), neither compassion levels nor attitudes towards donating differed significantly, regardless of whether the fade involved one identifiable family or multiple families. This outcome might be due to methodological differences compared to past studies using single vs. multiple non-identifiable victims [17, 31]. Our study contrasted a request with one identifiable family (mother and daughter) against multiple families. It suggests that for two or more victims, differences in compassion and attitudes may not be statistically significant. This could be due to cognitive overload or a diffused empathetic response when facing multiple victims, even identifiable ones, leading to a plateau in compassion.

However, an interesting pattern emerged in the relationship between compassion fade conditions and donation amounts. Though compassion and attitudes didn't differ significantly, participants were more willing to donate larger amounts in the specific group (one identifiable family) ($M = 3.57, SD = .97$) compared to the general group ($M = 2.93, SD = 1.13$), $t(196) = 4.24, p < .001$. This aligns with the identifiable victim effect, where people donate more readily when presented with a specific, identifiable individual or small group [17, 31]). Research shows that donors often feel a stronger connection to specific individuals or families [32]. In this study, participants exposed to the Shevchenko family story (a specific unit) were willing to donate more than those in the general group. This effect can be attributed to the human tendency to respond more generously to identifiable individuals, as their specific circumstances and needs are easier to relate to [32]).

5.3 The Mediating Role of Hope

This study's key discovery is the significant role of hope in mediating the connections between message framing, attitudes, and donation behavior. This finding aligns with the growing body of research highlighting the power of emotions in shaping human choices. Homer (2021) sheds light on how distinct emotions can differentially motivate charitable giving [37]. While sadness often sparks empathy and compassion, hope plays a more dynamic role. It not only evokes a sense of possibility but empowers individuals with the belief that their actions can make a difference. This dual nature of hope – both emotional response and motivator – is especially relevant here. The positive framing, found to be more effective, likely tapped into this double-edged sword of hope, influencing both attitudes and donation intentions.

Further support comes from Fredrickson's broaden-and-build theory of positive emotions (2001) [38]. This theory posits that positive emotions broaden an individual's "thought-action repertoire," building enduring personal resources like resilience and optimism. In the context of charitable giving, positive framing, by inducing hope, broadens individuals' perspectives, making them more receptive to donating. It also builds a sense of personal efficacy and optimism, crucial for translating attitudes into actual donations. Lazarus (1991) offers a deeper understanding of hope's unique character [39]. Unlike most positive emotions arising in safe situations, hope emerges in stressful contexts, where fear and hope coexist. In challenging situations, hope motivates individuals to draw on their capabilities and find creative solutions. This aspect of hope is particularly relevant to this study. The positive framing in messages about war victims might have created a scenario where the audience, despite recognizing the severity, could see a glimmer of hope – a chance that their contributions could lead to positive change. This hope could have been the driving force behind the increased willingness to donate, both in terms of intentions and amounts.

5.4 Limitations and Future Directions

This study, while shedding light on how frame valence and emotions influence charitable messaging, has limitations that also provides directions for future research.

Expanding the Emotional Landscape. Explore a wider range of emotions like guilt, fear, love, and happiness, each holding unique psychological underpinnings and motivational influences. Studies suggest guilt and fear's distinct impacts [40], while positive emotions like love and happiness could provide a contrast to traditional negative appeals.

Nuances of Compassion Fade. The future study could take the single-victim vs. multiple-victim dynamic in war contexts into consideration. Compare responses to individual stories, fostering personal connection, against collective narratives highlighting the crisis's scale. Understanding this impact informs designing effective campaigns.

Real-World Application. Move beyond controlled settings to test findings in real-world scenarios like actual social media campaigns. This assesses how emotional appeals work in dynamic, less controlled environments, enhancing practical applicability.

Accounting for Individual Differences. Explore the influence of personal differences like cultural background, values, and past experiences. These significantly impact responses to emotional appeals. Consider segmenting audiences and examining tailored appeals' effectiveness for each group.

Methodological Diversification. Utilize qualitative methods like interviews, focus groups, or ethnographic studies alongside quantitative data. This gains deeper insights into the emotional and cognitive processes driving donor behavior, providing a richer, more nuanced understanding.

Longitudinal Studies. Conduct longitudinal studies to understand how prolonged war exposure affects public empathy and donation behavior. Tracking changes in public response over time, unlike cross-sectional snapshots, reveals if compassion fade sets in or if strategies can maintain interest and compassion.

References

1. Chou, E.Y., Murnighan, J.K.: Life or death decisions: framing the call for help. PloS ONE **8**(3) (2013). https://doi.org/10.1371/journal.pone.0057351
2. Reinhart, A.M., Marshall, H.M., Feeley, T.H., Tutzauer, F.: The persuasive effects of message framing in organ donation: the mediating role of psychological reactance. Commun. Monogr. **74**(2), 229–255 (2007). https://doi.org/10.1080/03637750701397098
3. Cao, X.: Framing charitable appeals: the effect of message framing and perceived susceptibility to the negative consequences of inaction on donation intention. Int. J. Nonprofit Voluntary Sector Mark. **21**(1), 3–12 (2015)
4. Kandrack, R., Lundberg, G.: On the influence of emotion on decision making: the case of charitable giving. In: Guo, P., Pedrycz, W. (eds.) Human-Centric Decision-Making Models for Social Sciences. SCI, vol. 502, pp. 57–73. Springer, Heidelberg (2014). https://doi.org/10.1007/978-3-642-39307-5_3
5. van Doorn, J., Zeelenberg, M., Breugelmans, S.M.: The impact of anger on donations to victims. Int. Rev. Victimol. **23**(3), 303–312 (2017)
6. Västfjäll, D., Peters, E., Slovic, P.: Compassion fatigue: donations and affect are greatest for a single child in need. White paper, Decision Research (2012)
7. Tannenbaum, M.B., et al.: Appealing to fear: a meta-analysis of fear appeal effectiveness and theories. Psychol. Bull. **141**(6), 1178–1204 (2015). https://doi.org/10.1037/a0039729
8. Chang, C.-T., Lee, Y.-K.: Framing charity advertising: influences of message framing, image valence, and temporal framing on a charitable appeal1. J. Appl. Soc. Psychol. **39**(12), 2910–2935 (2009). https://doi.org/10.1111/j.1559-1816.2009.00555.x
9. Lindstrom, M.: Buyology: truth and lies about why we buy. Currency (2010)
10. Nabi, R.L.: The case for emphasizing discrete emotions in communication research. Commun. Monogr. **77**(2), 153–159 (2010)
11. Chen, Q., Wells, W.D.: Attitude toward the site. J. Advert. Res. **39**(5), 27–38 (1999)
12. Lerner, J.S., Keltner, D.: Beyond valence: toward a model of emotion-specific influences on judgement and choice. Cogn. Emot. **14**(4), 473–493 (2000)

13. Gross, J.J., Halperin, E., Porat, R.: Emotion regulation in intractable conflicts. Curr. Dir. Psychol. Sci. **22**(6), 423–429 (2013)
14. Armitage, C.J., Conner, M.: Efficacy of the theory of planned behaviour: a meta-analytic review. Br. J. Soc. Psychol. **40**(4), 471–499 (2001). https://doi.org/10.1348/014466601164939
15. Keltner, D., Oatley, K., Jenkins, J.M.: Understanding Emotions. Wiley, Hoboken (2014)
16. Keltner, D., Ellsworth, P.C., Edwards, K.: Beyond simple pessimism: effects of sadness and anger on social perception. J. Pers. Soc. Psychol. **64**(5), 740–752 (1993). https://doi.org/10.1037/0022-3514.64.5.740
17. Small, D.A., Verrochi, N.M.: The face of need: facial emotion expression on charity advertisements. J. Mark. Res. **46**(6), 777–787 (2009). https://doi.org/10.1509/jmkr.46.6.777
18. Septianto, F., Soegianto, B.: Being moral and doing good to others: re-examining the role of emotion, judgment, and identity on prosocial behavior. Mark. Intell. Plan. **35**(2), 180–191 (2017)
19. Saslow, L.R., et al.: My brother's keeper? Soc. Psychol. Personal. Sci. **4**(1), 31–38 (2012). https://doi.org/10.1177/1948550612444137
20. Lazarus, R.S.: Emotions and interpersonal relationships: toward a person-centered conceptualization of emotions and coping. J. Pers. **74**(1), 9–46 (2006). https://doi.org/10.1111/j.1467-6494.2005.00368.x
21. Kemp, E., Bui, M., Krishen, A., Homer, P.M., LaTour, M.S.: Understanding the power of hope and empathy in healthcare marketing. J. Consum. Mark. **34**(2), 85–95 (2017). https://doi.org/10.1108/jcm-04-2016-1765
22. Cavanaugh, L.A., Bettman, J.R., Luce, M.F.: Feeling love and doing more for distant others: specific positive emotions differentially affect prosocial consumption. J. Mark. Res. **52**(5), 657–673 (2015). https://doi.org/10.1509/jmr.10.0219
23. Decrop, A., Derbaix, C.: Pride in contemporary sport consumption: a marketing perspective. J. Acad. Mark. Sci. **38**(5), 586–603 (2010). https://doi.org/10.1007/s11747-009-0167-8
24. Antonetti, P., Maklan, S.: Exploring postconsumption guilt and pride in the context of sustainability. Psychol. Mark. **31**(9), 717–735 (2014)
25. Markowitz, E.M., Slovic, P., Västfjäll, D., Hodges, S.D.: Compassion fade and the challenge of environmental conservation. Judgm. Decis. Mak. **8**(4), 397–406 (2013)
26. Dunn, E.W., Ashton-James, C.: On emotional innumeracy: predicted and actual affective responses to grand-scale tragedies. J. Exp. Soc. Psychol. **44**(3), 692–698 (2008). https://doi.org/10.1016/j.jesp.2007.04.011
27. Gifford, R.: The dragons of inaction: psychological barriers that limit climate change mitigation and adaptation. Am. Psychol. **66**(4), 290–302 (2011). https://doi.org/10.1037/a0023566
28. Slovic, P.: "If I look at the mass I will never act": psychic numbing and genocide. Judgm. Decis. Mak. **2**(2), 79–95 (2007)
29. Smith, R.W., Faro, D., Burson, K.A.: More for the many: the influence of entitativity on charitable giving. J. Consum. Res. **39**(5), 961–976 (2013). https://doi.org/10.1086/666470
30. Cameron, C.D., Payne, B.K.: Escaping affect: how motivated emotion regulation creates insensitivity to mass suffering. J. Pers. Soc. Psychol. **100**(1), 1–15 (2011)
31. Kogut, T., Ritov, I.: The singularity effect of identified victims in separate and joint evaluations. Organ. Behav. Hum. Decis. Process. **97**(2), 106–116 (2005). https://doi.org/10.1016/j.obhdp.2005.02.003
32. Jenni, K., Loewenstein, G.: Explaining the identifiable victim effect. J. Risk Uncertain. **14**, 235–257 (1997)
33. Rottenberg, J., Gross, J.J.: Emotion and emotion regulation: a map for psychotherapy researchers. Clin. Psychol. Sci. Pract. **14**(4), 323–328 (2007)
34. Lerner, J.S., Keltner, D.: Fear, anger, and risk. J. Pers. Soc. Psychol. **81**(1), 146–159 (2001)

35. Hatfield, E., Cacioppo, J.T., Rapson, R.L.: Emotional contagion (1994). https://doi.org/10.1017/cbo9781139174138

36. Rozin, P., Royzman, E.B.: Negativity bias, negativity dominance, and contagion. Pers. Soc. Psychol. Rev. **5**(4), 296–320 (2001). https://doi.org/10.1207/s15327957pspr0504_2

37. Homer, P.M.: When sadness and hope work to motivate charitable giving. J. Bus. Res. **133**, 420–431 (2021)

38. Fredrickson, B.L.: The role of positive emotions in positive psychology: the Broaden-and-Build Theory of positive emotions. Am. Psychol. **56**(3), 218–226 (2001)

39. Lazarus, R.S.: Cognition and motivation in emotion. Am. Psychol. **46**(4), 352–367 (1991)

40. Brennan, L., Binney, W.: Fear, guilt, and shame appeals in social marketing. J. Bus. Res. **63**(2), 140–146 (2010)

Research on the Collaborative Mechanism of Project Robots in Online Knowledge Production Communities: An Analysis of GitHub

Ziyu Wang, Chengming Ma, and Wenhao Shen[✉]

Beihang University, Beijing, China
shenwenhao@buaa.edu.cn

Abstract. Bots are becoming more widely adopted in GitHub, with implications for online knowledge collaboration. It is necessary to study the extent of the impact of bots in online knowledge collaboration. A total of 843 projects with around 63125 aggregate data were acquired by crawling projects through GitHub API and filtering out projects that do not contain code or do not have any issues. Preliminary research found no correlation between the adoption of bots and the popularity of the project, while most of the literature support a positive correlation. But further classified observation according to the attributes of the bot, we found that projects with dedicated bots were more popular than projects with template bots. The study found that the adoption of dedicated bots for projects led to an increase in commit, fork, and issue count, which affected the addition, reorganization, and integration of knowledge collaboration. The study also found that projects with dedicated bots received more attention, with a positive correlation between fork count and star count, but no significant correlation between commit, issue count and star count. The impact of bots in online knowledge collaboration is still lacking in terms of adding and integrating knowledge.

Keywords: Human-bot interaction · online knowledge production · project robot · collaborative mechanism · GitHub

1 Introduction

As a hosting platform for open source software, GitHub represents the current community of online knowledge production and dissemination due to its large number of participants, high degree of internationalization of sources, and diversity of project types. The basic framework of multi-participation and dissemination after project launch includes: sharing basic information about the project with self-built wikis, opening channels to expand participation with pull requests, and improving code with issues to enhance the efficiency of collaboration. The knowledge production model of GitHub not only facilitates open collaboration among the core members of a project, but also expands the scope of public participation to co-construct knowledge in the online community in a more democratic way.

P.-L. P. Rau (Ed.): HCII 2024, LNCS 14700, pp. 147–161, 2024.
https://doi.org/10.1007/978-3-031-60901-5_11

In recent years, bots have been widely used in GitHub projects to operate mainly on highly automated and repetitive tasks such as error-checking, thereby enhancing feedback to developers, reducing the work of the maintainers, and ensuring standards of stability. Previous studies have illustrated that the use of bots has led to greater popularity of projects [1], but it does not declare that in what ways the use of project bots has affected the popularity of the projects. This study is dedicated to explore the impact of the use of project bots on knowledge production and collaboration, analyze the correlation between the use of different functions of project bots and the efficiency of the production and the collaboration of these code projects. Also, this study focuses on the impact of the main ways of using project bots on the popularity of the projects. Furthermore, based on the results, some feasible recommendations of future trends in the development of project bots will be given. The article will discuss the following research questions.

RQ1: The extent of the use of bots in GitHub projects that will affect the online knowledge collaboration process.

In the GitHub online community, the commit tag, fork tag, and issue tag reflect the actual involvement of project initiators and project participants in knowledge collaboration [2]. Project participants may: i) submit and update code, which is shown as "commit"; ii) rewrite and generate a new code project based on the current project code, which is shown as "fork"; and iii) propose changes or feedback requirements to the current code project, which is shown as "feedback". Feedback on the current code project is displayed as "issue". The project initiator or core team members have the rights to respond to the requirements, update iterations, merge forks, and modify errors, while the community participants have the rights to copy projects, modify forks, request merges, and raise issues. Project bots assist contributors by automatically performing predefined, repetitive tasks, mainly including repairing bugs, refactoring source code, suggesting code improvements, and predicting defects. First, we use the count of commits, forks, and issues as indicators to study the extent to which project bots affect online knowledge collaboration. Then, we classify the bots according to their functions and study the separated effect of the use of different types of project bots on the count of commits, forks, and issues, so as to explain how project bots can assist human users in adding, reorganizing, and integrating knowledge.

RQ2: The mode of the use of project bots that will affect the degree of concerns of the code-online-production projects.

The "star" in the GitHub community, which is open to community members, identifies community members' interest in the project. That is to say, this count can be used to measure the popularity of a project, which can also state the degree of concern among online community [3]. We explore the impact of project bots on the popularity in knowledge collaboration by clarifying whether the use of bots in a project has a significant correlation with the count of stars, and then indicating the impact of the different methods of using bots on the count of stars in a project.

This study may contribute to the bot-using trends in code-production and the discussion of participation of artificial intelligence in online knowledge production and collaboration: (i) verifying the extent to which the use of project bots affects knowledge collaboration on code-based projects; (ii) examining how project bots affect the popularity of a project.

2 Literature Review

Communities of code production and collaboration are one of the typical mode of online knowledge production. Increasingly, knowledge is created in the form of collaborator-generated content: consumer feedback systems, discussion boards, question-and-answer sites, open-source software, social networks, and online information repositories. Therefore, code production in online community is an important perspective to study knowledge production and collaboration. The motivations of collaborators to contribute code include the completeness, accuracy, and richness of the existing code [4], that is, the length, quality, and functionality of the code. Bots can provide timely feedback between contributors and maintainers in the form of code reviews [5], which improves the integrity and precision of the content of knowledge production. GitHub allows collaborators to work independently by cloning project repositories, making changes in their local environments, and committing the changes directly to the shared repositories, which makes it easier for collaborators to discuss and make modifications. This procedure develops the openness of the knowledge, which is conducive to increase public participation level [6].

Online knowledge collaboration is the sharing, transferring, accumulating, transforming and co-creation of knowledge, which involves the individual act of making knowledge available to others, as well as adding, reorganizing, modifying and integrating knowledge contributed by others [7]. It occurs when users view and amend co-edited documents [8]. Previous studies have explained that different aspects of the factors affecting online knowledge collaboration. Methods for evaluating code quality could be influenced by the organizational nature of open source projects. Open source software projects, whether company-driven or foundation-driven, provide complete software source code to collaborators, and the main difference between the projects is the way in which code quality is ensured. Company-driven projects are more closed, with only company employees able to accept new code contributions and maintain the software source code. Foundation-driven projects are more open, where outsiders can submit and modify new code once they have been approved by community members [9]. During the development of an open source software project, different interest orientations will lead to different impacts on the likelihood of developers making future contributions. Developers who are driven by material interests, are less likely to contribute code in the future, while developers who are driven by technical confidence, are more likely to make future code contributions [10]. Racial and cultural distinctions in developers affect the probability of code acceptance more than code quality. Code contributions submitted by European-American collaborators have a higher chance of being accepted as a major component of the final contribution merged into an open source project compared to Asian and African collaborators [11]. The reputation of contributors in open source projects influences the scope of public participation. Knowledge contributors with a high level of attention are more likely to attract potential knowledge contributors to the code production process [12]. The extent of a contributor's contribution in an open source project will change the size and scope of knowledge dissemination through the code review process. Core contributors, as representatives of the highest quality and attention of code contributions, are more active than peripheral contributors in disseminating knowledge [13].

Human-bot interaction also could be affected by the online knowledge collaboration process [14]. Previous researches have concluded that the involvement of bots positively influences knowledge collaboration. Bots support human-bot knowledge collaboration by manipulating simple, time-consuming or tedious automated tasks, collecting dispersed information and discovering what humans may have overlooked in the mass of available information [15]. Bots extend the function of GitHub by replacing some of the work of developers like committing, providing precise and focusing feedback on issues in the workflow and facilitating collaboration among developers [16]. Bots force human members of the team to discuss issues between different stages of the workflow by posting issue comments [17]. However, it has also been argued that bot intervention is detrimental to the development of online knowledge collaboration, reflected in the fact that user engagement was significantly reduced after the use of bots [18].

Currently, there is an academic debate about the impact of GitHub project bots in online knowledge collaboration. Therefore, we further investigate how GitHub project bots act in knowledge collaboration and how they have an influence on the popularity of projects. Based on the previous results, we select the count of commits, forks, and issues to represent the addition, reorganization, and integration of knowledge in order to investigate the extent of the bot's impact in knowledge collaboration. We also choose the count of stars to measure the popularity of the project, and analyze the correlation between commits, forks, issues and stars in order to explore what role bots will play in the dissemination of an online project. Figure 1 describes our technology roadmap.

Fig. 1. Overview of technology roadmap.

3 Data and Methods

3.1 Data Collection

Project Selection. In this study, we used the GitHub API to crawl all projects with at least one update since 1 January 2023 to 9 December 2023 with at least 1,000 forks. Then we obtained the top 1,000 projects sorted by star count, and filtered out the projects that do not contain code or do not have any issues acquiring a total of 843 projects. They have an average of 40,254.82 stars, an average of 6,083.98 commits, an average of 7,304.19 forks, and an average of 9483.85 issues.

Bots Detection. We obtained the usernames of all the contributors in the projects and the developers' names of the top 100 issues at the latest time of filing. Then we judged whether the projects have used bots by affirming the developers' names had the words "Bot" or "Robot" at the beginning or end. Of the 843 projects, 412 projects did not use bots and 431 projects used bots. More than half of the projects used bots.

Bots Classification. Further, depending on whether the username ends in "[bot]", it can be determined whether it is a template bot adapted from GitHub officially (e.g., "dependabot[bot]") or a bot built by some project itself (e.g., " flutter-pub-roller-bot"). of the 431 projects that used bots, 363 used template bots and 68 used dedicated bots. Only a few projects used dedicated bots.

3.2 Measurement Model

We use a linear regression model with dummy variable to quantitatively evaluate the effect of an intervention with bots on the commit count, fork count and issue count. To further discuss the possible pathways of how dedicated bots can affect the count of stars, we created the following model:

$$Stars = C_8 + C_1 \cdot DedicatedBot + (C_2 \cdot Forks + C_3 \cdot IssueCount + C_4 \cdot Commits)$$

$$+(C_5 \cdot Forks + C_6 \cdot IssueCount + C_7 \cdot Commits) \cdot DedicatedBot$$

DedicatedBot is a 0–1 dummy variable.

Star serves as the independent variable of the model and indicates the level of concerns of the project.

Commit shows the amount of activity contributed by developers in a GitHub project. To explain the contribution of the use of bots on the popularity of projects, we calculate the count of commits, which stands for the addition of knowledge in online knowledge collaboration.

Fork illustrates the richness of developer-contributed activities in GitHub projects. We estimate the count of forks after the use of bots, which represents the reorganization of knowledge contributed by others in online knowledge collaboration in order to account for the effect on the popularity of the projects.

Issue accounts for the completeness of developer contributions in GitHub projects. The count of issues as the integration of knowledge contributed by others in online knowledge collaboration. We compute it to declare the importance of the adoption of bots on the popularity of projects.

4   Results and Analysis

4.1   Template Bot and Dedicated Bot

We firstly explored the correlation between the use of bots in the projects and the count of project stars. Figure 2 shows the distribution of popularity (count of stars) in projects with and without bots. We found that, at the median, there is no significant difference between the count of stars in projects and the use of bots. Using the Kruskal-Wallis test, we discovered that the difference between the two groups was statistically significant ($p < 0.001$). This suggests that the use of a bot in a project does not correlate with the level of concerns in the project. However, previous studies demonstrated that the count of stars of projects with bots is higher than the count of stars of projects without bots [1], selected for projects that may contain irrelevant projects with only data and no code. We filtered projects with a number of forks greater than 1,000 and containing mainstream programming languages, showing a high level of public participation in the projects and improving the accuracy of the results.

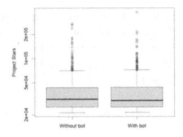

Fig. 2. Relation between bot and stars in GitHub project.

Then, GitHub projects are divided into two groups: projects with dedicated bot(s) and project without dedicated bot(s). The latter may contain template bots whose username ends with '[bot]' (such as GitHub-actions[bot]), or contain no bot at all. Table 1 summarizes the features of the template bots and dedicated bots.

Upgrading dependencies. Both template bots and dedicated bots have the ability to upgrade dependencies. Old dependencies can contain outdated usages, insecure vulnerabilities and lack supports from other developers. The bots can update the dependency versions required by the project to keep the project with up-to-date technologies and fix potential bugs.

Publishing new builds. Template bots and dedicated bots have the ability to publish new builds. Those bots may automatically bump the version number, compile and archive the source code to make an executable file, and publish it as a release. This allows general users to download and test the build without the need of compiling tools.

Making Suggestions. Making suggestions is a feature unique to dedicated bots. Dedicated bots are able to perform a number of tasks more autonomously, mainly including making suggestions for porting old to new requests; suggesting problems in running code; making requests (porting, rewriting, etc.); and suggesting automatic changes.

Table 1. Taxonomy table of bots used in GitHub projects.

Category	Topic	Explanation
template bot	update	update dependencies
	publish	publish new builds
dedicated bot	update	update dependencies
	publish	publish new builds
	suggest	suggest old transplant to new
		suggestions for modifying error-run code
		suggestions for automatic modification

We then determine if the distribution of 'star count' between those groups differs statistically. Table 2 manifests that the average number of stars without self-built projects is 39184, and the average number of stars with self-built projects is 52457. This is achieved using Kruskal-Wallis rank sum test. The result is displayed in the Table 2, showing a significant difference within $\alpha = 0.05$.

Table 2. Relativity between dedicated bots and stars.

	Without dedicated bots	With dedicated bots
Average	39184.14	52457.46
Standard Variance	26970.53	51820.76
Overall Kruskal Wallis Chi-squared	4.9398	
p-value	0.02624 < 0.05	

4.2 The Impact of Dedicated Bots on Online Knowledge Collaboration

In this section, we investigate the impact of commits, forks, and issues of projects employing dedicated bots on adding, reorganizing, and integrating knowledge in online knowledge collaboration.

Total Number of Commits. We explore the impact of the use of a dedicated bot in a project on the count of commits. Figure 3 demonstrates the distribution of knowledge addition (count of commits) in projects with and without a dedicated bot. We find that at the median, the count of commits in projects with dedicated bots is much higher than that in projects without dedicated bots. Using the Kruskal-Wallis test, we find that the difference between the two groups is statistically significant (P < 0.001). The projects with more commits may be due to the fact that the dedicated bot has the operation of providing suggestions, which makes it easier and faster for contributors to understand the problems of their code and thus commit their code in a more targeted way. On the other hand, the use of bots can help developers responsible for code review to shift their attention to other code quantity and quality improvement.

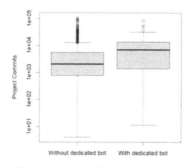

Fig. 3. The Effect of dedicated bots on the count of commits.

Total Number of Forks. We explored the influence of the use of dedicated bots in projects on the count of forks. Figure 4 displays the distribution of knowledge reorganization (count of forks) in projects with and without dedicated bots. We discovered that, at the median, the count of forks in projects with dedicated bots is slightly higher than the count of forks in projects without dedicated bots. Using the Kruskal-Wallis test, we found that the difference between the two groups was statistically significant (P < 0.05).

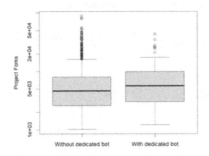

Fig. 4. The Effect of dedicated bots on the count of forks.

Total Number of Issues. We explored the effect of the use of dedicated bots in projects on the count of issues. Figure 5 shows the distribution of knowledge integration (count of issues) in projects with and without dedicated bots. We noticed that at the median, the count of commits in projects with dedicated bots is much higher than the count of commits in projects without dedicated bots. Using the Kruskal-Wallis test, we found that the difference between the two groups was statistically significant (P < 0.001).

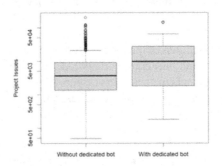

Fig. 5. The Effect of dedicated bots on the count of issues.

4.3 The Effect of Dedicated Bots on the Popularity of Projects in Knowledge Collaboration

It was indicated that projects with project dedicated bots in issue received more likes than those with official project bots, which clearly indicates that the dedicated bots effectively increased the concern of projects in terms of popularity. To further investigate the importance of dedicated bots on project popularity in online knowledge collaboration, we used the following metrics: (i) commit, (ii) fork, and (iii) issue. We investigated how commits, forks, and issues affect the count of stars. We fit an econometric model as described in Sect. 3.2:

$$\text{Stars} = C_8 + C_1 \cdot \text{DedicatedBot} + (C_2 \cdot \text{Forks} + C_3 \cdot \text{IssueCount} + C_4 \cdot \text{Commits})$$
$$+(C_5 \cdot \text{Forks} + C_6 \cdot \text{IssueCount} + C_7 \cdot \text{Commits}) \cdot \text{DedicatedBot}$$

In order to discover how the bots, influence the count of stars, we added both slope and intercept coefficient for the bots dummy variable. For this model, the count of commits, forks, and issues is the dependent variable. Table 3 summarizes the preliminary results of these models. In addition to the model coefficients, the table manifests the sum of squares, with each variable explaining Std.Error, t-Statistic, and Prob.

Using Ordinary Least Squares methods, we calculated the preliminary coefficient and the model's statistics is shown as Table 4.

Table 3. The effect of dedicated project bot on the count of commits, forks and issues.

	Coefficient	Std. Error	t-Statistic	Prob.
C_8	24572.17	1505.004	16.32698	0.0000
C_1	-6475.028	4031.612	-1.606064	0.1090
C_2	1.995909	0.135798	14.69766	0.0000
C_3	0.172176	0.142761	1.206041	0.2285
C_4	-0.279762	0.218894	-1.278073	0.2019
C_5	2.001682	0.364944	5.484902	0.0000
C_6	0.413669	0.239852	1.724688	0.0853
C_7	-0.859260	0.413675	-2.077137	0.0384

R-Squared	0.548419	Model F-Statistic	73.38699
Adjusted R-Squared	0.540946	Prob. Of F-Statistic	0.000000

We noticed that C_1, C_3, C_4 is insignificant in explaining how they affect star count of the project, thus we remove those variables and use weighted OLS to mitigate heteroscedasticity in the model:

$$\text{Stars} = C_8 + C_1 \cdot \text{DedicatedBot}$$
$$+ (C_2 \cdot \text{Forks} + C_3 \cdot \text{IssueCount} + C_4 \cdot \text{TotalCommits})$$
$$+ (C_5 \cdot \text{Forks} + C_6 \cdot \text{IssueCount} + C_7 \cdot \text{TotalCommits})$$
$$\cdot \text{DedicatedBot}$$

The results indicates that a project with only template bot(s) or no bots gain an average of 2.061 stars per fork. It displaces if equipped with dedicated bot(s), a project will gain 1.268 more stars per fork on average. It manifests issues and commits statistically have

Table 4. The effect of dedicated project bot on the count of commit, fork and issue.

	Coefficient	Std. Error	t-Statistic	Prob
C_8	23585.55	1.311460	17984.19	0.0000
C_1	0	(Removed Variable)		
C_2	2.060909	0.000507	4064.009	0.0000
C_3	0	(Removed Variable)		
C_4	0	(Removed Variable)		
C_5	1.267747	0.038675	9.352600	0.0000
C_6	0.478692	0.038675	12.37740	0.0000
C_7	−0.971980	0.045292	−21.46030	0.0000
Unweighed Statistics				
R-Squared	0.538360		Adjusted R-Squared	0.534026

no effect on the count of stars. However, an issue contributes 0.479 stars and a commit will reduce 0.972 stars for projects with dedicated bot(s).

As shown in Fig. 6, there is no significant correlation between commits and stars for projects using the template bot. There is also no correlation between commits and stars for projects using the dedicated bot, which indicates that the count of commits for the dedicated bot is not correlated with the popularity of the project. This means that in knowledge collaboration, using a dedicated bot to add the amount of knowledge contributed by others does not affect the popularity of the project.

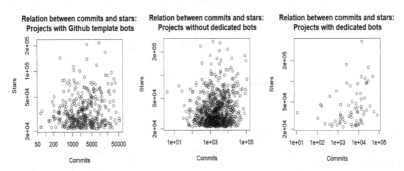

Fig. 6. Relation between commits and stars.

As seen in Fig. 7, there is no significant correlation between forks and stars using template bot in projects. There is a positive correlation between forks and stars for projects using dedicated bots, which indicates that the higher the count of forks in projects using dedicated bots, the higher the count of stars it will gain. It implies that the adoption of a dedicated bot in online knowledge collaboration is more conducive to restructuring the knowledge contributed by others, thus increasing the popularity of the project.

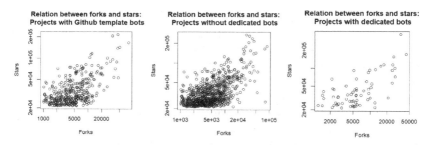

Fig. 7. Relation between forks and stars.

As illustrated in Fig. 8, there is no significant correlation between issues and stars using template bot projects. There is no correlation between issues and stars for projects using dedicated bots, which indicates that the count of issues of projects using dedicated bots does not have an impact on the count of stars. This implies that the adoption of dedicated bots in online knowledge collaboration, although more conducive to integrating knowledge contributed by others, does not affect the popularity of the project.

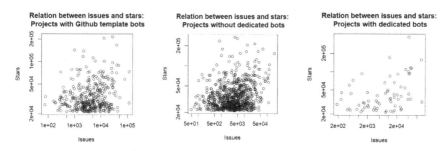

Fig. 8. Relation between issues and stars.

5 Further Discussion

The results of the study showed that the median number of commits on the project was higher after the adoption of dedicated bots in projects. This means that the assistance of the dedicated bot promoted the addition of knowledge among developers. This may due to the fact that the dedicated bot is responsible for suggesting developers to modify the problematic code, so that the developers get faster and clearer feedback, which leads to more targeted modifications to the code and improves the quality of the code. However, on the other hand, the increase in the count of commits makes the developers handle more code, which may become a maintenance burden for the developers [5].

We found that the count of forks in projects using the dedicated bot was higher than the count of forks in projects using the template bot. This suggests that the involvement of collaborators is higher with the intervention of the dedicated bot of self-built projects. As a result, with the adoption of the dedicated bot, the developers in the project are more willing to reorganize their knowledge in online knowledge collaboration.

The count of issues for projects using dedicated bots was higher than the count of issues for projects using template bots, but they did not act on the popularity of the project. Bots can help project contributors with issue-related tasks such as opening or closing issues, assigning issue assignees, adding labels, and locking issues [2], which increases the count of issues but does not affect the level of attention to the project.

From the results, we also note that among projects that use a dedicated bot, there is a correlation between the use of the bot to manipulate the submission of commits and the use of the bot to manipulate the submission of issues. That is, projects that use project bots in the commit section are more likely to use project bots in the issue section as a companion. This suggests that developers who invent dedicated bots are more likely to make the bot responsible for tracking the assistance aspects of raising and modifying issues, making the bot responsible for a more complete workflow, and thus improving the efficiency of knowledge collaboration.

In addition, there is a correlation between the average amount of code added per day and the presence of a commit bot in the project. Projects with a commit bot averaged a number of 45 lines of code more per day than projects without one. This seems to indicate that more collaborative knowledge is added with the involvement of a project bot, boosting productivity. However, in reality, projects with or without the use of bots had no significant correlation with their count of stars, forks, or project size. The possible explanation may be that project bots perform simple, repetitive, and mechanical operations in online knowledge production, and their workflows have more complex repetitive patterns, which are not practically relevant in terms of improving productivity [17].

The use of dedicated bots increases the count of commits and issues, and therefore influences addition and integration of knowledge. But commits, issues and stars have no correlation, so addition and integration of knowledge has no effect on the popularity of the project. The evidence points out the fact that the use of dedicated bots in projects still have limitations in advancing the knowledge collaboration process. The results also remind us a conjecture that when the bot is running automatically, developers do not have time to deal with the increased count of commits and issues. [19], which causes dissatisfaction among the contributors. The increase in the count of forks allows the contributors to discovery the multiple possibilities of the project code, which also enhances the activity of the contributors in online knowledge collaboration, and improves the richness of the code, which in turn plays a significant role in the popularity of the project.

6   Conclusion

In this study, we explore how project bots influence the process of online knowledge collaboration. By classifying the attributes of project bots, we distinguish the different impact between template bots and dedicated bots. Template bots have a low degree of autonomy and can only perform repetitive and simple operations such as updating dependencies and publishing builds. In contrast, dedicated bots have a higher degree of autonomy, and in addition to having the operations of template bots, they can also suggest code modifications, automatic updates, and porting code. The study appears that the count of commits, forks, and issues is more of projects with dedicated bots compared to projects with template bots. This means that the dedicated bot is more likely to impact on knowledge addition, reorganization, and integration.

We also investigated how project bots contribute to the popularity of projects. The study proved that projects with dedicated bots received more stars, which implies that projects with dedicated bots of projects will gain more concern in online community, which is more conducive to expanding the scope of knowledge dissemination. We further measure the significance of bots on adding, reorganizing, and integrating others' contributions in online knowledge collaboration by using commit, fork, and issue count as metrics. The results signify that the count of commits and issues of projects using dedicated bots is not correlated with the count of stars, while the count of forks is positively correlated with the count of stars. This symbolizes that forks as the reorganization of knowledge influences projects' popularity. Dedicated bots in projects are more autonomous and relevant in assisting the public to participate in knowledge production (co-generating project code, expanding project forks), which can effectively reduce the actual work of developers and allow them to have more energy and time to engage in more creative knowledge production. Only the adoption of dedicated bots can effectively improve productivity and promote more efficient co-operation between humans and machines, thus enabling projects to receive more attention, and thus increasing effectiveness and attracting more producers to participate in knowledge production and dissemination.

Commits and issues as the addition and integration of knowledge are not greatly involved in the popularity of the project, which suggests that there is still some room of improvement in the development of future project bots. In terms of knowledge addition, the future development of project bots can be improved in terms of accuracy (code redundancy, code running speed), security (degree of implementation of functions), relevance, etc., so that they can submit meaningful code automatically, which can enhance productivity and promote the development of human-bot collaboration mode. With regard to knowledge integration, the future development of project bots can be improved in relation to completeness (improving the bot workflow and increasing the degree of bot autonomy) and richness (updating and increasing the bot functionality), assisting developers to carry out their coding activities in a more explicit and targeted manner, and contributing to a more fluent process of online knowledge collaboration.

The knowledge production model of online communities expands the places where the traditional knowledge production model takes place and breaks the spatial limitation that collaborators must meet face-to-face to produce, share and disseminate knowledge. And also, the new mode has already shown its potential to occupy the edge of human-computer interaction in the way of bot-involvement in the field of code-producing. The knowledge production mode of online communities accumulates the knowledge acquired by human beings, as well as sharing the ability or potential of human thinking, changing the way human beings collaborate on knowledge. In open source communities, which are not directly profit-driven, collaborators contribute code more freely based on the wisdom of their predecessors, and there is a higher degree of openness and public participation in knowledge production. The addition of new production tools such as artificial intelligence, assists humans in generating complex, high-quality code from the point of the agency of things, and cooperates with them in the reorganization of future knowledge production, branching out the collaborative relationships in the view of social relationships.

Acknowledgments. This Work is Supported by Beijing Social Science Foundation Project (Youth Program, no. 22ZXC007).

References

1. Wu, X., Gao, A., Zhang, Y., Wang, T., Tang, Y.: A preliminary study of bots usage in open source community. In: Proceedings of the 13th Asia-Pacific Symposium on Internetware (Internetware 2022). Association for Computing Machinery, New York, pp. 175–180 (2022). https://doi.org/10.1145/3545258.3545284
2. Cheng, X., Zhang, Z., Yang, Y., Yan, Z.: Open collaboration between universities and enterprises: a case study on GitHub. Internet Res. **30**(4), 1251–1279 (2020)
3. Hu, Y., Wang, S., Ren, Y., Choo, K.-K.R.: User influence analysis for GitHub developer social networks. Expert Syst. Appl. **108**, 108–118 (2018). https://doi.org/10.1016/j.eswa. 2018.05.002
4. Hinnosaar, M., Hinnosaar, T., Kummer, M.E., et al.: Externalities in knowledge production: evidence from a randomized field experiment. Exp. Econ., 706–733 (2022). https://doi.org/ 10.1007/s10683-021-09730-x
5. Wessel, M., Serebrenik, A., Wiese, I., Steinmacher, I., Gerosa, M.A.: Effects of adopting code review bots on pull requests to OSS projects. In: 2020 IEEE International Conference on Software Maintenance and Evolution (ICSME), Adelaide, SA, Australia, pp. 1–11 (2020). https://doi.org/10.1109/ICSME46990.2020.00011
6. Pe-Than, E.P.P., Dabbish, L., Herbsleb, J.D.: Collaborative writing on GitHub: a case study of a book project. In: Companion of the 2018 ACM Conference on Computer Supported Cooperative Work and Social Computing (CSCW 2018 Companion), pp. 305–308. Association for Computing Machinery, New York (2018). https://doi.org/10.1145/3272973.3274083
7. Faraj, S., Jarvenpaa, S.L., Majchrzak, A.: Knowledge collaboration in online communities. Organ. Sci. **22**(5), 1224–1239 (2011)
8. Park, H., Park, S.J.: Communication behavior and online knowledge collaboration: evidence from Wikipedia. J. Knowl. Manage. **20**(4), 769–792 (2016)
9. Mäenpää, H., et al.: Organizing for openness: six models for developer involvement in hybrid OSS projects. J. Internet Serv. Appl. **9**(1), 1–14 (2018)
10. Taylor, J., Dantu, R.: For love or money? Examining reasons behind OSS developers' contributions. Inf. Syst. Manag. **39**, 122–137 (2022)
11. Nadri, R., Rodríguez-Pérez, G., Nagappan, M.: On the relationship between the developer's perceptible race and ethnicity and the evaluation of contributions in OSS. IEEE Trans. Softw. Eng. **48**, 2955–2968 (2022). https://doi.org/10.1109/TSE.2021.3073773
12. Dabbish, L., et al.: Social coding in GitHub: transparency and collaboration in an open software repository. In: The Conference on Computer Supported Cooperative Work, Seattle, WA, USA (2012)
13. Kerzazi, N., El Asri, I.: Knowledge flows within open source software projects: a social network perspective. In: El-Azouzi, R., Menasché, D.S., Sabir, E., Pellegrini, F.D., Benjillali, M. (eds.) Advances in Ubiquitous Networking 2. LNEE, vol. 397, pp. 247–258. Springer, Singapore (2017). https://doi.org/10.1007/978-981-10-1627-1_19
14. Ferrara, E., Varol, O., Davis, C., Menczer, F., Flammini, A.: The rise of social bots. Commun. ACM **59**(7), 96–104 (2016)

15. Wessel, M., Gerosa, M.A., Shihab, E.: Software bots in software engineering: benefits and challenges. In: Proceedings of the 19th International Conference on Mining Software Repositories (MSR 2022), pp. 724–725. Association for Computing Machinery, New York (2022). https://doi.org/10.1145/3524842.3528533
16. Hukal, P., Berente, N., Germonprez, M., Schecter, A.: Bots coordinating work in open source software projects. Computer **52**(9), 52–60 (2019). https://doi.org/10.1109/MC.2018.2885970
17. Saadat, S., Colmenares, N., Sukthankar, G.: Do bots modify the workflow of GitHub teams. In: 2021 IEEE/ACM Third International Workshop on Bots in Software Engineering (BotSE), pp. 1–5 (2021). https://doi.org/10.1109/BotSE52550.2021.00008
18. Palvannan, N., Brown, C.: Suggestion bot: analyzing the impact of automated suggested changes on code reviews. In: 2023 IEEE/ACM 5th International Workshop on Bots in Software Engineering (BotSE), Melbourne, Australia, pp. 33–37 (2023). https://doi.org/10.1109/BotSE59190.2023.00015
19. Mohayeji, H., Ebert, F., Arts, E., Constantinou, E., Serebrenik, A.: On the adoption of a TODO bot on GitHub: a preliminary study. In: Proceedings of the Fourth International Workshop on Bots in Software Engineering (BotSE 2022), pp. 23–27. Association for Computing Machinery, New York (2022). https://doi.org/10.1145/3528228.3528408

The Application of Immersive Virtual Digital Imaging Art in Cross-Cultural Communication of Internet Aesthetics Education

Weilong Wu[1]([envelope]), Kejia Chen[1], and Qifan Yang[2]

[1] School of Film Television and Communication, Xiamen University of Technology, Xiamen, China
wu_acedemic@163.com
[2] College of Education, Fujian Normal University, Fuzhou, China

Abstract. Objectives: In the Internet environment, the timeliness and scope of information communication has been dramatically improved. The mass media are able to reflect social and cultural norms through selective presentation and emphasis on certain themes, thus communicating with the audience and stimulating the greatest degree of emotional resonance, leaving a huge space for the realization of cross-cultural communication through Internet aesthetics education and diversified aesthetic standards.

The "Internet+" background has given birth to a brand new mobile aesthetic space, accompanied by the emergence of a brand new aesthetic orientation, which will certainly trigger new changes in contemporary aesthetic education methods and approaches. In today's media socialization, the Internet and mass media are quietly shaping people's aesthetic concepts and consciousness, however, while the Internet satisfies users' access to aesthetic information, it is also accompanied by the communication of a large amount of good and bad aesthetic information, and extremist and irrational mass aesthetic culture continues to grow on the Internet platform. Along with the development of science and technology, the concept of "meta-universe" was born, and virtual reality technology, as a key part of the digital form, has been used in more and more art forms and fields, and has created a new type of visual art for human aesthetic activities: virtual digital imaging art. Virtual digital imaging art is a kind of art form based on image, with technical means and auxiliary exploration of art space as the core. As an emerging medium that relies on technology and interaction, virtual image carries the social responsibility and mission of spreading culture and art. The integration of new technologies has become a new trend in foreign cultural communication in recent years. Inherent traditional cultural communication methods have been difficult to meet the needs of Internet aesthetics communication, there are barriers and limitations in the communication between aesthetic culture and the public, and the development of digital technology and its application in cross-cultural communication has become a feasible path to overcome these difficulties.

The study attempts to adopt a method that combines practical creation and theoretical deduction. First of all, based on the theory of cross-cultural communication, the virtual digital imaging art display space is built with the help of ue4

W. Wu and K. Chen—These authors contributed equally to this study

P.-L. P. Rau (Ed.): HCII 2024, LNCS 14700, pp. 162–178, 2024.
https://doi.org/10.1007/978-3-031-60901-5_12

software, and virtual reality technology is used to present the aesthetic works of the five artists, so as to construct the communication path of the idea of diversified aesthetic standards. Secondly, semi-structured user interviews and open-ended questionnaire survey method were integrated to obtain user experience evaluation indicators. Finally, based on the results of the research, the effectiveness of virtual digital imaging art in promoting the cross-cultural communication of Internet aesthetics education is assessed, and its significance and value in realizing the cross-cultural communication of Internet aesthetics education is explored, as well as the disadvantages and shortcomings that actually exist in the application. This study focuses on the brand-new mode of human-computer interaction in immersive virtual digital imaging art, trying to break the stereotypical impression of beauty under the stereotypical thinking of the Internet, to provide a good path for the communication of the diversified Internet view of aesthetics education in the new era, and to provide relevant theoretical support and practical cases for the research on the application of virtual digital imaging art in the cross-cultural communication of Internet aesthetics education.

Methods: In order to assess the effectiveness of the study and to obtain as large a sample size as possible, this study used an open-ended web-based questionnaire and semi-structured interviews to implement the research with users who participated in the art experience. In the open-ended web questionnaire, the design questions will inquire about four aspects, namely, aesthetic experience, interactive experience, immersion experience, and emotional experience, corresponding to their rating scales, and will be distributed through online social platforms. After that, interviews with typical users were conducted, and 30 users of different ages, professional backgrounds, and educational levels were selected from a number of artists, learners (students), scholars (researchers), and temporary visitors. After integrating the results, the virtual digital imaging art is further analyzed and evaluated in terms of enhancing the user's aesthetic experience, the effect of work display and the effect of Communicating of aesthetic ideas.

Results: The questionnaire data showed that participants gave high ratings in terms of interactive experience and overall satisfaction after concluding the immersive experience of the imaging artwork in the virtual space, which, combined with the results of the interviews, showed that the interviewees had a high degree of accuracy in the restoration and retelling of the information and details of the imaging artwork, and that they understood and remembered the content of the imaging artwork, and that the users' aesthetic experience was effective. However, in terms of immersion and emotional experience, some users reported that they were unable to fully immerse themselves in this art form, and that they were unable to gain sufficient emotional resonance from it.

Conclusions: It has been found that virtual digital imaging art, with the novel visual effect, open interactive experience and powerful communication advantages formed by a variety of artistic means having played an important role in expanding artistic expression, popularizing aesthetics education on the Internet, and cross-cultural communication of the idea of pluralistic aesthetic standards. It provides new ways and opportunities for cross-cultural communication of aesthetics education on the Internet, and effectively promotes the cross-cultural communication of aesthetics education.

Although virtual digital imaging art shows great potential for development in promoting the cross-cultural communication of aesthetics education on the Internet, its shortcomings and characteristics of lacking authenticity and physicality, being difficult to realize emotional resonance, being highly technology-dependent, and involving legal and ethical risks determine that we can only continue to learn and study it in the process of dynamic development. This paper addresses the research on the application of virtual digital imaging art in the cross-cultural communication of Internet aesthetics education, which only provides a perspective for studying new types of art, and the research is still very insufficient, and the research on virtual digital imaging art needs to be continuously excavated and updated, with a view to better theoretically supporting the development of new types of art represented by virtual digital imaging art.

Keywords: Virtual Reality · Virtual Digital · Digital Imaging Arts · Internet Aesthetics Education · Cross-cultural Communication

1   Introduction

1.1   The Formation of Aesthetic Education on the Internet

In the era of digitalization, mediatization as the core of the "Internet+", people are always in a huge flood of information, mobile networks have spawned a variety of information content to graphic design are full of "beauty" requirements. Along with the birth of the new aesthetic mobile space, people's aesthetic concepts have changed, the pursuit of aesthetic more personalized, the aesthetic value orientation presents utilitarianism, the aesthetic status tends to double.

The media integration in the Internet era has changed people's way of thinking, and also changed the way of aesthetic education, and the practice of aesthetic education is facing new challenges and opportunities, and the fusion of "Internet+" and aesthetic education has built up a brand new education model, which specifically affects all aspects of aesthetic education including the concept of aesthetic education, aesthetic activities, aesthetic education methods, and aesthetic education applications. In all aspects, aesthetic education has begun to develop in the direction of networked, intelligent and comprehensive. The Internet provides a rich resource base, a diversified display platform and a multi-dimensional research space for aesthetic education. It is thus clear that the in-depth integration of "Internet+" and aesthetic education is a necessary way to comply with the development of the times.

1.2   The Current Status of the Dissemination of Aesthetic Education on the Internet

Modern advertisements on the Internet, while disseminating commercial information, display the aesthetic culture and popular information of an era. The construction of the image of "beauty" in modern advertising is often shaped by the ideology of commercial value. The tendency to commercialize constantly reinforces and shapes the public's stereotypes of "beauty", and the Internet and the media attempt to propagate and amplify narrowly biased aesthetics, so that the issue of "aesthetic censure and homogeneity in the trend of Internet popularity", which should be taken seriously, is dissolved and distorted. The commercialization of cyberspace leads to the only flow of information on the network, this single flat "beauty" in a sense is the object of the gaze, is overemphasized by the formulaic beauty ultimately caused by the lack of public self-subjective cognition, triggering the public on the self-judgement of the misleading, people are no longer the recipients of aesthetic education, but after the flow of digital commercial users, aesthetic education is reduced to a tool of formalism. Digital commercial users, beauty education is reduced to a tool of formalism.

In the face of the many changes of aesthetic education in the network era, Inherent traditional ways of transmitting culture have been difficult to meet the needs of cross-cultural communication of aesthetic education, coupled with the influence of the social environment, the background of growth, linguistic symbols, and other factors, there are many barriers and limitations in the communication between the aesthetic culture and the public, and the path of cross-cultural communication of aesthetic education has been impeded by the traditional aesthetic education mode of the realistic dilemma faced by.

In today's media socialization, most of the information we receive comes from the network, and the Internet, as a new environment for the dissemination of aesthetic education, has widely penetrated into all aspects of society, promoting the transformation and integration of the traditional aesthetic education field into the network aesthetic education field. The digital era, with technology as the core driving force, has brought about profound changes in society, but also brought new opportunities for the realization of cross-cultural communication of aesthetic education, and the application of digital technology has become a feasible path to overcome the dilemma of the reality of aesthetic education: Technologies such as VR, AR and live broadcasting have expanded people's way of aesthetics; the emergence of various types of media has enriched the dissemination of aesthetic education; and the use of big data has transformed the process of people's aesthetic activities into quantifiable statistics. Technology has enabled the Internet platform to better enhance its own advantages in aesthetic education, help people better feel, explore and understand beauty, and realize high-quality cross-cultural dissemination of aesthetic education.

2 Literature Review

2.1 Immersive Virtual Digital Image Art

In the mid-1990s, American futurist Nicholas Negroponte painted a picture of a "digital" existence in his Digital Survival, declaring, "The digital revolution is changing the way we learn, the way we work, the way we play, in a word, the way we live. The digital revolution is changing the way we learn, the way we work, the way we play, in a word, the way we live." We can see that today, as we have entered the new millennium, the picture painted by Negroponte is gradually becoming a reality. Lee (2021) and others argue that the vast virtual physical cyberspace presents unprecedented opportunities for artists to merge every corner of the physical environment with digital creativity. In the context of contemporary digital art and documentary filmmaking, Favero (2019) suggests that practitioners are discovering that emerging image-based immersive practices, technologies, and tools (360-degree panoramic video and photography, virtual augmentation, mixed reality, and so on) wrap the viewer in the image, blurring the viewer and the viewed, "self" The distance between viewer and viewed, "self" and "other" is blurred. Since the 1990s so far, China's imaging academic research has experienced remarkable changes. With the rapid progress of modern technology, the application of computer technology and image processing technology has become more and more widespread, and nowadays, digital imaging has become a perfect combination of digital technology and art, which profoundly affects people's daily life. Li (2021) found that the controversy surrounding the right and wrong of digital image art has also never stopped. One viewpoint is that digital imaging has largely jeopardized the development of video art itself, while another viewpoint is that the era of traditional imaging has passed and the future belongs to digital imaging. In his review of digital artist Cao Fei's Stage of the Times UCCA exhibition, Meng (2022) said that the artist's expertise in video and media means-MR, VR, and AR technologies-builds a bridge between the virtual and the real, and that virtual reality, which breaks down technological barriers, relies on value-based strategies. Virtual reality technology strengthens the focus on real-world technology and politics, maps real life with the virtual world, and combines popular elements with art, which can make it easier for viewers to understand and appreciate the works.

Studies at home and abroad have shown that immersive virtual digital image art is constantly upgrading and developing, and is constantly penetrating into our daily life, giving the experiencer a multi-dimensional aesthetic experience through audio-visual communication and virtual environments. However, most of the existing studies stop at exploring the advantages and disadvantages of the rise of virtual digital image art for the public in terms of visual impact and perceptual experience, and have not yet paid attention to its role in public aesthetic education, and there is a lack of empirical assessment and analysis of the effect of its aesthetic communication. Immersive virtual digital image art is not only rich and diverse in visual experience, but also in the change of people's perception and cognition. It is not only a new art form, but also a cultural phenomenon leading to the future. In such a context, research on the application of virtual digital image art in aesthetic communication becomes necessary and indispensable.

2.2 Aesthetic Education on the Internet

Foreign scholars for the Internet aesthetic education research began at the end of the last century and the beginning of this century, Mike (1997) has pointed out that: "the media itself on the shaping of society's function is far greater than the role played by the content of the media. All technology has the property of being a bit of gold. Once a society introduces a new technology, all other functions in the society will be adapted to the form of the technology.

Once a new technology enters society, it immediately permeates every aspect of the social system. In this sense, new technology is a revolutionary force." Manuel Castor (2006) refers to the form of popular culture spawned by the computer Internet and multimedia technology as the culture of real virtuality. This virtuality is attached to popular culture, with new sensory experiences and a shift in the sense of space and time, which also triggers changes in aesthetic interests and moral constraints. Scholars such as Oluseyi Aliu (2021) suggest that Internet aesthetic education can be implemented using digital art galleries and museums, which can provide a wealth of artistic resources and educational opportunities through online exhibitions, virtual tours, and online education. Scholars such as Golovachev (2020) argue that Internet aesthetic education can be implemented through the development of art-based games and apps to implement Internet-based aesthetic education. These games and apps can provide interesting art experiences and help students learn about different art forms and techniques. Domestic scholars Zhang and Chen (2017) combined with the new situation of the development of "Internet+" and proposed that mobile aesthetic education is a new way of aesthetic education that allows people to have an aesthetic experience anytime, anywhere and be imbued with beauty and infection in a subtle way.

The Circular of the State Council on the Issuance of the Thirteenth Five-Year Plan for the Development of the National Education Industry emphasizes the need to "actively develop 'Internet + education'". To promote the deep integration of information technology and education and teaching" must be the most important, and "Internet+" and the deep integration of aesthetic education is precisely in such an era under the demands of the emergence. In recent years, the research and reform of Internet aesthetic education have mostly focused on hot issues such as the construction of Internet aesthetic education platform and the in-depth integration of aesthetic education and modern information technology, but the scope of Internet technology and art categories involved is relatively limited, and this study takes the virtual digital image art based on Internet technology as a specific case, which will help the research scope of Internet aesthetic education to expand and extend from a single aspect to multiple fields, and provide a more extensive development space for the subsequent technology-enabled education related research to provide a broader development space.

2.3 Cross-Cultural Communication

In today's world, globalization has brought individuals into increasingly frequent contact with different cultures, and multiculturalism has come to be regarded as a typical feature of contemporary society.

Aneas (2009) and other scholars say that the Internet enables easy access to information, and the multilingual character of individuals is extremely advantageous to their participation in globalization and cultural openness, and that language is the basis for the study of intercultural and cross-cultural communication, so that cross-cultural communication involves both the interactions and interactions between members of society with different cultural backgrounds, as well as the migration, diffusion and diffusion of various cultural elements in the global society, The process of change of various cultural elements in the global society and its impact on different groups, cultures, countries and even the human community.

As China's national economy continues to grow and science and technology continue to innovate, the dissemination of culture on the Internet has developed rapidly and steadily in China. Zhang (2022) proposes that network culture is essentially a collection of cultural activities, cultural products, cultural ways and cultural concepts formed in the Internet platform with Internet information technology as the core foundation, and they can all be characterized by continuous innovation in the Internet platform. The modern intercultural communication path is dominated by the integrated media vision.

Wang (2022) believes that based on the different advantages of various media, selectively combining, integrating and recreating a variety of visual cultural elements and images from different media, making the expression of cultural symbols diversified and rich, then the communication has taken place in this way the change of the main body of the communication, especially the rise of short videos accelerates the process of audience participation in the dissemination of the process, and everyone has the opportunity to independently create cultural content Everyone has the opportunity to create cultural content and short films on their own. The rise of network culture is essentially due to the background of the times and the social environment, while intercultural communication involves the process of diffusion, migration and change of all kinds of cultural elements in the global society, as well as its impact on different cultures, groups, countries and even the human community, and it is to help people better understand and cope with the cultural differences, and to promote the exchange, interoperability and integration between different cultures. According to Cui (2013), network culture has weakened the moral consciousness of young students to a certain extent, and cross-cultural communication is filled with a variety of information, among which there are many erroneous information and garbage that have a certain impact on people's ideological and moral consciousness and mental health, which have a negative impact on the values of young people.

With the further development of artificial intelligence, ushering in the era of Chat GPT, a general-purpose artificial intelligence with the significance of brain labor replacement. Taking current events into account, Wang (2023) argues that this phenomenon contributes to cross-cultural communication and the realization of a virtual "global village" or a meta-universe for all human beings. Compared with foreign countries, domestic cross-cultural visual communication research is more inclined to explore the connection between the semantics of visual symbols or visual culture and social topics, and the perspective of the research subject is relatively single, ignoring the research on other subjects and communication channels. Domestic research on virtual digital video art is still in its infancy, and research on the combination and application of immersive virtual digital video art and cross-cultural communication is very limited, with insufficient empirical cases, making it difficult to carry out follow-up research.

Therefore, it is particularly important to explore the application of immersive virtual digital image art in cross-cultural communication, and we urgently need more in-depth theoretical research and practical exploration in order to expand the depth and breadth of its application field and communication effect.

3 Practical Creation of Virtual Digital Image Art in Intercultural Communication of Internet Aesthetic Education

3.1 Content Overview

Considering the youthful nature of the audience of Internet aesthetic education, after searching and comparing a number of artists related to the theme of aesthetic education on online platforms, this exhibition invites five young Chinese contemporary artists. The exhibition simulates a virtual digital image art exhibition space with the help of ue4 software, and centers on the five artists' paintings, images, videos, and behaviors of the virtual digital art works to show their reflections on "aesthetic homogeneity under the trend of Internet popularity" and their explorations of multiple aesthetic boundaries. The exhibition is centered around the five artists' virtual digital artworks of painting, image, video and performance to show the artists' reflections on the "aesthetic singularity under the trend of internet popularity" and their exploration of the boundaries of multiple aesthetics.

3.2 Display Form

Layout of Exhibition Hall. The exhibition space is set against the backdrop of a city street, where seven groups of works by five artists (including two groups of photographs, two groups of paintings, and one performance art work) are placed. The exhibition starts from the subway station and extends to the end of the street. Utilizing the characteristics of urban public space, the artists' works are customized to blend into the environment, expanding the public nature of the works and bringing them closer to the audience (as shown in Fig. 1 and Fig. 2).

Fig. 1 . Exhibition Scenery

Background Arrangement of Works. In the exhibition space, media such as bus billboards, building billboards, and cafe backdrops are utilized as backdrops for the works (Fig. 3).

Fig. 2 . Artwork Setting Diagram

Fig. 3 . Artwork Setting Diagram

3.3 Exhibition Entrance

The exhibition utilizes the 720Cloud online platform to present a panoramic view of the virtual space. Visitors can scan the QR code or click on the browse link to enter the virtual space, and walk around and visit the virtual art space on their own, enjoying the artists' works and checking the introduction of the works. Link to the exhibition: http://720.vmdns.cn/tour/55e0f5e5e6fb6584.

4 Experimental Effect Evaluation

In order to assess the effect of virtual digital video art in the cross-cultural communication of aesthetic education on the Internet, and to reduce the subjective misjudgment caused by individual differences, the study designed an experiment by using the research methods of questionnaires and semi-structured interviews to compare the perceived effect of users' aesthetic education in virtual digital video art and traditional video art.

4.1 Experimental Object

A sample of 100 visitors from different regions and countries was selected for the experiment, and the members were randomly divided into two groups of 50 members each: the virtual digital image art group and the traditional image art group. The experimental group is the virtual digital image art group, members will enter the virtual exhibition space through online participation; the control group is the traditional image art group, members will visit the exhibition in reality. After the exhibition visit, questionnaires and follow-up interviews will be conducted with members of both groups. In order to ensure that there is no obvious difference between the experimental group and the control group in terms of the basic information of the personnel, 30 research samples are selected in each of the two experimental groups for the questionnaire results. Finally, the results of the questionnaire and interviews were synthesized to further analyze and evaluate user satisfaction, exhibition display effect, and perceived effect of user aesthetic education.

4.2 Experimental Design

Quantitative Research. The questionnaire was designed to cover the personal information of the experiencers, their feelings and evaluations of participating in aesthetic activities, etc. It aimed to collect the users' online and offline viewing of the exhibition respectively from a quantitative perspective, and to analyze the value and shortcomings of the current virtual digital image art in promoting the cross-cultural dissemination of Internet aesthetic education in view of the users' attitudes towards the interactive experience of virtual digital image art, the dissemination efficiency of aesthetic education, and other data and information. The questionnaire includes four parts: aesthetic experience, interactive experience, immersion experience, and emotional experience, and utilizes the Likert scale method to display five evaluation indicators of different magnitudes: very satisfied, satisfied, average, dissatisfied, and very dissatisfied. At the end of the questionnaire, an open-ended question about opinions and suggestions on virtual digital image art to enhance the effect of Internet aesthetic education dissemination and satisfaction with art aesthetic activities was set for users to follow up with follow-up interviews.

Qualitative Research. The study implements semi-structured interview research on the basis of the questionnaire survey, selecting five typical users of different ages, genders, occupational backgrounds and educational levels in each of the two experimental groups as the interview subjects, with the length of the interviews set at 30 min, and the forms of the interviews being telephone interviews and face-to-face interviews. At the end of the interviews, the high-frequency words provided by the interviewees were captured to gain an in-depth understanding of the users' behaviors and psychology during the online and offline exhibition viewing processes, as well as their cognition of the information of the art works during the aesthetic process, and the responses of the interviewees were further analyzed to summarize the performance of virtual digital image art in enhancing the users' aesthetic experience, the effect of the works' display, and the effect of the dissemination of the idea of beauty education, and other aspects. The content of the conversation is organized and analyzed after the interview.

5 Experimental Results

100 members were invited to participate in this experiment, and 60 members were finally selected through collection and screening to analyze the results, accessing the virtual exhibition space through online participation (n = 30), and visiting the exhibition on the ground in reality (n = 30). The above data, will lead to the following experimental results:

5.1 User Aesthetic Experience Evaluation

This experiment uses t-tests to study and analyze the effects of the aesthetic experience of users participating in the online exhibition of immersive virtual digital image art and the offline exhibition of traditional image art, respectively.

As can be seen from Table 1, for the overall environment of the exhibition: users who participated in the online exhibition (M = 4.03, SD = 0.98) were significantly higher than those who participated in the offline exhibition (M = 3.16, SD = 0.63), with $p = 0.000 < 0.05$.

For exhibition display effect: users participating in online exhibitions (M = 3.76, SD = 1.17) were significantly higher than those participating in offline exhibitions (M = 3.00, SD = 0.95), $p = 0.006 < 0.05$.

For exhibit placement design: users participating in online exhibitions (M = 3.61, SD = 0.93) were significantly higher than those participating in offline exhibitions (M = 2.88, SD = 0.83), $p = 0.001 < 0.05$.

For graphic quality: users participating in online exhibitions (M = 4.03, SD = 1.16) were significantly higher than those participating in offline exhibitions (M = 3.16, SD = 0.52), $p = 0.000 < 0.05$.

The above synthesis shows that in terms of users' aesthetic experience, there is a significant difference between participating in immersive virtual digital image art online exhibitions and traditional image art offline exhibitions, and the mean value of questionnaires obtained from participating in immersive virtual digital image art online exhibitions is higher than that of traditional image art offline exhibitions.

Table 1. Findings on users' aesthetic experience

Learning experience	group	N	average	SD	t	p
Overall environment of the exhibition	Participate in offline exhibitions	30	4.03	0.984	4.255	0.000
	Participate in the online exhibition	30	3.16	0.628		
Exhibition display effect	Participate in offline exhibitions	30	3.76	1.173	2.855	0.006
	Participate in the online exhibition	30	3	0.95		
Exhibit Placement Design	Participate in offline exhibitions	30	3.61	0.933	3.334	0.001
	Participate in the online exhibition	30	2.88	0.833		
Graphic Quality	Participate in offline exhibitions	30	4.03	1.159	3.908	0.000
	Participate in the online exhibition	30	3.16	0.515		

5.2 User Interaction Experience Evaluation

This experiment uses t-test to study and analyze the effect of user interaction experience of participating in immersive virtual digital image art online exhibition and traditional image art offline exhibition respectively.

As can be seen from Table 2, there is no significant difference between users who participated in the online exhibition (M = 3.42, SD = 0.79) and those who participated in the offline exhibition (M = 3.16, SD = 0.95) in terms of the sense of experience of viewing the exhibition, $p = 0.222 > 0.05$.

For the freedom of viewing: users who participated in the online exhibition (M = 4.27, SD = 0.94) were significantly higher than those who participated in the offline exhibition (M = 3.00, SD = 0.80), $p = 0.000 < 0.05$.

For fun interaction: users who participated in online exhibitions (M = 3.88, SD = 0.99) were significantly higher than those who participated in offline exhibitions (M = 3.09, SD = 0.93), $p = 0.002 < 0.05$.

For multimedia integration: users participating in online exhibitions (M = 3.58, SD = 0.79) were significantly higher than those participating in offline exhibitions (M = 2.88, SD = 0.66), $p = 0.000 < 0.05$.

The above synthesis shows that in terms of user interaction experience, there is a significant difference between participating in immersive virtual digital image art online exhibition and traditional image art offline exhibition except that there is no significant difference in the degree of freedom of viewing the exhibition, and there is a significant difference in other aspects, and the mean value of questionnaires obtained from participating in immersive virtual digital image art online exhibition is higher than that of traditional image art offline exhibition.

Table 2. Research results on user interaction experience

Learning experience	group	N	average	SD	t	p
Exhibition Experience	Participate in offline exhibitions	30	3.42	0.792	1.23	0.223
	Participate in the online exhibition	30	3.16	0.954		
Freedom of Viewing	Participate in offline exhibitions	30	4.27	0.944	5.844	0.000
	Participate in the online exhibition	30	3	0.803		
Interesting Interaction	Participate in offline exhibitions	30	3.88	0.992	3.295	0.002
	Participate in the online exhibition	30	3.09	0.928		
Multi-media integration	Participate in offline exhibitions	30	3.58	0.792	3.87	0.000
	Participate in the online exhibition	30	2.88	0.66		

5.3 User Immersion Experience Evaluation

This experiment uses t-test to study and analyze the effect of immersion experience of users participating in immersive virtual digital image art online exhibition and traditional image art offline exhibition respectively.

As can be seen from Table 3, for the overall exhibition atmosphere: users who participated in the offline exhibition (M = 4.19, SD = 1.06) were significantly higher than those who participated in the online exhibition (M = 3.03, SD = 0.77), with p = 0.000 < 0.05.

For the viewing angle: users participating in offline exhibitions (M = 4.03, SD = 0.97) were significantly higher than those participating in online exhibitions (M = 2.94, SD = 0.61), p = 0.000 < 0.05.

For the form of exhibit explanation: users who participated in the offline exhibition (M = 3.94, SD = 1.16) were significantly higher than those who participated in the online exhibition (M = 3.21, SD = 0.70), p = 0.003 < 0.05.

For the guidebook: users who participated in the offline exhibition (M = 4.03, SD = 0.86) were significantly higher than those who participated in the online exhibition (M = 2.94, SD = 0.61), p = 0.000 < 0.05.

The above synthesis shows that in terms of user immersion experience, there is a significant difference between participating in immersive virtual digital image art online exhibitions and traditional image art offline exhibitions, and the mean value of the questionnaire obtained from participating in traditional image art offline exhibitions is higher than that of immersive virtual digital image art online exhibitions.

Table 3. Research results on user immersion experience

Learning experience	group	N	average	SD	t	p
Overall exhibition atmosphere	Participate in offline exhibitions	30	3.03	0.77	−5.045	0.000
	Participate in the online exhibition	30	4.19	1.061		
Viewing Angle	Participate in offline exhibitions	30	2.94	0.609	−5.465	0.000
	Participate in the online exhibition	30	4.03	0.967		
Exhibit Explanation Format	Participate in offline exhibitions	30	3.21	0.696	−3.063	0.003
	Participate in the online exhibition	30	3.94	1.162		
Guide	Participate in offline exhibitions	30	2.94	0.609	−5.887	0.000
	Participate in the online exhibition	30	4.03	0.861		

5.4 User Emotional Experience Evaluation

As can be seen from Table 4, this experiment uses t-tests to study and analyze the effects of the emotional experience of users participating in the online exhibition of immersive virtual digital image art and the offline exhibition of traditional image art, respectively.

For the degree of emotional involvement in the exhibition: users who participated in the offline exhibition (M = 3.91, SD = 0.96) were significantly more involved than those who participated in the online exhibition (M = 2.85, SD = 0.51), $p = 0.000 < 0.05$.

For the resonance triggered by the works: users who participated in the offline exhibition (M = 4.09, SD = 0.96) were significantly higher than those who participated in the online exhibition (M = 2.94, SD = 0.79), $p = 0.000 < 0.05$.

The above synthesis shows that in terms of users' emotional experience, there is a significant difference between participating in immersive virtual digital image art online exhibitions and traditional image art offline exhibitions, and the mean value of questionnaires obtained from participating in traditional image art offline exhibitions is higher than that of immersive virtual digital image art online exhibitions.

Table 4. Research results on users' emotional experience

Learning experience	group	N	average	SD	t	p
Emotional engagement with the exhibition	Participate in offline exhibitions	30	2.85	0.508	−5.566	0.000
	Participate in the online exhibition	30	3.91	0.963		
Resonance of the works	Participate in offline exhibitions	30	2.94	0.788	−5.281	0.000
	Participate in the online exhibition	30	4.09	0.963		

5.5 Result

The questionnaire data showed that compared to the traditional video art group, the virtual digital video art group generally gave higher ratings after concluding the immersive experience of video artworks in the virtual space. In terms of interaction experience, participants generally found the operation interface in the virtual space friendly and convenient, and the interaction experience smooth and natural. In terms of overall satisfaction, participants generally expressed satisfaction with the art aesthetic activity. Combined with the results of the semi-structured interviews, the interviewees in the virtual digital image art group have a higher degree of accuracy in the restoration and retelling of the information and details of the video art works. This indicates that the members of the virtual digital image art experimental group have a deeper understanding and memory of the content of the video works, and that the virtual digital image art realizes the improvement of the aesthetic communication efficiency of the art works. In terms of users' aesthetic experience, respondents generally believe that the image art works in the virtual space have good visual effects and artistic aesthetics. They were able to intuitively feel the visual impact of the works and gained a good aesthetic experience from the mood created by the works. However, in terms of immersion experience and emotional experience, the interviewees gave feedback that they were unable to fully immerse themselves in this art form, and they indicated that there is still some room for improvement in terms of emotional engagement and immersion in video art works in virtual space.

After experimental evaluation, it is concluded that compared with traditional video art, virtual digital video art performs well in terms of aesthetic experience, interactive behavior, overall satisfaction, and aesthetic communication effect. However, there is still some room for development in terms of immersion experience and emotional experience. In the future, virtual digital video art needs to use technical means and innovative design to improve the emotional expression ability and immersion of video art works in virtual space, providing users with a richer and deeper aesthetic experience.

6 Discussion and Conclusions

Different from the aesthetic experience mode of traditional art, the interactive aesthetics of virtual digital image art provides the public with a space to perceive art works, becomes a link between the public and art, and continuously enriches the public's art aesthetic experience. In addition, the digital art field constructed by relying on virtual technology will also provide infinite possibilities for the development of human artistic process, and maximize the effect of art and cultural dissemination in a limited space.

The aesthetic education activities in the digital context effectively integrate the virtual digital image artworks with the media platform from the perspectives of perception, participation exploration and empathy, and through the digitization of perception, participation and promotion, digitalization is integrated into the Internet aesthetic education to help users carry out richer sensory perception, independent exploration and empathetic experience in the Internet platform. In this process, the idea of aesthetic education and the culture of aesthetic education can realize cross-cultural dissemination with the help of technological development, so as to achieve the goal of letting people perceive, recognize and disseminate beauty in the digital background, and to promote their in-depth understanding and application of beauty, so as to make them be able to examine beauty, pursue beauty and create beauty.

Although virtual digital image art has shown great development potential in promoting the cross-cultural communication of Internet aesthetic education, its deficiencies in the specific application process determine that the research on interactive aesthetics of virtual image art still needs to be continuously studied in theory and tested in practice. This study still has great deficiencies and there is room for further improvement.

Acknowledgement. This work was funded by Xiamen Education Scientific Planning Project: Application of VR in art design courses in the post-epidemic era Innovative Teaching Reform Study (Funding Number: 22002).

References

Lee, L.-H., et al.: When creators meet the metaverse: a survey on computational arts, ARXIV-CS.CY (2021). (IF: 3)

Isgrò, F., Trucco, E., Schreer, O.: Three-dimensional image processing in the future of immersive media. IEEE Trans. Circ. Syst. Video (2004). (IF: 4)

Favero, P.S.H.: A Journey from Virtual and Mixed Reality to Byzantine Icons Via Buddhist Philosophy (2019)

MeLuhan, E., Zingrone, F. (eds.): Essential Mcluhan, pp. 228–229. Routledge, London (1997)

Zhou, N.N., Deng, Y.L.: Virtual reality: a state-of-the-art survey. Int. J. Autom. Comput. **6**(4), 319–325 (2009)

The most spoken languages worldwide in 2023[EB/0L], 15 October 2023. https://www.statista.com/statistics/266808/the-most-spoken-languages-worldwide/

Aneas, M.A., Sandin, M.P.: Intercultural and cross-cultural communication research: some reflections about culture and qualitative methods. Forum Qual. Sozialforschung/Forum Qual. Soc. Res. **10**(1) (2009). Article 51

Negroponte, N.: Digital Survival D in. Translated by Hu Yong and Fan Haiyan, p. 15. Hainan Publishing House, Haikou (1996)

Lyotard, J.-F., translated by Che Shan. Postmodern state: report on knowledge, p. 113. Life-reading-Xinzhi Sanlianshubian, Beijing (1997)

[U.S.] Manuel Custer, translated by Xia Chujiu, The Rise of the Network Society. Social Science Literature Press, Beijing (2006). 310,353,1

Jiang, S.: On virtual image art and its aesthetic value. Hunan Normal University (2007). http://t.cn/A6joMi0s

Ma, C.: Exploring the dilemma of aesthetic education in the background of digitization. Popular Lit. Art (17), 170–171 (2020). http://t.cn/A6joxwQF

Hu, Y.: Exploration of the application of virtual reality technology in the teaching of aesthetic education. Daguan (Forum) (12), 147–149 (2022). http://t.cn/A6joxAi4

Liu, B.: Research on the application of interactive projection art in aesthetic education. Dalian University of Technology (2021). https://doi.org/10.26991/d.cnki.gdllu.2020.000833

Zhang, J.: Research on museum digital display technology and virtual exhibition. Chin. Museum (04), 88–92 (2017). http://t.cn/A6joJy8r

Zhao, T.: Research on interactive experience design of museum online exhibition based on contextual cognition theory. Jiangnan University (2023). https://doi.org/10.27169/d.cnki.gwqgu.2022.000996

Song, R.: Research on the innovative application of virtual reality technology in the display of ceramic art in Jingdezhen. Foshan Ceram. **33**(06), 62–64 (2023). http://t.cn/A6joJb1S

Hu, X.: Research on the aesthetic experience of VR images. Southwest University (2018). http://t.cn/A6joJq0I

Sun, B.: On the aesthetic characteristics of virtual reality art. China TV (10), 74–77 (2019). http://t.cn/A6joJ5rR

Liu, J.: Research on the interactive aesthetics of AR virtual image art from the perspective of acceptance aesthetics. Ningbo University (2020). https://doi.org/10.27256/d.cnki.gnbou.2019.000216

Chen, X.: Research on the application of immersive interaction design in virtual reality technology. Software **44**(09), 95–97 (2023). http://t.cn/A6joibJ3

Meng, S.: Digital art and virtual image strategy–a review of "Cao Fei: time Stage" UCCA exhibition. Beauty Times (Lower) **11**, 79–82 (2022). https://doi.org/10.16129/j.cnki.mysdx.2022.11.015

Zhang, J., Chen, B.: Research on "Internet+" mobile aesthetic education with cell phone as terminal. J. East China Normal Univ. (Educ. Sci. Edn.) **35**(05), 109–116+162 (2017). https://doi.org/10.16382/j.cnki.1000-5560.2017.05.009

General Office of the State Council: Opinions of the General Office of the State Council on Comprehensively Strengthening and Improving Aesthetic Education in Schools, 15 September 2015. http://t.cn/A6jo6SOd

State Council: State Council on actively promoting the "Internet +" action of the guiding opinions, 04 July 2015. http://t.cn/A6jo6OC0

Zhong, Q.: New era demands: the deep integration of "Internet+" and aesthetic education. Modern Educ. (04), 60–62 (2019). http://t.cn/A6joimpC

Zhang, J.: Research on the characteristics and influence of network culture communication under the view of media integration. Cult. Ind. (13), 1–3 (2022). http://t.cn/A6joiB9b

Wang, T.: Characteristics and strategies of visual culture communication in the context of integrated media. Commun. Copyright (05), 100–102 (2022). https://doi.org/10.16852/j.cnki.45-1390/g2.2022.05.019

Cui, Z.: The realization of socialist core value system popularization under the threshold of network culture communication. J. Guangxi Youth Cadre College **23**(06), 1–5 (2013). http://t.cn/A6jo6vkJ

Wang, W.: Generalized artificial intelligence in intercultural communication: changes, opportunities and challenges. External Commun. (05), 48–51 (2023). http://t.cn/A6jo6h9v

Golovachev, V.S., Zatsepina, M.B.: Model of interaction between libraries and preschool educational institutions in terms of the moral and aesthetic education of preschool children. Perspektivy nauki i obrazovania – Perspect. Sci. Educ. **47**(5), 170–185 (2020). https://doi.org/10.32744/pse.2020.5.12

Research on the Application of Design Thinking in Sustainable Food Design—Taking the Afternoon Tea on Earth Day as an Example

Weijian Yu, Qixuan Ni, and Jun Wu(✉)

School of Fine Arts and Design, Faculty of Arts, Shenzhen University, Shenzhen 518061, Guangdong, China

{2300505019,2020050003}@email.szu.edu.cn, junwu2006@hotmail.com

Abstract. This research focuses on the food crisis and examines how sustainable food design, an emerging discipline, can impact public food consumption behavior and help to re-establish food values. This study presents a research framework for sustainable food design based on the theory of the 'Four Orders of Design'. It analyzes and discusses the design practice of 'Earth Day Afternoon Tea' through a case study approach. The study concludes that the sustainable food design event involves four action steps: cognition, behavior, experience, and sympathy. It enables participants to stimulate the desire to explore in the process of eating, not only to obtain the satisfaction of tasting food, but also to develop a new view of food, to reflect on the relationship between people and food, and to establish new food values. This study proposes a model for fostering sustainability awareness through new eating behaviors under sustainable food design. The experience gained from this model can serve as a reference for other sustainable food design practices.

Keywords: Sustainable Food Design · Eating Design · design thinking · food crisis

1 Introduction

For the first time in 32 years of United Nations Development Program (UNDP) calculations, the Human Development Index (HDI) has declined globally for two consecutive years. The HDI measures a country's health, education, and standard of living. Human development has regressed to 2016 levels, undoing much of the progress made towards achieving the SDGs (UNDP 2022). The global food system is facing unprecedented pressures and challenges due to the increased frequency of extreme weather events such as pandemics, hurricanes, heavy rains, and high temperatures. In 2020, between 720 and 811 million people globally will be at risk of hunger, an increase of 161 million from 2019. Additionally, almost one-third of the food produced globally is lost or wasted. Approximately 3 billion tons of food is lost or wasted each year, with about 28% of arable land being affected. This results in greenhouse gas emissions as high as 3.3 billion tons. Food losses in farms and supply chains, as well as wastage at the retail

P.-L. P. Rau (Ed.): HCII 2024, LNCS 14700, pp. 179–192, 2024.
https://doi.org/10.1007/978-3-031-60901-5_13

and consumer levels, not only cause economic damage to farmers and consumers, but also exacerbate the human challenge of combating climate change and curbing biodiversity loss. It is important to address this issue to ensure food security and mitigate environmental damage. According to the World Wildlife Fund (WWF) in 2023, global agricultural production currently utilizes 70% of freshwater resources, 33% of land, and 30% of energy, while also emitting 20% of greenhouse gases (WWF 2023). Despite this, the Food and Agriculture Organization (FAO) reported in 2016 that 1/9 of the world's population still lacks access to sufficient food and nutrition (FAO 2016).

In recent years, the concept of food design has emerged in the design field. Food design is a new cross-disciplinary design category, food design as a way to make the relationship between food, people and the environment visible and transform it into a better practice (Ilieva 2020). This practice can offer diverse perspectives for comprehending the inherent qualities of food and cultural relationships. By utilizing design thinking, systematic exploration, and innovative research and design practices, new food experiences can be created to transform the relationship between humans and food. Further, it can promote healthier, more equitable, and sustainable food development in society. However, food design is a nascent field, and its theory, methodology, and practice have yet to be fully developed. Given the precarious state of our food system, it is crucial to explore ways to reduce food waste through food design and promote green and sustainable consumption patterns and lifestyles. This study aims to explore:

1. How to intervene in the food waste problem through design thinking, and how to explore the potential of food design in promoting green consumer awareness and lifestyle through the experience of food design at all stages from production, processing to consumption through design;
2. To construct a design framework for sustainable food design events through the analysis of design cases;
3. To construct a model of new eating behaviors to cultivate sustainable awareness under food design, in the hope that food design can bring about a new relationship between people and food, and raise awareness of reducing food waste and establishing new food values.

2   Literature Review

2.1   Food Design

Disciplinary Development. Food design is a cross-modal approach to the creation of food systems and behavioural impacts and interventions, involving design, psychology, sociology, and nutrition, and is dedicated to meaningful systemic service experiences of food, sustainable social cycles, healthy lifestyles, and experiential innovations in "eating". Martí Guixé, the Spanish pioneer of food design, first considered food design as a derivative of industrial design and held a food design exhibition in Barcelona in 1997, which triggered design research in the design community on the medium of food (Guixé 2003); Francesca Zampollo, a designer who also comes from an industrial design background, goes beyond the focus on the physical characteristics of food to correlate the broad field of socio-cultural factors associated with food, arguing that the focus is not only on the food itself, but also on the different contexts in which it interacts with people.

Therefore, she believes that the goal of food design is to enhance people's eating habits and experiences through innovative approaches that take into account sustainability and cultural values (Zampollo 2016a). She offers practical ideas and methodological applications to stimulate creativity and generate ideas for food design; In 2014, the Eindhoven School of Design in the Netherlands established the world's first department focused on food design, "Food non Food". Marije Vogelzang, who is responsible for teaching food design as the head of the department, as well as many foods design practices, emphasizes that she is a Marije Vogelzang, who is responsible for teaching food design as well as practicing food design, emphasizes that she is an eating designer, not a food designer, because she believes that food is already designed by nature, and that it is only in the process of eating that food can be called food. Marije points out that food is a more political substance, and that food, unlike products, is a substance that is internalized as part of the human body, and that the moment a person takes a bite of food, he or she becomes connected to culture, identity, agriculture, technology, the senses, and the psyche through food (Zampollo 2016b). These ideas suggest that human cognition can be shaped by the ways in which design thinking can be combined with food, and that food design can deepen a deeper relationship between people and food in ways that create new ideas about food. Nowadays, the concept of food design is still in the process of deepening and evolving as new ideas are created.

Food design has been developing in Europe for nearly 20 years and shows an increasing trend of multidisciplinary intersection and integration, with more and more related fields focusing on food design, combining art and technology to address many of the problems facing humanity, such as dietary structure, multimodal and multisensory, behavioural interventions (obesity, cardiovascular and other major health issues) and social sustainability (global warming, overconsumption and biodiversity). In addition to designers and scholars practicing and researching in food design, in Europe, institutions such as Polytechnic University of Milan in Italy, Delft University of Technology in the Netherlands, University of Oxford, University of Leeds and so on have successively offered professional degrees related to food design. In China, the Eecology crisis design program at the Central Academy of Fine Arts, the School of Design at the China Academy of Fine Arts, the School of Food Engineering at Jiangnan University, the Academy of Fine Arts at Tsinghua University, the Beijing Institute of Fashion Technology, the School of Design and Creativity at Tongji University, the School of Design at Shanghai Jiao tong University, Yangzhou University, and the School of Public Health at Zhejiang University also offer courses related to food design. In addition to educational institutions, there are many large companies that focus on food design, such as IKEA's space10 studio, which creatively explores the future of kitchens and restaurant food, McDonald's green restaurants, and KFC, which has installed Love Fridges in its stores. In terms of organizations, Zampollo has created the International Center for Food Design, which offers open days, "expert advice" events, social events, debates, seminars, online webinars, career days, project sharing events, etc., and also teaches practical approaches to food design; and in China, by food designer Chi Wei, who launched the +86 Food Design Alliance in 2019, curated the Future Food International Food Design Festival, and launched the +86 Future Food Award. This means that the role and influence of food design is also gradually being recognized in all sectors of society.

Food Design Approach. The design methodology of food design is still in the stage of ambiguous exploration, and depending on how it is categorized, there will be different requirements for designers with different professional backgrounds. One of the most popular categorizations is the discipline of food design proposed by Francesca Zampollo: Food Product Design is a design method for companies to produce finished food products through mass production of food raw materials, and is most closely related to agriculture and farming, which is the primary industry. Design For Food refers to the design of food containers, such as placement, transportation, cooking containers, utensils and other tools, more like a branch of industrial design; Design With Food is the method of cooking, seasoning, processing and adjusting the taste, temperature and color of food, which is closer to the work of a chef or scientist. Food Space Design is a method of designing the cooking space and eating space, which is usually carried out by a space designer; Food Product Design, Design With Food, Design For Food, and Food Space Design are combined to form Eating Design, which includes Food Service Design. Eating Design is also an activity in addition to the entire dining scene, so it also has its own independent structure, such as the theme of the activity, community, and decorations. Food Policy Design and Activism, Critical/Speculative/Future Food Design, Digital Media/Marketing/Communication, Food System Design, Sustainable Food Design, etc. are among the more metaphysical types of design (Zampollo and Peacock 2016). This means that food design is not the exclusive domain of designers with design degrees, but that people without design training, but with specific knowledge about food, are also designers of food design, even more important than some designers at some point. Hu argues that combining food design with systems thinking divides food design into three systems according to the links of food consumption and distribution: 1. The perceptual system of taste, 2. The aesthetics of food design, and 3. The recyclable food economy (Hu 2021). Under systems thinking, by emphasizing the following points in food design: 1. Holistic perspective: understanding the interconnections and interactions within the food system to design more sustainable and environmentally friendly solutions, 2. Interdisciplinary collaboration: designers are able to understand the food system in a more comprehensive way by collaborating with experts from different fields and create integrated design solutions, 3. Circular economy: by studying the waste and by-products in the food chain and finding ways to turn them into new resources, designers are thinking in a way that helps reduce waste and promotes the recycling of resources, 4. Long-term impact: this means that food design considers the long-term environmental, social and economic impact of the design to ensure that the design solution meets the needs of the present without harming the interests of future generations, 5. Social engagement: the importance of social engagement and public awareness is emphasized in food design. Designers need to consider how design can raise public awareness of food system issues and encourage consumers to make more sustainable choices.

2.2 Design Thinking

Design thinking is a concrete representation of innovative thinking in design activities and a unique contribution of the design field to human cognitive activities (Hu 2022). Design thinking as a methodology for innovative design is currently the dominant concept in design thinking research (Chu 2020). Tim Brown, the founder of IDEO, describes design thinking as a way of using the tools and mindset of designers to explore human needs and create entirely new solutions that can be used to creatively address personal, social, and business challenges (Brown 2008). While Horst Rittel and Melvin M. Webber argued that design thinking as a solution to intractable problems presents universal applicability and interdisciplinary properties in research (Rittel 1973). Buchanan proposed the "Four Orders of Design" to categorize design objects into four types: Symbols & Signs, Physical Objects, Event & Services, and Idea & systems. He pointed out that the four domains are interrelated and interpenetrating, and are jointly integrated in contemporary design thinking, which can be applied to any area of solving uncertain problems about people (Buchanan 1995); Klaus Krippendorff, on the other hand, argues that design and design thinking are about creating meaning, and that value and meaning are at the heart of design creation, with artifacts being the medium for communicating meaning rather than the core (Klaus 2006); Jonathan Leroy Biderman argues that the process of applying design thinking may artificially simplify the context and scope of a project by defining this idealized space for a particular design effort or project (Jonathan 2017).

Although design thinking is broadly defined and constantly updated as the field of design time expands, the evolution from design to design thinking actually evolved from creating products to analyzing the relationship between people and products, then to analyzing the relationship between people and people, and then to expanding to the relationship of the whole system that includes things, people, communities and the environment.

2.3 Food Design and Sustainable Design

Food design is inextricably linked to sustainable design and incorporates the concept of sustainability, which is one of the pillars of food design. Due to the biological properties of food, food is alive and highly perishable. Consumers have a demand for freshness and food scientists are constantly trying to extend the shelf life of food through preservation techniques (Bordewijk 2020). Food design is not only about the food itself, but also about multiple dimensions of food production, consumption, culture, society and economy. Food design must consider the entire food system, including food production, processing, packaging, distribution, marketing and consumer behavior (Van Boeijen 2023). Because food is a source of basic human needs and designers are challenged to provide safe and nutritious food to keep people healthy, food design involves design decisions that may impact human health and well-being (Biderman 2017).

Slow Food is a global movement that promotes food sustainability, and the organization works to ensure that everyone has access to quality, clean, and fair food (SFF 2023), with specific goals for food sustainability, an idea revered by many, including food designers. Marije Vogelzang's food design work "Volumes" is a plate decoration made of silicone-impregnated stones that aims to control overeating by using a stylized presentation to visually trick the brain into thinking the plate contains more food. Marije argues that sustainability in food design needs to be balanced with people's emotional needs, and that if the design is somewhat sustainable but frustrating, it loses its meaning (Marije 2020); Makeat Studios uses 3D printing technology to create coasters, meals, cutlery and other items from restaurant back-of-house waste, and Makeat founder Juan

Manuel Umbert believes waste is a lack of creativity; Food designer Alexa Tirlla created the Zero Waste Dinners, which were held in various locations to raise awareness of climate and environmental issues and to minimize the use of plastic in everyday life by combining architectural design methods with creative cooking, using only essential materials and ingredients to complete the meal; Siyang Jing Sustainable food design is defined as a systematic, future-oriented design that uses food design as a tool for human health and environmental sustainability. It is argued that in the post-COVID19 and post-carbon context, the importance of food design as a pathway to sustainable development has been gradually highlighted. (Jing 2023). The above suggests that food design is closely related to sustainable design, and suggests requirements and goals for sustainable food design practices.

3 Research Methods

This paper outlines research frame work (see Fig. 1). For sustainable food design based on the above information. According to the Four Orders of Design theory (Buchanan 1995), design practices are analyzed in four main fields: (1) Symbols & Signs, (2) Physical Objects, (3) Events & Services, and (4) Ideas & Systems. Design practices within each field utilize different dimensions of design thinking and focus on different core tasks: the task of communicating meaning, the task of constructing objects, the task of realizing interactions, and the task of integrating systems. Each of these fields is a site for provoking thought and establishing new food values. Therefore, sustainable food design may alternately address the issues of communicating meaning, constructing objects, realizing interactions, and integrating systems. There is no priority among the four orders. They integrate the horizontal expansion of fields and the vertical deepening of complexity, so that there is a more organic correlation among them.

The research framework is oriented to the food crisis and combines the strategy of sustainable design, including education and awareness, community engagement, sustainable material selection, life cycle assessment, longevity and timeless design, zero waste

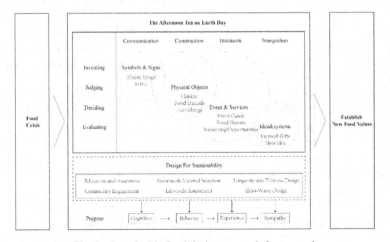

Fig. 1. Sustainable food design research frame work

design, through the four design fields of symbols & signs, physical objects, events & services, and ideas & systems as the touch points of sustainable design, and the four action steps of participants' cognition, behavior, experience, and sympathy as the joints that form the process of building new food values.

4 Design Case Analysis

The afternoon tea on Earth Day is an event within the 2019 graduation season of Hubei Institute of Fine Arts, which started on April 22, Earth Day. Earth Day is the world's largest civil holiday for environmental protection, which was established to publicize and practice the concept of environmental protection (Global citizen 2015).The afternoon tea on Earth Day is a buffet afternoon tea on sustainable food design in the lobby of Wuhan Landing Design Studio, inviting students and faculty members of Hubei Institute of Fine Arts to participate in the event. Throughout The afternoon tea on Earth Day, the event was named "all done", a word taken from "all done", which expresses the main idea of the event - an exploration of the possibilities of consuming a range of substances in the event to their fullest potential. -It is an exploration of the possibilities for the full consumption of a range of substances in the event. In this afternoon tea, the concept of sustainability is emphasized from the symbols to the systems, and the ingredients, tableware, and decorations are all utilized in a way that does not produce waste, while at the same time taking into account the aesthetics and the design of a fun experience. Through the food design, participants will be stimulated to explore the process of eating, not only to get the satisfaction of tasting food, but also to create a new awareness of the food, reflect on the relationship between human and food, and establish a new value of food.

4.1 Cognitions of The Afternoon Tea on Earth Day

Before the event starts, the event must take into account the need to publicize it externally and send out invitations, and this stage mainly deals with information and communication (see Fig. 2). The main way to publicize the event is to push it through the Internet to reduce the use of paper. Based on the theme image symbols, posters and peripheral materials were designed for promotion, and printed materials were printed with eco-friendly ink. In order to match the atmosphere of "Earth Day", we chose green and transparent materials to express the layout of the event venue; green has the meaning of green and environmental protection, and has the meaning of returning to close to nature; the attribute of transparent comes from the characteristics of the material of our napkin glutinous rice paper, and at the same time has the characteristics of "all done", which means "full consumption".

During an afternoon tea, the menu serves as an instruction manual for the meal, allowing participants to get a sense of the event by conveying information on the surface. Clipped to stainless steel receipt holders, the menus are made of edible materials such as starch paper, sugar paper, and tortilla skins, with different dishes corresponding to different flavors. Edible materials with colors such as coffee, honey mustard, and icing were used as ink to print the ingredient list, suggested serving method, and presentation of the dishes on the surface of the menu. This ensured that participants had access to information about the food and that the menu was edible as part of the meal.

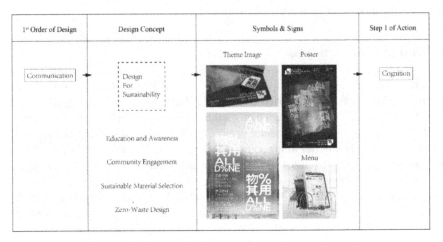

Fig. 2. Sustainable food design strategies on the step of cognition.

4.2 Behaviors of The Afternoon Tea on Earth Day

The natural constraints and predefined uses of an item can correspond to the possible uses, operational procedures, and functions of the item. Through factors such as constraints on the physical structure of the item, semantic constraints, cultural constraints, and logical constraints, it is possible to demonstrate explicit and correct operational procedures in different situations (Norman 2015). The whole afternoon tea is in the form of a relaxed buffet, and there are no complicated table manners in the event, so you can choose the food you want to eat based on your own interests and eat where you feel comfortable. There is enough freedom in the activity to create a relaxed atmosphere that allows participants to maximize their immersion in the afternoon tea exploration process, while keeping them within the flow of the activity. This phase focuses on the issue of constructed objects, which appear to be designed as objects in the event space, but actually aim to frame the boundaries of participants' behavior (see Fig. 3).The key design touchpoints in the problem domain with built constructs are at the points of cuisine, food utensils, and furnishings, which are subordinate to Design With Food, Design For Food, and Food Space Design, respectively (Zampollo 2016a). Prior to participating in the event, each participant receives an invitation letter, which itself is made of a usable material, as well as a fire-paint stamp imitated in white chocolate on the envelope, which is written with information related to the event as well as the suggestion that the invitation letter and the fire-paint stamp can be eaten after reading it, implanting the participant in advance with pre-determined uses and constraints. At the beginning of the event, participants will be given their own cutlery, made of a dinner plate and a round fork. All items are displayed on a long table with a small area of manila grass in the center of the table and on the floor to enhance the atmosphere and match the green theme of Earth Day. At the front of the table were several types of menus, which as mentioned above are dining instructions made of edible materials and are part of the dish. Participants chose their favorite menu and chose the one that suited them, and ate it along with the menu. The design of the dishes mimics objects in nature, creating a sense of strangeness from daily meals and enhancing the freshness of the participants' meals. The dishes consist of fruit desserts, meat savory snacks, and beverages, of which the fruit portion utilizes fruits that have been collected and returned to the store because of transportation problems and have been damaged, as well as fruits that have been rejected by the merchants as commodities due to their poor appearance but have not actually decayed; the meat consists of two types of meat: shrimp and beef, both of which are slow-cooked in low temperatures. Meat, shrimp and beef, are cooked through low-temperature slow cooking, can maximize the retention of the original flavor of the food, more than steaming, boiling, frying can retain more vitamin components, and reduce the use of oil and salt; the use of the liquid containing seaweed gum and calcium-containing liquids react to the surface of the rapid condensation of a layer of condensate film characteristics of the liquid drinks wrapped up to form a "beverage bubbles The liquid is wrapped around the drink to form a "drink bubble", so that the liquid can be dispensed without disposable paper cups, and placed in cup-shaped ice cubes made of frozen soda water, changing the previous method of mixing ice cubes with drinks, while achieving the effect of chilling. The design utilizes two design principles, Sustainable Material Selection and Life-cycle Assessment, to achieve Zero-Waste Design, by setting up different cuisines, food utensils, and furnishings. Through the setting of different cuisines, food utensils, and furnishings, participants can perceive different aesthetics and pleasures in the process of eating, so that they can enjoy multiple aesthetic experiences while eating. It also allows participants to frame their behavior within the physical, semantic, cultural and logical constraints of the objects, thus controlling their behavior within the predefined framework of the activity.

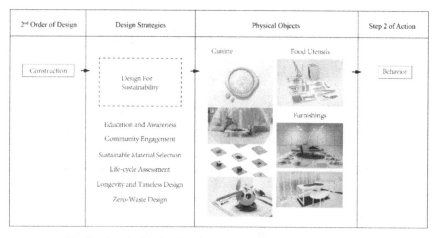

Fig. 3. Sustainable food design strategies on the step of behavior.

4.3 Experiences of The Afternoon Tea on Earth Day

Like eating in a restaurant, people do not only pay attention to tangible objects, but also expect good service to bring a better experience. The design of events and services in the problem domain of realizing interactions emphasizes the human experience more than the construction of the design of tangible objects in the problem domain of having constructs. But designing based on emotions, physical states, mental processes (e.g., goals and moods), and expectations is difficult because these are subjective, they change, and therefore are nearly impossible to predict. Therefore, the design of the event experience focuses on ensuring the integrity of the experience and having channels for communication and feedback, with specific touchpoints being event guide, food flavors, and socializing opportunity (see Fig. 4). Event guide is to provide guidance for the entire event, including the waiter talking about the concept of the event, guiding the food pairing, the bar, and serving drinks and the food with a drink. The event guide was to provide guidance for the entire event, including waiters describing the concept of the event, guidance on food pairings, bar service, and dishes with guide cards describing the flavors and textures. The entire event site was originally a meeting room at work, with a bar and a square table with eight seats, providing the possibility of communication and interaction, which can still be done after the event, which adopts the sustainable design strategy of Longevity and Timeless Design. By shaping the spatial environment with physical objects and human participations, it creates an open, qualitative and exploratory environment that attracts participants to explore immersively and continuously stimulates the interaction of idea generation and exchange.

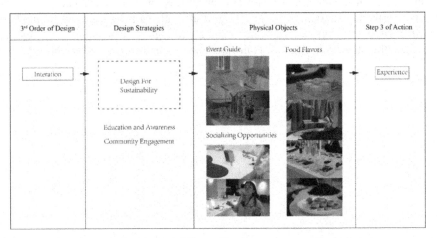

Fig. 4. Sustainable food design strategies on the step of experience.

4.4 Sympathies of The Afternoon Tea on Earth Day

Food-centered design explores the value of food in social relations under self-reflection, mapping out people's current and expected forms of life. Facing the problematic area of the fourth order integration system, in The afternoon tea on Earth Day, Symbols & Signs and Physical objects are the foundation layer, through which the Events & Services of food design are organized, and the participants use a series of sensory stimulation as an opportunity to generate ideas about the relationship between people and food during or after the activities. Participants will use a series of sensory stimuli as an opportunity to think about the relationship between humans and food, rethink the relationship between humans and nature, and sympathize with the concept of sustainable development during and after the event (see Fig. 5). At the end of the party, the food was packaged in boxes made of discarded paper pulp from the printing store near the campus, in accordance with the concept of Sustainable Material Selection, and made into a tabletop landscape that was distributed to the party participants as a souvenir. The Manila lawn still retains a living root structure, and in addition to being used as a tablescape, the souvenir lawn can also be placed on a larger lawn nearby, continuing to grow and add a piece of greenery to the land around it to promote Community Engagement. New ideas generated during this phase are also design touchpoints that implant the idea of a new human-food relationship into the minds of the participants who, in addition to feeling a sense of sustainable food design in the event in a small system, are also able to experience the benefits of sustainable food design. In addition to feeling the significance of sustainable food design in the small system of the event, the participants, as a member of the ecology in the larger system, reflect and urge on their own behavioral style, everyone is alerted to their own role in the ecology, and this new idea is the basis for the establishment of new food values.

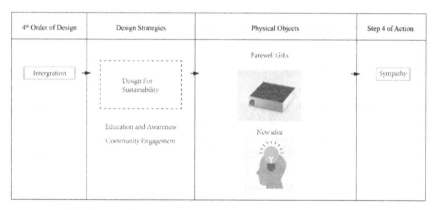

Fig. 5. Sustainable food design strategies on the step of sympath

5   Discussion

Based on existing scholars' research on the generalization, methodology and practice of food design and the application of design thinking to innovative design (Zampollo 2016a and Buchanan 1995), this paper explores the role and methodology of food crisis-oriented sustainable food design in establishing new food values, and proposes a research framework for the application of design thinking in sustainable food design design strategies. The sustainable food design practices and case studies at The Afternoon Tea on Earth Day are verified.

This paper constructs a modeling framework for food crisis-oriented sustainable food design, which is concerned with food-mediated food-related design. Food design, as an emerging interdisciplinary research direction, plays a great role in improving eating experience and ecosystem innovation (Jing 2023). Sustainable design objects are classified into four main areas: Symbols & Signs, Physical Objects, Events & Services, and Ideas & Systems through the four orders of design, which deal with conveying meanings, constructing objects, realizing interactions, and integrating systems, respectively. Adopting sustainable design strategies such as education and awareness, community engagement, sustainable material selection, life cycle assessment, longevity and timeless design, and zero waste design, we are committed to developing sustainable design to design touchpoints, intervening in the four stages of cognition, behavior, experience, and sympathy as a design starting point, prompting people to develop new ideas about the relationship between people and food, and facilitating the establishment of new food values in the future.

The Earth Day Afternoon Tea aims to transform external knowledge into brain knowledge by organizing external knowledge and integrating design issues in various fields, and to instill sustainable development awareness in the minds of participants in the form of an attractive, non-didactic, and rich sensory experience of afternoon tea. In addition, there are still many shortcomings in the process of actual implementation. The Earth Day afternoon tea is a small-scale food design activity centered on designers, and the dissemination capacity of the activity is limited, so if the activity fails to target a wider range of people and attract enough attention, it will not be beneficial to the promotion of the concept. At the same time, a small event with a small budget is the most critical, which makes the choice of sustainable materials limited, as the price of environmentally friendly materials for sustainable materials is much more expensive than disposable items such as plastics and foams. On the one hand, due to the lack of relevant knowledge background on the nutritional balance of food, an event planned by a designer as a centerpiece may lack consideration of this aspect of food pairing. In addition, the balance between sustainability and aesthetics can sometimes be misjudged from a designer's perspective. This is precisely why interdisciplinary and multidisciplinary collaboration is important and necessary for sustainable food design practices. In the future, companies and schools should take social responsibility and encourage designers to combine and innovate aesthetics and sustainable materials so that sustainable concepts can be promoted through design aesthetics and even become fashionable. In the long term, suppliers and manufacturers of sustainable materials in the future will be encouraged to facilitate economies of scale, reduce the cost of purchasing sustainable materials, and promote the development of sustainable materials, thus further increasing the possibilities of sustainable food design, and consumers will have more choices for sustainable lifestyles. Bringing sustainable food design into existence is not a special event, but our daily life itself.

6 Conclusions

Food design is a new multidisciplinary design discipline, food design as a way to make the relationship between food, people and the environment visible and transform it into a better practice (Ilieva 2020). In the context of today's food crisis, the food system is exposed to unprecedented risks, and sustainable design plays a key role in addressing these challenges. Through the research and practice of sustainable food design, the public's food consumption behavior can be influenced and new food values can be established.

This study proposes to construct a model of sustainable food design to promote sustainability awareness (see Fig. 6), which is verified in the case of The Afternoon Tea on Earth Day. In sustainable food design, symbols & signs and physical objects are used as the foundation layer, and through the foundation layer, events & services of food design are developed to provide a series of cognitive, behavioral, and experiential opportunities for participants, and to sympathize with the four steps of action, so that they can generate ideas about the relationship between people and food in the process of participating in the event or at the end of the event. In the process of participating in the activity or after the activity, participants will generate ideas about the relationship between human and food, rethink the relationship between human and nature, and sympathize with sustainable development, in which the idea & system is formed throughout the process of sustainable food design, and such a model is aimed at establishing new food values, and it is the practice of applying design thinking in the field of food design. The establishment

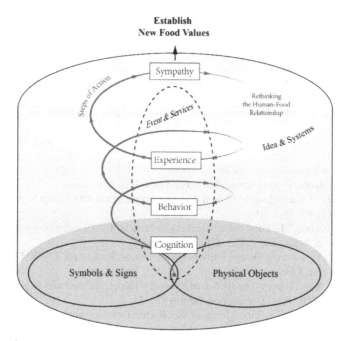

Fig. 6. A model of sustainable food design to promote sustainability awareness

of sustainable food values has long-term social effects, and it is hoped that the experience of this study could provide a reference for other sustainable food design practices.

References

FAO: Food Loss and Waste Database (2016). https://www.fao.org/platform-food-loss-waste/flw-data/en. Accessed 24 Oct 2023

SSF. Slow Food. https://www.slowfood.com/about-us/. Accessed 24 Oct 2023

Globalcitizen (2015). https://www.globalcitizen.org/fr/content/the-history-of-earth-day-3/?gclid=CjwKCAiA_OetBhAtEiwAPTeQZ5JELAoaV3xisxd6-v8E63-MlptqXMwq-jPFfjV-H30eN5BQ1NxsYBoCVHkQAvD_BwE. Accessed 24 Dec 2023

WWF:ZERO WASTE COOKBOOK (2023). https://www.wwf-opf.org.cn/news/2172. Accessed 30 Oct 2023

Biderman, J.L.: Embracing complexity in food, design and food design. Int. J. Food Design 2(1), 27–44 (2017)

Bordewijk, M., Schifferstein, H.N.: The specifics of Food Design: insights from professional design practice. Int. J. Food Des. 4(2), 101–138 (2020)

Brown, T.: Design thinking. Harv. Bus. Rev. 86(6), 84 (2008)

Chu, D., Li, J., Jiang, J.: From qualitative method practice to quantitative process cognition: status and progress of research on design thinking. Zhuangshi (10), 88–92 (2020)

Hu, F.: Systematic food-centered design conceives the idea of future lifestyle. Zhuangshi (03), 48–60 (2021)

Hu, Y., Bai, Y., Zhou, Z., Du, X.: Capture, cognition and interpretation of design thinking. Zhuangshi (05), 78–83 (2022)

Ilieva, R.T.: Experiencing food, designing dialogues. In: proceedings of the 1st international conference on food design and food studies (EFOOD 2017)," Ricardo Bonacho, Alcinda Pinheiro de Sousa, Cláudia Viegas, João Paulo Martins, Maria José Pires and Sara Velez Estêvão (eds). Int. J. Food Design 4(2), 181–187 (2020)

Jing, S.: Sustainable food design: a four-dimensional transformation of theory and methodology towards post carbon era. In: International Conference on Human-Computer Interaction, pp. 310–323. Springer, Cham (2023)

Rittel, H.W., Webber, M.M.: Dilemmas in a general theory of planning. Policy Sci. 4(2), 155–169 (1973)

van Boeijen, A.G., Schifferstein, H.N.: How to include the sociocultural context in food design: Insights, tools and strategies. Int. J. Food Des. 9, 73–99 (2024)

Vogelzang, M.: Volumes. Marije Vogelzang (2023)

Zampollo, F.: Welcome to food design. Int. J. Food Des. 1(1), 3–9 (2016)

Zampollo, F.: The wonderful world of food design: a conversation with Marije Vogelzang. Int. J. Food Des. 1(1), 65–71 (2016)

Zampollo, F., Peacock, M.: Food design thinking: a branch of design thinking specific to food design. J. Creat. Behav. 50(3), 203–210 (2016)

Buchanan, R.W.: Discovering Design Explorations in Design Studies, pp. 23–68. The University of Chicago Press, Chicago (1995)

Norman, D., (K. Xiao, Trans.): The Design of Everyday Things: Revised and Expanded Edition. Basic books. CITIC Press Corporation, Beijing (2015)

UNDP (United Nations Development Programme), Human Development Report 2021–22: Uncertain Times, Unsettled Lives: Shaping our Future in a Transforming World. New York (2022)

Guixé, M., Millet, J.R., Planella, A.: Food design. Galería H2O (2003)

To Split or Not to Split? Evaluating IA Roles Providing Knowledge and Emotional Support

Jingyu Zhao, Pei-Luen Patrick Rau$^{(\boxtimes)}$ ⓘ, and Yankuan Liu ⓘ

Department of Industrial Engineering, Tsinghua University, Beijing, China
rpl@tsinghua.edu.cn

Abstract. As intelligent agents (IAs) become increasingly integrated into human-machine systems, understanding the dynamics of collaboration between individuals and IAs is crucial. This study explores the impact of different IA roles and users' knowledge levels on collaborative task performance and subjective evaluations. Three IA role design approaches are investigated: expert-type IA providing only knowledge support, mentor-type IA (combined-persona) providing both knowledge and emotional support, and IA group (split-persona) providing knowledge and emotional support separately. Participants with high and low task-related knowledge levels were involved. Results reveal that the combined-persona IA enhances task performance but receives lower subjective evaluations, whereas the split-persona IA receives higher subjective evaluations but reduces task performance, indicating a trade-off between objective and subjective measures. Additionally, users' knowledge levels influence preferences for IA roles, with low-knowledge participants favoring emotional support. Recommendations are made for adjusting IA roles based on task requirements and user characteristics.

Keywords: Intelligent Agents · Human-Machine Collaboration · Split-persona Effect

1 Introduction

With the rapid advancement of artificial intelligence, machine learning, and cognitive modeling, the levels of automation and intelligence in machines are progressively increasing. The introduction of automation and intelligent agents (IAs) has brought about changes in human-machine systems [1], allowing IA to assume roles as team members. Intelligent agents, defined as autonomous agents with a certain degree of self-regulation and service capabilities in communication, decision-making, and application scenarios, have become integral [2–4]. In people's daily lives, IAs, serving as communication carriers, are embedded in smartphones, computers, or smart speakers, providing voice-based IA services [5], For example, the recently launched voice interaction version of GPT has once again captured people's attention with its exceptional naturalness and professionalism. IAs are also widely used by numerous enterprises to enhance vitality, productivity, and efficiency [6]. The diverse types, varied functionalities, and multidimensional interactions of IA s have transformed human-machine interaction, driving the development

P.-L. P. Rau (Ed.): HCII 2024, LNCS 14700, pp. 193–205, 2024.
https://doi.org/10.1007/978-3-031-60901-5_14

of human-machine collaboration. A manifestation of this collaboration is the changing role establishment and function allocation between humans and machines. Under the concept of human-machine symbiosis, human-machine teams are beginning to form.

The highly anthropomorphic appearance and roles of IAs, coupled with perceptual intelligence supported by multi-channel data processing, have transformed IAs from tools for task completion into entities with human-like attributes as team members [7, 8]. IAs are now establishing anthropomorphic roles and the concept of social presence. During interactions with users, they form expected role positions and exert relevant functions within those identities, thereby establishing social roles. IAs in interactions may function as work assistants or life managers, taking on roles such as leaders, colleagues, or subordinates with different power distances. In educational contexts, IAs may act as teachers or teaching assistants. The establishment of different social roles through the anthropomorphism of IAs is a crucial factor influencing human-machine interaction. On the other hand, the user's position in human-machine collaboration, including their knowledge background, mental models, and operational proficiency, introduces uncertainty in interactions with IAs. Therefore, the alignment between user backgrounds and Intelligent agents also deserves attention.

This study aims to investigate the impact of collaboration between individuals and IAs in task scenarios from two perspectives: the combination or split of IA roles when providing support and the users' knowledge levels. Specifically, the study explores three design approaches for IA roles, namely, an expert-type IA providing knowledge support only, a mentor-type IA (combined-persona IA) providing both knowledge and emotional support, and a group consists of two independent IAs (split-persona IAs) in which one IA provides knowledge support as an expert-type while the other provides emotional support as a peer-type IA. Additionally, the study considers the dimension of user knowledge, categorizing participants into groups with and without task-related knowledge. This research provides new insights into the design of IAs in human-machine collaboration and offers recommendations for IA role design based on individual differences and the provision of different support needs.

2 Related Studies and Hypotheses

IAs are computer systems equipped with artificial intelligence and machine learning technologies. They can intelligently interact with users in natural language, catering to a diverse range of goals and a vast user base [9]. With the development of natural language processing and speech recognition technologies, the conversational abilities of intelligent agents have continually improved [10]. They are gradually gaining the capacity to independently conduct teaching, design, support, and supervise learning processes, thus enabling personalized learning experiences [11, 12]. Despite some skepticism regarding the effectiveness of intelligent agents in learning contexts [13–15], numerous studies have affirmed the assistance provided by intelligent agents to learners, particularly their effectiveness as guides [16–19]. For instance, Tegos, Demetriadis [20] compared the impact of intelligent agent interventions on learning outcomes, finding that interventions significantly improved students' grades and task performance. Targeted interventions tailored to individual needs were found to be more effective.

In the realm of human-machine collaboration involving intelligent agents, as per the Autonomous Agent Teammate-likeness model, factors such as IA capabilities, task relevance, and communication richness contribute to users perceiving intelligent agents as more human-like than mere tools [21]. This tendency propels intelligent agents toward a more anthropomorphic role. Regarding the role design of intelligent agents in learning, a classic model proposed by Kim and Baylor outlines three teaching roles: expert, motivator, and mentor, expanding the support scope of intelligent agents from providing knowledge support to offering social and emotional support [22, 23]. The study revealed that mentor and motivator roles, which include emotional support, were perceived as more human-like, enhancing learners' self-efficacy. Roles providing knowledge support, such as expert and mentor, were more effective in improving learning outcomes. Among the roles, the mentor, capable of providing both knowledge and emotional support, demonstrated the most effective guidance [10]. Researchers have also discovered the split-persona effect, where dividing an intelligent agent into two roles for knowledge and emotional support separately is more effective than consolidating them into a single role [24]. When learning with two intelligent agents assuming different roles, learners can easily distinguish information sources, resulting in deeper learning and increased motivation [25].

On the other hand, as members of human-machine teams, human users often exhibit individual differences due to personality, culture, past experiences, knowledge, and skills, influencing team performance and cognition [26, 27]. Particularly in the context of learning assistants, Choi and Clark [28] compared the performance of users with different levels of knowledge when facing intelligent agents and regular prompts, finding that users with lower knowledge levels performed better when assisted by intelligent agents. Kim [29] investigated the impact of different capabilities of learning assistants on users with varying knowledge levels, revealing that learners exhibit higher motivation and performance when collaborating with learning assistants of similar knowledge levels. Besides users' cognitive abilities and knowledge levels, their interaction experiences with intelligent agents and experiences using multimedia may also influence the overall performance of the human-machine team [30, 31].

In terms of task design, the presentation of information by intelligent agents during interactions with learners and the effort to minimize learners' cognitive load are closely related to the anthropomorphic features of intelligent agents and the types and styles of information they convey. According to cognitive load theory, the sources of load include intrinsic load, extraneous load, and germane load [32]. Studies have explored how intelligent agents express task-related and non-task-related information during communication, revealing that task-related information enhances learning effectiveness, while non-task-related information impairs perception and interaction, leading to attention diversion [33].

Based on the literature review above, this study proposes that, compared to an expert-type IA offering only knowledge support or a mentor-type IA (combined-persona IA) providing both knowledge and emotional support, users are likely to give higher evaluations to an IA group (split-persona IAs) which consists of an expert-type IA offering knowledge support and a peer-type IA providing emotional support. Additionally, given that an increased number of interactive entities can lead to attention dispersion, diminishing work efficiency, it is anticipated that in terms of task performance and cognitive load, the mentor-type IA that provides both knowledge and emotional support will outperform the IA group where these two forms of support are provided separately. In terms of user knowledge levels, this study posits that users with high knowledge levels may prefer the expert-type IA providing only knowledge support, while users with low knowledge levels may prefer the IA providing emotional support. Furthermore, among users with low knowledge levels, there may be a preference for the IA group. Specifically, this study proposes the following hypotheses:

H1: Users collaborating with the combined-persona IA that provides both knowledge and emotional support will demonstrate better task performance and lower cognitive load compared to those collaborating with the split-persona IAs that provides knowledge and emotional support separately.

H2: The split-persona IAs that provides knowledge and emotional support separately will receive higher subjective evaluation compared to the combined-persona IA that provides both knowledge and emotional support.

H3: Users with high task-related knowledge level will give higher subjective evaluation to the expert-type IA that provides knowledge support only, while users with low task-related knowledge levels will give higher subjective evaluation to the IAs that provide emotional support, particularly the split-persona IAs that provides knowledge and emotional support separately.

3   Method

3.1 Experiment Design

This study conducted a 2 (task-related knowledge level: high or low) * 3 (IA role: expert-type IA, mentor-type IA, or IA group) mixed design experiment. The participants' task-related knowledge levels serve as between-group variables, they are pre-screened based on whether they have studied or prepared for the task-related test. The IA role serves as a within-group variable, with the expert-type IA providing only knowledge support during interactions and not offering emotional support such as encouragement and reassurance. The mentor-type IA (combined-persona IA) provides both knowledge and emotional support during interactions. The IA group (split-persona IA) is designed based on the split-persona effect, comprising an expert-type IA and a peer-type IA. The former provides only knowledge support, while the latter provides only emotional support. All participants interacted with the three types of IA roles and completed the experimental tasks in a randomized sequence.

3.2 Participants and Task

A total of 40 subjects were recruited in the experiment, 19 females and 21 males. 9 females and 11 males were in the low task-related knowledge level group; 10 females and 10 males were in the high task-related knowledge level group. All participants have prior experience using IAs. Other participant attributes such as age and professional background, are balanced across all groups.

In each collaboration task with each IA role, participants were required to complete 8 administrative ability test questions under the assistance of the corresponding IA role. This set included 4 language comprehension questions and 4 graphic reasoning questions, all sourced from real administrative ability test questions from various provinces on the Huatu Education official website. To maintain consistency in the difficulty level of the three sets of tasks, the overall correctness rates of each question in the sets were balanced.

3.3 Procedure

Upon the arrival of the participants, they would be briefed on the experiment's content and procedures, sign an informed consent form, and then proceed to the formal experiment. Participants would be randomly assigned an IA role. Before the collaborative task, participants would listen to a segment of the current IA role's voice for testing purposes. Following the collaborative task, participants would fill out a questionnaire, assessing their subjective experiences during the answering process, and submit their answers to the 8 questions. Subsequently, participants would take a brief break and then proceed sequentially with the collaboration with the second and third IA roles following the same process. Once the collaboration task with all three IA roles was completed, participants would fill out a post-experiment questionnaire. Upon completion of the questionnaire, the experiment would conclude.

In the collaborative task, each question has a response time of 1 min. After the question appears, participants have a reading time of 30 s, during which expert-type or mentor-type IA will speak after the reading time is over. For the IA group, 5 s after the question appears, the peer-type IA will speak to provide encouragement. After 30 s, the expert-type IA will provide advice, followed by continued encouragement from the peer-type IA. Five seconds before the end of the 1-min answering time, the screen will prompt participants to record their answers. Participants cannot switch between questions on their own, and each question will be displayed and switched according to the designated time.

The entire experiment has a duration of approximately 45 min. Participants will receive an experimental reward of 40–50 CNY based on performance.

3.4 Measures

The experiment collected objective and subjective measures of multiple dependent variables to assess task completion quality and interaction experience. Objective variables included task performance measured by question accuracy rates, while subjective variables encompassed cognitive load, emotions, perceived usefulness, satisfaction, and trust.

Cognitive load was measured using the NASA-TLX [34], which rates six dimensions (mental demand, physical demand, temporal demand, own performance, effort, and frustration) ranging from 1–20, and involves pairwise comparisons to determine weights. The emotion scale utilized the SAM scale [35] to measure emotional valence and arousal, with scores ranging from 1–9. Perceived usefulness covered four related questions [36] ranging from 1–7. Satisfaction was assessed through four questions measuring satisfaction [37], ranging from 1–7. Trust was obtained by having participants rate their trust in the IA role they collaborated with on a scale of 1–10.

3.5 Apparatus and Manipulation

The experiment was conducted remotely through an online network. Experimenters initiated an online meeting room in advance, and participants joined the meeting to engage in voice communication with the experimenters. Videos displaying various IA roles and questions were pre-recorded according to the task sequence and rhythm. Experimenters shared their screen and computer audio during the experiment, allowing participants to understand the experiment progress, access question information, and differentiate and interact with different IA roles through the screen.

To avoid the impact of appearance and voice, all IA roles were represented by identical icons with different colors: black for the expert-type IA, blue for the mentor-type IA, and pink for the peer-type IA. The IA group consisted of two icons representing the expert-type IA and peer-type IA. IA icons were consistently displayed on one side of the screen during collaborative tasks. When an IA role was not speaking, the corresponding icon blinked continuously to indicate that the IA was active. When an IA role spoke, a voice waveform icon appeared below the respective icon. Regarding audio, the experiment used the online website https://ttsmaker.com/zh-cn for text-to-speech conversion. Female voices were employed for all roles, but different voice numbers were selected from the voice library: voice number 1051 for the expert-type IA, voice number 1003 for the mentor-type IA, and voice number 204 for the peer-type IA.

Participants were informed throughout the experiment that they would interact with three different IA roles. The participants were explicitly told that different colors represented different roles. However, the specific correspondence between colors and roles, as well as the specific identities and order of the roles, was not disclosed to the participants. The experimental interface faced by the participants is shown in the Fig. 1 and Fig. 2.

2. (Multiple Choice Question) In terms of calligraphy, there is a distinction between Han stone inscriptions and Han bamboo slips. Han stone inscriptions are carved after calligraphic practice, then ink-imprinted, while Han bamboo slips are directly written on with a brush. This leads to differences in writing attitude: stone inscriptions are formal, with strict adherence to language, content, font, and engraving process, while bamboo slips reflect a more relaxed state without the pressure to write perfectly. The saying "calligraphy has no intention of being good" applies, contrasting the meticulousness of stone inscriptions with the spontaneity of bamboo slips, offering different aesthetic pleasures. The inspiration from Han bamboo slip calligraphy today lies in its natural and spontaneous attitude. Understanding these differences is crucial when studying ancient calligraphy to grasp their respective characteristics. This passage aims to explain:

A. The direct influence of writing attitude on calligraphy style
B. Han stone inscriptions and Han bamboo slips as representatives of different writing styles
C. How to correctly understand the calligraphic value of Han stone inscriptions and Han bamboo slips
D. Calligraphy works as a synthesis of writing tools and behavior

Fig. 1. Language comprehension task with support from Blue IA (given in native language)

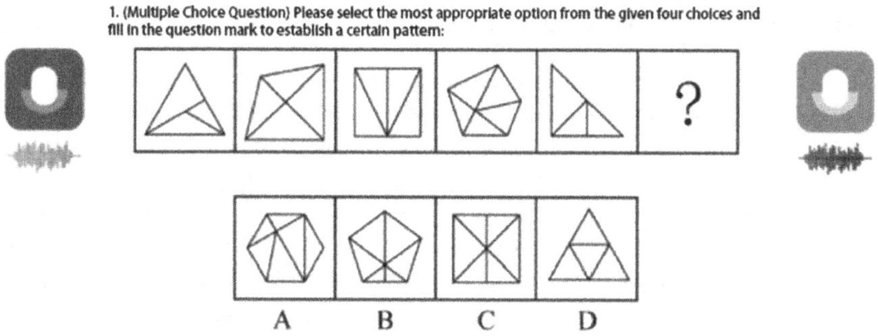

1. (Multiple Choice Question) Please select the most appropriate option from the given four choices and fill in the question mark to establish a certain pattern:

Fig. 2. The graphic reasoning task with support from Black and Red IAs

4 Results

For the dependent variables measured in the experiment, the normality and homogeneity of variance of the dependent variables were first examined using the Shapiro-Wilk test and Levene's test, respectively. Variables that passed the tests were analyzed using analysis of variance (ANOVA), while other variables were subjected to analysis using the non-parametric Scheirer-Ray-Hare test. Data analysis was conducted using SPSS and R software. Descriptive statistics for each dependent variable are presented in Table 1.

Table 1. Descriptive statistics for each dependent variable ($* = p < 0.05$; $** = p < 0.01$)

		knowledge level		Sig.	IA role			Sig.
		low	high		expert	mentor	group	
accuracy rates %	mean	59.8	71.9	**	66.3	72.8	58.4	**
	sd	18.0	18.5		19.5	17.0	18.7	
cognitive load	mean	13.13	11.73	*	12.42	13.34	11.53	*
	sd	2.73	3.48		3.28	2.91	3.19	
emotion valence	mean	5.65	5.58		5.58	5.22	6.05	
	sd	1.59	1.72		1.72	1.75	1.40	
Emotion arousal	mean	5.77	6.17		5.85	6.10	5.95	
	sd	1.63	1.64		1.64	1.45	1.84	
perceived usefulness	mean	5.80	5.73		5.95	5.43	5.92	*
	sd	0.94	1.05		0.88	1.08	0.94	
satisfaction	mean	5.52	5.28		5.59	5.09	5.52	*
	sd	0.91	1.07		1.02	0.97	0.95	
Trust	mean	8.03	7.55		8.05	7.23	8.10	*
	sd	1.52	2.38		1.85	2.06	2.01	

4.1 Task Performance and Cognitive Load

The Scheirer-Ray-Hare nonparametric test was used to test the effect of the IA roles and the levels of task-related knowledge on question accuracy rates of the collaborative task.

The results showed a significant main effect of task-related knowledge level on question accuracy rates ($p < 0.05$). Participants with high level of task-related knowledge had a significantly higher accuracy rates (mean = 71.9%, sd = 18.5%) than those with low level of task-related knowledge (mean = 59.2%, sd = 18.0%). Also, there was a significant main effect of IA roles on accuracy rates ($p < 0.05$). Using pairwise comparisons, participants who collaborated with the mentor-type IA had a significantly higher accuracy rates (mean = 72.8%, sd = 17.0%) than those who worked with the IA group consist of an exprt-type IA and a peer-type IA (mean = 58.4%, sd = 18.7%) ($p < 0.05$). Accuracy rates for collaborating with the expert-type IA (mean = 66.3%, sd = 19.5%) did not present a significant difference from the other two levels.

As the cognitive load, the result of ANOVA showed a significant main effect of IA roles on cognitive load ($p < 0.05$). Using pairwise comparisons, participants who collaborated with the mentor-type IA (mean = 13.34, sd = 2.91) had significantly higher cognitive load than those who collaborated with the IA group (mean = 11.53, sd = 3.19) ($p < 0.05$). The results also showed a significant main effect of task-related knowledge level on cognitive load ($p < 0.05$). The cognitive load of participants with high level of task-related knowledge (mean = 11.73, sd = 3.48) was significantly lower than that of participants with low level of task-related knowledge (mean = 13.13, sd = 2.73).

H1 concerns the impact of combined-persona IA and split-persona IAs on task performance and cognitive load. The experimental results indicate that H1 is supported.

4.2 Subjective Evaluation

The Scheirer-Ray-Hare test was used to test the effect of roles IA roles and the levels of task-related knowledge on the results of the subjective evaluation.

In terms of emotions, both emotion valence and arousal showed no significant differences based on task-related knowledge levels and IA roles. Overall, participants exhibited positive emotions towards all IA roles. Participants with low level of task-relevant knowledge showed the highest emotion valence when collaborating with the IA group, while those with high level of task-related knowledge exhibited the highest emotion valence when collaborating with the expert-type IA.

In terms of perceived usefulness, the results indicate a significant main effect of IA roles on participants' perceived usefulness ($p < 0.05$). Pairwise comparisons revealed a marginally significant difference in perceived usefulness between mentor-type IA (mean = 5.43, sd = 1.08) and expert-type IA (mean = 5.95, sd = 0.88) ($p < 0.1$). Similarly, a marginally significant difference was observed in perceived usefulness between mentor-type IA and the IA group (mean = 5.92, sd = 1.84) ($p < 0.1$). This suggests that participants perceived the usefulness of mentor-type IA to be lower compared to the other two IA roles. The results did not reveal any significant impact of levels of task-related knowledge on perceived usefulness.

In terms of satisfaction, the results reveal a significant main effect of IA roles on satisfaction ($p < 0.05$). Pairwise comparisons indicate a marginally significant difference in satisfaction between participants collaborating with mentor-type IA (mean = 5.09, sd = 0.97) and those collaborating with expert-type IA (mean = 5.59, sd = 1.02) (p < 0.1). This suggests that satisfaction was slightly lower when collaborating with mentor-type IA compared to expert-type IA. There were no significant differences in satisfaction between expert-type IA and the IA group.

In terms of trust, the results indicate a significant main effect of IA roles on participants' trust (p < 0.05). Pairwise comparisons reveal that participants' trust in collaboration with mentor-type IA (mean = 7.23, sd = 2.06) is significantly lower than their trust with the IA group (mean = 8.10, sd = 2.01) (p < 0.05). No significant effects of participants' task-related knowledge levels on trust were observed.

H2 concerns the impact of combined-persona IA and split-persona IAs on various subjective evaluations. The experimental results indicate that H2 is supported.

H3 concerns the impact of task-related knowledge levels on preferences of IA roles. This hypothesis is partially supported as it shows a trend in the aspect of emotional valence.

4.3 Discussion

The research results indicate that the combined-persona IA leads to higher task performance, whereas the split-persona IAs result in higher subjective evaluations. Built upon the foundation of an expert-type AI that provides only knowledge support, the mentor-type IA (combined-persona IA) is capable of simultaneously offering emotional support, providing dual support in knowledge and emotion during collaboration. On the other hand, the IA group (split-persona IAs) involves the addition of another peer-type IA responsible solely for emotional support. The results show that, compared to split-persona IAs, the combined-persona IA results in significantly higher cognitive load, lower perceived usefulness, satisfaction, and trust, but brings about significantly higher task performance. This suggests that there is a trade-off between objective performance and subjective evaluation in the choice of whether to split functionalities, providing guidance and insights for the future design of IAs. For example, when various tasks assigned to different intelligent agents lead to efficiency issues, it may be beneficial to consider adjusting from a split-persona mode to a combined-persona mode. This adjustment could reduce task switching and interruptions during multitasking, improving user cognition and experience. However, in cases where integrating roles is challenging, another approach could involve establishing connections between different intelligent agents. This involves sharing information and coordinating actions among the agents to decrease the burden of task switching, while simultaneously enhancing the entertainment value of role interplay.

In terms of differences in subjective evaluations, insights can be gleaned from participants' feedback in the post-test questionnaire. Participants expressed the view that the mentor-type IA (combined-persona IA) was perceived as more verbose compared to the expert-type IA, with some participants suggesting that the encouraging statements from the mentor-type IA actually reduced the effectiveness by decreasing the amount of useful information. On the other hand, the prompts provided by the expert-type IA were considered straightforward and efficient, saving time in answering questions. However, for the peer-type IA, participants rarely found the encouraging statements bothersome;

instead, some considered its presence very thoughtful. Some studies argue that IA's emotional support stems from the social cues provided by the IA [38], given the experimental task's level of difficulty in this study, participants were more inclined toward pragmatic motivations for using IA, downplaying social purposes. Consequently, the emotional support provided by the mentor-type IA led to participant dissatisfaction, as it did not fulfill the role of completing knowledge support quickly and efficiently, as observed with the expert-type IA. In contrast, the IA group operated differently. Under this split-persona mode, participants had already formed certain expectations about the roles of the two IAs. Therefore, the encouragement from the peer-type IA did not contradict participants' expectations. Additionally, participants' interaction with the IA during collaboration involved interruptions and shifts in attention. The split-persona mode facilitated a clear distinction between knowledge and emotional support from different IAs. This allowed participants to choose and shift their attention to interact with different IAs, thereby avoiding the process of filtering effective information during interactions with the mentor-type IA (combined-persona IA).

The reasons behind the differences in task performance may be attributed to the fact that different IAs occupied varying amounts of time and attention. In collaborations with a single IA, the experiment allocated 30 s for participants to read the question before the AI intervention. However, in collaborations with the IA group, the peer-type IA would initiate encouragement during question-reading stage, thus occupying a portion of the reading time. During the subsequent speaking phase after reading the question, the expert-type IA had the most concise and shortest speaking time, followed by the mentor-type IA, and the IA group had the longest speaking time. Since the total answering time for each question was set at 1 min, the longer speaking time of the IA group led to shorter reading and thinking time, which could be a contributing factor to the differences in task performance. Another potential reason is that even though participants had a clear role assignment in the split-persona mode, communicating with two IAs still resulted in more attention shifts, leading to longer recovery times before returning to the original task. Hence, despite participants' higher evaluations of the IA group, it objectively caused more task interruptions and attention interference.

In the experiment, participants with different knowledge levels also exhibited variations in their evaluations of different IA roles. In the assessment of emotional valence, participants with lower knowledge levels reported the highest emotional valence when collaborating with the IA group, while participants with higher knowledge levels experienced the highest emotional valence when collaborating with expert-type IA. This result aligns with the different motivations and needs of participants with varying knowledge levels when collaborating with different IA roles. For participants with higher knowledge levels, they are more familiar with the tasks and have a clearer understanding of the thought process and their own capabilities, making them less reliant on IAs to provide additional emotional support. However, for participants with lower knowledge levels, the tasks are more unfamiliar, leading to a stronger sense of frustration and anxiety. In such situations, an IA that can provide emotional support tends to enhance their motivation and cooperation.

5   Conclusion

This research investigated the effectiveness of various Intelligent Agent (IA) roles in providing knowledge and emotional support in human-machine collaboration. The study compared an expert-type IA (knowledge support only), a mentor-type IA (combined-persona IA providing both knowledge and emotional support), and a split-persona IA group. Results revealed a distinct trade-off between objective task performance and subjective user evaluations across different IA roles.

The combined-persona IA enhanced task performance, signifying its efficacy in aiding users in achieving higher accuracy in tasks. However, this approach resulted in a higher cognitive load and lower subjective evaluations in terms of perceived usefulness, satisfaction, and trust. This indicates that while the combined-persona IA is effective in task facilitation, it may impose a greater cognitive burden on users, leading to reduced overall user satisfaction. In contrast, the split-persona IAs, although resulting in a reduction in task performance, received more favorable subjective evaluations. This suggests a user preference for distinct roles when it comes to knowledge and emotional support, possibly due to clearer role delineation and reduced cognitive effort in distinguishing between types of support.

Furthermore, this study found that users' knowledge levels influenced their preferences for IA roles. Participants with lower task-related knowledge favored emotional support, which aligns with their need for reassurance in unfamiliar task scenarios. This highlights the importance of tailoring IA roles based on user characteristics and task requirements.

In conclusion, this study underscores the complexity of designing IAs for human-machine collaboration. It suggests that while combined-persona IAs can enhance task efficiency, they may not always align with user preferences for a less cognitively demanding experience. Therefore, designers of IAs should consider the trade-offs between task performance and user experience, possibly adopting a more flexible approach that allows customization of IA roles based on the specific needs and knowledge levels of users.

Disclosure of Interests.   The authors have no competing interests to declare that are relevant to the content of this article.

References

1. Malin, J.T., et al.: Making intelligent systems team players: case studies and design issues. In: Human-Computer Interaction Design, vol. 1 (1991)
2. Demir, M., McNeese, N.J., Cooke, N.J.: Team communication behaviors of the human-automation teaming. In: 2016 IEEE International Multi-disciplinary Conference on Cognitive Methods in Situation Awareness and Decision Support (CogSIMA). IEEE (2016)
3. Mercado, J.E., et al.: Intelligent agent transparency in human–agent teaming for Multi-UxV management. Hum. Factors **58**(3), 401–415 (2016)
4. Myers, C., et al.: Autonomous intelligent agents for team training. IEEE Intell. Syst. **34**(2), 3–14 (2018)
5. Hoy, M.B., et al.: An introduction to voice assistants. Med. Ref. Serv. Q. **37**(1), 81–88 (2018)
6. Quarteroni, S.: Natural language processing for industry: ELCA's experience. Informatik-Spektrum **41**(2), 105–112 (2018)

7. Grimm, D.A., et al.: Team situation awareness in human-autonomy teaming: a systems level approach. In: Proceedings of the Human Factors and Ergonomics Society Annual Meeting. SAGE Publications Sage, Los Angeles (2018)
8. Lyons, J.B., et al.: Viewing machines as teammates: a qualitative study. In: 2018 AAAI Spring Symposium Series (2018)
9. Islas-Cota, E., et al.: A systematic review of intelligent assistants. Futur. Gener. Comput. Syst. **128**, 45–62 (2022)
10. Kim, Y., Baylor, A.L.: Based design of pedagogical agent roles: a review, progress, and recommendations. Int. J. Artif. Intell. Educ. **26**, 160–169 (2016)
11. Edwards, C., et al.: I, teacher: using artificial intelligence (AI) and social robots in communication and instruction. Commun. Educ. **67**(4), 473–480 (2018)
12. Pane, J.F., et al.: Continued Progress: Promising Evidence on Personalized Learning. Rand Corporation (2015)
13. Heidig, S., Clarebout, G.: Do pedagogical agents make a difference to student motivation and learning? Educ. Res. Rev. **6**(1), 27–54 (2011)
14. Schroeder, N.L., Adesope, O.O., Gilbert, R.B.: How effective are pedagogical agents for learning? a meta-analytic review. J. Educ. Comput. Res. **49**(1), 1–39 (2013)
15. Schroeder, N.L., Romine, W.L., Craig, S.D.: Measuring pedagogical agent persona and the influence of agent persona on learning. Comput. Educ. **109**, 176–186 (2017)
16. Akcora, D.E., et al.: Conversational support for education. In: Artificial Intelligence in Education: 19th International Conference, AIED 2018, London, UK, 27–30 June 2018, Proceedings, Part II 19. Springer, Heidelberg (2018)
17. Chen, L., Chen, P., Lin, Z.: Artificial intelligence in education: a review. IEEE Access **8**, 75264–75278 (2020)
18. Hiremath, G., et al.: Chatbot for education system. Int. J. Adv. Res. Ideas Innov. Technol. **4**(3), 37–43 (2018)
19. Pham, X.L., et al.: Chatbot as an intelligent personal assistant for mobile language learning. In: Proceedings of the 2018 2nd International Conference on Education and E-Learning (2018)
20. Tegos, S., et al.: Conversational agents for academically productive talk: a comparison of directed and undirected agent interventions. Int. J. Comput.-Support. Collab. Learn. **11**, 417–440 (2016)
21. Wynne, K.T., Lyons, J.B.: An integrative model of autonomous agent teammate-likeness. Theor. Issues Ergon. Sci. **19**(3), 353–374 (2018)
22. Baylor, A., Kim, Y.: Validating pedagogical agent roles: expert, motivator, and mentor. In: EdMedia+ Innovate Learning. Association for the Advancement of Computing in Education (AACE) (2003)
23. Baylor, A.L., Kim, Y.: Simulating instructional roles through pedagogical agents. Int. J. Artif. Intell. Educ. **15**(2), 95–115 (2005)
24. Baylor, A.L., Ebbers, S.: Evidence that multiple agents facilitate greater learning. In: Artificial Intelligence in Education: Shaping the Future of Learning Through Intelligent Technologies, pp. 377–379 (2003)
25. Baylor, A.L.: The design of motivational agents and avatars. Educ. Tech. Res. Dev. **59**, 291–300 (2011)
26. Anderson, M., Gavan, C.: Engaging undergraduate programming students: experiences using lego mindstorms NXT. In: Proceedings of the 13th Annual Conference on Information Technology Education (2012)
27. O'Neill, T., et al.: Human–autonomy teaming: A review and analysis of the empirical literature. Hum. Factors **64**(5), 904–938 (2022)
28. Choi, S., Clark, R.E.: Cognitive and affective benefits of an animated pedagogical agent for learning English as a second language. J. Educ. Comput. Res. **34**(4), 441–466 (2006)

29. Kim, Y.: Desirable characteristics of learning companions. Int. J. Artif. Intell. Educ. **17**(4), 371–388 (2007)
30. Cummings, M.L., Clare, A., Hart, C.: The role of human-automation consensus in multiple unmanned vehicle scheduling. Hum. Factors **52**(1), 17–27 (2010)
31. Hoff, K.A., Bashir, M.: Trust in automation: Integrating empirical evidence on factors that influence trust. Hum. Factors **57**(3), 407–434 (2015)
32. Paas, F., Renkl, A., Sweller, J.: Cognitive load theory and instructional design: recent developments. Educ. Psychol. **38**(1), 1–4 (2003)
33. Veletsianos, G.: How do learners respond to pedagogical agents that deliver social-oriented non-task messages? impact on student learning, perceptions, and experiences. Comput. Hum. Behav. **28**(1), 275–283 (2012)
34. Hart, S.G., Staveland, L.E.: Development of NASA-TLX (Task Load Index): results of empirical and theoretical research. In: Advances in Psychology, pp. 139–183. Elsevier (1988)
35. Pyatt, G.: A SAM approach to modeling. J. Policy Model. **10**(3), 327–352 (1988)
36. Bhattacherjee, A., Perols, J., Sanford, C.: Information technology continuance: a theoretic extension and empirical test. J. Comput. Inf. Syst. **49**(1), 17–26 (2008)
37. Davis, F.D.: Perceived usefulness, perceived ease of use, and user acceptance of information technology. MIS Q. 319–340 (1989)
38. Schneider, S., et al.: The cognitive-affective-social theory of learning in digital environments (CASTLE). Educ. Psychol. Rev. **34**(1), 1–38 (2022)

Cultural Perception, Attention and Information Processing

A Study of Differences in Audience Affective Perceptions of Non-heritage Documentaries

Lijuan Guo[1] , Yingying Hang[1], Wen Zhang[2] , Tiantian Cao[3] , and Jun Wu[4(✉)]

[1] School of Art and Media, Taishan College of Science and Technology, Taian 271000,
Shandong, China
[2] School of Art and Design, Lijiang College of Culture and Tourism, Lijiang 674100,
Yunnan, China
[3] School of Film and Media, Anhui Wenda Information Engineering College, Hefei 230000,
Anhui, China
[4] School of Fine Arts and Design, Faculty of Arts, Shenzhen University, Shenzhen 518061,
Guangdong, China
junwu2006@hotmail.com

Abstract. In the milieu of globalization, a kaleidoscope of cultures is intricately weaving together, catalyzing a heightened consciousness towards the pivotal role of safeguarding and bequeathing the ethereal vestiges of intangible cultural heritage. This quintessential facet of China's venerable traditional ethos serves as a conduit for engendering a profound resonance of cultural empathy among the populace. Our scholarly inquiry delves into the realm of documentary cinematography, spotlighting the intangible cultural legacies emblematic of four distinct provinces: Anhui, Shandong, Shanxi, and Yunnan. This exploration seeks to discern the variegated emotional and cognitive perceptions harbored by audiences of diverse provenances in relation to these cinematic chronicles of intangible cultural heritage. The empirical evidence unearthed reveals several nuanced insights: (1) The emotional and cognitive engagement with these documentaries manifests a remarkable uniformity across gender lines, evidencing no substantial disparities; (2) A predilection for higher appraisal of these documentaries was notably more pronounced among the younger demographic as opposed to those aged 50 and beyond; (3) Viewers possessing an academic or professional background in film, television, and the arts accorded significantly loftier evaluations than their counterparts from the realms of design and the liberal arts; (4) Evaluations tendered by individuals with educational attainments spanning from high school to doctoral studies markedly outstripped those emanating from junior college affiliates; (5) Notably, audiences hailing from Yunnan Province bestowed upon the quartet of documentaries concerning intangible cultural heritage, ratings that significantly eclipsed those proffered by viewers from other provinces.

Keywords: Intangible Cultural Heritage · Documentary Film · Emotional Cognition · Cognitive Differences

P.-L. P. Rau (Ed.): HCII 2024, LNCS 14700, pp. 209–226, 2024.
https://doi.org/10.1007/978-3-031-60901-5_15

1 Introduction

In the era of globalization and the advent of technological innovation, the safeguarding and propagation of intangible cultural heritage have emerged as a global discourse. Intangible heritage represents not merely the cultural mnemonic and historical emblem of a nation but also constitutes the shared patrimony of humanity at large. Of late, the utilization of documentary film as a medium for the recording and dissemination of intangible cultural heritage has ascended to prominence as a pivotal strategy for its preservation. Documentaries dedicated to intangible heritage transcend the mere conveyance of information, imbuing deep cultural resonance and emotional significance. Through the lens of documentary filmmaking, the essence, narrative, and cultural underpinnings of Non-Heritage Foundations (NHF) are afforded broader exposition and diffusion. Nonetheless, divergences in cultural backgrounds, value systems, aesthetic inclinations, and other subjective factors engender distinct emotional responses to the same documentary among audiences. Such cognitive disparities not only shape the viewing experience but also influence the comprehension and appreciation of intangible heritage. This scholarly endeavor selected four quintessential documentaries on intangible heritage from disparate provinces as focal points of analysis: *Rice Paper* from Anhui Province, *Taishan Shadow* from Shandong Province, *Square Floating Fragrance* from Shanxi Province, and *Yi Hai Cai Cavity* from Yunnan Province. Employing independent samples T-test and ANOVA analysis, the study aims to elucidate the variance in emotional cognition among audiences of diverse backgrounds towards these documentaries, with objectives outlined as follows:

- To investigate the differential affective perceptions of intangible heritage documentaries among audiences from varied backgrounds;
- To explore the discrepancies in affective responses towards intangible heritage documentaries across different provinces.

2 Literature Review

2.1 Documentary on Intangible Cultural Heritage

Intangible cultural heritage (ICH) is a unique cultural resource of a country or even a region, which includes oral traditions, performing arts, social practices, handicrafts and technologies, etc. It not only reflects the history and culture, but also contains profound wisdom of life, which is of great significance for maintaining cultural diversity and promoting the construction of human community. Intangible Cultural Heritage Protection", the General Office of the State Council proposed to encourage news media to set up special topics and columns on intangible cultural heritage, and to support the strengthening of the creation of documentaries on related subjects to increase the dissemination and popularization of intangible cultural heritage [1]. Cultural self-confidence is the full affirmation of a country or a nation of its own cultural value and the firm belief in its own cultural vitality [2]. Intangible cultural heritage is a high degree of condensation of the excellent traditional culture of the Chinese nation, a condensation of the cultural memory and identity of the people of a region or nation, and its inheritance is also a historical continuation of the cohesion and centripetal force of the people who are in the same cultural community [3]. Along with the deepening influence of globalization in the field of film and media, the function of documentaries in telling objective events, observing social changes, portraying the spirit of the times, and preserving collective memory is particularly prominent, and it has become an important part of the national cultural strategy and cultural soft power [4]. It is also an important window for the world to understand China's social history and observe the development of Chinese reality [5]. Non-heritage documentaries take recording and dissemination of non-heritage or related content as the theme, take non-heritage projects and inheritors as the subject of filming, and bring the audience audio-visual enjoyment and emotional resonance with exquisite and vivid video images and profound cultural values, which is an important carrier to enhance cultural confidence, highlight national culture and disseminate non-heritage skills in the new era [6].

2.2 Emotional Cognition

Art is the creation of symbolic forms of human emotion [7], and Plutchik [8] believes that emotion is a system of action, which has existential value for individuals and human beings, and will guide behavioral responses. Movies are essentially an emotional art form. Through compelling stories, sympathetic characters, and a cinematic world presented through audio-visual means, it attempts to stimulate emotion in the viewer [9, 10]. This so-called cinematic emotional experience is considered an important aspect of narrative comprehension [11] and engagement [12]. Indeed, the abstract meaning of a movie and the "message" it conveys are entirely shaped by emotional experience [13]. A movie is not only a way of seeing, but also a way of hearing, feeling, thinking and reacting. It presents not just a mental world (perception and cognition) but a holistic experience connected to emotions, feelings and the body [9]. The core of intangible cultural heritage video recording is to empathize with the audience, through the video writing of intangible cultural heritage masters with apprentices, skills inheritance, folklore forms, etc., to construct some kind of emotional bond with the general audience, bring some kind of emotional touch to the audience, and then form a kind of cultural identity [14]. Its role expression emphasizes the role of "people" in the construction of the documentary with the help of a specific role, leading the audience to observe, experience and think from the perspective of the specific role, so as to realize the empathy between the creator and the receiver. The emotional connection between people and characters is the link that triggers empathy, and viewers can form emotional communication through their understanding of each real character [15]. From the perspective of artistic acceptance, when audiences face documentaries, emotions induce image memory and emotional memory and form certain emotional experiences, and audiences are touched by the life emotions encompassed in the text through the art form of documentaries as an intermediary. Only when the audience enters the artistic acceptance of emotional communication, can the audience more deeply recognize, experience and think about the apparent form, inheritance changes, inner implication, traditional spirit of "non-heritage" [16], while generating a strong sense of identity with the creative content and realizing the creative value of the work [17].

2.3 Audience

Since the birth of movie, it has been inseparable from the era and the audience. From silent movie to sound movie, from wide screen to stereoscopic movie, the external manifestation is the change of time and technology, while the driving force behind is actually the audience and the market [18]. Documentary communication is always closely related to the audience's psychology, and movie planners usually set the content of the movie according to the audience's psychological needs in the process of making documentaries. Only by mastering the psychological laws and characteristics of the audience, can we find and satisfy the audience's psychological needs in order to improve the communication effect of the movie [19]. In the process of aesthetic consumption of intangible cultural heritage, the consumption of culture as a product is characterized more by providing the audience with aesthetic pleasure and emotional experience. Intangible heritage resources as a form of culture, in the process of its inheritance and dissemination to meet the audience's aesthetic consumption and emotional experience is an important part [14]. The relationship between documentaries and audiences is mutual influence and molding. Through continuous innovation and change, documentaries satisfy the diversified needs of the audience, and at the same time influence the audience's cultural cognition and aesthetic interests.

3 Research Objects and Methods

In this study, we employed a quantitative research methodology, selecting four emblematic documentaries on intangible cultural heritage from Anhui, Shandong, Shanxi, and Yunnan provinces as the focal points of our study. These documentaries, namely *Taishan Shadow*, *Rice Paper*, *Square Floating Fragrance*, and *Yi Hai Cai Cavity* (P1, P2, P3, and P4 respectively), serve as the research cases. The survey instrument was bifurcated into two sections: the initial segment encompassed demographic queries—gender, age, field of specialization, educational attainment, and province of residence; the subsequent segment consisted of evaluative queries, totaling eight in number. These inquiries aimed to gauge the enhancement of the respondents' comprehension of intangible cultural heritage, the bolstering of their cultural self-assurance, the ignition of interest or a sense of duty towards the preservation and transmission of intangible cultural heritage, the inclination to recommend these documentaries for viewing or discussion, the propensity to engage in related ICH activities or experiences, the willingness to support or participate in ICH conservation and dissemination initiatives, the curiosity to learn about ICH from other regions, and their preference for the documentary in question, as delineated in Table 1. The evaluation employed a five-point Likert scale, with options ranging from "Strongly Disagree" to "Strongly Agree," assigned scores from 1 to 5, respectively. This approach facilitated a structured and nuanced understanding of audience perceptions. The survey was integrated with the video content of the pertinent documentaries, thereby enabling respondents to directly engage with the intangible cultural heritage documentaries while providing their feedback, enhancing the relevance and immediacy of their responses.

Table 1. Questionnaire general assessment questions.

number	General assessment issues
A1	Your knowledge of intangible cultural heritage has increased
A2	Your cultural self-confidence has been enhanced
A3	Stimulated your interest in or sense of responsibility for the safeguarding and transmission of ICH
A4	Whether you have the desire to recommend others to watch or discuss these contents
A5	Whether you have the desire to participate in relevant ICH activities or experiences
A6	Whether you are more willing to support or participate in ICH safeguarding and transmission programs
A7	Your desire to learn about intangible cultural heritage in other regions
A8	Your preference for this movie

4   Results

4.1   Reliability and Validity Analysis

The reliability of the questionnaire was tested by exploring the internal consistency of the various constructs of the scale and the magnitude of the impairment of the Cronbach's alpha coefficient in each direction after the deletion of a single question as a reference standard for the selection of the questions and for assessing the strength of the reliability of the scale. The questionnaire analysis found that the Cronbach's alpha coefficient is 0.957, Sapp [20] pointed out that the Cronbach's alpha coefficient of 0.8–0.9 is acceptable, and more than 0.9 has good reliability, so it can be seen that the questionnaire in this study has good reliability. The corrected total correlation of the single questions of each construct and content of the characteristics ranges from 0.813–0.869, and the alpha coefficient after deletion ranges from 0.950–0.953, which shows that the internal consistency between the selected questions is high, and the selection of the questions is reasonable. Through the validity analysis, it can be seen that the KMO coefficient is 0.955, which has a high value, the Sig value is 0.000, which is highly significant, the eigenvalue is 6.130, which can explain 76.62% of the variance of the preset use, the factor loadings of each question are from 0.862–0.892, and the commonality is from 0.743–0.796. Sapp pointed out that the factor loading of 0.5 or more is good, and 0.7 or more is ideal. 0.7 or more is ideal, and commonality of 0.3 or more is good and 0.5 or more is ideal. The factor loadings and commonality of each question in this study are higher than the standard value of ideal state, which has good validity.

4.2   Analysis of the Differences Between Gender and Each of the Variables

Utilizing the audience's gender as the independent variable and the responses to the eight comprehensive evaluation questions as the dependent variables, an independent samples t-test was conducted to examine the variance in emotional responses between male and female audiences towards the documentaries of non-heritage from distinct regions. The documentaries in question, *Taishan Shadow, Rice Paper, Square Floating Fragrance,* and *Yi Hai Cai Cavity,* were scrutinized to assess gender-based differences in emotional cognition. The findings indicate a remarkable consistency in the ratings provided by audiences of different genders across all four documentaries, demonstrating an absence of significant disparity in emotional cognition. Consequently, both male and female viewers derived a comparably profound emotional experience from these non-heritage-related documentaries, underscoring the universal appeal and impact of these cultural narratives.

4.3 Analysis of Differences Between Age and Variables

Employing the age demographic of the audience as the independent variable and the responses to the eight overarching assessment queries as the dependent variables, this study delved into the variances in emotional perception among different age cohorts towards the four documentaries. The outcomes, as encapsulated in Table 2, reveal pronounced disparities in the affective responses of audiences across varying age brackets to the documentaries. There were significant distinctions noted in the responses to the eight general assessment questions, exhibiting a consistent pattern in the ratings, with each of the queries demonstrating substantial significance. The analysis indicated that the appraisal scores from audiences aged 19 and under, 20–29, 30–39, and 40–49 years were markedly higher than those from individuals aged 50 and above. This trend underscores a greater appreciation of the documentaries among younger viewers, in contrast to the more subdued responses observed within the older demographic segments. Such findings highlight a generational divide in the reception and valuation of these cultural narratives, with younger audiences showing a heightened engagement and valuation compared to their older counterparts.

Table 2. Cognitive differences among audiences of different age backgrounds.

Documentary	Variable	LEVEN test for equality of variances	Mean relative T test		
		F	Mean	St	Post-Hoc
P1 *Taishan Shadow*	A1	103.504***	4.19	1.071	1 > 5,2 > 5,3 > 5,4 > 5
	A2	89.350***	4.23	1.049	1 > 5,2 > 5,3 > 5,4 > 5
	A3	108.524***	4.19	1.070	1 > 5,2 > 5,3 > 5,4 > 5
	A4	79.628***	4.16	1.047	1 > 5,2 > 5,3 > 5,4 > 5
	A5	117.848***	4.22	1.049	1 > 5,2 > 5,3 > 5,4 > 5
	A6	90.306***	4.21	0.991	1 > 5,2 > 5,3 > 5,4 > 5
	A7	103.908***	4.15	1.062	1 > 5,2 > 5,3 > 5,4 > 5
	A8	106.744***	4.22	1.005	1 > 5,2 > 5,3 > 5,4 > 5

(continued)

Table 2. (*continued*)

Documentary	Variable	LEVEN test for equality of variances	Mean relative T test		
		F	Mean	St	Post-Hoc
P2 *Rice paper*	A1	91.531***	4.28	1.06	1 > 5,2 > 5,3 > 5,4 > 5
	A2	94.057***	4.26	1.021	1 > 5,2 > 5,3 > 5,4 > 5
	A3	104.965***	4.16	1.057	1 > 5,2 > 5,3 > 5,4 > 5
	A4	90.035***	4.18	1.027	1 > 5,2 > 5,3 > 5,4 > 5
	A5	113.622***	4.25	1.081	1 > 5,2 > 5,3 > 5,4 > 5
	A6	113.428***	4.19	1.082	1 > 5,2 > 5,3 > 5,4 > 5
	A7	92.732***	4.16	1.080	1 > 5,2 > 5,3 > 5,4 > 5
	A8	97.539***	4.23	0.985	1 > 5,2 > 5,3 > 5,4 > 5
P3 *Square Floating Fragrance*	A1	125.671***	4.30	1.045	1 > 5,2 > 5,3 > 5,4 > 5
	A2	94.582***	4.28	1.059	1 > 5,2 > 5,3 > 5,4 > 5
	A3	89.061***	4.25	1.042	1 > 5,2 > 5,3 > 5,4 > 5
	A4	77.875***	4.19	1.017	1 > 5,2 > 5,3 > 5,4 > 5
	A5	87.718***	4.26	1.024	1 > 5,2 > 5,3 > 5,4 > 5
	A6	94.700***	4.26	1.053	1 > 5,2 > 5,3 > 5,4 > 5
	A7	100.667***	4.20	1.081	1 > 5,2 > 5,3 > 5,4 > 5
	A8	73.765***	4.26	0.994	1 > 5,2 > 5,3 > 5,4 > 5
P4 *Yi Hai Cai Cavity*	A1	84.579***	4.16	1.065	1 > 5,2 > 5,3 > 5,4 > 5
	A2	112.332***	4.19	1.048	1 > 5,2 > 5,3 > 5,4 > 5
	A3	84.898***	4.21	1.027	1 > 5,2 > 5,3 > 5,4 > 5
	A4	82.502***	4.15	1.025	1 > 5,2 > 5,3 > 5,4 > 5
	A5	91.214***	4.22	1.067	1 > 5,2 > 5,3 > 5,4 > 5
	A6	95.213***	4.18	1.083	1 > 5,2 > 5,3 > 5,4 > 5
	A7	61.919***	4.15	1.026	1 > 5,2 > 5,3 > 5,4 > 5
	A8	87.762***	4.20	1.037	1 > 5,2 > 5,3 > 5,4 > 5

*p < .05.** p < .01. *** p < .001 1 = 19 and under; 2 = 19–29; 3 = 30–39; 4 = 40–49; 5 = 50 and over

4.4 Analysis of the Differences Between Specialties and Variables

Considering the professional background of the audience as the independent variable, and the responses to the eight comprehensive assessment questions as the dependent variables, this study sought to unearth the variances in emotional cognition among audiences with different academic specializations towards the four documentaries. The findings, presented in Table 3, elucidate distinct patterns in the appraisal of the documentary

Taishan Shadow. Notably, audiences with backgrounds in film and television disciplines awarded significantly higher ratings compared to those from liberal arts fields. Furthermore, ratings from individuals in art-related majors markedly surpassed those from participants with design specializations across most evaluative dimensions.

These outcomes highlight the impact of diverse academic backgrounds and aesthetic preferences on the emotional cognition of the audience. It demonstrates how the knowledge base and aesthetic inclinations inherent to specific fields of study can influence the reception and valuation of cultural narratives, underscoring the nuanced interplay between educational specialization and the appreciation of intangible cultural heritage documentaries.

Table 3. Differences in perceptions of audiences from different professional backgrounds.

Documentary	Variable	LEVEN test for equality of variances	Mean relative T test		
		F	Mean	St	Post-Hoc
P1 *Taishan Shadow*	A1	3.883**	4.19	1.071	
	A2	4.383***	4.23	1.049	1 > 4
	A3	3.471**	4.19	1.070	
	A4	3.327**	4.16	1.047	
	A5	2.803*	4.22	1.049	
	A6	2.979*	4.21	0.991	
	A7	5.017***	4.15	1.062	5 > 2, 5 > 3
	A8	3.899**	4.22	1.005	
P2 *Rice paper*	A1	4.178***	4.28	1.006	
	A2	4.379***	4.26	1.021	5 > 2,5 > 4
	A3	6.839***	4.16	1.057	5 > 2,5 > 3
	A4	3.168**	4.18	1.027	
	A5	3.692**	4.25	1.081	5 > 2
	A6	5.857***	4.19	1.082	1 > 4,5 > 2
	A7	5.765***	4.16	1.080	1 > 2,5 > 2
	A8	4.461***	4.23	0.985	5 > 2
P3 *Square Floating Fragrance*	A1	4.241***	4.30	1.045	1 > 2
	A2	5.224***	4.28	1.059	1 > 2,5 > 2
	A3	5.686***	4.25	1.042	1 > 2,5 > 2
	A4	3.953**	4.19	1.017	5 > 2
	A5	2.777*	4.26	1.024	

(continued)

Table 3. (*continued*)

Documentary	Variable	LEVEN test for equality of variances	Mean relative T test		
		F	Mean	St	Post-Hoc
	A6	5.917***	4.26	1.053	1 > 4,5 > 4
	A7	3.616**	4.20	1.081	
	A8	3.823**	4.26	0.994	5 > 2
P4 *Yi Hai Cai Cavity*	A1	5.089***	4.16	1.065	5 > 2,5 > 4
	A2	4.198***	4.19	1.048	5 > 2,5 > 4
	A3	5.041***	4.21	1.027	1 > 4,5 > 4
	A4	3.672**	4.15	1.025	5 > 2
	A5	4.410***	4.22	1.067	
	A6	3.610**	4.18	1.083	
	A7	3.287**	4.15	1.026	
	A8	3.406**	4.20	1.037	

* p < .05.** p < .01. *** p < .001 1 = Film and television related; 2 = Design related; 3 = Science and engineering related; 4 = Arts related; 5 = Art related; 6 = Other
P1A1: 5(4.43) > 1(4.37) > 6(4.15) > 2(3.95) > 3(3.85) > 4(3.81) P1A3: 5(4.39) > 1(4.37) > 6(4.22) > 2(4.05) > 3(3.88) > 4(3.72)
P1A4: 5(4.36) > 6(4.41) > 1(4.28) > 3(3.94) > 2(3.93) > 4(3.75) P1A5: 5(4.43) > 6(4.37) > 1(4.31) > 2(4.02) > 3(3.97) > 4(3.86)
P1A6: 5(4.43) > 1(4.42) > 6(4.41) > 2(3.85) > 3(3.82) > 4(3.69) P1A8: 6(4.52) > 5(4.44) > 1(4.36) > 3(3.97) > 4(3.94) > 2(3.88)
P2A 1: 5(4.51) > 6(4.44) > 1(4.43) > 4(4.00) > 2(3.97) > 3(3.94) P2A 4: 6(4.44) > 5(4.42) > 1(4.20) > 3(4.00) > 2(3.93) > 4(3.86)
P3A 5: 5(4.48) > 6(4.37) > 1(4.31) > 3(4.12) > 2(4.03) > 4(3.89) P3A 7: 1(4.39) > 5(4.41) > 6(4.33) > 4(4.03) > 2(3.85) = 3(3.85)
P4A 5: 6(4.59) > 1(4.41) > 5(4.38) > 4(4.06) > 2(3.85) > 3(3.82) P4A 6: 5(4.48) > 6(4.30) > 1(4.22) > 4(3.94) > 2(3.93) > 3(3.79)
P4A 7: 6(4.41) > 5(4.34) > 1(4.24) > 3(4.00) > 4(3.89) > 2(3.80) P4A 8: 5(4.42) > 6(4.37) > 1(4.30) > 3(3.97) > 2(3.95) > 4(3.81)

4.5 Analysis of Differences Between Education and Variables

By setting the educational background of the audience as the independent variable and utilizing the responses to the eight comprehensive rating questions as the dependent variables, this study aimed to investigate the variance in affective perceptions towards the non-heritage documentaries among audiences with differing levels of education. The findings, as delineated in Table 4, reveal that in the analysis of the four documentaries, the appraisal scores from audiences with educational attainments of high school or lower, bachelor's degree, and master's degree were significantly higher compared to those from individuals holding specialized degrees. This pattern suggests that the level of formal education plays a role in shaping the audience's emotional response and appreciation of non-heritage documentaries. It indicates that audiences with general education levels—ranging from high school to graduate studies—tend to have a more favorable affective perception of these documentaries than those with more specialized, perhaps more narrowly focused, academic training.

Table 4. Differences in Perceptions of Audiences with Different Educational Backgrounds.

Documentary	Variable	LEVEN test for equality of variances	Mean relative T test		
		F	Mean	St	Post-Hoc
P1 *Taishan Shadow*	A1	21.101***	4.19	1.071	1 > 2,3 > 2,4 > 2
	A2	21.004***	4.23	1.049	1 > 2,3 > 2,4 > 2,5 > 2
	A3	23.752***	4.19	1.070	1 > 2,3 > 2,4 > 2
	A4	22.899***	4.16	1.047	1 > 2,3 > 2,4 > 2,5 > 2
	A5	20.043***	4.22	1.049	1 > 2,3 > 2,4 > 2
	A6	16.188***	4.21	0.991	1 > 2,3 > 2,4 > 2
	A7	25.204***	4.15	1.062	1 > 2,3 > 2,4 > 2
	A8	17.413***	4.22	1.005	1 > 2,3 > 2,4 > 2
P2 *Rice paper*	A1	21.945***	4.28	1.006	1 > 2,3 > 2,4 > 2
	A2	18.640***	4.26	1.021	1 > 2,3 > 2,4 > 2
	A3	22.527***	4.16	1.057	1 > 2,3 > 2,4 > 2
	A4	21.463***	4.18	1.027	1 > 2,3 > 2,4 > 2,5 > 2
	A5	21.503***	4.25	1.081	1 > 2,3 > 2,4 > 2,5 > 2
	A6	23.693***	4.19	1.082	1 > 2,3 > 2,4 > 2
	A7	20.417***	4.16	1.080	1 > 2,3 > 2,4 > 2
	A8	17.124***	4.23	0.985	1 > 2,3 > 2,4 > 2
P3 *Square Floating Fragrance*	A1	24.408***	4.30	1.045	1 > 2,3 > 2,4 > 2
	A2	23.457***	4.28	1.059	1 > 2,3 > 2,4 > 2,5 > 2
	A3	21.327***	4.25	1.042	1 > 2,3 > 2,4 > 2,5 > 2
	A4	23.778***	4.19	1.017	1 > 2,3 > 2,4 > 2,5 > 2
	A5	20.110***	4.26	1.024	1 > 2,3 > 2,4 > 2,5 > 2
	A6	24.560***	4.26	1.053	1 > 2,3 > 2,4 > 2
	A7	19.959***	4.20	1.081	1 > 2,3 > 2,4 > 2
	A8	21.904***	4.26	0.994	1 > 2,3 > 2,4 > 2,5 > 2

(continued)

Table 4. (*continued*)

Documentary	Variable	LEVEN test for equality of variances	Mean relative T test		
		F	Mean	St	Post-Hoc
P4 *Yi Hai Cai Cavity*	A1	19.223***	4.16	1.065	1 > 2,3 > 2,4 > 2
	A2	29.642***	4.19	1.048	1 > 2,3 > 2,4 > 2,5 > 2
	A3	21.507***	4.21	1.027	1 > 2,3 > 2,4 > 2,5 > 2
	A4	19.616***	4.15	1.025	1 > 2,3 > 2,4 > 2,5 > 2
	A5	24.384***	4.22	1.067	1 > 2,3 > 2,4 > 2
	A6	17.970***	4.18	1.083	1 > 2,3 > 2,4 > 2
	A7	17.878***	4.15	1.026	1 > 2,3 > 2,4 > 2,5 > 2
	A8	18.410***	4.20	1.037	1 > 2,3 > 2,4 > 2

* $p < .05.$ ** $p < .01.$ *** $p < .001$ 1 = High school and below; 2 = Specialist; 3 = Bachelor's degree; 4 = Master's degree; 5 = Doctoral degree

4.6 Analysis of Differences Between Provinces and Variables

By considering the province of upbringing of the audience as the independent variable and employing the responses to the eight comprehensive rating questions as the dependent variables, this investigation sought to discern the variances in emotional perceptions amongst audiences from different provinces towards the four documentaries. The outcomes, as outlined in Table 5, demonstrated that across the board for the four documentaries, significant disparities were observed in all eight questions. A notable trend emerged, indicating that the ratings from audiences who grew up in Yunnan were consistently higher than those from Anhui. This finding highlights the influence of geographical and cultural background on the reception and appreciation of documentaries on intangible cultural heritage. It suggests that audiences from Yunnan, possibly due to cultural, environmental, or educational influences specific to their province, exhibit a more profound engagement and positive emotional response to the documentaries compared to their counterparts from Anhui. This differential response underscores the importance of regional cultural identity and its impact on the perception and valuation of cultural narratives.

Table 5. Differences in perceptions of audiences from different provincial backgrounds.

Documentary	Variable	LEVEN test for equality of variances	Mean relative T test		
		F	Mean	St	Post-Hoc
P1 *Taishan Shadow*	A1	6.125***	4.19	1.071	2 > 1,4 > 1,5 > 1
	A2	8.015***	4.23	1.049	2 > 1,4 > 1,5 > 1
	A3	7.562***	4.19	1.070	2 > 1,4 > 1
	A4	6.050***	4.16	1.047	2 > 1,4 > 1
	A5	4.370**	4.22	1.049	4 > 1
	A6	3.673**	4.21	0.991	2 > 1,4 > 1
	A7	5.115***	4.15	1.062	2 > 1,4 > 1
	A8	6.118***	4.22	1.005	4 > 1
P2 *Rice paper*	A1	3.836**	4.28	1.006	
	A2	5.047***	4.26	1.021	4 > 1
	A3	3.516**	4.16	1.057	4 > 1
	A4	4.457**	4.18	1.027	4 > 1
	A5	4.752***	4.25	1.081	4 > 1,2 > 1,
	A6	4.016**	4.19	1.082	4 > 1,4 > 3
	A7	3.077*	4.16	1.080	
	A8	4.348**	4.23	0.985	4 > 1
P3 *Square Floating Fragrance*	A1	6.762***	4.30	1.045	4 > 1,4 > 3
	A2	7.045***	4.28	1.059	4 > 1,2 > 1
	A3	5.477***	4.25	1.042	4 > 1,2 > 1,4 > 3
	A4	5.545***	4.19	1.017	4 > 1,2 > 1
	A5	5.032***	4.26	1.024	4 > 1,4 > 3
	A6	3.363*	4.26	1.053	4 > 1
	A7	6.274***	4.20	1.081	4 > 1,2 > 1
	A8	3.301*	4.26	0.994	4 > 1
P4 *Yi Hai Cai Cavity*	A1	4.504***	4.16	1.065	4 > 1
	A2	3.948**	4.19	1.048	4 > 1
	A3	4.755***	4.21	1.027	4 > 1,4 > 3
	A4	3.360*	4.15	1.025	
	A5	4.279**	4.22	1.067	4 > 1

(*continued*)

Table 5. (continued)

Documentary	Variable	LEVEN test for equality of variances	Mean relative T test		
		F	Mean	St	Post-Hoc
	A6	2.891*	4.18	1.083	4 > 1
	A7	3.143*	4.15	1.026	4 > 1
	A8	4.539***	4.20	1.037	4 > 1,4 > 3

* p < .05.** p < .01. *** p < .001 1 = Anhui; 2 = Shanxi; 3 = Shandong; 4 = Yunnan; 5 = Other provinces

P2A1:5(4.55) > 4(4.49) > 2(4.44) > 3(4.12) > 1(3.98)
P2A7: 2(4.40) > 4(4.34) > 5(4.27) > 3(3.99) > 1(3.90)
P4A4:4(4.40) > 2(4.43) > 5(4.09) > 3(3.98) > 1(3.97)

5 Discussion

1. Spectators of diverse genders demonstrate a notably uniform emotional response to documentaries on intangible cultural heritage (ICH), devoid of substantial variances. This uniformity may be attributed to the differences in their life journeys, cultural matrices, and ethical frameworks. The younger demographic often shows a preference for cutting-edge and contemporary narrative strategies, whereas the more mature audience gravitates towards a presentation imbued with traditional richness and historical profundity. Primarily, the essence of ICH possesses a universal allure. Ventures like the *Taishan Shadow* from Tai'an, Shandong, and the *Rice Paper* tradition of Anhui, captivate a broad spectrum of viewers, transcending gender boundaries with their deep cultural implications and enduring historical worth. The comprehensive scope and depth of these cultural manifestations resonate with the shared emotional and cognitive fabric of both male and female viewers, thereby underscoring the pervasive charm and impact of ICH documentaries in the articulation of cultural virtues. In addition, the process of documentary filmmaking frequently seeks objectivity and factual integrity, which could mitigate the effect of gender disparities on the audience's emotional interaction. This pursuit of objectivity entails that the creators and directors concentrate more on the exposition of the stories and intrinsic values within ICH, rather than focusing on gender-specific themes or narrative perspectives. Lastly, in the contemporary societal context, viewers of different genders are increasingly aligning in their cognition and embracement of cultural heritage. This convergence, fostered by enhanced educational levels and expanded cultural understandings, suggests that viewers irrespective of gender are likely to perceive and engage with ICH documentary content through a similar lens, achieving comparable emotional profundity.
2. Viewers of varying age brackets display pronounced disparities in their emotional engagement with documentaries on intangible cultural heritage (ICH), with the younger cohorts typically assigning higher ratings compared to those over 50 years of age. The quartet of documentaries in question delves into ICH narratives such as the

Taishan Shadow of Tai'an, Shandong, the *Rice Paper* of Anhui, the *Square Floating Fragrance* from Shanxi, and the *Yi Hai Cai Cavity* in Yunnan. Younger viewers, likely owing to their access to a wider array of information sources and broader cultural interactions, tend to be more open to documentaries featuring novel concepts and advanced techniques. Their heightened sensitivity to new technologies and contemporary narrative forms could lead to more favorable assessments of documentaries that reinterpret traditional culture through modernized approaches. Additionally, the younger demographic might exhibit more eclectic and liberal cultural and aesthetic tastes, gravitating towards works that integrate fresh perspectives and modern aesthetics—features increasingly prevalent in contemporary documentaries. In contrast, the older viewership might hold a greater appreciation for traditional methods of expression and historical fidelity, and could be less receptive to innovative narrative styles and elements. Furthermore, the connection of younger audiences with ICH might be primarily about rediscovering and exploring traditional cultures in new lights, positioning ICH as a vital medium for them to express cultural pride and delve into ancestral cultures. Conversely, older viewers might derive their interest more from a sense of familiarity and nostalgia. This divergence in cultural perception and emotional attachment may significantly influence their respective evaluations of the documentaries. Lastly, the variation in life experiences and value systems across age groups plays a crucial role. Younger individuals might prioritize the contemporary application and innovation of ICH over its historical and traditional essence. On the other hand, older audiences may emphasize the traditional preservation and historical conveyance of ICH more profoundly.

3. Viewers from distinct professional backgrounds exhibit notable variations in their emotional perception of documentaries on intangible cultural heritage (ICH), with those in the realms of film and art generally assigning higher ratings than their counterparts in design and the liberal arts. Individuals engaged in film-related professions, armed with an in-depth understanding of cinematic production techniques, are likely to possess a heightened recognition and appreciation of the documentaries' filmmaking prowess, editing caliber, visual effects, and narrative architecture, leading them to award more favorable evaluations. Conversely, audiences from liberal arts disciplines may place greater emphasis on the profundity of content and the cultural significance, potentially resulting in a sense of underwhelm in these areas. Furthermore, the elevated scores from art-centric viewers could be attributed to their affinity for artistic expression and creative portrayal. In the documentary *Rice Paper*, those with an art background markedly outscored viewers from design fields. In *Square Floating Fragrance*, the scoring pattern diverged, with film-affiliated evaluations surpassing those from design, and art-related scores exceeding both. In the documentary Yi Hai Cai Cavity, art-oriented viewers significantly outperformed those in design and liberal arts in terms of scoring. Audiences hailing from the art and film sectors, by virtue of their specialized training, may possess a deeper comprehension and a more profound appreciation for the artistic renditions, storytelling techniques, and the finer technical aspects present in the documentaries. Their expertise allows them to appraise the quality of these documentaries from a nuanced professional standpoint, likely culminating in higher scores. Audiences from the design field typically esteem innovation, practicality, and visual aestheticism. In contrast, those from the liberal arts sphere are

more inclined to concentrate on the cultural essence and societal resonance of the documentaries, which could explain their relatively lower scoring tendencies.

4. Viewers from varied educational echelons exhibit notable divergences in their emotional cognition towards documentaries on intangible cultural heritage (ICH), with those possessing associate degrees registering lower scores compared to other educational cohorts. Post-viewing of ICH documentaries, individuals with associate degrees demonstrate a diminished emotional cognition in aspects such as comprehending intangible culture, bolstered cultural confidence, interest or sense of duty in safeguarding and perpetuating intangible cultural heritage, propensity to recommend others to view or discuss these subjects, eagerness to engage in pertinent ICH cultural activities or experiences, readiness to support or partake in ICH conservation and inheritance initiatives, aspiration to grasp ICH from disparate regions, and personal preferences. Primarily, audiences with an education of high school level or lower may lean more on instinctual sensations and rudimentary cognition to assess ICH documentaries. This approach enables them to extract immediate gratification from the narrative storytelling and visual allure, without the necessity to profoundly comprehend cultural contexts or artistic methodologies. Secondly, from a pedagogical perspective, associate degree programs typically prioritize the development of technical and practical skills, potentially resulting in a constrained accrual of knowledge and diminished interest in the realms of humanities, history, and cultural arts among students. This educational framework may shape their cognitive paradigms, restricting the depth of their understanding and appreciation of intangible cultural heritage. Particularly in ICH documentaries, a genre demanding cross-cultural comprehension and deep emotional engagement, students with associate degrees might not fully discern or connect with the intricate layers and profound significances embedded in these works. Lastly, groups with higher educational backgrounds often have greater access to a plethora of cultural content and activities, likely leading to a more profound understanding and elevated appraisal of ICH documentaries. In contrast, those with associate degrees may experience a dearth in this aspect, attributed to limited resources and opportunities.

5. Viewers hailing from disparate provinces exhibit pronounced variations in their emotional engagement with documentaries on intangible cultural heritage (ICH), with those from Yunnan Province demonstrating a higher inclination to rate these documentaries favorably. Nestled in Southwest China, adjacent to Vietnam, Laos, and Myanmar, Yunnan stands as the most ethnically diverse province in the nation, home to groups like the Yi, Bai, Dai, and more. This rich tapestry of cultures likely engenders a deeper resonance and appreciation among local viewers for documentaries that illuminate a variety of cultural narratives. In stark contrast, Anhui Province, situated in Eastern China, predominantly features a Han ethnic majority with fewer minority groups. This demographic composition might result in a comparatively muted sensitivity and emotional investment in such themes among Anhui's populace, as opposed to their Yunnan counterparts. Moreover, Yunnan's inherent multiculturalism may influence its educational framework to place a greater emphasis on multicultural studies, in contrast to Anhui where education and media might lean more towards the mainstream cultural narrative. Additionally, elements such as the level of economic development, the urban-rural dynamic, and the fluidity of population, particularly

the influx of migrant workers, can subtly shape individuals' cultural perceptions and aesthetic inclinations. For instance, Yunnan's proximity and border with several neighboring countries could foster more extensive cross-border cultural interactions and demographic flux, potentially endowing its residents with a wider range of experiences and a more open-minded approach towards understanding and valuing diverse cultures. This factor could consequently influence their cultural tastes and aesthetic judgements, leading to a more rapid assimilation and heightened appraisal of ICH from other provinces.

6 Conclusion and Suggestions

The research presented reveals that audiences of varying backgrounds have both similarities and significant differences in their emotional cognition towards intangible cultural heritage (ICH) documentaries. The conclusions are summarized as follows:

1. Universal Appeal Across Genders: The negligible disparity in gender responses underscores the universal allure of culture: Gender appears to have a minimal impact on the emotional cognition concerning ICH documentaries. This phenomenon highlights the inclusive nature and widespread appeal of ICH, suggesting these documentaries successfully bridge gender divides, resonating with shared cultural values and collective emotional experiences.
2. Narrative Techniques and Age Dynamics: The preference of younger audiences for innovative and contemporary narrative styles underscores the critical need to evolve traditional ICH communication strategies. This pivot is essential to resonate with the
 • sensibilities of modern viewers. Future endeavors in ICH documentary filmmaking must incorporate pioneering narrative methods to captivate and engage a younger demographic effectively.
3. Influence of Professional Background on Perception: The professional background of viewers markedly influences their assessment of documentary craftsmanship and artistic representation. This diversity in evaluation underscores the importance of considering the varied perspectives of a multifaceted audience in documentary production. Those from film and art sectors possess an acute insight into the technical and artistic intricacies, while viewers from design and liberal arts spheres are likely to prioritize the depth of content and the intrinsic cultural values portrayed.
4. Educational Background and Cultural Engagement: The variance in documentary evaluation by individuals with associate degrees may reflect a broader issue of unequal cultural education and resource allocation across educational strata. This disparity accentuates the necessity for a differentiated and inclusive approach in the educational dissemination of ICH, catering to audiences with diverse educational backgrounds.
5. Geographic Influence and Cultural Resonance: The regional variance in audience ratings of ICH documentaries could be attributed to the distinct cultural landscapes and heritages of different provinces. For instance, viewers from Yunnan, enriched by the province's extensive cultural diversity, may find a deeper connection and resonance with documentaries that explore a spectrum of cultural themes.

In the realm of future production of intangible cultural heritage (ICH) documentaries, it is imperative for teams to delve profoundly into the emotional requirements and cultural sentiments of diverse audience demographics, weaving these elements intricately into both the narrative and visual fabric of the documentaries. For younger viewers, an innovative approach could involve the incorporation of cutting-edge technologies like virtual reality (VR) and augmented reality (AR), coupled with more dynamic and interactive storytelling methods. This strategy aims to ignite their curiosity and engagement with ICH. Conversely, for older viewers, narratives that delve into the rich history and traditional roots of ICH projects could resonate deeply, evoking a sense of nostalgia and cultural identity. Furthermore, ICH documentary production transcends mere documentation of cultural heritage; it embodies a journey of emotional exchange. By artfully presenting the life stories of ICH practitioners, the intricate process of skill transmission, and the role of ICH in the fabric of contemporary society, these documentaries can significantly fortify the emotional bond and cultural resonance with their audience. Establishing this deep-seated emotional connection is pivotal in heightening public awareness and participation in the preservation of ICH, thus fostering its perpetuation and evolution. Consequently, upcoming ICH documentary projects ought to prioritize the exploration and application of emotional cognition. By constructing a bridge of emotional resonance, they can effectively link diverse audience groups to the essence of intangible cultural heritage, achieving a harmonious blend of depth and expansiveness in cultural transmission. Future research might expand to include documentaries from additional provinces, aiming to comprehensively discern the pivotal factors that influence audience emotional cognition.

Funding. This research was supported by the General Projects of Shenzhen Philosophy and Social Science Planning under Grants, grant number No. SZ2022B037.

References

1. The Central People's Government of the People's Republic of China: Opinions on Further Accelerating the Work of Intangible Cultural Heritage Protection Issued by the General Office of the Central Committee of the Communist Party of China and the General Office of the State Council (2021). http://www.gov.cn/zhengce/2021-08/12/content_5630974.htm. Accessed 25 Oct 2023
2. Sun, C.J.: The Charm and Experience of Emotional Expression in Visual Media. China Film Press, Beijing (2010)
3. Li, B.X., Hu, G.L.: The truth unveiling and value expression of 'intangible cultural heritage' documentaries. China Telev. **12**, 81–85 (2020)
4. Tang, Y.: On the cultural space construction of minority intangible cultural heritage documentaries. Jianghuai Forum **02**, 97–101 (2019)
5. Li, Z.: The visual representation and dissemination of intangible cultural heritage documentaries in the context of converged media. J. Soc. Sci. Jiamusi Univ. **39**(06), 60–62, 70 (2021)
6. Wang, L.D.: The challenges and breakthroughs in the dissemination of intangible cultural heritage documentaries: a case study of popular ICH documentaries on Bilibili. In: Publishing Wide Angle, vol. 23, pp. 82–85 (2021)
7. Langer, S.K., Liu, D.J., et al.: Feeling and Form. China Social Sciences Press, Beijing (1986)
8. Plutchik, R.: Emotion: A Psychoevolutionary Synthesis. Harper & Row, New York (1980)
9. Plantinga, C.: Moving Viewers: American Film and the Spectator's Experience. University of California Press, Berkeley (2009)

The Cross-Cultural Differences in Consumers' Personality Type of Thinking or Feeling Influence the Judgments of Hedonic or Utilitarian Value

Ling-Wen Huamg and Tseng-Ping Chiu[✉]

Department of Industrial Design, National Cheng Kung University, Tainan, Taiwan
p36124097@gs.ncku.edu.tw

Abstract. This article explores whether personality type influences consumer preferences for hedonic versus functional aspects differences across cultures. Selects MBTI T-type and F-type as the focus of personality observation. The main reason is that T-type and F-type were related to judgment and appearance in the past. This experiment uses flat posters as stimulus samples, and posters are divided into high and low dimensions due to cross-cultural context, and illustration-style pictures are high-context and have higher visual enjoyment.

It is assumed that photographic images have low context and high visual utility. The process will be through literature collection to explore the correlation between cross-cultural collectivism, personality, and visual choices, using the MBTI map and Hofstede hedonic numerical comparison to conduct secondary analysis and initially discover the hedonic numerical values in various countries around the world. The higher it is, the greater the percentage of F. The next step is to use two groups of questionnaires to be distributed separately, so that the subjects can judge hedonic or utilitarian decisions under the visual stimulation of a unified vector or illustration, and use the questions selected from the hedonic and utilitarian scales to make the subjects fill in the questions. The degree of visual perception. We hypothesize that personality and cross-culture will mutually influence consumers' judgments and operations. This paper provides implications for the fields of visual design, marketing, and social psychology to better understand how different cultural experiences and personalities influence judgments of functionality versus hedonistic in global markets.

Keywords: Personality Trait · Thinking versus Feeling · Consumer Behavior · Hedonic versus Utilitarian · Cross-Cultural Studies

1 Introduction

Psychological tests are a marketing tool that always has imagination. Starting around 2018, various test marketing has become popular on various social software. Young people of Generation Z even use the results of psychological tests to become basis for daily conversations, making friends, and starting topics.

© The Author(s), under exclusive license to Springer Nature Switzerland AG 2024
P.-L. P. Rau (Ed.): HCII 2024, LNCS 14700, pp. 227–241, 2024.
https://doi.org/10.1007/978-3-031-60901-5_16

It is also what we often call UCG marketing. UCG marketing is advertising centered on psychological testing and using marketing tools to trigger the masses to spontaneously produce content and generate their own willingness to share, triggering a popular effect. This kind of marketing method can not only achieve the purpose of promoting the brand, but also allow potential customers to attract their attention through semi-customized product marketing. It can be seen from this that personality plays a very important part in this marketing link. According to past literature, we know that graphic vision occupies a large part in consumers' shopping behavior, and it is also a very important impression.

In an eye-tracking study, it was found that graphic components in print ads attract significant attention regardless of size [1] (Pieters, Wedel, 2004). This also tells us that the image component in print advertising is of high importance, so this experiment chose flat posters will be used as the main experimental stimulus sample. In fact, there are more trajectories that can prove the importance of personality and marketing. The characteristics and features of a new product are key factors in whether consumers are willing to adopt the new product [2] (Rogers, 1983). This means that consumers will choose goods that match their personality. From a cross-cultural perspective, there is collectivism and individualism. Their consumption habits for pleasure and utilitarianism are also significantly different. So, when personality and cross-culture collide, will it have an impact on consumers' judgment or consideration? Therefore, given the current focus on hedonic versus utilitarian aspects of visual design and the general lack of academic activity in the field, there is a clear need for research on this issue. This study investigated consumers' judgments of hedonic and functional aspects from the perspective of cross-cultural differences in self-construal. Based on quantitative research, it verified the correlation between personality and cross-cultural consumer behavior.

In short, this article makes it easier for the public to understand how different cultural experiences and personalities influence visual judgments of function and pleasure in global markets, examines current and potential customers, and thereby provides guidance for visual design and marketing communication strategies. Therefore, the main objectives of this study include: 1. Secondary data analysis to investigate the association between personality and hedonic and judge visual illustrations and actual photos; 3. Understand how people with different personalities and collectivism feel and judge visual illustrations and actual photos; 3. Understand the influence of cross-culture and personality, will the judgment of pleasure and utilitarianism be affected? The above are the three main parts of this article.

First, we discuss the theoretical background and previous research in this area. Second, we present findings on cross-cultural, personality, and hedonic utility and discuss our findings considering existing theory. On this basis, we conducted a questionnaire experimental test. Third, we present the results of experiments designed to verify whether our hypotheses are correct. We conclude with a general discussion of the findings, as well as limitations of the study and directions for future research.

2 Background and Review of Literature

2.1 Hedonic or Utilitarian with Visual

Utilitarianism refers to instrumental, task-oriented, rational, functional, and cognitive evaluations of feelings [3] (Pieter M.A. Desmet, Juan Carlos Ortíz Nicolás, Jan P. Schoormans, 2008). For many years, scholars have devoted themselves to research on functional consumption, hoping that consumers can complete the action of "purchasing goods" more quickly.

But when trends such as experience economy and emotion research became more and more common, hedonic consumption emerged at this time and was also valued by scholars and researchers. Hedonic is often a multi-sensory, fantasy and emotional aspect. And it reflects consumers' emotional value, non-profit orientation, experience orientation and emotion orientation [4] (Babin et al., 1994). People who enjoy hedonic consumption consider the shopping experience to be more important than simply purchasing the product.

2.2 High and Low Context

High-context cultures are those that communicate in ways that are a deeply meaningful message. And their culture relationships usually deeply. Low-context cultures usually highly personal culture and have the direct expression ways [5] (Edward T. Hall, 1976).

For example, we can easily find this difference in print advertisements. Most Eastern countries are accustomed to using illustrations to present pictures on posters, while in the West, they are accustomed to using actual photos. Compared with illustrations, actual photos are more direct and faster in terms of context. It can also be said to be an expression that favors utilitarian consumption.

H1: Illustration images are more hedonic, while real images are more utilitarian.

2.3 Myers-Briggs Type Indicator (MBTI)

The MBTI was developed by Isabel Briggs Myers and her mother. Katherine Briggs designed the scale based on the psychological type theory of the famous Swiss psychoanalyst Jung and the mother and daughter's long-term research and observation of human personality differences.

MBTI is a forced-choice, self-reported personality assessment tool. There are 4 indicators of personality assessment, including the way of generating energy (E/I), thinking mode (S/N), and the basis for making decisions. (T/F), and reactive attitudes to life (J/P). The research design of this scale is to enable the measurer to know himself better, and it can also be used in the workplace, such as assisting human resources in placing employees in appropriate positions. MBTI has become one of the most widely used personality trait testing tools today [6] (David J. Pittenger, 1993).

2.4 Thinking (T-Type) and Feeling (F-Type)

Most of us will discuss Thinking and Feeling as the basis for decision-making or appearance preference in academic circles. This is why this study will select this set of traits as independent variables. Usually, these two types of people have many differences, as shown in the following table (Table 1):

Table 1. Comparison chart of the differences between thinkers and feelers.

Thinking vs. Feeling	
Logic and facts	Emotional
Credibility	Empathy
Appearance preference rectangular	Appearance preference round and high acceptance of irregularities

As can be seen from the above table, the two types of people have very different judgment systems, and they also have many different cognitions in consumption and visual preferences.

2.5 Brand Personality

Brand will reflect the brand's personality and help align personality types with specific customer personas [7] (Aaker, 1997). Brand personality is formally defined here as "a set of human characteristics associated with a brand." For example, Coca-Cola is often defined as happy, family, and cool in consumers' minds. It has been argued that the symbolic use of brands is possible because consumers often imbue brands with human personality traits. [8] (Gilmore, 1919). This may be partly due to the strategies used by advertisers to inject personality into brands, such as personification and the creation of user personas.

H2: In the MBTI personality, F-type focus on hedonic when making decisions, while T-type focus on utilitarianism when making decisions.

2.6 Consumer Purchase Decision-Making Process

There are five stages of consumer decision-making behavior, namely: Need recognition, Information search, Evaluation, Purchase and Post purchase behavior. The stages of need recognition and information search refer to the needs or desires in life, which will prompt consumers to start searching products or advertising they need.

Evaluation is the most influential part of hedonic and personality. During this stage the individual will evaluate alternatives. The process of evaluating various products will depend on the consumer's underlying goals, motivations, and personality. There are many different products on the market, and consumers have certain beliefs about different brands or products. At this stage, it is easiest to have choice barriers, and it is also easiest to feel and judge products through your own values [9] (Jisana T. K, 2014).

The last two behaviors are the easier-to-understand terms of buying and selling. Post-service, he is the behavioral pattern after making a decision [10] (SHEIKH QAZZAFI, 2019).

2.7 The Influence of Hedonic and Utility in Consumption

There is an obvious gap in the consumption behavior of hedonic and utilitarian consumers. This also reminds businessmen that we need to sell our products in different ways, as shown in the following table (Table 2):

Table 2. Comparison chart of the differences between Hedonic and Utility.

Hedonic	Utility
Pursue sensual	Reason
Entertainment	Target
Diversified	Efficiency
Enjoyment	Task oriented
Personal preferences	Willing to listen to Suggestions from people

We can see that hedonic consumers care more about their thoughts and feelings and the fun of shopping. On the contrary, utilitarian consumers care more about shopping efficiency and may listen to the opinions of their trusted partners to achieve their goals faster [11] (Michael A. Jones, Kristy E. Reynolds, Mark J. Arnold, 2006).

2.8 Cross-Cultural and Culture Difference

From a cross-cultural perspective, we can know that the cultural dimension is divided into individualism and collectivism. It is very similar to independent and interdependent in the cultural dimension, and in some ways, some of their differences coincide with the personality and enjoyment mentioned above, as shown in the following table (Table 3):

Table 3. Comparison chart of the differences between Independent and Interdependent.

Individualism	Collectivism
Analytical	Holistic thinking
Individualism	Collectivism
Preference and atmosphere	CP value, durable and practical
Hedonic Value	Utilitarian Value

To put it simply, we can see that the independent self is like the F-type personality and hedonistic consumers in the MBTI test. For example, they all tend to have strong personal preferences when shopping or making judgments. On the other hand, the interdependent self has many similarities with the T-type personality in the MBTI test. For example, they both tend to judge the durability, applicability, and even monetary value of items. This is also the most critical factor in extending the assumptions behind this article.

H3: Individualism people focus on hedonic when making decisions, while Collectivism people focus on utility.

3 Method

The experiment is mainly divided into two parts: secondary data analysis and questionnaire distribution. In the follow-up, statistical single-factor variation analysis, Univariate analysis, chi-square analysis and correlation analysis are used to draw conclusions.

3.1 Step 1: MBTI and Indulgence Values Secondary Analysis

After comparing the secondary data, it was found that areas with high hedonistic also have a higher proportion of the population of F, showing a significant positive correlation, as shown in the following the chart (Fig. 1):

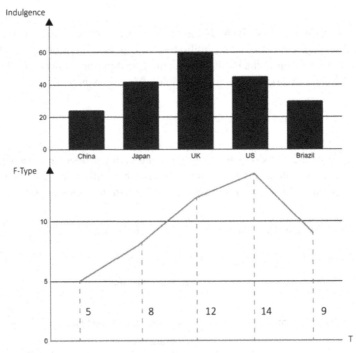

Fig. 1. The percentage of areas with more F-types than T-types is compared with the hedonic level of the area.

3.2 Step 2: Questionnaire Preparation and Scale

The questionnaire is divided into the following parts. First, the subject will enter the MBTI scale test, then the self-construction test, and finally the basic information and image decision-making and feelings test.

3.2.1 MBTI Scale

This article uses the 96-item MBTI test scale compiled by South China Normal University, and only uses the number of T and F questions in the scale, a total of 24 questions. The subjects choose the value from 1 to 7 according to their own personality according to the description of the question, the larger the value, the more you agree with the point of view discussed in the question. Finally, by summing and averaging the values, we can know the subject's personality TF tendency value.

3.2.2 Self-construal Scale

Hofstede's five-dimensional measure of culture has been the overwhelmingly dominant metric of culture. Using Hofstede's metric, researchers have found meaningful relationships between national culture and important demographic, geographic, economic, and political indicators of a society. This famous metric has been widely accepted and applied at both country and individual levels in cross-cultural studies. The experiment in this article uses six questions on collectivism as part of the test. If the value is high, it means that the tested case is biased toward collectivism, and if the value is low, the opposite is true.

3.2.3 Image Test

Based on the hypothesis, this article uses the between subject experiment method to group posters with illustrations and real photos, and randomly divide the subjects according to odd and even the last number of cellphone number. In each section, a total of eight posters for music festivals and career resume lectures will appear, and at the same time, the subject will be given a situation to make him decide which activities he most wants to participate in. The situation is as follows: You are a college student who is about to graduate today. Today, the school holds two paid graduation activities, and each graduate is given enough money to participate in one activity. Please answer the questions according to the following poster. The following are illustrations and real image samples. All images have an average of warm and cold colors, multiple characters, and the same amount of language and text (Fig. 2).

In the last part, the subjects will be asked to fill in whether they want to participate in activities, enjoyment, and utilitarian level. There are seven questions in each sample. There are seven levels in total from strongly disagree to strongly agree. The subjects will be asked to fill in the questions based on the picture samples they see. Respond to your feelings.

Fig. 2. All stimulus sample images.

4   Results

In this study, 61 responses were received, with a total of 60 valid questionnaires, 52.5% of which were completed by girls and 47.5% by boys. Approximately 40% of Westerners and 60% of Taiwanese answered the questions (Fig. 3).

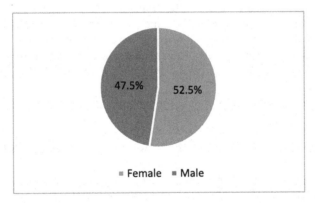

Fig. 3. Pie chart of male to female ratio of questionnaire respondents.

4.1   The Impact of Real Photo Posters and Illustration Posters on Joy

When we use illustrated posters, the hedonic quality is significantly increased. A one-way between subjects ANOVA was conducted to compare the effect of hedonic vision vs. utilitarian vision on hedonic activity nature of pleasure conditions. There was a significant effect of IV hedonic vision vs. utilitarian vision on DV hedonic activity Nature's joy level at the $p < .05$ level for the three conditions (Fig. 4).

4.2   Hedonic and Utilitarian Activities and the Influence of Vision in Experiments

Without considering vision, the subject has some differences in the nature preferences of the activity itself.

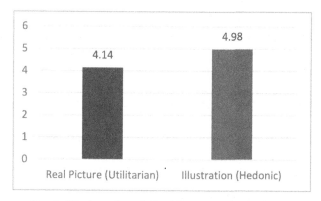

Fig. 4. The joy value of all subjects towards the picture.

The Impact on Hedonic and Utilitarian Activities Without Visual Influence. In the state where vision was not affected, there was a significant main effect of attend, $F = 3.008$, $P = .049$, $P < .05$. And there was a significant main effect of joy, $F = 20.636$, $P < .001$. Next was a significant main effect of fantasy, $F = 20.686$, $P < .001$. There was a significant main effect of hedonic, $F = 39.421$, $P < .001$. The significant main effect of wise, $F = 12.332$, $P < .001$. The last one is significant main effect of utility, $F = 16.719$, $P < .001$. This means that activities of hedonic and utilitarian nature, without being affected by vision, have a greater impact on willingness to participate, sense of joy, and There are already significant differences in the degree of fantasy, sense of enjoyment, intelligence, and utilitarianism.

Effects of Visual Grouping on Hedonic Versus Utilitarian Activities. After visual grouping, only some indicators interacted with it. There was a significant main effect of joy, $F = 22.222$, $P < .001$. Next, there was a significant main effect of fantasy, $F = 4.44$, $P = .039$, $P < .05$. There was a significant main effect of hedonic, $F = 8.999$, $P = .004$, $P < .05$. The last one is significant main effect of wise, $F = 5.740$, $P = .02$, $P < .05$. After adding visual considerations, the four feelings that have significant responses are joy, fantasy, enjoyment, and intelligence.

4.3 The Impact of FT-Type in Personality MBTI on Hedonic and Functional Vision

Different personality tendencies will also affect the perception of vision, but T-type personality was not significant for all feelings in this experiment. This may be related to the fact that T-type subjects rely on logical judgment rather than feelings.

The Visual Impact of F-type on the Degree of Fantasy of Utilitarian Activities in Personality MBTI. Through univariate analysis and Pearson correlation was conducted to compare the effect of hedonic vision (posters made with illustration elements) and utilitarian vision (posters made with real photo elements) on the ideal conditions of utilitarian activity nature (workplace resume lectures). There was a significant effect of IV hedonic vision (posters made with illustration elements) and utilitarian vision (posters made with real photo elements) on DV The degree of fantasy of utilitarian activity nature (workplace resume lectures) at the p < .05 level for the two conditions [F = 6.267, p = .015] and there was a positive correlation between the two variables, r (58) = [.328], p = [.01].

Post hoc comparisons using the Tukey HSD test indicated that the mean score for the real picture condition (M = 4.07, SD = 1.11) was significantly different than the illustration condition (M = 2.78, SD = 0.99).

This represents F-type personality. When seeing the visual representation of utilitarian activities as real picture posters, they are more likely to have fantasies than illustration visual posters.

The Visual Impact of F-type on the Degree of Fantasy of Utilitarian Activities in Personality MBTI. Through univariate analysis and Pearson correlation was conducted to compare the effect of hedonic vision (posters made with illustration elements) and utilitarian vision (posters made with real photo elements) on the utilitarian conditions of utilitarian activity nature (workplace resume lectures). There was a significant effect of IV hedonic vision (posters made with illustration elements) and utilitarian vision (posters made with real photo elements) on DV The utilitarian nature of the activity (workplace resume lecture) at the p < .05 level for the two conditions [F = 4.52, p = .038] and there was a positive correlation between the two variables, r (58) = [.292], p = [.024]. Post hoc comparisons using the Tukey HSD test indicated that the mean score for the real picture condition (M = 4.49, SD = 1.19) was significantly different than the illustration condition (M = 4.04, SD = 1.08).

This represents F-type personality. When seeing the visual representation of utilitarian activities as real picture posters, they feel more utilitarian than illustration visual posters.

The Visual Impact of F-type on the Degree of Fantasy of Utilitarian Activities in Personality MBTI. Through univariate analysis and Pearson correlation was conducted to compare the effect of hedonic vision (posters made with illustration elements) and utilitarian vision (posters made with real photo elements) on the fantasy level conditions. There was a significant effect of IV hedonic vision (posters made with illustration elements) and utilitarian vision (posters made with real photo elements) on DV Fantasy level of hedonic activity (music festival) at the p < .05 level for the two conditions [F = 6.15, p = .02] and there was a positive correlation between the two variables, r (58) = [.296], p = [.022]. Post hoc comparisons using the Tukey HSD test indicated that the mean score for the illustration condition (M = 4.40, SD = .82) was significantly different than the real picture condition (M = 4.24, SD = 1.22).

This represents the F-type personality. When seeing the visual representation of hedonic activities in the form of an illustration visual poster, it is easier to feel fantasy than in a real photo visual poster.

The Visual Impact of F-type in Personality MBTI on the Degree of Enjoyment of Hedonic Activities. Through univariate analysis and Pearson correlation was conducted to compare the effect of hedonic vision (posters made with illustration elements) and utilitarian vision (posters made with real photo elements) on the hedonic conditions of the nature of hedonic activities (music festivals). There was a significant effect of IV hedonic vision (posters made with illustration elements) and utilitarian vision (posters made with real photo elements) on DV The level of hedonic activity (music festival) at the p < .05 level for the two conditions [F = 10.86, p = .02] and there was a positive correlation between the two variables, r (58) = [.359], p = [.005]. Post hoc comparisons using the Tukey HSD test indicated that the mean score for the illustration condition (M = 4.74, SD = .96) was significantly different than the real picture condition (M = 4.33, SD = 1.09).

This represents F-type personality. When seeing the visual representation of hedonic activities in the form of illustration visual posters, they feel more hedonic than in real photo visual posters.

The Visual Impact of F-type in Personality MBTI on the Degree of Enjoyment of Hedonic Activities. Through univariate analysis and Pearson correlation was conducted to compare the effect of hedonic vision (posters made with illustration elements) and utilitarian vision (posters made with real photo elements) on intelligence conditions of hedonic activity nature (music festival). There was a significant effect of IV hedonic vision (posters made with illustration elements) and utilitarian vision (posters made with real photo elements) on DV Hedonic activity (music festival) intelligence at the p < .05 level for the two conditions [F = 4.87, p = .03] and there was a positive correlation between the two variables, r (58) = [.262], p = [.043]. Post hoc comparisons using the Tukey HSD test indicated that the mean score for the illustration condition (M = 3.94, SD = .93) was significantly different than the real picture condition (M = 3.73, SD = 1.21).

This represents F-type personality. When seeing the visual representation of hedonic activities in the form of illustration visual posters, they feel smarter than real photo visual posters.

4.4   The Influence of FT-Type in Personality MBTI on Hedonic and Functional Visual Participation Willingness and Decision-Making

Through univariate analysis and Pearson correlation was conducted to compare the effect of hedonic vision (posters made with illustration elements) and utilitarian vision (posters made with real photo elements) on conditions of willingness to participate in hedonic activities (music festivals). There was a significant effect of IV hedonic vision (posters made with illustration elements) and utilitarian vision (posters made with real photo elements) on DV Hedonic activity (music festival) willingness to participate at the p < .05 level for the two conditions [F = 11.29, p = .001] and there was a positive correlation between the two variables, r (58) = [.382], p = [.003]. Post hoc comparisons using the Tukey HSD test indicated that the mean score for the illustration condition (M = 4.56, SD = 1.04) was significantly different than the real picture condition (M = 4.29, SD = 1.21).

This represents the F-type personality. When seeing the visual representation of hedonic activities in the form of illustration visual posters, they are significantly more willing to participate in the activities or adopt the decision than in the real photo visual posters.

4.5   The Cross-Cultural Correlation Between Collectivism and Personality F-Type in This Experiment

A Pearson correlation coefficient was performed to evaluate the relationship between F-Type and Collectivism. There was a significant relationship between them, r (58) = .240, p = .065. This means that type F is related to collectivism, which is also different from what was discussed in the previous objective data.

4.6   Cross-Cultural Effects of Collectivism on Hedonic and Functional Visual Fantasy Levels

Through univariate analysis and Pearson correlation was conducted to compare the effect of hedonic vision (posters made with illustration elements) and utilitarian vision (posters made with real photo elements) on conditions of willingness to participate in hedonic activities (music festivals). There was a significant effect of IV hedonic vision (posters made with illustration elements) and utilitarian vision (posters made with real photo elements) on DV Fantasy level of hedonic activity (music festival) at the p < .06 level for the two conditions [F = 3.56, p = .06] and there was a positive correlation between the two variables, r (58) = [.249], p = [.055]. Post hoc comparisons using the Tukey HSD test indicated that the mean score for the illustration condition (M = 4.40, SD = .08) was significantly different than the real picture condition (M = 4.23, SD = 1.22).

There was a significant effect of IV hedonic vision (posters made with illustration elements) and utilitarian vision (posters made with real photo elements) on DV The degree of fantasy of utilitarian activity nature (workplace resume lecture) at the p < .06 level for the two conditions [F = 4.65, p = .04] and there was a positive correlation between the two variables, r(58) = [.255], p = [.055]. Post hoc comparisons using the Tukey HSD test indicated that the mean score for the real picture condition (M = 3.78, SD = .99) was significantly different than the illustration condition (M = 4.29, SD = 1.11).

This means that cross-culturally, people who are more collectivistic are significantly more likely to have imagination when they see the visual representation of hedonic activities in the form of illustration visual posters than in real photo visual posters. Interestingly. When the nature of the activity changes to a utilitarian one, it is easier for them to have illusions when seeing posters with real photos.

5   Discuss

The purpose of this study was to examine whether personality type influences consumer preferences for hedonic versus functional aspects of cross-cultural differences. We started from secondary data analysis to subsequent extended questionnaire research, using a series of statistical analysis methods to obtain more convincing data results. From the secondary data analysis, we can find from the interactive comparison between Hofstede and the personality map that the higher the F-Type area in the MBTI personality, the higher the hedonic value. The results of the analysis generated through the questionnaire showed that in a state like visual stimulation, F-Type subjects did choose hedonic music festival activities. On the contrary, T-Type subjects also chose lecture activities tend to be utilitarian. These all support our second hypothesis: In the MBTI personality, F-type focus on hedonic when making decisions, while T-type focus on utilitarianism when making decisions. From the statistical data, we can see that the illustration-type visual Joy and enjoyment were high for subjects regardless of personality or self-construction. This confirms our first hypothesis: Illustration images are more hedonic, while real images are more utilitarian. Based on these quantitative data, through questionnaires and statistical analysis, we found that self-construal was not related to judgment and vision in the experiment. There was no correlation with the hedonic and utility, and there was no interaction with personality.

Therefore, we conclude that among Generation Z and Y, cultural self-construal does not affect the judgment of hedonic and utilitarianism. However, this does not mean that it is a certain situation. In this experiment, the age and nationality of the subjects were similar, which means that when they are all Eastern, even if they tend to be independent, the average value of the correlation analysis shows that the two the group differences are not obvious, leading to quantitative data that affects statistics and ultimately the results. Second, the personality TF-type data in this experiment was analyzed using the dichotomy method, which can easily polarize the values and lead to extreme values in the data. This data can help designers use illustrative images to make ads or web pages more enjoyable; If you want to express information and efficiency more directly, you can use a larger number of real photos for drawing. As for the marketing team, if your consumers tend to have F-type personalities, please provide more experiential marketing activities; on the contrary, please provide practical marketing methods or products to T-type consumer groups (Fig. 5).

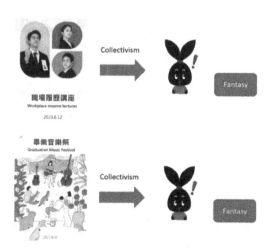

Fig. 5. Significant responses among subjects who tend to be collectivists

Under the influence of personality, subjects who tend to have an F-type personality are more likely to have fantasies when they see utilitarian activities with a utilitarian vision. Like cross-cultural reactions, only when hedonic activities are presented in a hedonic vision Easier to fantasize. When seeing the visual presentation of hedonic activities as hedonic visual posters, they feel smarter than utilitarian visual posters. But for T-type personality, there is no significant correlation. This may also be since T-type personality is accustomed to making judgments based on contextual thinking rather than feelings, so they don't have many feelings about the posters. The data also shows that subjects with F-type personality do prefer hedonic activities such as meals and music festivals (Figs. 6 and 7).

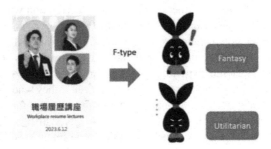

Fig. 6. Subjects with Type F tendencies saw significant responses to utilitarian activities paired with utilitarian vision.

Fig. 7. Subjects with Type F tendencies saw significant responses to hedonic activities paired with hedonic visions.

This data can help designers use illustrative images to make ads or web pages more enjoyable; As for the marketing team, if your consumers tend to have F-type personalities, please provide more experiential marketing activities or adjust the design style according to different natures of activities. Different regions and personalities will have different results.

References

1. Pieters, R., Wedel, M.: Attention capture and transfer in advertising: brand, pictorial, and text-size effects. J. Mark. **68**(2), 36–50 (2004)
2. Maddux, J.E., Rogers, R.W.: Protection motivation and self-efficacy: a revised theory of fear appeals and attitude change. J. Exp. Soc. Psychol. **19**(5), 469–479 (1983)

3. Desmet, P.M., et al.: Product personality in physical interaction. Des. Stud. **29**(5), 458–477 (2008)
4. Babin, B.J., Darden, W.R., Griffin, M.: Work and or fun measuring hedonic and utilitarian. J. Consum. Res. **20**(4), 644–656 (1994)
5. Hall, E.T.: Beyond culture, Anchor (1976)
6. Pittenger, D.J.: The utility of the Myers-Briggs type indicator. Rev. Educ. Res. **63**(4), 467–488 (1993)
7. Aaker, J.L.: Dimensions of brand personality. J. Mark. Res. **34**(3), 347–356 (1997)
8. Gilmore, C.W.: Reptilian faunas of the Torrejon, Puerco, and underlying Upper Cretaceous formations of San Juan County, New Mexico, US Government Printing Office (1919)
9. Markus, H.R., Kitayama, S.: Cultures and selves-a cycle of mutual constit. Perspect. Psychol. Sci. **5**, 420–430 (2010)
10. Kim, D., et al.: High-versus low-context culture: a comparison of Chinese, Korean, and American cultures. Psychol. Mark. **15**(6), 507–521 (1998)
11. Mugge, R., et al.: The development and testing of a product personality scale. Des. Stud. **30**(3), 287–302 (2009)
12. Hardin, E.E., et al.: Factor structure of the self-construal scale revisited: Implications for the multidimensionality of self-construal. J. Cross Cult. Psychol. **35**(3), 327–345 (2004)
13. Masuda, T., Nisbett, R.E.: Attending holistically versus analytically: comparing the context sensitivity of Japanese and Americans. J. Pers. Soc. Psychol. **81**(5), 922 (2001)
14. Jisana, T.K.: Consumer behaviour models: an overview. Sai Om J. Commer. Manag. **1**(5), 34–43 (2014)
15. Qazzafi, S.: Consumer buying decision process toward products. Int. J. Sci. Res. Eng. Dev. **2**(5), 130–134 (2019)
16. 张进辅, 曾. MBTI 人格类型量表的理论研究与实践应用. Adv. Psychol. Sci. 14 (2006)
17. Ott-Holland, C.J., et al.: The effects of culture and gender on perceived self-other similarity in personality. J. Res. Pers. **53**, 13–21 (2014)
18. Arnold, M.J., Reynolds, K.E.: Hedonic shopping motivations. J. Retail. **79**(2), 77–95 (2003)
19. Bartikowski, B., Walsh, G.: Attitude contagion in consumer opinion platforms: posters and lurkers. Electron. Mark. **24**(3), 207–217 (2014)
20. Masuda, T., Wang, H., Ito, K., Senzaki, S.: Culture and the mind: implications for art, design and advertisement (2012)
21. Pittenger, D.J.: Measuring the MBTI… and coming up short. J. Career Plan. Employ. **54**(1), 48–52 (1993)
22. Wang, C.-Y.: Does personality type affect people preference for the golden ratio? An MBTI personality approach. Case Stud. J. **6**(1) (2017)
23. Di, W., et al.: Is a picture really worth a thousand words? In: Proceedings of the 7th ACM International Conference on Web Search and Data Mining, pp. 633–642 (2014)
24. Diefenbach, S., et al.: The 'hedonic' in human-computer interaction. In: Proceedings of the 2014 Conference on Designing Interactive Systems, pp. 305–314 (2014)
25. Safari, A.: Customers' international online trust - insights from focus group interviews. J. Theor. Appl. Electron. Commer. Res. **7**(2), 13–14 (2012)
26. Hardin, E.E., et al.: Factor structure of the self-construal scale revisited. J. Cross Cult. Psychol. **35**(3), 327–345 (2016)
27. ND. Country Comparison Tool. https://www.hofstede-insights.com/. Hofstede tool
28. ND. MBTI MAP. https://www.16personalities.com/country-profiles/global/world#global
29. Boztepe, S.: Toward a framework of product development for global markets: a user-value-based approach. Des. Stud. **28**(5), 513–533 (2007)
30. Torelli, C., Cheng, S.: Cultural meanings of brands and consumption: a window into the cultural psychology of globalization. Soc. Pers. Psychol. Compass **5**, 251–262 (2011)
31. Fetvadjiev, V.H., van de Vijver, F.J.R.: Measures of personality across cultures. In: Measures of Personality and Social Psychological Constructs, pp. 752–776 (2015)

How Augmented Visual Feedback Aids Patrons' Reading and Interaction with Rare Books – Evidence from Eye Movement

Weijane Lin[1(✉)] ⓘ, Koji Masumoto[2], Koh Kakusho[2], and Hsiu-Ping Yueh[1] ⓘ

[1] National Taiwan University, No. 1, Sec. 4, Roosevelt Rd., Taipei 10617, Taiwan
{vjlin,yueh}@ntu.edu.tw
[2] Kwansei Gakuin University, 1 Gakuen Uegahara, Sanda 669-1330, Japan
{gdt56894,kakusho}@kwansei.ac.jp

Abstract. Library rare books are crucial resources in libraries that add specializations to library collections. These rare books are valuable in their content, which documents significant research achievements, historical events in various fields, and their forms. To improve the accessibility of the useful library collection, this study developed different types of visual representations using augmented reality technology. As a study of our serial research endeavors, this study further investigates how participants used different augmented visual elements during their reading, and if their use of these visual materials affected their understanding. A total of 63 college students' eye movements when reading the assigned rare book were recorded and analyzed. The participants were assigned into 4 groups to read the rare book on medical plants with augmented visual feedback in terms of different media elements. Their attention to the layout elements and plant parts, as well as their referencing behaviors between semantic sections, were recorded and analyzed to understand how the augmented visual feedback affected and aided them in reading rare books.

Keywords: Eye Movement · Rare Books · Augmented Feedback · Augmented Reality

1 Introduction

Rare books are a genre of library special collections that support research, education of primary sources skills, and informal learning in exhibitions in an academic library. Limited by their fragile condition, rare books are usually preserved in closed and temperature-controlled bookshelves or displayed in locked glass cases with a fixed page open on a book holder. To unveil meaningful book content and to attract visitors, such as university students who are frequent users of academic libraries, many libraries and researchers have used virtual technology, such as virtual reality (VR) and augmented reality (AR), to resolve the problem [1, 2].

Based on the nature of simulation technology, AR provides a highly interactive experience by superimposing computer-generated virtual objects, such as images, videos,

P.-L. P. Rau (Ed.): HCII 2024, LNCS 14700, pp. 242–250, 2024.
https://doi.org/10.1007/978-3-031-60901-5_17

and 3D models, on reality in real-time [3]. The interactivity of AR transforms learners from passive information recipients to active knowledge acquirers, which backs up the constructive learning pedagogy [4]. Targeting the three major challenges of exhibiting, researching, and teaching rare books [5–7], alternatives and solutions were testified and suggested, such as offering explanations [8] to the original Latin texts, placing illustrations and texts to increase interaction [9], and even using multimodal channels to engage patrons [10]. Current studies adopted AR to further represent these solutions in synchronous ways, such as augmenting the original text of rare books by project-based AR [11], providing explanations and music mentioned in a manuscript [12], or augmenting 3D rare book models for students to learn Medieval literature [13]. However, despite the prosperous applications and positive reputations of AR, few studies answered whether and why AR raised a sense of engagement and motivation.

Therefore, as part of our series of investigations into patrons' reading of rare books aided by AR [14, 15], this study pays particular attention to readers' actual use of the augmented visual feedback by tracking their eye movement. Meanwhile, this study discovers if any behavioral patterns exist through our analytics [14]. It is hoped to collect objective data on patrons' reading behaviors and generalize from the behavioral patterns to understand how AR facilitates readers' engagement and motivation. We focused on the visual feedback that engages the readers and initiates the recognition and comprehension of domain-specific terminology and concepts. Based on the existing AR supplemental information position and the common supplemental materials provided aside from rare books, including translation and pictures, this study investigated four different layouts consisting of two original media possessed by the rare book: botanical illustration and Latin text, and two augmented visual feedback of botanical color photographs and Chinese translated texts. This study explores how augmented visual feedback represented by different media influences readers' reading behaviors in terms of their eye movement to provide a more comprehensive understanding of patrons' reading and interaction with rare books.

2 Research Design

2.1 Methodology

Eye tracking is one of the physiological measures that directly reflects human cognitive processing. Parameters like the increase in pupil dilation and the decrease in fixation duration have proven to be related to mental effort [14, 15]. Stolk and Brok [16] categorized transition patterns of reading into one-way and two-way. One-way transitions occur when a text has been finished, and the graphics are then read without any connected return. Two-way transitions, on the other hand, have back and forth between the two visual representations. Two-way transitions could be analogous to "return" in general eye-tracking events, which suggest transitions to ROIs (Region of Interest) that have already been visited. Moving back and forth is seen as a sign of actual integration; thus, studies on textbook design and reading have used ROI transitions as an indication of making sense. For example, a previous study [17] found that students with lower prerequisites have more transitions when reading biological textbooks because they need more time for referencing. Empirical pieces of evidence from the above studies showed that eye-tracking data is highly associated with users' reading motivation and performance. Therefore, this study tracks participants' eye movement to conduct an experimental investigation of readers' behaviors in reading rare books.

A between-group quasi-experiment design was adopted to investigate the causal relationship and interaction effect among different arrangements of visual elements. 66 university students were recruited but 3 were excluded for failed eye tracking data and outliers. At the individual level, participants were randomly assigned to one out of the four experimental groups as between-subjects factors: (a) augmented Chinese translated text with original illustration, (b) augmented Chinese-translated text to the initially integrated layout with illustration and Latin texts, (c) augmented Chinese-translated text and augmented color photographs to the initially integrated layout with illustration and Latin texts, and (d) augmented Chinese-translated text and augmented color photographs replaced the original Latin texts and illustration. Each group was reading the same content only with a different page layout (as shown in Fig. 1). All conditions were provided with the same learning materials and post-test questionnaires.

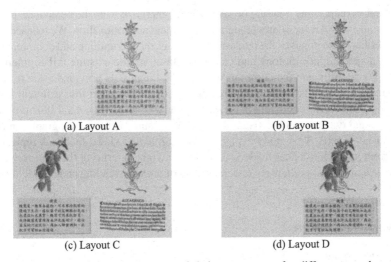

(a) Layout A   (b) Layout B

(c) Layout C   (d) Layout D

Fig. 1. Combinations of the components and their arrangement for different page layouts for alkakenge as an example. Adapted from Tanaka Collection of National Taiwan University [16]

The participants were tested individually in a single session lasting approximately 40 min. The participants were first administered the informed consent and an exemplary scientific passage for practice. After the practice session, they were allowed as much time as needed to read the texts. The participants were asked to take the reading comprehension test when they finished reading.

2.2 Reading Materials

The reading materials were adapted from a rare book of the University Library's special collection entitled De virtutibus herbarum (The Nature of Herbs) [16]. The book introduced more than 200 medicinal herbs in medieval Europe with botanical illustrations and

Latin text. Based on the accessibility of information and the level of difficulty, 7 herbs including daffodil, absinthe, acorus, alkekengi, bugloss, marrubium, and verbascum were selected as the basis of reading materials for the experiment.

Two different virtual pieces of information were augmented to the book: translated Chinese texts to the original Latin texts, and the color photograph that illustrates the traits and habitats of the selected herb. Subject matter experts and linguistic professionals proofread each medicinal herb's translated passages to ensure the content's accuracy. Each translated passage was controlled to be in 100 Chinese characteristics to ensure the quantity and difficulty of reading content are equivalent across different herbs. The 4 visual elements, namely the original Latin texts, original botanical illustration, augmented Chinese translation, and augmented color photograph, were arranged in four different layouts accordingly. Sample pages describing alkakenge with the four layouts are illustrated as Fig. 1.

2.3 Data Collection and Analysis

The eye tracker used in this study is Tobii EyeX with 50 Hz. We assigned one participant to each group and read the reading materials according to the designated page layout shown in Fig. 1, allowing each participant to read a page for each medical herb. Participants' coordinate data on gaze point and gaze time were recorded, in total, we collected the eye movement data from 63 patrons, including 15 in group (a), 16 in group (b), 16 in group (c), and 16 in group (d).

This study employed the machine learning method and analytics developed in our previous studies [14, 15] to record eye movement at a frequency of once every 0.1 s for all participants staying on all pages. Critical event data collected included fixation, transitions, and regression scanpaths for each page and each visual element (original Latin texts, original illustration, augmented Chinese translation, and augmented botanical color photographs). Furthermore, temporal data were calculated and analyzed on a page-by-page basis, including first fixation duration, total fixation duration, and mean fixation duration. In addition to the visual element of each layout, readers' semantic references between textual keywords and graphical sections were also recorded and analyzed in order to understand readers' cross-referencing behaviors.

3 Preliminary Findings

3.1 Patrons' Gaze Movement Through All Visual Elements

To investigate the patterns of correspondence between each visual element and the learner's eye movement, we use the following function to obtain the simulated 4D data for clustering.

$$c_\lambda^h(k) = \frac{1}{|C_\lambda^h(k)|} \sum\nolimits_{\Phi_\lambda^h \in C_\lambda^h(k)} \Phi_\lambda^h \tag{1}$$

Figure 2 gives several examples of the preliminary clustering results of the major gaze movements among different participants (in color). Based on the cluster centers, the participants' transitions could be classified into two main patterns: (1) dwelling mainly on the same visual element of augmented Chinese translation, and (2) heavily cross-referencing between two visual elements of augmented Chinese translation and the graphical elements of augmented color photographs or botanical illustration.

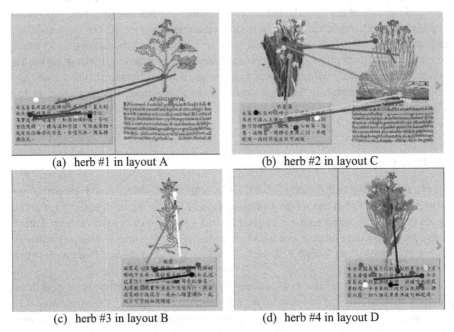

(a) herb #1 in layout A   (b) herb #2 in layout C

(c) herb #3 in layout B   (d) herb #4 in layout D

Fig. 2. Examples of visualizing the cluster centers for 4D data of different herbs and different page layout

3.2 Patrons' Transition Among Different Visual Elements

Further looking at the transitions between different visual elements among all page layouts, as shown in Fig. 3, it is found that Layout C (augmented Chinese-translated text and augmented color photographs to the initially integrated layout with illustration and Latin texts) has the most transitions between different visual elements, followed by Layout D (augmented Chinese-translated text and augmented color photographs replaced the original Latin texts and illustration), then Layout A (augmented Chinese-translated text with original illustration), and Layout B (augmented Chinese-translated text to the initially integrated layout with illustration and Latin texts) is the least.

With the 4 types of visual elements (original Latin text, original botanical illustration, augmented Chinese-translated text, and augmented color photograph), there are up to 6 possible transition ways across different visual elements. In order to find out which elements were used more frequently among different page layouts, we compared the number with the type of transitions in all pages. It was found that despite the different page layouts, participants made the most transitions between the original botanical

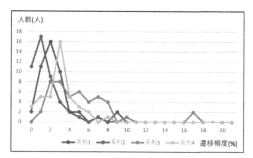

Fig. 3. Transitions between different visual elements in all 4 page layouts (blue – A, red – B, green – C, yellow – D) (Color figure online)

illustration and the augmented Chinese-translated text, followed by transitions between the augmented color photographs and the augmented Chinese-translated text. The preliminary results also confirmed that many of the transitions involved augmented color photographs. This may be due to the fact that the augmented color photographs showed the physical characteristics, such as parts and color of the herbs more clearly, thus serving to supplement the verbal description.

3.3   Patrons' Cross-Referencing Between Semantic and Visual Elements

Based on the results regarding the frequencies of transitions reported in 3.2, it is found that participants frequently cross-reference the Chinese-translated text with the graphical elements of the original botanical illustrations and augmented color photo-graphs. To further examine how patrons refer to the graphical elements semantically, we defined the descriptions of plant parts in the Chinese-translated text as a subset of semantic ROIs. We also labeled the corresponding plant parts in the botanical illustrations and the color photographs to examine how the subjects' gaze trajectories shifted between these semantic parts. Figure 4 shows an example of gaze movement on the semantic ROIs.

Fig. 4. Example of how semantic ROIs to corresponding plant parts was labeled

In this way, we were able to quantify and visualize the subjects' cross-referencing behaviors for these semantic parts. Although we are still in the process of analyzing all data, the preliminary findings suggest that the subjects are more likely to find the corresponding plant parts at a glance when referencing augmented color photographs, resulting in slightly fewer cross-references between color photographs and the Chinese-translated text. On the other hand, when referencing the botanical illustrations, there appeared more transitions within the visual element of illustration, suggesting that the subjects were not sure about the plant parts in the illustration and thus performed a reading behavior of iterative search for confirmation, resulting in the most cross-references between the illustration and the Chinese-translated text.

4 Discussion and Conclusions

This study examined the readers' eye movement using augmented visual feedback in varied page layouts of rare books. Based on our previous endeavors in designing AR rare books featuring visual elements of illustrations, photos, and texts [15], this study further explored whether the readers may utilize these elements differently and the connections across different elements to discover the relationship manifest through changes in the readers' eye movement patterns. Four distinct page designs featuring different combinations of visual elements associated with medicinal herbs were utilized for the study. 63 participants were divided into four groups, each group assigned to read the AR rare book using one of the page layouts, focusing on 7 pages detailing various medicinal herbs. The participant's eye movement data, including the gazing position coordinates and gazing time, was collected for analysis using machine learning methods [14].

The preliminary observations indicated that Layout C, which augmented Chinese-translated text and color photographs to the initially integrated layout with botanical illustration and Latin texts, had a high frequency of transitions between different visual elements. The findings implied that all visual elements on the page captured readers' attention and facilitated their movement across different visual elements. Further examination of how participants utilized augmented color photographs or original botanical illustrations to aid comprehension when reading the Chinese-translated text revealed that cross-references using color photographs were more precise, required less time to read, and enhanced referencing efficiency. In contrast, the intentional emphasis and potential distortion found in botanical illustrations [15, 17] led to increased within-element fixations as well as prolonged viewing time. Finally, this study successfully linked eye movement data to the meaning of the content. By identifying semantic ROIs in Chinese-translated text, botanical illustrations, and color photographs, we collected data on readers' attention paths and reading behaviors for various semantic content. This allowed us to examine differences in gaze transition frequency between different semantic sections and clarify the usage and effectiveness of each augmented visual feedback on participants' reading of AR rare books. These findings suggest that the integration of augmented visual elements, such as color photographs and botanical illustrations, can enhance readers' comprehension and attention when reading rare books.

Based on the understanding of how participants use and integrate different types of augmented visual feedback in rare book reading, we will complete the ongoing analysis of the semantic parts and achieve a comprehensive understanding of participants' retrieval and cross-reference of the exhibiting AR rare books. In addition, our further studies will keep associating data on learning performance, including memory and comprehension test scores, to investigate how the quality and quantity of augmented visual feedback affect rare book reading performance.

Acknowledgments. This study was supported by the National Science and Technology Council in Taiwan (NSTC111-2628-H-002-006-MY3; NSTC112-2410-H-002-121-MY3), and JSPS KAKEN Grant (JP18H01063).

Disclosure of Interests. The authors have no competing interests to declare that are relevant to the content of this article.

References

1. Lin, W., Chang, H.-J.: Understanding taxonomical botanist's usage of special collection in the academic library: a bibliometrics study of NTU Tanaka collection. J. Libr. Inform. Stud. **20**(1), 101–129 (2022)
2. Lin, W., Lo, W.-T., Yueh, H.-P.: Effects of learner control design in an AR-based exhibit on visitors' museum learning. PLoS ONE **17**, e0274826 (2022)
3. Azuma, R.T.: A survey of augmented reality. Presence: Teleoperators Virtual Environ. **6**(4), 355–385 (1997). https://doi.org/10.1162/pres.1997.6.4.355
4. Wojciechowski, R., Cellary, W.: Evaluation of learners' attitude toward learning in ARIES augmented reality environments. Comput. Educ. **68**, 570–585 (2013)
5. Loxley, J., Vincent, H., Marshall, J., Otty, L.: Exhibiting the Written Word (2011)
6. Cauchard, J.R., Ainsworth, P.F., Romano, D.M., Banks, B.: Virtual manuscripts for an enhanced museum and web experience 'living manuscripts.' In: Zha, H., Pan, Z., Thwaites, H., Addison, A.C., Forte, M. (eds.) VSMM 2006. LNCS, vol. 4270, pp. 418–427. Springer, Heidelberg (2006). https://doi.org/10.1007/11890881_46
7. Tranouez, P., et al.: DocExplore: overcoming cultural and physical barriers to access ancient documents. In: Proceedings of the 2012 ACM Symposium on Document engineering, pp. 205–208 (2012)
8. Vincent, H.: The library and the display of text. World Library and Information Congress. In: 78th IFLA General Conference and Assembly. IFLA, Helsinki, Finland (2012)
9. Ke, H.-R., Tseng, S.-H.: Digital curation for cultural and intellectual assets: a Taiwan perspective. LIBRES: Libr. Inform.n Sci. Res. Electron. J. **26**, 64 (2016)
10. Mitchell, E., Seiden, P., Taraba, S.: Past or portal?: Enhancing undergraduate learning through special collections and archives. Assoc of Cllge & Rsrch Libr (2012)
11. Todd-Diaz, A., Jr Givens, E.: Watch your materials perform: shattering conventions and display cases with augmented reality. GIRONA 2014 Archives & Cultural Industries, Girona, Spain (2014)
12. British library, Turning the pages. https://ttp.onlineculture.co.uk/
13. Armstrong, G., Hodgson, J., Manista, F., Ramirez, M.: The SCARLET Project AR in special collections. SCONUL Focus **54**, 52–57 (2012)
14. Lin, W., Kotakehara, Y., Hirota, Y., Murakami, M., Kakusho, K., Yueh, H.P.: Modeling reading behaviors: an automatic approach to eye movement analytics. IEEE Access **9**, 63580–63590 (2021)

15. Lin, W., Masumoto, K., Kakusho, K., Yueh, H.-P.: How scientific illustration and photography aid learners' reading–evidence from eye movements. In: International Conference on Human-Computer Interaction, pp. 255–264. Springer, (2023). https://doi.org/10.1007/978-3-031-35946-0_21

16. Avicenna, S.: De virtutibus herbarum. Gioăni Andrea Vauassore, Venetia (1524)

17. Hickman, E.J., Yates, C.J., Hopper, S.D.: Botanical illustration and photography: a southern hemisphere perspective. Aust. Syst. Bot. **30**, 291–325 (2017)

Enhancement Methods of Sustained Attention in Complex Systems: A Review

Haijing Tang and Qin Gao[✉]

Department of Industrial Engineering, Tsinghua University, Beijing, China
gaoqin@tsinghua.edu.cn

Abstract. In complex systems, sustained attention has become a key factor affecting operators' performance. Many studies have focused on how to enhance sustained attention to avoid performance decline caused by attention distraction, decline, and insufficiency. The present review summarized the research results in this field. From the perspectives of task design, personnel selection, personnel training, and process intervention, we summarized and sorted out the latest enhancement methods of sustained attention in complex systems. Also, we compared the means, effects, and application scenarios of these methods. While the findings of most enhancement methods to date were either solitary or contradictory in nature, they exerted a positive effect on sustained attention, in general. Besides, the effects of enhancement were seemingly influenced by several factors, such as time-on-task and overall experimental protocol, and may not last so long.

Keywords: Sustained Attention · Vigilance · Enhancement Methods

1 Introduction

Sustained attention is differentiated from other classes of attention and requires an observer to maintain engagement in a specific task over an extended period of time [1, 2]. It has become a critical factor affecting the performance of human operators in various complex systems. Applications that need sustained attention include military surveillance, air traffic control, cockpit monitoring, seaboard navigation, industrial process/quality control, long-distance driving, and agricultural inspection [3–7]. In these scenarios, operators need to maintain long-term focus on the current task, which consumes a significant amount of cognitive resources, resulting in increased mental workload, fatigue, and decreased performance [7]. Besides, due to the repetition and monotony of the stimulus signal, operators are also more likely to experience low arousal and scattered attention, leading to difficulty in maintaining performance levels [1, 8]. Many factors are shown to influence the timing and magnitude of sustained attention, including signal duration, source complexity, and declarative memory usage in the task [9].

Numerous studies have been conducted on the mechanisms and characteristics of attention maintenance in sustained attention tasks. Most of them involved the detection of rare targets amongst non-targets, over long durations (minutes to hours) and was essential to the characterization of vigilance decrement, or performance decline over time [1]. However, many studies are from the field of psychology and carried out through simple sustained attention tasks (e.g., continuous performance tasks, CPT). For example, Temple et al. designed the abbreviated vigilance task (AVT), where participants were asked to identify a key signal (letter "O") from a series of character signals presented on a screen, including letters "D" and reversed letter "D" [10]. The stimuli were presented on a white background and covered by unfilled circles at a frequency of 57.5 times per minute for a duration of 12 min. This experimental paradigm has been validated and widely used in subsequent studies on sustained attention tasks [11–13]. Although many studies using the AVT in laboratory settings have observed vigilance decrement similar to that of real-world sustained attention tasks, there is still controversy over whether the results of these experiments can be generalized to complex systems [4, 10].

Operators in complex systems not only need to focus on a sustained attention task, but also need to deal with other parallel tasks, which forms a scenario of multitasking and depletes their cognitive resources, such as nuclear power plants, unmanned aerial systems, and air traffic control systems [14]. In recent years, in order to narrow the gap between laboratory and real-world scenarios caused by system complexity, more research on sustained attention tasks has been conducted on multitasking simulation platforms, including the unmanned aerial systems (UAS) simulation platform provided by the ALOA research testbed [15], the simulation aircraft driving platform represented by NASA's MATB-II (Multi-Attribute Task Battery II) [16], and many other simulation driving platforms [17–20]. These platforms typically prototype a certain type of task in real-world application scenarios and provide several subtasks containing different sensory modalities. For example, the MATB-II platform provides auditory communication tasks and visual system monitoring tasks, resource management tasks, and tracking tasks, while simulation driving platforms typically include visual driving primary tasks and auditory phone answering subtasks. By using these higher-fidelity simulation platforms, researchers can conduct in-depth exploration of the performance and cognitive mechanisms of sustained attention tasks.

Among the related studies, many studies have focused on how to manage or enhance sustained attention to avoid performance decline in complex systems, which helps to reduce vigilance decrement with the use of cognitive enhancement methods and leads to better safety, active control, and improvement in overall performance. The literature contains a large number of means for sustained attention enhancement, such as mental training, yoga, integrating new challenges into the primary task, music, and video games [21–25]. Resulting studies have reported contradictory findings regarding the efficacy of the enhancement methods, which have hampered the progress of further investigations. To address these ambiguities, a comprehensive review of sustained attention enhancement methods is undertaken in this paper to summarize the research results in this field and highlight the most promising direction for further research.

For the purpose of our review, we obtained research publications (journal/conference papers, books, and book chapters) by searching research databases (e.g. Google Scholar and Web of Science) using relevant terms ("sustained attention", "vigilance", "vigilant attention") coupled with the terms "enhancement," "intervention," "manage," "task," and "complex systems". We identified two foundational articles in the field of cognitive psychology [1, 26] and several more from other disciplines (e.g., [27–32]). We then searched for research publications focused on sustained attention/vigilance that cited the above articles. In addition to the searching databases, the reference list for all selected articles was examined to identify any additional articles that might have been overlooked during the primary search. The main variables examined in each article were (i) the involved complex system of the study, (ii) the manipulations or the time duration of stimulation of each type of enhancer, (iii) sustained attention test, (iv) number of subjects participating in the study, (v) summary of results, (vi) effects on sustained attention, and (vii) comments on the findings. According to the type of enhancer, this resulted in a total of 127 publications that were coded for task design, personnel selection, personnel training, and process intervention. This helped us identify themes to organize the below review.

2 Enhancement Methods of Sustained Attention

2.1 Methods Related to Task Design

In complex systems, the design of the task is closely related to the sustained attention performance of the participants, including signal discrimination type, signal type, sensory modality, signal salience, temporal uncertainty of stimulus, spatial uncertainty of stimulus, and attributes of the background event [4]. Accordingly, in order to improve operators' performance in sustained attention tasks, each of these factors should be checked and targeted in the task design of the complex system.

Signal Discrimination Type. According to the signal discrimination type, sustained attention tasks can be divided into simultaneous discrimination and successive discrimination [33]. In simultaneous discrimination tasks, the signal is presented together with other signals for the operator to distinguish and compare. In successive discrimination tasks, the critical signal does not appear at the same time as other signals, and the operator needs to compare the current signal with the standard signal in memory to determine whether it is the critical signal. Research has found that successive discrimination require more cognitive resources than simultaneous discrimination, which means that operators' sustained attention performance in simultaneous discrimination tasks is better than that in successive discrimination tasks [34]. In addition, factors such as event rate, event asynchrony, spatial uncertainty, and multitasking also have a greater impact on sustained attention performance in successive discrimination tasks [35].

Sensory Modality. In sustained attention tasks, the sensory modality of signals is a key factor affecting operators' performance. Research based on auditory, visual, and tactile signals has shown that sustained attention performance in auditory tasks is often better than in visual and tactile tasks [36]. There are some technical methods that can improve operators' sustained attention performance in visual tasks, such as bringing them closer to the visual display so that they cannot focus their gaze elsewhere [37]. Signals can also be presented simultaneously to both the visual and auditory channels to obtain higher levels of sustained attention performance than single-modality signals [38, 39]. Overall, the sensory modality should be selected according to the features of the complex system. For example, researchers used auditory signals to indicate lane position and distance to support driver activity, resulting in increased time spent by drivers in the central area of the lane and improved driver performance [40, 41].

Signal Salience. Sustained attention performance is closely related to the signal salience, which can usually be measured by the amplitude and duration of signal changes. By increasing the amplitude of signal-to-noise ratio changes, operators' sustained attention performance and stability in complex systems can be improved [10, 42]. As the amplitude of signal changes increases, if the duration is also increased, the signal can become more salient, but the benefits to sustained attention usually decreases with time until about four seconds [43]. In addition, stimulus salience can also be enhanced through graphical representation in the digital system[44]. When operators receive hints from graphical displays, their sustained attention performance is significantly higher than that of operators without graphical hints [44, 45]. Thus, to improve operators' performance in complex systems, the signal salience should be designed properly and graphical representation is a good way when designing the sustained attention tasks.

Temporal Uncertainty. Temporal uncertainty can be controlled by the density of target signals appearing within a period of time or the time intervals between two signals. The more target signals that appear within a period of time, the lower the uncertainty for operators as to when the target signals will appear, resulting in better sustained attention performance, higher accuracy and faster response speed [46]. When the time intervals between two signals are irregular and unpredictable, operators' detection speed and accuracy for target signals are lower [47]. Additionally, researchers have found that operators who were trained under high signal density conditions perform better in sustained attention tasks than those who were trained under low signal density conditions, regardless of whether the signal density in the formal task is high or low [48]. These results suggest that designing tasks and training sessions specifically to control operators' expectations of temporal uncertainty for target signals can enhance their sustained attention in complex systems.

Spatial Uncertainty. Spatial uncertainty usually refers to the randomness of the location of target signals appearing on the display or system, which may be unpredictable or fixed. When the spatial uncertainty of the target signal is high, operators tend to focus their attention on the most likely location for the signal to appear [49]. Neurological evidence from changes in cerebral blood flow velocity and eye movements shows that under the condition of high spatial uncertainty, the cerebral blood flow velocity decreases over time, the blink frequency and the eye closure time increase, indicating that sustained attention tasks with high spatial uncertainty are accompanied by higher levels of fatigue [50]. Therefore, to improve operators' performance in complex systems, spatial uncertainty of signals in sustained attention tasks should be minimized as much as possible.

Other Signal-Related Features. There are other signal-related features that can affect sustained attention performance. Firstly, the goal of the detection in the signal can impact sustained attention performance. When an operator's task involves detecting the occurrence of a certain feature in the signal, their sustained attention performance is generally better than when they are required to check whether a feature is absent in the signal [51–53]. Secondly, when operators need to focus on local features of the signal, their sustained attention performance is better than when they need to focus on overall features of the signal [42]. Functional magnetic resonance imaging (fMRI), positron emission tomography (PET), and cerebral blood flow velocity measurements suggests that sustained attention is dominated by the right hemisphere of the brain, while local feature detection is dominated by the left hemisphere [54–57]. Researchers believe that in sustained attention tasks that require attention to local features, the left and right hemispheres of the brain share the information processing burden, while sustained attention and overall feature detection both place a load on the right hemisphere of the brain [42]. Therefore, focusing on local features may improve sustained attention performance compared to focusing on overall features. Lastly, the motion characteristics of target signals may also affect sustained attention performance. Detecting motion features is almost an automated function for humans and requires little attention processing, but sustained attention performance can decrease under unfavorable conditions [58].

Background Events. Sustained attention tasks typically involve operators detecting target signals in a series of dynamic background events, where the frequency and regularity of background events affect their sustained attention performance. Overall, the response speed and accuracy are negatively correlated with event frequency, and vigilance decrement is more pronounced in high event frequency situations compared to low event frequency situations [47]. The frequency of background events also serves as a moderator for the salience and temporal uncertainty of signals or stimuli, helping operators improve sustained attention [59]. The regularity of background events also affects sustained attention performance. When events occur in a regular manner, operators perform better than when events occur irregularly [60]. These results indicate that sustained attention in complex systems is not only influenced by the characteristics of the signals themselves, but also by the background events in which they occur. Thus, both of them should be considered in sustained attention task design.

Feedback. When operators can receive feedback on their performance, they are more motivated and adjust their state to achieve better performance [26]. This can be effective in the design of sustained attention tasks. It not only carries an informational value but also offers motivational properties capable of influencing learning processes [61]. Providing performance feedback to operators during sustained attention tasks has been found to improve performance in both the testing phase and subsequent formal experimental phases [62].

2.2 Methods Related to Personnel Selection

Due to differences in brain structure and function, individual differences are significant in sustained attention. Research using fMRI has shown that the frontal and parietal regions of the right hemisphere are crucial for sustained attention [63]. Additionally, analysis of the brain cortex's vertical direction using sMRI (structural magnetic resonance imaging) indicates that better sustained attention is associated with increased thickness in the visual, somatosensory, frontal, and parietal cortices [63]. Therefore, individual differences in sustained attention make screening operators before the sustained attention task begins a beneficial way, especially when selecting operators for complex systems.

Researchers have designed several sustained attention tasks to evaluate individuals' ability to sustain attention, most of which rely on sustained external stimuli, such as CPT, AVT, and multitasking platforms like UAS and MATB-II. In recent years, many new experimental paradigms have been developed, such as the gradCPT (gradual-onset CPT) developed by Rosenberg et al. based on the CPT [64]. In this task, a central face stimulus gradually transitions at a constant speed (1200 ms), and participants are required to respond to each male face but not to infrequent target female faces. The innovation of this task is that it can eliminate the exogenous clues of stimulus change signals between trials. Unlike other sustained attention task paradigms, the performance indicator of the gradCPT task is VTC (variance time course), which measures the trial-to-trial variability of reaction time. In this task, periods of very fast or very slow reaction times have been found to be associated with decreased target recognition accuracy [64, 65].

Another sustained attention experimental paradigms include the S-PFT test (a sustained version of the Paced Finger Tapping), in which participants are required to maintain a stable finger tapping rhythm for several minutes [66]. The S-PFT test does not involve any stimulus recognition or detection, so there is no measurement of accuracy, but it allows researchers to estimate the fluctuation of reaction time without external stimuli. Based on the above sustained attention tasks designed in previous studies, we can implement specific procedures for sustained attention testing to select individuals with good ability of sustained attention, enabling them to perform well in scenarios and tasks of complex systems.

2.3 Methods Related to Personnel Training

Although there are individual differences in the ability of sustained attention, performance on sustained attention tasks can be improved through appropriate training. Studies have shown that effective sustained attention training methods include cognitive training directly related to the task, meditation, and action video games [26, 32, 67, 68]. Some of these trainings are believed to improve individuals' attention networks and enhance their cognitive control abilities, known as attention network training. Other trainings aim to enhance individuals' attentional functions by reducing habitual and reactive thoughts, emotions, and behaviors unrelated to the current task, known as attention state training [69, 70]. The remaining part of this section will introduce the two most widely studied types of attention training: meditation and action video games.

Meditation. Conscious meditation is believed to improve mind wandering in sustained attention tasks. The meditative state refers to reaching a state of restful alertness, good awareness, and balance of the body, mind, and environment [70]. Research has found that short-term meditation can prevent the generation of task-unrelated thoughts and reduce the impact of mind wandering on task performance [67]. Longer-term meditation training has a more significant impact on cognitive task performance. Meditation training for about a week enhances working memory and cognitive control, while training for about two weeks significantly reduces the number of task-unrelated thoughts generated during cognitive tasks. Studies on longer-term meditation training have also found positive effects on task performance [69, 71]. In addition, short-term meditation reduces the number of negative thoughts generated, while five weeks of meditation overall reduces the level of anxiety and the number of anxiety episodes [67].

The sustained attention improvement of meditation has been found to be related to the co-regulation of the central nervous system (CNS) and the autonomic nervous system (ANS) in regulating the mind-body state [70]. During and after meditation training, positive changes were observed in physiological indicators of ANS activity, such as heart rate, skin conductance, respiratory rate, and amplitude. Compared to other relaxation activities, meditators had significantly lower levels of heart rates and skin conductance, higher level of abdominal respiratory amplitude, and lower level of chest respiratory rate. Studies based on heart rate variability (HRV) measurements also found a significant increase in high-frequency HRV during meditation training, indicating successful suppression of sympathetic nervous system activity and activation of parasympathetic nervous system activity. In addition, regular meditation training has been shown to affect attention-related neural networks, including sustained attention, emotional regulation, and monitoring performance [67, 72]. Meditators were found to perform better than non-meditators in perceiving complex and ambiguous visual stimuli [73].

Meditation training can be further divided into focused attention and open monitoring [67, 69, 72]. Focused attention meditation requires operators to constantly focus their attention on a target (such as their own breath), which can be seen as a self-regulating attention training [74]. Open monitoring meditation requires operators to feel the emergence and disappearance of thoughts during meditation and seems to be a way to relax the mind. Compared to traditional mindfulness meditation, open monitoring meditation requires less cognitive resource and mainly improves attentional recovery [69]. Focused attention meditation, on the other hand, involves activation of the brain's cognitive control regions, which requires monitoring performance and active regulation of attention and behavior, consistent with the demand for sustained attention [72].

Action Video Games (AVG). Action video games refer to a type of electronic game that involves fast motion and requires vigilant monitoring of visual periphery and simultaneous tracking of multiple targets [75]. Research has found that this type of game has benefits for players' cognitive abilities, such as perception, attention, and cognitive control [76]. Skilled action game players perform better than others in sustained attention and multitasking, with higher signal recognition accuracy, shorter response times, and lower false alarm rates [26, 77]. It is believed that playing action games improves players' visual attention abilities, allowing them to capture and understand more visual items. Therefore, when task-related information appears in the periphery, it is more likely to attract attention and receive the necessary processing [75]. In addition, in Chiappe et al.'s study, operators of the MATB task also performed better in communication tasks, indicating that the benefits of electronic games are not limited to visual forms but can also extend to auditory and other tasks [77]. That is, the general attentional resources are improved through training.

2.4 Methods Related to Process Intervention

Drug and Caffeine Intake. Drugs and caffeine intakes are believed to enhance cognitive abilities, including sustained attention of complex systems. When using drugs for intervention, even small doses can have a significant impact on alertness (such as nootropic, methylphenidate, and modafinil). Studies have shown that nootropics can improve performance in attention, alertness, and memory potential and enhance cognitive function in healthy subjects [78–80]. Methylphenidate and modafinil are used by military personnel who need to stay alert during long-term tasks [81]. These drugs generally improve brain oxygen supply by stimulating neural growth or altering the production of neurochemicals from organs [82]. A study gathered 10 pilots who had been awake for 37 h and asked them to take 100mg of modafinil. Results showed their self-ratings of depression and anger decreased, while their self-ratings of vitality, vigilance, and confidence increased [83]. In a helicopter simulation task, 6 pilots who had been awake for 40 h twice and took 200mg of modafinil reported fewer emotional and vigilance problems than those who took a placebo [84]. Another study found that the performance and vigilance of 50 healthy subjects who took 200mg and 400mg doses of modafinil significantly improved compared to those who took 600mg of caffeine [85]. These empirical findings indicate the promising potential of drugs as an intervention in sustained attention tasks of complex systems.

Drinking coffee to stay vigilant is a daily habit for many people, and its effect on the central nervous system is well known [86, 87]. Many studies have reported that caffeine has a positive impact on sustained attention [26, 88]. However, the duration and degree of this effect may depend on the dose. Low to moderate doses (e.g., 40 mg~300 mg) have been shown to improve operators' accuracy in sustained attention tasks and reduce their response time to stimuli during long-time tasks [89, 90]. High doses (e.g., 500mg), on the other hand, have been shown to impair the performance of healthy participants in attention and vigilance after 45 min of ingestion [91]. There are also individual differences in the reaction to caffeine intake, which are usually attributed to differences in people's daily coffee consumption habits and dosage [92, 93].

Although research suggests that drugs can have a positive effect on improving attention and increasing vigilance, it is still unknown whether these drugs can promote useful task execution in complex systems. Some drugs may have side effects, such as headaches, diarrhea, insomnia, fatigue, tremors, and nausea [94]. Some drugs are not legally approved, and their consumption and intake may be illegal. Overall, more studies are needed to reduce their side effects. As for caffeine intake, its positive effect on improving and maintaining sustained attention is consistent in research, but its impact on higher cognitive functions is still controversial. Although caffeine can improve a person's sustained attention, it may not necessarily help them make the right decisions, which is a crucial step in complex human-machine systems. In addition, excessive caffeine intake may increase the risk of dehydration, cardiovascular dysfunction, headaches, and sleep disorders, making it unsuitable for operators [95].

Sensory Stimulation. Sensory stimulations can help operators improve their attention and arousal levels. Typical sensory stimulations include fragrance, transcranial direct current stimulation (tDCS), haptic stimulation, and auditory beats.

Multiple studies have shown that introducing certain types of fragrance can improve attention and vigilance and reduce stress [96–98]. For example, when scents from peppermint and cinnamon are introduced, operators show improved sustained attention and response times [99, 100]. When comparing odorless conditions with peppermint-scented conditions, participants showed higher accuracy and faster speed in typing task and letter sorting task [101]. In signal detecting tasks, inhaling peppermint or pleasant scents can improve participants' detection performance and accuracy [102]. Also, introducing pleasant scents during driving tasks also improves drivers' sustained attention performance [96]. Furthermore, research based on scent types suggests that peppermint scent can generally promote sustained attention in most studies, while lemon and ylang-ylang scents may have negative effects on operators' sustained attention [103, 104]. Scent concentration and the emotional state caused by the scent can also affect sustained attention. For example, participants show high level of sustained attention under low concentration conditions of cinnamon leaf volatiles, which is believed that low concentration conditions enhance physiological arousal without causing negative emotion that damages the task performance [105].

Transcranial direct current stimulation (tDCS) is a neural regulation technique to enhance sustained attention. The tDCS involves applying a small electric current of 1-2mA to the scalp, which has been shown to be safe for up to 30 min [106]. The tDCS causes changes in neuronal excitability via membrane polarization and alterations of the synaptic strength [107]. Many studies have shown that tDCS can have a positive impact on improving sustained attention in individuals, but this is influenced by factors such as duration, intensity, frequency, electrode position, and control settings [108–111]. For example, when a 1mA current is applied for 10 min to the dorsolateral prefrontal cortex (F3 and F4 positions), participants reported higher levels of sustained attention, along with improved target detection performance and discrimination ability [112]. However, the effectiveness of tDCS can also be affected by task difficulty, individual differences (such as genetics, age, and gender), and baseline variability [113]. Therefore, whether tDCS will become a practical intervention method in sustained attention tasks still needs to be explored.

Music and binaural auditory beats are two typical auditory simulations that can be applied to enhance sustained attention. Studies have shown that playing background music during sustained attention tasks can improve performance, especially when the operator is expected to reach a state of fatigue [26, 114]. The effectiveness of music can also depend on individual preferences and familiarity with the music. Listening to familiar or preferred music can better improve emotions and increase sustained attention, while listening to unfamiliar music may increase the risk of distraction[115]. Binaural auditory beats is related to the binaural beat effect, which refers to the perception of sound coming directly from the depths of the brain when both ears receive music beats with slightly different frequencies. For example, when sound waves with a frequency of less than or equal to 10 Hz are simultaneously given to both ears, the two sound waves are integrated in the brain, resulting in a frequency difference of less than or equal to 10 Hz, which can be called the "third tone." The "third tone" is only perceived by the brain and can be observed through electroencephalogram (EEG) brain waves. Low-frequency binaural beats (8–13 Hz) are usually associated with mental calmness and relaxation, while high-frequency binaural beats (14–30 Hz) are usually associated with sustained attention and concentration [116]. Several studies have shown that binaural beats can help improve people's sustained attention performance [117, 118]. However, it may be difficult for listening to music or binaural beats in complex systems, which limits the application of the auditory stimulation method.

Haptic stimulation has been established as a technique to enhance sustained attention, usually achieved through tactile perception from the skin (e.g., vibration). A typical application of haptic stimulation in driving is deployed in locations (e.g., steering wheel, seat, and pedals) by maintaining continuous contact with the driver's body (e.g., placing hands on the steering wheel) to produce haptic stimulation [119]. These tactile signals are seen as warning signals to alert drivers of impending events or dangers, reminding them to be more attentive. Research has shown that rhythmic 15 Hz signals improves operators' short-term attention, response speed, and accuracy in sustained attention tasks [120]. Similar results have also been found in flight task studies for pilots, where haptic stimulation provides higher detection rates and shorter response times to unexpected events compared to visual stimulation [121]. Although haptic stimulation has great value as an intervention to improve sustained attention, continuous haptic stimulation may interfere with operator performance and increase stress levels because repetitive haptic stimulation may cause discomfort, increase workload, and shift the operator's attention away from the task [26]. In addition, the effects of haptic stimulation are influenced by factors such as age, gender, and skin sensitivity [122]. Therefore, when using haptic stimulation as an intervention for sustained attention tasks, the influence of factors such as tactile type, age, gender, and skin sensitivity should be fully considered.

Cognitive load modulation. Cognitive load modulation has recently been proposed to improve the phenomenon of vigilance decrement in video monitoring tasks. This is achieved by incorporating challenging events (e.g., simulated rainfall) into the primary task, and the results show that operators' sustained attention performance is significantly improved, with shortened response times to stimuli [21]. The essence of this intervention is to increase workload to a certain extent to stimulate participants to invest more attention resources, thereby improving their sustained attention. However, more large-scale studies are needed to further improve the effectiveness of this technique in improving sustained attention.

Rest and Break. By allowing cognitive resources to recover, breaks between tasks can effectively alleviate the pressure and fatigue that arise during sustained attention tasks. Helton et al. studied the changes in task performance after inserting different activities (rest, tasks of the same type, and tasks of different types) during sustained attention tasks[123, 124]. The results showed that task performance after the rest was best and gradually decreased as the overlap between the cognitive resources required for the inserted task and the original task increased. In recent years, more and more research has focused on other types of rest activities, including listening to music, playing electronic games, exercising, and appreciating natural scenery. On the one hand, according to the attention restoration theory, providing stimuli with soft fascination during rest can evoke indirect/involuntary attention, thereby restoring the attention required to complete tasks and relieving cognitive fatigue [125]. On the other hand, providing appropriate stimuli during rest can increase individuals' arousal and enhance brain activity, thereby maintaining their sustained attention to input signals and avoiding performance decline [26]. For example, regardless of the type of music, subjects who had no feeling or negative evaluation of the music they listened to during rest showed a higher miss rate in the task after rest [115]. Like other rest activities, music is also believed to reduce stress and anxiety and regulate mood [115, 126]. Listening to music has low requirements for environment, equipment, and time, making it very easy to implement in various work environments. This makes listening to music a low-cost but effective rest activity. In addition, single sessions of aerobic exercise have been found to have positive behavioral outcomes on sustained attention, selective attention, and directed attention. This means that cognitive task performance improves after exercise, especially with moderate aerobic exercise lasting 20 to 30 min, which has the best enhancing effect on sustained attention in subsequent tasks [127].

3 Summary

Over all, the current review presents a comprehensive review of conventional and unconventional means of enhancement techniques on sustained attention in complex systems. While the findings of most conventional enhancement techniques to date were either solitary or contradictory in nature, modern unconventional enhancement techniques exerted a positive effect on sustained attention, in general. Besides, the effects of enhancement were seemingly influenced by several factors, such as time-on-task and overall experimental protocol, and may not last so long. Additionally, the underlying neural mechanisms are yet to be fully elucidated.

3.1 Task Design

In sustained attention tasks, the design of the task is closely related to the sustained attention performance of the participants. The factors include signal recognition type, perceptual modality, signal salience, temporal uncertainty of signal occurrence, spatial uncertainty of signal occurrence, and background events. Accordingly, in order to improve the performance of participants in sustained attention tasks, each of these factors should be examined and targeted in the task design.

3.2 Personnel Selection

Due to differences in brain structure and function, there are individual differences in sustained attention. Research using functional magnetic resonance imaging has shown that the frontal and parietal regions of the right hemisphere are crucial for sustained attention. Additionally, analysis of the brain cortex's vertical direction using structural magnetic resonance imaging has shown that better sustained attention is associated with increased thickness in the visual, somatosensory, frontal, and parietal cortices. Therefore, individual differences in sustained attention make screening task performers before the task as an important step, especially when selecting operators that have to keep high-level sustained attention for complex systems.

3.3 Personnel Training

Operators' performance in sustained attention tasks can be improved through appropriate training. Research suggests that effective sustained attention training methods include cognitive training directly related to the task, meditation, and action video games. Some of these trainings, such as cognitive training, are believed to improve individuals' attention networks, enhancing their cognitive control abilities, i.e., attention network training.

Other trainings enhance individuals' attentional functioning by reducing habitual and reactive thoughts, emotions, and behaviors unrelated to the current task, i.e., attention state training.

3.4 Process Intervention

Conventional and mundane means of sustained attention enhancement are often well-established techniques and are culturally accepted by societies. They include drug and caffeine intake, sensory stimulation, cognitive load modulation, and rest and break. These elements have been investigated for decades. Their intervention occurs across the wide cognitive domains of memory, perception, attention and understanding. Overall, process intervention is quite potential and promising in enhancing sustained attention in complex systems. The challenges are mainly from the safety, the health, and the cost, which deserves more researches.

4 Future Directions

Based on the present review, a number of aspects should be considered by researchers when investigating the effects of interventions/enhancements on sustained attention. The following section summarizes the future directions in this field.

Firstly, as previously mentioned, there are multiple dimensions to consider when evaluating the target signals and background events of sustained attention tasks. These dimensions collectively contribute to the complexity of sustained attention tasks, which is one of the most confusing issues in this field. Depending on the design of the task, the complexity can be amplified, eliminated, or improved to mitigate alertness decline. Therefore, task complexity is an important factor for sustained, and research is still needed to systematically investigate the different dimensions of task complexity and to improve relevant designs or interventions to enhance operator sustained attention in complex systems.

Secondly, operators in complex systems not only need to focus on a sustained attention task, but also need to deal with other parallel tasks, which forms a scenario of multi-tasking and depletes their cognitive resources, such as nuclear power plants, unmanned aerial systems, and air traffic control systems [14]. Some studies that focus on the complex system have taken two or more tasks into consideration. However, those studies are inadequate. Researchers have to consider the effect of other tasks on sustained attention tasks, which will affect the application of various enhancement methods. Also, more simulated platforms that is prototyped from the real complex system are expected to support the experimental design.

Thirdly, when investigating the effect of various methods for enhancing sustained attention, the experimental tasks are often too simple. Compared to normal control conditions, these simple tasks can lead to habituation and a decline in the effect of the enhancement methods. Therefore, in future research, researchers should choose sustained attention tasks based on complex systems, especially those involving planning, problem-solving, and decision-making, as they reflect sustained attention in complex systems. In addition, some studies have not attempted to link neural activation with task performance, so future research should link these two factors in the analysis.

Acknowledgments. This study received no external funding.

Disclosure of Interests. The authors have no competing interests to declare that are relevant to the content of this article.

References

1. Esterman, M., Rothlein, D.: Models of sustained attention. Curr. Opin. Psychol. **29**, 174–180 (2019)
2. Unsworth, N., Robison, M.K.: Working memory capacity and sustained attention: a cognitive-energetic perspective. J. Exp. Psychol. Learn. Mem. Cognit. **46**, 77 (2020)
3. Brookings, J.B., Wilson, G.F., Swain, C.R.: Psychophysiological responses to changes in workload during simulated air traffic control. Biol. Psychol. **42**, 361–377 (1996)
4. Donald, F.M.: The classification of vigilance tasks in the real world. Ergonomics **51**, 1643–1655 (2008). https://doi.org/10.1080/00140130802327219
5. Körber, M., Cingel, A., Zimmermann, M., Bengler, K.: Vigilance decrement and passive fatigue caused by monotony in automated driving. Procedia Manuf. **3**, 2403–2409 (2015)
6. Reinerman-Jones, L., Matthews, G., Mercado, J.E.: Detection tasks in nuclear power plant operation: vigilance decrement and physiological workload monitoring. Saf. Sci. **88**, 97–107 (2016)
7. Warm, J.S., Parasuraman, R., Matthews, G.: Vigilance requires hard mental work and is stressful. Hum. Factors **50**, 433–441 (2008). https://doi.org/10.1518/001872008X312152
8. Lenartowicz, A., Simpson, G.V., Cohen, M.S.: Perspective: causes and functional significance of temporal variations in attention control. Front. Hum. Neurosci. **7**, 381 (2013)
9. Gartenberg, D., Gunzelmann, G., Hassanzadeh-Behbaha, S., Trafton, J.G.: Examining the role of task requirements in the magnitude of the vigilance decrement. Front. Psychol. **9**, 1504 (2018)
10. Temple, J.G., Warm, J.S., Dember, W.N., Jones, K.S., LaGrange, C.M., Matthews, G.: The effects of signal salience and caffeine on performance, work-load, and stress in an abbreviated vigilance task. Hum. Factors **42**, 183–194 (2000). https://doi.org/10.1518/001872000779656480
11. Craig, C.M., Klein, M.I.: The abbreviated vigilance task and its attentional contributors. Hum. Factors **61**, 426–439 (2019)
12. Helton, W.S., Russell, P.N.: Working memory load and the vigilance decrement. Exp. Brain Res. **212**, 429–437 (2011)
13. Helton, W.S., Russell, P.N.: Visuospatial and verbal working memory load: effects on visuospatial vigilance. Exp. Brain Res. **224**, 429–436 (2013)
14. Laarni, J.: Multitasking and interruption handling in control room operator work. In: Human Factors in The Nuclear Industry, pp. 127–149. Elsevier (2021)
15. Wohleber, R.W., et al.: Vigilance and automation dependence in operation of multiple Unmanned Aerial Systems (UAS): a simulation study. Hum. Factors **61**, 488–505 (2019). https://doi.org/10.1177/0018720818799468
16. Hsu, B.-W., Wang, M.-J.J., Chen, C.-Y., Chen, F.: Effective indices for monitoring mental workload while performing multiple tasks. Percept. Mot. Skills **121**, 94–117 (2015). https://doi.org/10.2466/22.PMS.121c12x5

17. Atchley, P., Chan, M.: Potential benefits and costs of concurrent task engagement to maintain vigilance: a driving simulator investigation. Hum. Factors **53**, 3–12 (2011). https://doi.org/10.1177/0018720810391215

18. Cao, S., Liu, Y.: Concurrent processing of vehicle lane keeping and speech comprehension tasks. Accid. Anal. Prev. **59**, 46–54 (2013). https://doi.org/10.1016/j.aap.2013.04.038

19. McManus, B., Heaton, K., Stavrinos, D.: Commercial motor vehicle driving performance: an examination of attentional resources and control using a driving simulator. J. Exp. Psychol. Appl. **23**(2), 191–203 (2017). https://doi.org/10.1037/xap0000120

20. Steinborn, M.B., Huestegge, L.: Phone conversation while processing information: chronometric analysis of load effects in everyday-media multitasking. Front. Psychol. **8**, 896 (2017). https://doi.org/10.3389/fpsyg.2017.00896

21. Bodala, I.P., Li, J., Thakor, N.V., Al-Nashash, H.: EEG and eye tracking demonstrate vigilance enhancement with challenge integration. Front. Hum. Neurosci. **10**, 273 (2016)

22. Gupta, A., Bhushan, B., Behera, L.: Short-term enhancement of cognitive functions and music: a three-channel model. Sci. Rep. **8**, 15528 (2018)

23. Lutz, A., Slagter, H.A., Rawlings, N.B., Francis, A.D., Greischar, L.L., Davidson, R.J.: Mental training enhances attentional stability: neural and behavioral evidence. J. Neurosci. **29**, 13418–13427 (2009)

24. Szalma, J., Daly, T., Teo, G., Hancock, G., Hancock, P.: Training for vigilance on the move: a video game-based paradigm for sustained attention. Ergonomics **61**, 482–505 (2018)

25. Telles, S., Gupta, R.K., Verma, S., Kala, N., Balkrishna, A.: Changes in vigilance, self-rated sleep and state anxiety in military personnel in India following yoga. BMC. Res. Notes **11**, 1–5 (2018)

26. Al-Shargie, F., Tariq, U., Mir, H., Alawar, H., Babiloni, F., Al-Nashash, H.: Vigilance decrement and enhancement techniques: a review. Brain Sci. **9**, 178 (2019). https://doi.org/10.3390/brainsci9080178

27. Clayton, M.S., Yeung, N., Kadosh, R.C.: The roles of cortical oscillations in sustained attention. Trends Cogn. Sci. **19**, 188–195 (2015)

28. Li, F., Chen, C.-H., Lee, C.-H., Feng, S.: Artificial intelligence-enabled non-intrusive vigilance assessment approach to reducing traffic controller's human errors. Knowl.-Based Syst. **239**, 108047 (2022)

29. Sanchis, C., Blasco, E., Luna, F.G., Lupiáñez, J.: Effects of caffeine intake and exercise intensity on executive and arousal vigilance. Sci. Rep. **10**, 8393 (2020)

30. Schallhorn, C.S.: Vigilance aid use and aircraft carrier landing performance in pilots of tactical aircraft. Aerosp. Med. Hum. Perform. **91**, 518–524 (2020)

31. Tamanani, R., Muresan, R., Al-Dweik, A.: Estimation of driver vigilance status using real-time facial expression and deep learning. IEEE Sens. Lett. **5**, 1–4 (2021)

32. Ueberholz, R.Y., Fiocco, A.J.: The effect of a brief mindfulness practice on perceived stress and sustained attention: does priming matter? Mindfulness **13**, 1757–1768 (2022)

33. Parasuraman, R.: Memory load and event rate control sensitivity decrements in sustained attention. Science **205**, 924–927 (1979). https://doi.org/10.1126/science.472714

34. Caggiano, D.M., Parasuraman, R.: The role of memory representation in the vigilance decrement. Psychon. Bull. Rev. **11**, 932–937 (2004)

35. Warm, J.S., Dember, W.N.: Tests of vigilance taxonomy (1998)

36. Szalma, J.L., et al.: Effects of sensory modality and task duration on performance, workload, and stress in sustained attention. Hum. Factors **46**, 219–233 (2004)

37. Galinsky, T.L., Warm, J.S., Dember, W.N., Weiler, E.M., Scerbo, M.W.: Sensory alternation and vigilance performance: the role of pathway inhibition. Hum. Factors **32**, 717–728 (1990)

38. Buckner, D.N., MC Grath, J.J.: A Comparison of Performances on Single and Dual Sensory Mode Vigilance Tasks. Human Factors Research Inc., Los Angeles (1961)

39. Doll, T.J., Hanna, T.E.: Enhanced detection with bimodal sonar displays. Hum. Factors **31**, 539–550 (1989)
40. Skrypchuk, L., Langdon, P., Sawyer, B.D., Mouzakitis, A., Clarkson, P.J.: Enabling multitasking by designing for situation awareness within the vehicle environment. Theor. Issues Ergon. Sci. **20**, 105–128 (2019)
41. Skrypchuk, L., Langdon, P., Sawyer, B.D., Clarkson, P.J.: Unconstrained design: improving multitasking with in-vehicle information systems through enhanced situation awareness. Theor. Issues Ergon. Sci. **21**, 183–219 (2020)
42. Helton, W.S., Hayrynen, L., Schaeffer, D.: Sustained attention to local and global target features is different: performance and tympanic membrane temperature. Brain Cogn. **71**, 9–13 (2009)
43. Warm, J.S., Loeb, M., Alluisi, E.A.: Variations in watch keeping performance as a function of the rate and duration of visual signals. Percept. Psychophysics **7**, 97–99 (1970)
44. Szalma, J.L.: Workload and stress in vigilance: the impact of display format and task type. Am. J. Psychol. **124**, 441–454 (2011)
45. Bennett, K.B., Flach, J.M.: Display and Interface Design: Subtle Science, Exact Art. CRC Press (2011)
46. Wickens, C.: Attention: theory, principles, models and applications. Int. J. Hum.-Comput. Interact. **37**, 403–417 (2021)
47. Warm, J.S., Finomore, V.S., Vidulich, M.A., Funke, M.E.: Vigilance: a perceptual challenge (2015)
48. Griffin, J.A., Dember, W.N., Warm, J.S.: Effects of depression on expectancy in sustained attention. Motiv. Emot. **10**, 195–205 (1986)
49. Helton, W.S., Weil, L., Middlemiss, A., Sawers, A.: Global interference and spatial uncertainty in the Sustained Attention to Response Task (SART). Conscious. Cognit. **19**, 77–85 (2010)
50. Funke, M.E., et al.: The neuroergonomics of vigilance: effects of spatial uncertain-ty on cerebral blood flow velocity and oculomotor fatigue. Hum. Factors **59**, 62–75 (2017)
51. Finomore, V.S., Shaw, T.H., Warm, J.S., Matthews, G., Boles, D.B.: Viewing the workload of vigilance through the lenses of the NASA-TLX and the MRQ. Hum. Factors **55**, 1044–1063 (2013). https://doi.org/10.1177/0018720813484498
52. Hollander, T.D., et al.: Feature presence/absence modifies the event rate effect and cerebral hemovelocity in vigilance performance. In: Presented at the Proceedings of the Human Factors and Ergonomics Society Annual Meeting (2004)
53. Quinlan, P.T.: Visual feature integration theory: past, present, and future. Psychol. Bull. **129**, 643 (2003)
54. Helton, W.S., et al.: The abbreviated vigilance task and cerebral hemodynamics. J. Clin. Exp. Neuropsychol. **29**, 545–552 (2007)
55. Langner, R., Eickhoff, S.B.: Sustaining attention to simple tasks: a meta-analytic review of the neural mechanisms of vigilant attention. Psychol. Bull. **139**, 870 (2013)
56. Sarter, M., Givens, B., Bruno, J.P.: The cognitive neuroscience of sustained attention: where top-down meets bottom-up. Brain Res. Rev. **35**, 146–160 (2001)
57. Warm, J.S., Matthews, G., Parasuraman, R.: Cerebral hemodynamics and vigilance performance. Mil. Psychol. **21**, S75–S100 (2009)
58. Parasuraman, R., et al.: Detecting threat-related intentional actions of others: effects of image quality, response mode, and target cuing on vigilance. J. Exp. Psychol. Appl. **15**, 275 (2009)
59. Parasuraman, R., Warm, J.S., Dember, W.N.: Vigilance: Taxonomy and utility. In: Mark, L.S., Warm, J.S., Huston, R.L. (eds.) Ergonomics and human factors, pp. 11–32. Springer New York, New York, NY (1987). https://doi.org/10.1007/978-1-4612-4756-2_2

60. Shaw, T., Finomore, V., Warm, J., Matthews, G.: Effects of regular or irregular event schedules on cerebral hemovelocity during a sustained attention task. J. Clin. Exp. Neuropsychol. **34**, 57–66 (2012)

61. Kluger, A.N., DeNisi, A.: The effects of feedback interventions on performance: a historical review, a meta-analysis, and a preliminary feedback intervention theory. Psychol. Bull. **119**, 254 (1996)

62. Teo, G.W., Schmidt, T.N., Szalma, J.L., Hancock, G.M., Hancock, P.A.: The effects of feedback in vigilance training on performance, workload, stress and coping. In: Presented at the Proceedings of the Human Factors and Ergonomics Society Annual Meeting (2013)

63. Mitko, A., et al.: Individual differences in sustained attention are associated with cortical thickness. Hum. Brain Mapp. **40**, 3243–3253 (2019). https://doi.org/10.1002/hbm.24594

64. Rosenberg, M., Noonan, S., DeGutis, J., Esterman, M.: Sustaining visual attention in the face of distraction: a novel gradual-onset continuous performance task. Atten. Percept. Psychophys. **75**, 426–439 (2013). https://doi.org/10.3758/s13414-012-0413-x

65. Fortenbaugh, F.C., DeGutis, J., Esterman, M.: Recent theoretical, neural, and clinical advances in sustained attention research. Ann. N. Y. Acad. Sci. **1396**, 70–91 (2017). https://doi.org/10.1111/nyas.13318

66. Petilli, M.A., Trisolini, D.C., Daini, R.: Sustained-paced finger tapping: a novel approach to measure internal sustained attention. Front. Psychol. 9 (2018)

67. Feruglio, S., Matiz, A., Pagnoni, G., Fabbro, F., Crescentini, C.: The impact of mindfulness meditation on the wandering mind: a systematic review. Neurosci. Biobehav. Rev. **131**, 313–330 (2021). https://doi.org/10.1016/j.neubiorev.2021.09.032

68. Rupp, M.A., Sweetman, R., Sosa, A.E., Smither, J.A., McConnell, D.S.: Searching for affective and cognitive restoration: examining the restorative effects of casual video game play. Hum. Factors **59**, 1096–1107 (2017). https://doi.org/10.1177/0018720817715360

69. Lymeus, F., Lindberg, P., Hartig, T.: Building mindfulness bottom-up: meditation in natural settings supports open monitoring and attention restoration. Conscious. Cogn. **59**, 40–56 (2018). https://doi.org/10.1016/j.concog.2018.01.008

70. Rothbart, M.K., Posner, M.I.: The developing brain in a multitasking world. Dev. Rev. **35**, 42–63 (2015). https://doi.org/10.1016/j.dr.2014.12.006

71. MacLean, K.A., et al.: Intensive Meditation training improves perceptual discrimination and sustained attention. Psychol. Sci. **21**, 829–839 (2010). https://doi.org/10.1177/0956797610371339

72. Brandmeyer, T., Delorme, A., Wahbeh, H.: Chapter 1 - The neuroscience of meditation: classification, phenomenology, correlates, and mechanisms. In: Srinivasan, N. (ed.) Progress in Brain Research, pp. 1–29. Elsevier (2019). https://doi.org/10.1016/bs.pbr.2018.10.020

73. Boccia, M., Piccardi, L., Guariglia, P.: The meditative mind: a comprehensive meta-analysis of MRI studies. Biomed. Res. Int. **2015**, 1–11 (2015). https://doi.org/10.1155/2015/419808

74. Weng, H.Y., et al.: Focus on the breath: brain decoding reveals internal states of attention during meditation. Front. Hum. Neurosci. **14**, 336 (2020)

75. Green, C.S., Bavelier, D.: Action video game modifies visual selective attention. Nature **423**, 534–537 (2003). https://doi.org/10.1038/nature01647

76. Bediou, B., Adams, D.M., Mayer, R.E., Tipton, E., Green, C.S., Bavelier, D.: Meta-analysis of action video game impact on perceptual, attentional, and cognitive skills. Psychol. Bull. **144**, 77 (2018)

77. Chiappe, D., Conger, M., Liao, J., Caldwell, J.L., Vu, K.-P.L.: Improving multi-tasking ability through action videogames. Appl. Ergon. **44**, 278–284 (2013). https://doi.org/10.1016/j.apergo.2012.08.002

78. Greely, H., et al.: Towards responsible use of cognitive-enhancing drugs by the healthy. Nature **456**, 702–705 (2008)

79. Kim, D.: Practical use and risk of modafinil, a novel waking drug. Environ. Health Toxicol. **27**, (2012)

80. Turner, D.C., Robbins, T.W., Clark, L., Aron, A.R., Dowson, J., Sahakian, B.J.: Cognitive enhancing effects of modafinil in healthy volunteers. Psychophar-macology. **165**, 260–269 (2003)

81. Repantis, D., Schlattmann, P., Laisney, O., Heuser, I.: Modafinil and methylphenidate for neuroenhancement in healthy individuals: a systematic review. Pharmacol. Res. **62**, 187–206 (2010)

82. Husain, M., Mehta, M.A.: Cognitive enhancement by drugs in health and disease. Trends Cogn. Sci. **15**, 28–36 (2011)

83. Caldwell, J.A., Caldwell, J.L., Smith, J.K., Brown, D.L.: Modafinil's effects on simulator performance and mood in pilots during 37 h without sleep. Aviat. Space Environ. Med. **75**, 777–784 (2004)

84. Caldwell, J.A., Caldwell, J.L., Smyth, N.K., Hall, K.K.: A double-blind, placebo-controlled investigation of the efficacy of modafinil for sustaining the alertness and performance of aviators: a helicopter simulator study. Psychopharmacology **150**, 272–282 (2000)

85. Wesensten, N., Belenky, G., Kautz, M.A., Thorne, D.R., Reichardt, R.M., Bal-kin, T.J.: Maintaining alertness and performance during sleep deprivation: modafinil versus caffeine. Psychopharmacology **159**, 238–247 (2002)

86. Cappelletti, S., Daria, P., Sani, G., Aromatario, M.: Caffeine: cognitive and physical performance enhancer or psychoactive drug? Curr. Neuropharmacol. **13**, 71–88 (2015)

87. Porciúncula, L.O., Sallaberry, C., Mioranzza, S., Botton, P.H.S., Rosemberg, D.B.: The Janus face of caffeine. Neurochem. Int. **63**, 594–609 (2013)

88. Kamimori, G.H., McLellan, T.M., Tate, C.M., Voss, D.M., Niro, P., Lieberman, H.R.: Caffeine improves reaction time, vigilance and logical reasoning during extended periods with restricted opportunities for sleep. Psychopharmacology **232**, 2031–2042 (2015)

89. Kilpeläinen, A.A., Huttunen, K.H., Lohi, J.J., Lyytinen, H.: Effect of caffeine on vigilance and cognitive performance during extended wakefulness. Int. J. Aviat. Psychol. **20**, 144–159 (2010)

90. Lanini, J., Galduróz, J.C.F., Pompéia, S.: Acute personalized habitual caffeine doses improve attention and have selective effects when considering the fractionation of executive functions. Hum. Psychopharmacol. Clin. Exp. **31**, 29–43 (2016)

91. Frewer, L., Lader, M.: The effects of caffeine on two computerized tests of attention and vigilance. Hum. Psychopharmacol. Clin. Exp. **6**, 119–128 (1991)

92. Evans, S.M., Griffiths, R.R.: Caffeine tolerance and choice in humans. Psychopharmacology **108**, 51–59 (1992)

93. Fillmore, M.T.: Investigating the behavioral effects of caffeine: the contribution of drug-related expectancies. Pharmacopsychoecologia (1994)

94. Talih, F., Ajaltouni, J.: Probable nootropicinduced psychiatric adverse effects: a series of four cases. Innov. Clin. Neurosci. **12**, 21 (2015)

95. Temple, J.L., Bernard, C., Lipshultz, S.E., Czachor, J.D., Westphal, J.A., Mestre, M.A.: The safety of ingested caffeine: a comprehensive review. Front. Psych. **8**, 80 (2017)

96. Baron, R.A., Kalsher, M.J.: Effects of a pleasant ambient fragrance on simulated driving performance: the sweet smell of... safety?. Environ. Behav. **30**, 535–552 (1998)

97. Heuberger, E., Ilmberger, J.: The influence of essential oils on human vigilance. Nat. Prod. Commun. 5, 1934578X1000500919 (2010)

98. Milotic, D.: The impact of fragrance on consumer choice. J. Consum. Behav. An Int. Res. Rev. **3**, 179–191 (2003)

99. Parasuraman, R., Warm, J., Dember, W.: Effects of olfactory stimulation on skin conductance and event-related potentials during visual sustained attention. Progress Report1992 (1992)

100. Raudenbush, B., Grayhem, R., Sears, T., Wilson, I.: Effects of peppermint and cinnamon odor administration on simulated driving alertness, mood and work-load. N. Am. J. Psychol. **11**, 245 (2009)

101. Herz, R.S.: Influences of odors on mood and affective cognition. Olfaction taste cognition. **160**, 177 (2002)

102. Jones, K., Ruhl, R., Warm, J., Dember, W.: Olfaction and vigilance: the role of hedonic value. Autom. Technol. Hum. Perform. Curr. Res. Trends. **6**, 193 (1999)

103. Gould, A., Martin, G.N.: 'A good odour to breathe?' The effect of pleasant ambient odour on human visual vigilance. Appl. Cognit. Psychol. Official J. Soc. Appl. Res. Mem. Cognit. **15**, 225–232 (2001)

104. Moss, M., Hewitt, S., Moss, L., Wesnes, K.: Modulation of cognitive performance and mood by aromas of peppermint and ylang-ylang. Int. J. Neurosci. **118**, 59–77 (2008)

105. Matsubara, E., et al.: Volatiles emitted from the leaves of Laurus nobilis L. improve vigilance performance in visual discrimination task. Biomed. Res. **32**(1), 19–28 (2011). https://doi.org/10.2220/biomedres.32.19

106. Bikson, M., Datta, A., Elwassif, M.: Establishing safety limits for transcranial direct current stimulation. Clin. Neurophysiol. Official J. Int. Fed. Clin. Neurophysiol. **120**, 1033 (2009)

107. Arul-Anandam, A.P., Loo, C.: Transcranial direct current stimulation: a new tool for the treatment of depression? J. Affect. Disord. **117**, 137–145 (2009)

108. Gonzalez, P.C., Fong, K.N.K., Brown, T.: The effects of transcranial direct current stimulation on the cognitive functions in older adults with mild cognitive impairment: a pilot study. Behav. Neurol. **2018**, 1–14 (2018)

109. McKinley, R.A., Bridges, N., Walters, C.M., Nelson, J.: Modulating the brain at work using noninvasive transcranial stimulation. Neuroimage **59**, 129–137 (2012)

110. Schuijer, J.W., De Jong, I.M., Kupper, F., Van Atteveldt, N.M.: Transcranial electrical stimulation to enhance cognitive performance of healthy minors: a complex governance challenge. Front. Hum. Neurosci. **11**, 142 (2017)

111. Simonsmeier, B.A., Grabner, R.H., Hein, J., Krenz, U., Schneider, M.: Electrical brain stimulation (tES) improves learning more than performance: a meta-analysis. Neurosci. Biobehav. Rev. **84**, 171–181 (2018)

112. Nelson, J.T., McKinley, R.A., Golob, E.J., Warm, J.S., Parasuraman, R.: Enhancing vigilance in operators with prefrontal cortex transcranial direct current stimulation (tDCS). Neuroimage **85**, 909–917 (2014). https://doi.org/10.1016/j.neuroimage.2012.11.061

113. Hsu, T.-Y., Juan, C.-H., Tseng, P.: Individual differences and state-dependent responses in transcranial direct current stimulation. Front. Hum. Neuro-Sci. **10**, 643 (2016)

114. Ünal, A.B., Steg, L., Epstude, K.: The influence of music on mental effort and driving performance. Accid. Anal. Prev. **48**, 271–278 (2012)

115. Baldwin, C.L., Lewis, B.A.: Positive valence music restores executive control over sustained attention. PLoS ONE **12**, e0186231 (2017). https://doi.org/10.1371/journal.pone.0186231

116. Vernon, D.: Human Potential: Exploring Techniques Used to Enhance Human Performance. Routledge (2009)

117. Lane, J.D., Kasian, S.J., Owens, J.E., Marsh, G.R.: Binaural auditory beats affect vigilance performance and mood. Physiol. Behav. **63**, 249–252 (1998)

118. Reedijk, S.A., Bolders, A., Colzato, L.S., Hommel, B.: Eliminating the attentional blink through binaural beats: a case for tailored cognitive enhancement. Front. Psych. **6**, 82 (2015)

119. Gaffary, Y., Lécuyer, A.: The use of haptic and tactile information in the car to improve driving safety: a review of current technologies. Front. ICT **5**, 5 (2018)

120. Zhang, S., Wang, D., Afzal, N., Zhang, Y., Wu, R.: Rhythmic haptic stimuli improve short-term attention. IEEE Trans. Haptics **9**, 437–442 (2016)

121. Arrabito, G.R., Ho, G., Aghaei, B., Burns, C., Hou, M.: Effects of vibrotactile stimulation for sustaining performance in a vigilance task: a pilot study. In: Presented at the Proceedings of the Human Factors and Ergonomics Society Annual Meeting (2011)

122. Kalisch, T., Kattenstroth, J.-C., Kowalewski, R., Tegenthoff, M., Dinse, H.R.: Cognitive and tactile factors affecting human haptic performance in later life. PLoS ONE 7, e30420 (2012)

123. Helton, W.S., Russell, P.N.: Rest is best: the role of rest and task interruptions on vigilance. Cognition 134, 165–173 (2015). https://doi.org/10.1016/j.cognition.2014.10.001

124. Helton, W.S., Russell, P.N.: Rest is still best: the role of the qualitative and quantitative load of interruptions on vigilance. Hum. Factors 59, 91–100 (2017). https://doi.org/10.1177/001 8720816683509

125. Kaplan, S.: The restorative benefits of nature: toward an integrative frame-work. J. Environ. Psychol. 15, 169–182 (1995). https://doi.org/10.1016/0272-4944(95)90001-2

126. Knight, W.E.J., Rickard, N.S.: Relaxing music prevents stress-induced increases in subjective anxiety, systolic blood pressure, and heart rate in healthy males and females. J. Music Ther. 38, 254–272 (2001). https://doi.org/10.1093/jmt/38.4.254

127. de Fernandes, M., Sousa, A., Medeiros, A.R., Del Rosso, S., Stults-Kolehmainen, M., Boullosa, D.A.: The influence of exercise and physical fitness status on attention: a systematic review. Int. Rev. Sport Exerc. Psychol. 12, 202–234 (2019). https://doi.org/10.1080/175 0984X.2018.1455889

Commanding Consumers' Visual Attention: Enhancement and Attenuation

Minqian Yang[1], Xin Lei[1,2], and Pei-Luen Patrick Rau[1(✉)]

[1] Department of Industrial Engineering, Tsinghua University, Beijing 100084, China
`rpl@tsinghua.edu.cn`
[2] School of Management, Zhejiang University of Technology, Zhejiang Province,
Hangzhou 310014, China

Abstract. Visual salience method has been proven to be an effective way to emphasize important visual information. This study designed and evaluated six visualization approaches based on two techniques of utilizing visual salience. Three of them used enhancement techniques to enhance useful information—enlarging, light background, highlight frame. The other three used attenuation techniques to attenuate distracting information—shrinking, shadowing, and covering. An experimental visual searching task simulating online shopping was designed to evaluate these visualization approaches using the eye-tracking method. The evaluation assessed three aspects: performance, eye workload and subjective experience. The results showed different degrees of significant reduction in completion time and saccade frequency for the six visualization approaches compared to the control approach. Light background, highlight frame and covering approaches all performed well in reducing completion time and eye saccade frequency, thus also received the most positive subjective ratings. Shrinking and enlarging performed not well and received the most negative ratings. The results also indicated that some approaches of attenuation (shrinking and covering) would perform better for information presentation under complicated searching conditions. Our findings can be utilized as a guideline for online shopping interface design.

Keywords: Human-computer interaction · Interaction design · Visual salience · Visualization design and evaluation

1 Introduction

Online shopping is a popular method of consumption because of price transparency and convenience [1], benefiting from its information capacity and web page flexibility. Despite the advantages offered by the internet, consumers are forced to face overwhelming information daily [2]. Information overload can lead to irrational decision-making which can lead to negative consequences [3]. The proper organization and presentation of information is important for decision makers. If current presentation cannot be modified, visualizations can assist in information searching and processing.

© The Author(s), under exclusive license to Springer Nature Switzerland AG 2024
P.-L. P. Rau (Ed.): HCII 2024, LNCS 14700, pp. 270–284, 2024.
https://doi.org/10.1007/978-3-031-60901-5_19

The visual salience effect occurs when an object has a unique feature that distinguishes it from the background, such as color, luminance, size, etc. [4]. This can affect people's attention allocation resources [5] particularly where graphic information is concerned [6]. Previous studies have separately investigated different visualizations that implement visual salience, such as highlighting, covering up, and changing size. A recent study has revealed that a website link's color salience influences users' attention and affective experience [7]. As visual design has been proved essential for consumers' attitudes toward e-commerce, exploring more salience approaches is necessary for the interface design of shopping websites [4].

This study aimed to explore the application of visual salience through a visual searching task simulating online shopping for healthier food product, including ameliorating products that meet nutritional requirements and diluting those that do not. In this way, the visual salience method was utilized from two aspects: enhancing useful information and attenuating distracting information. Three visualization approaches were designed for each of the two aspects. The scenario of this experiment was inspired by the social tendency of eating healthily, since studies had shown that displaying nutrition information before customers buy or eat food could help them make healthier choices [8]. The six visualization approaches were evaluated through three metrics: improving search performance, decreasing eye workload, and promoting subjective experience. Our findings improved the understanding of the visual salience effect, determined how different visualizations influence users and helped streamline the interface design for shopping webpages and applications.

2 Theoretical Background

2.1 Information Overload and Visual Salience Approach

Information overload occurs when people with limited cognitive resources are overwhelmed by too much information and cannot process all of it. Studies have shown that when faced with overly complex problems in a limited time frame, people tend to allocate their attention to specific information to simplify their decision-making process [9–11]. They tend to restructure the original problem and selectively allocate attention resources to accomplish the task [12]. The restructuring process includes information transformation, rearrangement, and deletion. Visual salience provides a practical approach to help restructure information to avoid information overload. Salience refers to the phenomenon in which one's attention is directed to the portions of the environment [13]. The most salient information items are most likely to be acquired and tended to first, especially when the information is represented graphically [6]. This study classified visualization saliency into two aspects: enhancing useful information (for transformation and rearrangement) and attenuating distracting information (for deletion). Still and Still [14] showed that the application of visual salience could increase search efficiency in complex displays under realistic, goal-driven task conditions, including reducing reaction time and scan path. Salience was realized through product label and target image in the study, which could both be classified into the "enhancement" category. However, Schroder, Driver [15] developed an inverted U model explaining the relationship between the amount of information and its utilization, which suggested an optimal level of information for decision-makers. Streufert, Clardy [16] also found that people required certain load conditions when integrating data and making decisions, which meant there existed an optimal number of alternatives when consumers made choices [17]. These results indicated that it is necessary to attenuate distracting information in complex conditions, while adding or strengthening information in simple conditions to achieve optimal utilization.

Former studies proposed some different approaches to realize salience through both enhancement and attenuation, such as highlighting, covering up, and changing the picture size. Highlighting emphasized the target, thus affecting the way people allocate their attention [18]. Hard highlights drew boxes around the target regions, and soft highlights enhanced light regions of the visual field [19]. Julier, Livingston [20] proposed a method of filtering information on augmented reality devices by suppressing irrelevant information. Codispoti and De Cesarei [21] showed that using larger pictures could result in more persistent memories [22]. These approaches of saliency were all studied in different studies without a comparison. This study systematically evaluated the effect of different salience approaches utilizing both enhancement and attenuation methods.

A visual searching task was used in this study, referring to the method of Still and Still [14]. On the one side, since all the methods of visualization saliency were designed to help people restructure information, thus all of them could improve users' searching performance. On the other side, since enhancement and attenuation were aimed to help different aspects of restructuring information process, they could have different degrees of effect on improving searching performance. Also, we assumed that attenuation would be better for challenging tasks, while enhancement would be better for easy tasks. Therefore, Hypothesis 1 was proposed as:

- **H1.1** All the visualization approaches adopting enhancement and attenuation can improve search performance and user experience.
- **H1.2** The visualization approaches adopting enhancement and attenuation have different degrees of improvement on search performance and user experience.
- **H1.3** Attenuation approaches perform better on improving performance in difficult tasks than in easy tasks.
- **H1.4** Enhancement approaches perform better on improving performance in easy tasks than in difficult tasks.

2.2 Eye Movement and Workload

Major eye movement indicators include saccade, fixation, pupil state, and blink time [23]. Many studies have suggested eye movement indirectly reflects mental workload [24, 25]. Fixation and saccades were the most common indicators. The fixation state is the maintenance of the visual gaze on a single location, which represent the attention to that position and obtain information [26]. de Greef, Lafeber [27] found that fixation duration increased with the mental workload. A saccade is a rapid conjugate eye movement that shifts the center of gaze from one part of the visual field to another. It has been confirmed that a high frequency of saccade means more muscle movement and more visual fatigue [28]. As the workload increases, faster and more frequent saccades are required to process information.

In this study, we also applied the eye-tracking method to evaluate users' workload. As mentioned in Sect. 2.1, visual salience helped people focus on the target more quickly, thus could reduce eye movement and therefore decrease mental workload. We used saccade times and fixation duration as main metrices. Due to the different principles enhancement and attenuation have on helping people process information, we hypothesized that they had different effects on reducing eye workload:

- **H2.1** All the visualization approaches adopting enhancement and attenuation can reduce eye workload.
- **H2.2** The visualization approaches adopting enhancement and attenuation have different degrees of reduction on eye workload.

3 Methods

3.1 Experiment Design

The experiment was to evaluate different visualization approaches on the efficiency and user experience to get consumers' attention when searching for satisfying products during online shopping. The main dependent variable was the visualization approach, while task difficulty was also taken into consideration.

The experiment used a within-sections design with repeated measures. Each experiment consisted of seven sections made up of six sections of salience visualization approaches and a blank control section. There were 12 tasks for each section, each containing four tasks for each of the three difficulty levels (seven visualization approaches × three difficulty levels × four tasks). Each participant needed to complete 84 searching tasks in total, and none of them was repeated. The order of the twelve tasks in each section was random. A Latin square design was adopted to exclude the influence of section order, generating seven order groups.

3.2 Materials and Tasks

The experimental tasks were set based on an online food shopping scenario, through which we aimed to guide consumers to buy healthy food. On each shopping page, 15 food products with a (3 rows × 5 columns) grid layout were presented. The image of each product was laid in one cell, next to which some other information was provide in text, including basic information such as the net content, production date, price, and the nutrition information such as GI and the content of all kinds of nutrients per 100 g such as carbohydrate, protein, fat, NSP, etc. To increase the diversity of the task, the kind of information provided might be different on different task pages. An example of product information cell and task page is shown in Fig. 1. The platform used for the user interface design was Mockplus[1](version 3.6.2.1). It was a practical software to create interactive prototypes for mobile and web.

This study applied the methods of enhancement and attenuation to present the images of products and the relative information to help consumers lock on the target more easily. In the pages that applied enhancement method, there were 6 to 8 products out of the

---

[1] https://www.mockplus.cn/.

15 products were enhanced, among which must contain the target. In the pages that applied attenuation method, there were 6 to 8 products out of the 15 products were attenuated, among which mustn't contain the target. This simulate the situations during online shopping that several candidates meeting requirements were picked out (or the ones that don't meet were excluded) by the website, so that the consumer only need to make the final decision. The reason not to present only the candidates is to save the integrity of information, so that consumers can also catch a glimpse of other products in case that they change their mind. Referring to the visualization in the literature, the two methods were designed into six specific approaches. Enhancement included light background, highlight frame, and size enlarging. Light background applied light green color background with 80% opacity to highlight relevant objects, while highlight frame applied dark green bold frames around them. Enlarging increased the image and font size of objects by 30%. Attenuation included covering, shadowing, and size shrinking. Covering used heavily colored area at 100% opacity to cover some irrelevant goods, while shadowing used 80% opacity. Opposite to enlarging, shrinking reduced the image and font size of objects by 30%. The overview of the visualizations is shown in Fig. 2.

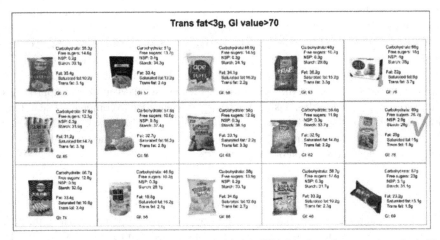

Fig. 1. An example of the searching task page (level 2 difficulty, from the control section). The green tick on the right side shows the target of this page.

The task was to find the only one target product that meet the search requirements on top of each page. The requirements were set according to the information we provided, aiming to lead consumers to food that contains less fat, less sugar, more protein and more NSP. Only when choosing the right answer can they reach the next page. If choosing the wrong one, they will get a warning for re-choosing. There were three difficulty levels for searching tasks, which were distinguished by the number of requirement conditions. For level 1, only one searching condition was required. For level 2 there were two, and for level 3 there were three conditions.

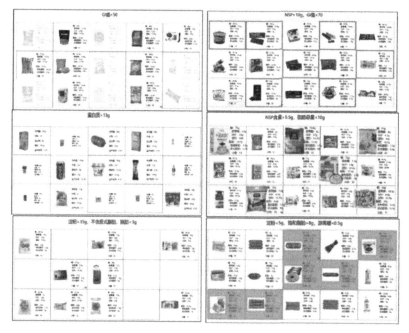

Fig. 2. The Overview of the salience visualizations in the experiment. The three in the left column are attenuation pages: shadowing, shrinking, covering (from up to down). The three in the right column are enhancement pages: highlight frame, enlarging, light background (from up to down).

3.3 Measures

This study adopted three main dimensions to evaluate the visualizations for the searching tasks: performance, eye movement, and subjective ratings: 1) **Performance.** The performance was evaluated according to two metrics: completion time and the number of errors. The completion time of a task refers to the total time from the task page was open till it was completed. The number of errors of a task refer to the total counts of choosing the wrong product before the right answer. During the experiment, clicking behavior data were recorded using a Python ver3.8 program for mouse listening. 2) **Eye movement.** The eye movement data in this study was evaluated according to two metrics: saccade frequency and fixation duration. The saccade frequency of a task was defined as the saccade times per second during the task (times per second, from the task page was open till it was completed). The fixation duration of a task referred to the mean of the lasting time of all the fixations during the task. For each participant, one section of visualization contained twelve tasks including four for each difficult level. We then calculated the mean of the data of the four tasks at the same level, which generated a sequence of three numbers for each metric in performance and eye movement for each visualization. 3) **Subjective ratings.** Subjective ratings for a visualization were collected using questionnaires on the laptop as soon as the twelve searching tasks in this section were finished. The five metrics evaluated were liking, perceived usability, degree of concentration and task load. Task load consisted of six items from the NASA-TXL and one item about the perceived difficulty. The evaluation of perceived liking, usability, degree of concentration consisted of several items, respectively, as is shown in Table 1.

Table 1. Questionnaire items for subjective ratings with the reversed items marked (R)

Liking (1 ~ 7)	Please score for the way of presentation in the task section I'd like to continue using the way of presentation for other tasks I was satisfied with the way of presentation in the task section
Perceived Usability (1 ~ 7)	I think this way of presentation can effectively weaken irrelevant information I think this way of presentation can effectively strengthen useful information This way of presentation made the search task simpler This way of presentation helped me find the target more quickly This way of presentation distracted me during the task (R) This way of presentation improved my efficiency This way of presentation increased difficulty of the task (R)
Degree of Concentration (1 ~ 7)	With this way of presentation, I could focus on the useful information With this way of presentation, I got distracted by irrelevant information (R) I had a high level of concentration during the task I lost my concentration during the task (R)
Task Load (1 ~ 7)	How difficult do you think the task in the section is?
	[Mental demands] How much mental effort (thinking, making decisions, calculating, remembering, searching, etc.) is required to complete the task?
	[Physical demand] How much physical effort (pushing, pulling, turning, controlling, moving, etc.) did you take to complete the task?
	[Time requirement] How much confusion did time pressure cause for you to complete the task?
	[Performance Level] How satisfied are you with the results you have achieved in the tasks?
	[Effort level] How much effort did you put into completing the task?
	[Frustration level] How frustrated or annoyed were you during the task?

3.4 Experiment Equipment

The experimental lab was equipped with two laptops: one was for the researcher to control the eye tracker, and the other one was for the participants to complete the visual search tasks. The laptop for the task had a 32 × 18 cm screen. The vertical viewing distance of the participants was about 50 cm. The eye-tracker used in this experiment was Tobii Pro Glass 2, a wearable eye-tracking tool with a 100-Hz sampling rate (Tobii Technology, 2018). The Tobii Controller software (version 1.25) was used to control the eye tracker. Eye movement data was stored on an SD card and exported using Tobii Pro Lab software.

3.5 Participants

The sample size was calculated using the G Power method by R (version 4.0.5). We chose a medium effect size f $= 0.3$, setting the Type I error rate α as 0.05 and the statistical power (1-β) as 0.8. In this way, a minimal sample size of twenty-three of was required for this seven-block experiment. To make the result more convincing, we recruited forty undergraduate Chinese college students as participants. Among which four participants' eye movement data were eliminated because of calibration problems. The final number of valid data points was thirty-six, including eighteen males and eighteen females. They were randomly assigned to the seven groups generated by Lain-square mentioned in Sect. 3.1. Sixteen participants were under the age of 21 years, seventeen were between 22 and 24 years, and the other three were over 25 years old.

3.6 Procedure

Upon arrival, participants were told about the detailed task rules and procedure of the experiment. After completing a questionnaire for demographic information, they wore the eye tracker and performed the calibration. The calibration was done using the single-point method. Then, they would do all the following tasks on the experiment laptop. There were five practice task pages at the beginning to ensure the participants had fully understood the task. They were free to ask any question during this stage. After that, the formal experimental process containing seven sections began. Participants needed to follow the instructions on the laptop screen and finish the subjective evaluation questionnaire every time a task section was finished. After the experiment, there was a brief interview containing several simple questions: "Which was your favorite visualization? Why? Which was your least favorite visualization? Why?" The whole experiment took approximately 40–50 min, during which participants would wear the Tobii eye tracker. Each participant was paid around ¥50.

3.7 Data Analysis

Data in this study were processed and analyzed using Python (version 3.8) and R (version 4.0.5). For performance and subjective ratings, data were recorded directly as required. For eye movement, raw data were initially processed through a Python program to count saccade counts and calculate the fixation duration for further analysis. The data of performance time, error and eye movement were all proved to fit normality using the Shapiro-Wilks test ($\alpha = 0.05$). Repeated-measures ANOVA was the main method to test the hypotheses. Post-hoc test was also used for further comparison with Bonferroni adjustment for p-value. For subjective ratings, the consistency of items in each metric were tested using the Cronbach's α. Most of the subjective ratings data didn't fit normality, so the Kruskal-Wallis test and the Dunn test (p-value adjustment method: Bonferroni) were used for analysis.

4 Results

4.1 Performance

Completion Time. The ANOVA results showed that the main effects of visualization approach (F (3.8, 133.6) = 43.93, p < .001), difficulty level (F (1.6, 57.7) = 296.13, p < .001) and the interaction effect of visualization and difficulty (f (7.4, 260.4) = 9.39, p < .001) were all significant. firstly, the completion time of difficult level 1 was significantly shorter than level 2 (p < .001), the completion time of difficult level 2 was significantly shorter than level 3 (p < .001). secondly, the results of one-sided post-hoc test showed that the completion time of all the visualization sections was significantly shorter than the blank control section (all p < .001) except for shrinking (p = 0.145). the completion time of enlarging was significantly shorter than shrinking (p = 0.0015), while neither the difference between shadowing and enlarging nor between shadowing and shrinking was significant. the completion time of light background was significantly shorter than all the other visualization sections (all p < .001) except for highlight frame (p = 0.077). the completion time of highlight frame was significantly shorter than all the other visualization sections (all p < .001) except for covering (p = 0.051) and light background (p = 0.077). the completion time of covering was significantly shorter than all the other visualization sections (all p < .001) except for highlight frame (p = 0.051) and light background(p = 0.145). the distribution of completion time is demonstrated in Fig. 3. There also existed an interaction effect, which caused the different results of significance when conducting pairwise t-tests in three groups of different levels. in level 1, only the completion time of light background section was significant shorter than others (p < .001), while the other visualization sections almost have no difference except that they were all shorter than the control group. in level 2, the completion time of highlight frame section also became significantly shorter than others as the light background (all p < .001). while in level 3, the completion time all the visualization approaches were significantly shorter than the blank control group including shrinking. also, the completion time of covering also became significantly shorter (p < .05) in level 3.

Number of Errors. The ANOVA results didn't show any significant result the number of errors among the seven sections since most of the participants made no mistake (thirty out of thirty-six). neither did the interactions between task difficulty.

4.2 Eye Movement

Saccade Frequency. The ANOVA results showed that the main effect of visualization approach (F (3.8, 132.8) = 3.23, p = 0.016) and difficulty level (F (1.5, 54.0) = 3.75, p = 0.042) was significant, while the interaction effect was not significant. post-hoc tests showed that the saccade frequency of difficult level 3 was significantly more than level 1 and level 2 (p < .01). as for visualization approaches, one-sided post-hoc tests showed that only the saccade frequency of enlarging is significantly more than light background(P < .001), Covering (P = 0.008) and Highlight Frame (P = 0.021). The saccade frequency of light background was also significantly less than the blank control section (p = 0.015), shadowing (p = 0.009), shrinking (p = 0.007), as is shown in

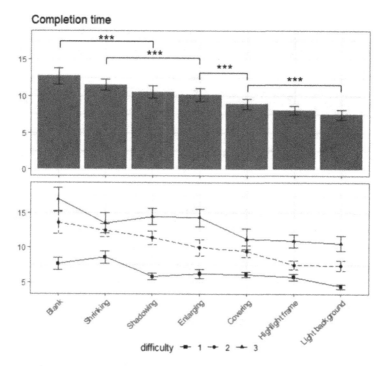

Fig. 3. The completion time of different visualization approaches and difficulty levels (*p < 0.05, **p < 0.01, ***p < 0.001)

Fig. 4. Overall, light background always performed significantly well, and the enlarging performed the worst. but when the task became difficult, covering and shrinking went forward, although the difference was not significance.

Fixation Duration. The ANOVA results didn't show any significant result the fixation duration among the seven sections. neither did the interactions between task difficulty.

Subjective Ratings

The Cronbach's α of each metric was firstly calculated after the reversed items being reversed: liking (0.959), usability (0.957), degree of concentration (0.845), task load (0.672). The results indicated a good consistency, thus the average of the containing items' score was used for the following analysis of each metric.

Kruskal-Willias test showed significant difference on liking, perceived usability, degree of concentration and task load (p < .001). The results of Dunn test showed that for liking, perceived usability, and degree of concentration, the difference between light background, highlight frame and covering was not significant, while the difference between blank, enlarging, and shrinking was also not significant, but the difference between these two groups was significant (all p < 0.001). The ratings of shadowing didn't show a significant difference compared to either group. For the task load, the significant

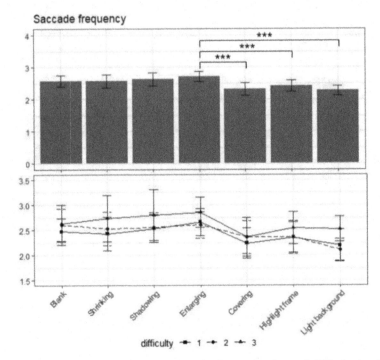

Fig. 4. The saccade frequency of different visualization approaches and difficulty levels (*p < 0.05, **p < 0.01, ***p < 0.001)

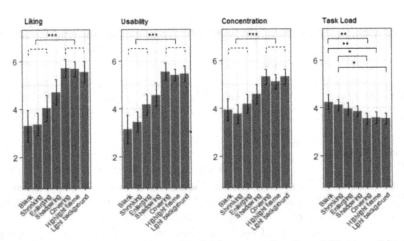

Fig. 5. The subjective ratings of different visualization approaches (*p < 0.05, **p < 0.01, ***p < 0.001)

difference was only found between blank and covering, blank and highlight frame, shrinking and covering, shrinking and light background ($p < 0.05$). The comparisons of these metrics are shown in Fig. 5.

5 Discussion and Conclusion

This study focuses on enhancement and attenuation, the two main methods of the visual salience approach. Three visualizations are designed and evaluated for each method. The evaluation dimensions include participants' performance, eye workload, and subjective ratings based on a visual searching experiment simulating online shopping.

Compared to the blank section, completion time is significantly reduced for all other sections except for shrinking, and there existed significant difference in completion time among the six visualization approaches. Participants reported significantly higher likeness, perceived usability and degree of concentration for light background, highlight frame and covering than shrinking, enlarging and the blank approaches. Also, the perceived task load of light background, highlight frame and covering was significantly lower than some other approaches. **H1.1** and **H1.2** were mostly supported. Shrinking wasn't helpful when the difficulty level of the task was 1 or 2. However, it was observed that the performance of shrinking and covering increased significantly when task difficulty reached level 3. This indicated that attenuation could become more helpful when the task is complex. **H1.3** was partially supported. However, the performance of enhancement approaches stayed well in both easy and difficult tasks. Thus, **H1.4** was not supported. Saccade frequency was significantly reduced for the light background section compared to all other sections. The covering and highlight frame also showed significant reduction compared to enlarging. **H2.1** and **H2.2** were not fully supported. Fixation duration didn't show significant differences. Neither the number of errors nor the fixation duration showed significant differences among the visualization sections, which is consistent with the conclusions of Still and Still [14].

In summary, the approaches of light background, highlight frame, and covering have better performance in this experiment than other approaches, including improving participants' searching performance, reducing their eye workload and getting better subjective ratings. Light background always performed the best for all the evaluation metrics. Fifteen out of the thirty-six participants chose the light background as their favorite. Participants noted it was "the most conspicuous," "the easiest to notice," and "easy to distinguish from irrelevant information." The theories of covert attention can explain this. A large area of color provided a cued location that allowed participants to select visual information even without eye movement, granting priority to processing that information [29]. Also, the dark green, bold highlighting frame performed well. It provided a cue similar to the light background but was not that conspicuous. Results showed that as task difficulty increased, relative saccade times in the highlight frame became less than in the light background, which can be explained by its clarity. When the amount of information increased, the highlight frame had less interference, while the large color area of the light background looked obscured. Participants said it was "both obvious and clear," "simple and effective," and "had less disturbance." Last but not least, covering also showed promising results, making it the best in the attenuating section.

Fifteen out of thirty-six participants chose covering as their favorite aspect. It directly reducing the amount of information, making the tasks more manageable. Participants said that it "directly narrow down" and "effectively removed irrelevant information." However, in a practical scenario, the decision to cover information should be carefully considered, as it might impair information integrity.

The other three approaches got worse results both on objective and subjective metrices. Shadowing made irrelevant obscured, thus receiving less attention. The participants' reviews of shadowing were different. Some said it "effectively weakened the irrelevant information," while others said "it did not help much since the irrelevant information can still be seen." In general, it is a relatively effective approach in the attenuating section. Shrinking and enlarging consistently yielded the poorest results. Thirteen out of thirty-six participants chose shrinking as their least favorite, and ten chose enlarging. Although they were shown to help improve performance and eye movement data, participants felt they were of little help in filtering information. Common feedback included: "It's messy and intrusive," "It's not easy to tell which is bigger and which is smaller," "The different sizes make the interface cluttered and unclear," and "Enlarging made me annoyed." This is evident in the saccade times of shrinking, which exceeded even those in the blank section, hence the saccade times of enlarging when the difficulty level was three. This meant that shrinking did not make irrelevant information unnoticeable while enlarging was visually disruptive when information was complex.

It was worth mentioning that shrinking and covering both showed a slight increase in reducing searching time as tasks became more complex. This could be explained by the information utilization curve [15, 30]. When information processing becomes complicated, attenuating saves users from overloading. Enhancing, however, might make people more overwhelmed when the information volume exceeds the optimal level.

This study had some limitations. Firstly, our participants were all college students, which decreased the diversity of the sample. Secondly, our tasks were all goal-driven searching tasks, excluding other tasks such as browsing. Thirdly, the task difficulty in this study was distinguished only by changing the number of requirement conditions, regardless of the amount of product information. Further studies should explore the interactions between the amount of information provided and visualization methods. Furthermore, the visualizations for visual salience were limited, and more approaches should be designed and evaluated.

Disclosure of Interests. The Authors Have no Competing Interests to Declare that Are Relevant to the Content of This Article.

References

1. Yang, J., Zhao, H., Wan, J.: Research on the advantages and disadvantages of online shopping and corresponding strategies. In: 2010 International Conference on E-Product E-Service and E-Entertainment. IEEE (2010)
2. Holton, A.E., Chyi, H.I.: News and the overloaded consumer: factors influencing information overload among news consumers. Cyberpsychol. Behav. Soc. Netw. **15**(11), 619–624 (2012)
3. Driver Michael, J., Mock Theodore, J.: Human information processing, decision style theory, and accounting information systems. Account. Rev. **50**(3), 490–508 (1975)

4. Wang, Y.D., Emurian, H.H.: Trust in e-commerce: consideration of interface design factors. J. Electron. Comm. Organ. (JECO) 3(4), 42–60 (2005)
5. Wolfe, J.M., Cave, K.R., Franzel, S.L.: Guided search: an alternative to the feature integration model for visual search. J. Exp. Psychol. Hum. Percept. Perform. 15(3), 419 (1989)
6. Jarvenpaa Sirkka, L.: Graphic displays in decision making—the visual salience effect. J. Behav. Decis. Mak. 3(4), 247–262 (1990)
7. Cao, Y., Proctor, R.W., Ding, Y., Duffy, V.G., Zhang, Y., Zhang, X.: Influences of color salience and location of website links on user performance and affective experience with a mobile web directory. Int. J. Hum. Comp. Interact. 37(6), 547–559 (2021)
8. Flaherty, S.J., McCarthy, M.B., Collins, A.M., McAuliffe, F.M.: A different perspective on consumer engagement: exploring the experience of using health apps to support healthier food purchasing. J. Market. Manage. 35(3–4), 310–337 (2019)
9. Keller, K.L., Staelin, R.: Effects of quality and quantity of information on decision effectiveness. J. Consum. Res. 14(2), 200–213 (1987)
10. Shields, M.D.: Effects of information supply and demand on judgment accuracy: evidence from corporate managers. Account. Rev. 58, 284–303 (1983)
11. Sundström Gunilla, A.: Information search and decision making: the effects of information displays. Acta Physiol (Oxf.) 65(2), 165–179 (1987)
12. Payne John, W., Bettman James, R., Johnson Eric, J.: Behavioral decision research: a constructive processing perspective. Annu. Rev. Psychol. 43(1), 87–131 (1992)
13. Taylor, S.E, Thompson, S.C: Stalking the elusive" vividness" effect. Psychol. Rev. 89(2), 155 (1982)
14. Still, J., Still, M.: Influence of visual salience on webpage product searches. ACM Trans. Appl. Percept. (TAP) 16(1), 1–11 (2019)
15. Schroder, H.M., Driver, M.J., Streufert, S.: Human Information Processing: Individuals and Groups Functioning in Complex Social Situations, Holt, Rinehart and Winston (1967)
16. Streufert, S., Clardy, M.A., Driver, M.J., Karlins, M., Schroder, H.M., Suedfeld, P.: A tactical game for the analysis of complex decision making in individuals and groups. Psychol. Rep. 17(3), 723–729 (1965)
17. Malhotra Naresh, K.: Information load and consumer decision making. J. Consum. Res. 8(4), 419–430 (1982)
18. Freer Timothy, W., Ulissey Michael, J.: Screening mammography with computer-aided detection: prospective study of 12,860 patients in a community breast center. Radiology 220(3), 781–786 (2001)
19. Kneusel Ronald, T., Mozer Michael, C.: Improving human-machine cooperative visual search with soft highlighting. ACM Trans. Appl. Percept. (TAP) 15(1), 1–21 (2017)
20. Simon, J., Livingston, M.A., Edward Swan II, J.E., Baillot, Y., Brown, D.: Adaptive user interfaces in augmented reality. In: Workshop on Software Technology for Augmented Reality Systems (STARS) (2003)
21. Codispoti, M., De Cesarei, A.: Arousal and attention: picture size and emotional reactions. Psychophysiology 44(5), 680–686 (2007)
22. Huh H.-J.L.: The Effect of Newspaper Picture Size on Readers' Attention, Recall, and Comprehension of Stories (1993)
23. Zhan, Z., Zhang, L., Mei, H., Fong, P.S.W.: Online learners' reading ability detection based on eye-tracking sensors. Sensors 16(9), 1457 (2016)
24. Feng, C., Wanyan, X., Yang, K., Zhuang, D., Wu, X.: A comprehensive prediction and evaluation method of pilot workload, technology and health care 26(S1), 65–78 (2018)
25. May James, G., Kennedy Robert, S., Williams Mary, C., Dunlap William, P., Brannan Julie, R.: Eye movement indices of mental workload. Acta Physiol. (Oxf) 75(1), 75–89 (1990)
26. Kenneth, H., Marcus, N., Andersson, R., Dewhurst, R., Jarodzka, H., Van de Weijer, J.: Eye Tracking: A Comprehensive Guide to Methods and Measures, OUP Oxford (2011)

27. de Greef, T., Lafeber, H., van Oostendorp, H., Lindenberg, J.: Eye movement as indicators of mental workload to trigger adaptive automation. In: Schmorrow, D.D., Estabrooke, I.V., Grootjen, M. (eds.) International Conference on Foundations of Augmented Cognition. 2009. Springer, Heidelberg (2009) https://doi.org/10.1007/978-3-642-02812-0_26

28. Billones Robert, K.C., et al.: Digital eye strain and fatigue recognition using electrooculogram signals and ultrasonic distance measurements. In: 2018 IEEE 10th International Conference on Humanoid, Nanotechnology, Information Technology, Communication and Control, Environment and Management (HNICEM). IEEE (2018)

29. Carrasco, M., McElree, B.: Covert attention accelerates the rate of visual information processing. Proc. Nat. Acad. Sci. **98**(9), 5363–5367 (2001)

30. Streufert, S., Suedfeld, P., Driver Michael, J.: Conceptual structure, information search, and information utilization. J. Personal. Soc. Psychol. **2**(5), 736 (1965)

The Impact of Media Multitasking Behavior Among College Freshmen on Information Processing: A Study Based on Academic Performance

Yongmei Zhang[1,2,3], Ting Tao[1,2(✉)], Wenbin Gao[1,2], Ligang Wang[1,2], and Chunlei Fan[1,2]

[1] Key Laboratory of Mental Health, Institute of Psychology, Chinese Academy of Sciences, Beijing 100101, China
taot@psych.ac.cn

[2] Department of Psychology, University of Chinese Academy of Sciences, Beijing 100049, China

[3] School of Mechanical Engineering, University of Science and Technology Beijing, Beijing 100083, China

Abstract. Objective: To explore the impact of media multitasking behavior on the depth of information processing by analyzing the relationship between media multitasking behavior and academic performance of college freshmen in terms of ecological validity. Method: A total of 178 college freshmen were selected, and the media multitasking index was measured using a media usage questionnaire. The heavy media multitasking behavior group (HMM) and light media multitasking behavior group (LMM) were selected, and the differences in demographic information, mobile phone usage, and academic performance in the college entrance examination, professional courses, and public courses between the HMM and LMM groups were analyzed and compared. Result: There was no significant difference in demographic information, mobile phone usage, and college entrance examination scores between the HMM and LMM groups, as well as subjective and objective scores in professional courses. However, there was a significant difference in objective scores in public courses ($P < 0.05$), and there was a marginal difference in subjective scores in public courses, all of which were lower in the HMM group than in the LMM group. Long term media multitasking behavior can weaken individuals' ability to deeply process information and affect the academic performance of college students. Innovation: There has been limited research on the impact of media multitasking behavior on information processing in the past. This study starts from the perspective of ecological validity, analyzes the differences in the impact of media multitasking behavior on the academic performance of college freshmen in professional and public courses, and concludes the relationship between media multitasking behavior and information processing. That is, the more media multitasking behavior, the shallower the individual's information processing level.

Keywords: Media multitasking behavior · Information processing · Academic performance

P.-L. P. Rau (Ed.): HCII 2024, LNCS 14700, pp. 285–294, 2024.
https://doi.org/10.1007/978-3-031-60901-5_20

1   Introduction

1.1   A Subsection Sample

With the rapid development of information technology, media products such as smart-phones and portable computers are constantly evolving, and new technologies such as big data, artificial intelligence, and mobile internet are widely used. These hardware devices and technological means are integrated with each other, bringing great conve-nience to people's learning, work, and life. Individuals can access the internet more conveniently through various media such as mobile phones and computers, achieving seamless switching of media functions such as learning, work, entertainment, and social media. Media multitasking behavior is becoming a new way of life for the younger generation.

Media multitasking behavior refers to participating in multiple media activities simultaneously, such as reading e-books while listening to music, or replying to emails while making voice calls [1]. Research data shows that college students are an impor-tant group of people who use media for multitasking operations [2]. Due to the needs of scientific research and learning, college students often use various media forms in a short period of time, such as instant messaging apps, electronic games, online videos, etc. These media forms provide rich social, entertainment, and information resources for college students. They can browse, comment, and reply to social media on multi-ple different media simultaneously to maintain contact with friends and classmates, or to more efficiently obtain and utilize information, while browsing multiple web pages, search engines, and databases for information filtering and integration.

Media multitasking behavior refers to participating in multiple media activities simultaneously, such as reading e-books while listening to music, or replying to emails while making voice calls [1]. Research data shows that college students are an impor-tant group of people who use media for multitasking operations [2]. Due to the needs of scientific research and learning, college students often use various media forms in a short period of time, such as instant messaging apps, electronic games, online videos, etc. These media forms provide rich social, entertainment, and information resources for college students. They can browse, comment, and reply to social media on multi-ple different media simultaneously to maintain contact with friends and classmates, or to more efficiently obtain and utilize information, while browsing multiple web pages, search engines, and databases for information filtering and integration.

Media multitasking behavior is changing the learning situation of college students. Compared to the elderly, college students switch their attention more frequently between different media and maintain their attention more briefly [3]. When individuals develop the habit of diverting their attention to multiple types of information and cannot elim-inate the influence of irrelevant stimuli in the environment, it can affect information processing and memory. The field of cognitive psychology places great emphasis on the role of working memory in complex psychological abilities such as learning and reasoning [4]. During the learning process, college students need to memorize a large number of knowledge points and concepts. Working memory can help them quickly absorb information in the classroom and also help them quickly extract the necessary knowledge points in exams. In addition, working memory can help students establish connections between different disciplines, promote interdisciplinary thinking and learning. Therefore, frequent media multitasking behavior causes college students to exhibit more distracting behaviors in their studies, leading to a decline in working memory and thus affecting their academic performance. Experiments have shown that the use of instant messaging tools by young people in the classroom significantly leads to a decrease in the accuracy of completing exam questions [5].

At present, university courses are divided into professional courses and public courses. Professional courses are mandatory courses that must be studied and mastered in this subject, which are related to mastering skills and abilities as well as future employment prospects. They are usually more than ten interrelated courses, each of which accounts for a relatively high number of credits and corresponding learning hours. Public courses are courses that students of any major must study, with the main purpose of cultivating talents with comprehensive development in morality, intelligence, physical fitness, aesthetics, and labor skills, and providing methodology for learning. Generally, public courses are not closely related to each other and are not within the scope of their respective majors, making them relatively novel for college students. In terms of evaluating academic performance, the types of exam questions in the final exam of the course are divided into objective questions and subjective questions. Objective questions specifically refer to multiple-choice questions, while subjective questions include non-multiple-choice questions such as fill in the blank questions, short answer questions, essay questions, material questions, answer questions, essay questions, etc. From the perspective of information processing, objective questions test the re recognition of correct knowledge among several options, which belongs to surface processing, while subjective questions re test the depth of students' understanding of the problem and their ability to apply knowledge, with more components of deep processing [6].

Based on the above discussion, this study speculates that long-term media multitasking behavior will reduce the academic performance of college students and weaken their ability to deeply process information. Therefore, based on a media usage questionnaire survey, this study focuses on college students and analyzes the impact of media multitasking behavior on information processing ability by comparing their academic performance in the college entrance examination, professional courses, and public courses.

2 Object and Method

2.1 Object

Selecting freshmen majoring in engineering from a certain engineering university in Beijing as subjects, a questionnaire survey was conducted on a class basis, and 178 valid questionnaires were collected. Among them, there are 148 males and 30 females.

2.2 Tools

General Situation Survey Form. Including gender, place of origin, and college entrance examination scores.

Media Use Questionnaire (MUQ). The media use questionnaire developed by Ophir et al. and revised by Yang Xiaohui et al. [7] was used to measure media multitasking behavior. This questionnaire measures the media multitasking situation of 12 different forms of daily activities, namely ① print media, ② television, ③ computer video, ④ music, ⑤ non-music audio, ⑥ electronic games, ⑦ making phone calls, ⑧ instant messaging software, ⑨ sending text messages, ⑩ email, 11 browsing web pages, and 12 other computer applications. The participants first answered the total amount of time they spent on a certain primary media activity per week, and then answered the frequency of using other secondary media while using the primary media. There were four options: most of the time, sometimes, very little time, and never.

Media Multitasking Index (MMI): assigns a value to each answer option in the matrix, with "most of the time" assigned as 1, "sometimes" assigned as 0.67, "very little time" assigned as 0.33, and "never" assigned as 0. The MMI calculation formula is as follows:

$$MMI = \sum_{i=1}^{n} \frac{m_i \times h_i}{h_{total}}$$

where n = 12, m_i refers to the frequency of using other media while using the main media i; h_i refers to the total weekly usage time of the main media i (in hours); h_{total} refers to the total weekly usage time of all major media. The higher the MMI value, the higher the level of media multitasking.

Academic performance. There are three indicators for academic performance, including the college entrance examination (Gaokao) score, the final exam score for one major course and one public course in the first semester of university, where the final exam score records both objective and subjective questions.

2.3 Statistical Methods

SPSS 22 was used for statistical analysis of the data, with x ± s representing mean and standard deviation. T-tests and univariate analysis were performed on the data, and p < 0.05 was considered statistically significant.

3 Results

The mean MMI of 178 college students is 2.98, with a standard deviation of 2.34. Heavy media multitaskers (HMM) are defined as those with MMI scores higher than one standard deviation (2.98 + 2.34 = 5.32), and light media multitaskers (LMM) are defined as those with MMI scores lower than one standard deviation (2.98–2.34 = 0.64). According to statistics, there are 32 people in the HMM group and 24 people in the LMM group.

3.1 Comparison of Demographic Information Between HMM and LMM Groups

The chi-square test was conducted on the gender composition of the two groups of participants, as shown in Fig. 1. It can be concluded that $\chi^2 = 3.26$ and $p = 0.196$. The results indicate that there is no significant difference in the gender composition between the two groups of participants.

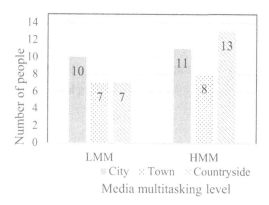

Fig. 1. Gender comparison.

A chi-square test was conducted to classify the source areas of the two groups of participants, as shown in Fig. 2. It can be concluded that $\chi 2 = 0.929$ and $p = 0.92$. The results indicate that there was no significant difference in the source areas (city, town, countryside) between the two groups of participants.

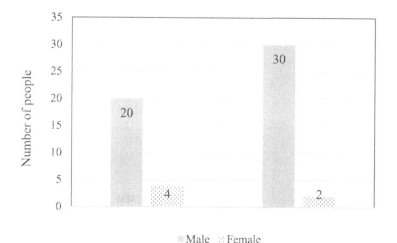

Fig. 2. Comparison of Hometowns.

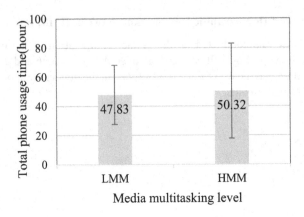

(a)

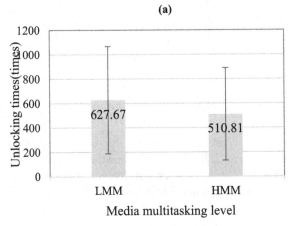

(b)

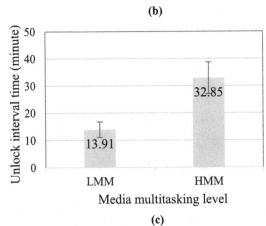

(c)

Fig. 3. **(a-c)** Comparison of mobile phone usage between HMM group and LMM group participants.

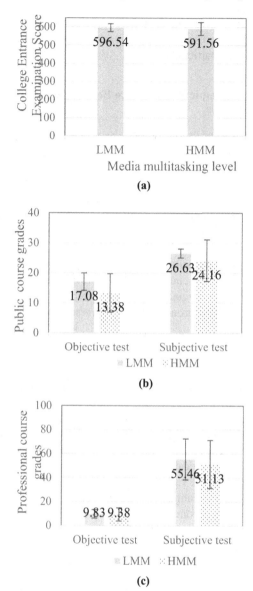

Fig. 4. (a-c) Comparison of academic performance between HMM group and LMM group participants.

3.2 Comparison of Mobile Phone Usage Between HMM Group and LMM Group

An independent sample t-test was conducted on the total duration of mobile phone usage, the number of phone unlocks within the past 7 days, and the unlocking interval between the two groups of participants. As shown in Fig. 3(a-c), obtained: the total usage time of the phone in the past 7 days was t = 0.329, $p = 0.743$, the number of unlocks within

7 days was t $= 1.067, p = 0.291$, and the unlocking interval was t $= -0.805, p = 0.424$. The results showed that there was no significant difference in these three indicators between the two groups of participants.

3.3 Comparison of Academic Performance Between HMM Group and LMM Group

Conduct independent sample t-tests on the scores of the HMM and LMM groups in the college entrance examination, professional courses, and public courses. As shown in Fig. 4(a-c), obtained: college entrance examination score t $= 0.611, p = 0.543$, objective question score t $= 0.360, p = 0.721$ for professional courses, subjective question score t $= 0.853, p = 0.397$ for professional courses, objective question score t $= 2.636, p = 0.011$ for public courses, subjective question score t $= 1.710, p = 0.093$ for public courses. The results showed that there was no significant difference in the scores of the college entrance examination, subjective and objective questions in professional courses between the two groups of participants. There is a significant difference in the scores of objective questions in public courses, with the HMM group performing worse than the LMM group. There is a marginal significant difference in subjective test scores in public courses, with the HMM group performing worse than the LMM group.

4 Discussion

Through analysis, it was found that basic demographic information such as gender and place of origin of the participants did not have an impact on media multitasking behavior. Before the college entrance examination, students have heavy academic tasks, and even if there is media multitasking behavior, the frequency may not be high, which has little impact on them. The results of this study also indicate that there is no significant difference in the college entrance examination scores between the HMM group and the LMM group, indicating that the various situations of the participants in the initial state are homogeneous and can be compared in the future.

After the college entrance examination, students have ample time. Even if they enter university, their academic tasks are relatively easier than in high school, and they have full control over their media usage rights. After a summer and a semester of media multitasking behavior accumulation, there was a difference in final exam scores. In terms of academic performance in public courses, the HMM group had poorer objective test scores than the LMM group. The reason behind this may be that objective questions are all multiple-choice questions, and compared to subjective questions, they rely more on whether the subjects have clearly remembered this information. But the reality is that when we need to know the specific details of a certain information, we usually turn to search engines for help. Sparrow et al.'s research shows that due to the convenience of using multimedia to search for information, people tend to use various search engines when encountering difficulties. When they want to retrieve this information later, they will have a harder time recalling the information itself [4]. In practice, we know the name of a concept and where to find its relevant information, but other specific information cannot be extracted from memory because it has not been deeply processed. In terms of subjective questions, the HMM group participants also scored lower than the LMM group participants, which is consistent with our previous expectations. This result indicates that long-term experience in media multitasking behavior does to some extent weaken individuals' ability to deeply process information and lower their academic performance.

In terms of academic performance in professional courses, the results of this study indicate that there is no significant difference between the HMM group and the LMM group, indicating that the performance of the subjects in professional courses is not affected by media multitasking behavior experience. This result is different from the change in grades in public courses, which may be due to the fact that the subjects do not only learn this professional course, but also have other professional courses at the same time. Other professional courses may have a certain promoting effect on the subjects' understanding of the chosen professional course. In addition, the number of courses in professional courses is also higher. Through the staggered arrangement and extraction exercises in the relevant professional course settings, all participants have accumulated professional knowledge in terms of quantity, whether active or passive, and achieved a certain depth of processing and understanding of the professional course, thereby promoting effective learning [8]. Therefore, there was no difference in academic performance in professional courses at the end of the semester.

5 Conclusion

The above research indicates that in public courses for college students, which mainly focus on testing their accurate memory, long-term media multitasking behavior leads to damage to individual short-term memory through frequent switching of different media content, making it difficult to maintain memory and understanding of information for a long time, and unable to process information at a deeper level, thereby weakening the individual's ability to process information deeply. Therefore, it has a negative impact on the academic performance of college students in public courses. However, due to the alternation of courses and practice arrangements, professional courses have increased the accumulation of learning and improved the depth of information processing and understanding among college students. Therefore, long-term media multitasking behavior has not had a significant impact on the academic performance of professional courses.

Acknowledgments. This study was funded by the National Natural Science Foundation of China (grant number 62107038).

Disclosure of Interests. The authors have no competing interests to declare that are relevant to the content of this article.

References

1. Wallis, C: The impacts of media multitasking on children's learning and development: report from a research seminar. In: The Joan Ganz Cooney Center at Sesame Workshop, New York (2010)

Exploring Preferences for Temporal and Spatial Frame in Navigation Context

Yanqing Zhu$^{(\boxtimes)}$ and Hao Tan

School of Design, Hunan University, Changsha 410000, China
s220800508@hnu.edu.cn

Abstract. With the development of mobile communication technology and geographic information technology, in-vehicle navigation has become more and more intelligent and convenient, and has become an important aid for people's daily traveling. It is necessary to study how to make the navigation information more favorable for drivers to understand, and to improve the stability of driving and human-computer interaction experience. Auditory channel reminder is an important transmission channel, which is mainly realized by voice announcement. The information content, i.e., corpus wording, is an important dimension of speech announcing, and most current studies have been conducted from the perspective of wording complexity, with few studies on temporal and spatial information, but in navigation scenarios, spatio-temporal information is one of the key elements constituting human spatial cognition.

Existing studies have shown that a given spatial distance can be measured in either spatial or temporal units, and after constant velocity conversion, representing the same distance in spatial and temporal frames is logically equivalent, and although spatio-temporal frame effects affect people's willingness to travel, there are fewer studies on the impact on driving wayfinding behavior.

The findings suggest that different descriptions of spatial choice problems significantly change people's preference order. The study conducted an information framing study from the perspective of people's experiential preferences, which has significant potential from the perspective of human-computer co-development. The findings of the study can support the creation of new forms of choice information frames under different conditions to increase the efficacy of human-machine collaboration and improve the user experience.

Keywords: Navigation · Spatial-temporal Framework · Wording · Effect

1 Introduction

In the context of today's complex transportation networks and traffic environments, navigation systems have emerged to help people complete driving tasks more efficiently and conveniently. Moreover, they have become an essential tool for daily travel. Navigating while driving has become a common behavior in present driving scenarios. According to industry reports [1, 2], as of 2019, the user base of mobile map services in China has reached 755 million, with 92% of drivers actively using mobile navigation apps during

© The Author(s), under exclusive license to Springer Nature Switzerland AG 2024
P.-L. P. Rau (Ed.): HCII 2024, LNCS 14700, pp. 295–307, 2024.
https://doi.org/10.1007/978-3-031-60901-5_21

driving. Knapper et al. [3] collected natural driving data from 21 drivers over a month using cameras and sensors. Analysis of this data revealed that drivers used navigation devices for about 23% of their trips, indicating a significant reliance on navigation during travel.

The current methods of navigation information delivery primarily include a combination of visual and auditory channels, auditory channel, or visual channel. Auditory channel plays a vital role and is typically delivered through voice instructions. However, human cognitive and mental workload capacities (perception, analysis, decision-making, and execution) are inherently limited. Driving is a complex task that requires the coordinated use of visual, auditory, motor, and cognitive resources [4]. Frequently, drivers need to perform several concurrent driving tasks while also engaging in a considerable number of non-driving activities. Using navigation systems while driving undoubtedly consumes resources allocated for driving tasks, thereby impacting driving performance. Voice instructions as a key method of navigation information delivery and their content (i.e., the wording of instructions) have attracted widespread attention among scholars. Still, research has primarily focused on the complexity of the instructions and not much on the aspect of timing and spatial information, which are essential components of human spatial cognition in navigation scenarios.

Existing studies show that a given spatial distance can be measured using spatial or temporal units and, after conversion at a constant speed, representation of the same distance in spatial and temporal frameworks is logically equivalent: Describing a distance in a spatial framework (e. g., shopping a few kilometers away) and in a temporal framework (e. g., shopping a few dozen minutes' walk away) are descriptions of the same thing. Yet, different descriptions significantly change people's preferences, resulting in the time–space framing effect [5]. Although the time–space framing effect influences people's travel intentions, studies on its impact on driving navigation behavior are scarce.

Against this backdrop, this study will analyze the importance and role of timing and spatial information in navigation instructions, explore the impact of time–space framing effect on driving behavior, and investigate how to guide drivers more effectively in correct navigation by changing frames to enhance driving performance. This research aims to reveal the role and impact of the time–space framing effect on people's travel intentions and driving behavior, to help drivers better understand and respond to different situations. It will also provide theoretical support and practical guidance for the design of navigation systems and in-vehicle devices to improve the driving experience and safety.

2 Related Research

2.1 Human-Machine Interaction Issues in Navigation Driving Scenarios

Utilizing navigation for route-finding during driving is a classic case of human-machine collaboration to complete spatial tasks. With the development of technologies such as artificial intelligence and automation, the autonomy and intelligence of machines have gradually increased. Coordination and collaboration between humans and robots are inevitable. How to improve the efficiency of human-machine interaction is a key issue. Human-machine interaction generally includes three types of spatial tasks [6]: (1) locating a specified object, (2) placing an object at a designated location, and (3) navigating a machine to a specified position. To achieve higher interaction efficiency when humans and machines cooperate to complete spatial tasks, machines must possess spatial cognition abilities similar to humans. During human-machine collaboration, the exchange of spatial information is a form of spatial language interaction, belonging to natural language expression, with certain cognitive mechanisms. This process tests whether the information emitted by the machine conforms to human spatial cognition and also the human's ability to understand and analyze machine-generated information.

However, errors in the context of navigation driving are a common phenomenon. Simon [7] suggests that humans are "boundedly rational," meaning errors are always present. For example, misreading navigation prompts in unfamiliar traffic environments is often due to a series of internal psychological states when users are distracted or tense, combined with improper display of navigation prompts, causing difficulties in recognition or rapid understanding by the user. In fact, most human errors are not caused by irresponsible behavior but rather by poor design. From the perspective of human information processing and driving behavior, human errors can be divided into five categories: recognition errors, comprehension errors, planning errors, omission errors, and execution errors [8]. In the process of navigation driving, comprehension and omission errors are particularly prominent, with comprehension errors often being a matter of language design.

Furthermore, driving scenarios are complex and diverse. According to navigation industry standards such as Data classification and coding for navigation electronic map [9], Classification and codes for fundamental geographic information feature [10], and Data specification for road high definition navigation electronic map [11], we can identify over 1500 navigation driving scenarios, including left turns on city main roads, going straight on city side roads, and so on. Therefore, on the premise that research has confirmed that simple prompt messages are more understandable to drivers, the accuracy of the wording used in voice prompts is challenged. That is, whether the vocabulary usage in the broadcast sentences conforms to its correct semantic rhyme. Deviations in semantic rhyme have led to a series of comprehension errors, including those related to the content of spatial-temporal information.

2.2   The Time–Space Framing Effect

In classical physics, the concepts of time and space are absolute. We can discuss space without specifying time, for instance, when measuring the length of a geometric object without considering time. We can also discuss time without referring to space, such as describing two simultaneous events without involving the observer's location. Since space and time can be separated, they are considered independent, with space composed of three independent dimensions (e. g., an object moving along the x, y, z axes) and time consisting of one independent dimension.

Linguistically, phrases that describe time and space according to their respective dimensions constitute temporal and spatial information frameworks. In the field of computing, this results in the formation of space-time code matrices, which are essentially temporal-spatial frameworks.

Empirical research indicates that our mental representations of time and space are interrelated [12], and the spatial representation of numbers and temporal information is thought to be rooted in multisensory experiences [13]. Given that time is usually integrated into travel (i.e., traveling longer distances requires more time), the issues of spatial and temporal choice are not independent of each other [14].

While adults with strong mathematical abilities are less likely to be influenced by the time–space framing effect compared to those with weaker abilities [5, 15], because individuals with higher computational capabilities can more easily retrieve and use appropriate numerical principles and conversions compared to those with lower capabilities, according to Dual-process theory, human thinking and behavior are influenced by two different cognitive processes: intuitive and rational. The intuitive process is fast, automatic, effortless, implicit, and emotional, whereas the rational process is slow, conscious, effortful, explicit, and logical [16]. During driving, the driver needs to perceive changes in the environment and react quickly, which is an intuitive process. When adding the use of in-vehicle navigation, the driver's process of receiving navigation information requires rational processing, reflecting the complexity of navigation while driving.

Based on a series of studies, Kuang et al. [5] proposed a new type of framing effect, the time–space framing effect. It utilizes the conversion relationship between space and time to develop a spatial-temporal framework, extending the classic framing effect from the domain of risk choice to the domains of time and space selection, belonging to the general category of "nudging." In this research, Kuang et al. provided a series of proofs through experiments that seemingly trivial changes in the presentation of spatial choice problems (i. e., a given distance described by either a temporal or spatial framework) lead to significant preference shifts. However, in the everyday transfer of information in human-machine interaction, situations often arise where framing is combined, and the study does not compare single-factor frames with combined frames.

2.3 The Spatial-Temporal Framework in In-Vehicle Navigation Instructions

To facilitate the understanding of information by recipients, the broadcast content standards of navigation systems vary under different language systems. Yang Liping et al. [17] categorize the complexity based on the number of information units and divide voice information elements into "directional information," "directional information + road information," "distance information + directional information + road information," and "distance information + directional information + road information + lane information." However, in practical applications, in order to accurately describe spatial relationships, the expression of a certain type of information may be supplemented by a series of words to indicate the direction of a spatial displacement, which increases the potential for information transmission deviation. For example, the phrase "You will soon be entering the service road to the front right" contains "directional information" and "road information," but in expression, it is also explained with adverbs of time and verbs. In the Chinese language system, adverbs of time are a relatively abstract concept, easily leading to vague judgment and behavioral deviations in the listener.

At the same time, under different driving conditions (such as normal or emergency situations), existing navigation voice broadcasts can be classified and broadcasted according to different scenarios. That is, in different scenarios, the narrative style and language style of the voice broadcasts may differ.

Existing research on the time–space framing effect has analytically isolated spatial framework and temporal framework through virtual driving experiments. However, in the context of navigation driving, the two are integrated to form a complete dynamic description of space. The impact of different combined frames on the performance of drivers in navigation and whether the time–space framing effect will occur remains unknown.

2.4 Present Study

The purpose of this study is to test whether navigation broadcast information under different spatial-temporal frameworks can affect our common driving behaviors and judgments. In this study, we conducted a simulated driving experiment to investigate how navigation broadcast information under different spatial-temporal frameworks would influence drivers' experiences and efficiency. To replicate driving scenarios as closely as possible, we asked participants to drive their personal vehicles to a designated parking spot before commencing the simulated driving experiment. During the simulated driving experiment, participants were seated in the driver's seat of their own vehicles in a parked context. We prepared three video segments that were completed from the driver's first-person perspective with the task of "reaching the destination." The navigation broadcast information in the three video segments was based on different spatial-temporal frameworks. Participants were asked to watch the three standardized videos in a random order and then score them using a scale.

3 Method

3.1 Participants

All participants were recruited online through the questionnaire platform WJX (https:// www.wjx.cn/). The questionnaire consisted of several parts, including participants' basic personal information, fundamental driving-related information and operational behavior questions, questions unrelated to this study, and a section to express willingness to participate in the experiment. By default, participants who did not meet the basic information criteria, did not express their willingness, or failed to express their intention to participate in the experiment were automatically excluded by the WJX system, thus enhancing the statistical power and reliability of the online survey dataset. Among all the participants, 20 (66.7%) were male, and 10 (33.3%) were female, with an average age of 31 years. All participants had a clear understanding of the purpose of the experiment and received compensation upon completion.

3.2 Scenarios

The selection of scenarios was based on typical driving situations that drivers frequently encounter during their daily natural driving processes. Taking into account the typicality of the scenarios, the degree of relevance of existing navigational broadcast script content to the spatial-temporal framework for corresponding scenarios, as well as considerations for variable control, we ultimately chose "reaching the destination" as the final experimental scenario. This allowed experienced drivers to evaluate the navigational broadcast script content through the method of watching simulated driving videos.

3.3 Variables

In this study, the independent variable was the type of navigational broadcast script framework. We designed three different navigational broadcast contents based on the scripts used by Amap, a popular navigation software in China, for the scenario of "reaching the destination." These scripts were: "You will arrive at your destination in 140 m," "You will soon reach your destination," and "You will soon reach your destination in 140 m," representing temporal framework information, spatial framework information, and combined spatial-temporal framework information, respectively. By altering the spatial-temporal framework information in the navigational broadcast scripts, the user's driving experience is affected.

The dependent variable was user experience, which included seven dimensions: identifiability, understandability, executability, overall experience, perceived efficiency, experience, and perceived safety. Each dimension comprised several sub-indicators, measured in different ways. These indicators were assessed through scale scores and in-depth interviews.

3.4 Subjective Scales

We designed a voice experience questionnaire to evaluate the drivers' subjective perception of the navigation broadcast scripts in terms of identifiability, understandability, and executability.

Executability and overall experience were drawn from the user experience questionnaire by Laugwitz [18]. A 7-point Likert scale scoring was used to arrange the options as: strongly disagree, disagree, somewhat disagree, neutral, agree, somewhat agree, strongly agree, with corresponding scores of 1, 2, 3, 4, 5, 6, and 7, respectively.

Identifiability, perceived efficiency, and experience were taken from Polkosky's [19] speech interface usability scale, which also utilized a 7-point Likert scale with the options arranged as mentioned above and scored accordingly.

Understandability was derived from Hone's [20] Subjective Assessment of Speech System Interface (SASSI) tool, adopting the same 7-point Likert scale scoring method.

Perceived safety was referenced from Shi's [21] SURVEY ON AV & CAV questionnaire, which again used the 7-point Likert scale for the options and scoring as previously described.

In addition to extracting relevant questions from the above research questionnaires, we supplemented some questions according to the objectives of our experiment.

Furthermore, we conducted in-depth interviews, allowing participants to describe and evaluate the navigation broadcast scripts within the scenarios, to reflect their feelings and reactions to the script content. The main questions included: (a) Did you recognize the differences in script content between the three broadcasts? (b) How would you rate the three broadcast scripts? (c) Please tell us your most and least favorite broadcast scripts and why? (d) In the scenario of arriving at the destination, which aspects of information do you pay attention to? These questions aimed to understand their feelings towards the scripts under the spatial-temporal framework.

3.5 Procedure

Firstly, we will ask participants to fill out an informed consent form and provide them with written instructions about the experiment, informing them to pay attention to the navigation broadcast content while watching the simulation driving videos. After the participants have read the instructions and clearly understood the experiment, the experimenter will randomly play three video clips. After each video, participants will need to fill out a voice experience questionnaire, which takes about one minute to complete. Finally, we will conduct in-depth interviews and record the participants' responses to the designed questions (Fig. 1).

Fig. 1. Experimental Scenario

4 Data Analysis

In this study, we explored the impact of different spatial-temporal frameworks on drivers' experience scores. To systematically assess this impact, we designed an experiment with three independent groups, each representing a specific spatial-temporal framework setting. We hypothesized that these different spatial-temporal frameworks would have a significant effect on the drivers' experience scores. To test this hypothesis, we collected experience scores from drivers under each spatial-temporal framework condition and performed an Analysis of Variance (ANOVA).

ANOVA is a powerful statistical tool that allows us to detect whether there is a statistically significant difference in the average experience scores between different groups. In the ANOVA, we first checked the data for normality and homogeneity of variances to ensure that the basic assumptions of ANOVA were met. After confirming these assumptions, we conducted a one-way ANOVA, a test specifically used to compare mean differences among three or more independent samples. In this way, we could determine whether the drivers' experience scores were significantly affected under different spatial-temporal frameworks.

As shown in Table 1, spatial-temporal frameworks had a significant effect on drivers' experience scores, $F(2) = 10.454, p < 0.001$, indicating that there were significant differences in scores between different spatial-temporal frameworks, and that this effect was statistically significant. To ensure that the data analysis of our study accurately detected potential differences between treatment groups and provided specific and reliable statistical evidence, we selected the Tukey's LSD (Least Significant Difference) as our main post hoc analysis method.

Table 1. Analysis of Variance of Drivers' Experience Scores Under Different Spatial-Temporal Frameworks

ANOVA					
Source of Variation					
	Sum of Squares	Degrees of Freedom	Mean Square	F	P
Between Groups	20.885	2	10.442	10.454	<0.001
Within Groups	86.900	87	0.999		
Total	107.785	89			

As shown in Table 2, when comparing the spatial-temporal framework with the spatial framework, the mean difference (I-J) is -0.097, with a 95% confidence interval of $[-0.610, 0.416]$, and $p = 0.708 > 0.05$, which is not statistically significant. When comparing the spatial-temporal framework with the temporal framework, the mean difference (I-J) is 0.970, with a 95% confidence interval of $[0.457, 1.483]$, and $p < 0.001$, indicating that the difference between the spatial-temporal framework and the temporal framework is statistically significant, with the driver experience score in the spatial-temporal framework being significantly higher than that of the temporal framework. When comparing the spatial framework with the temporal framework, the mean difference (I-J) is 1.067, with a 95% confidence interval of $[0.554, 1.580]$, and $p < 0.001$, indicating that the difference between the spatial framework and the temporal framework is statistically significant, with the driver experience score in the spatial framework being significantly higher than that of the temporal framework.

In summary, we found significant differences between the spatial-temporal framework and the temporal framework, as well as between the spatial framework and the temporal framework. However, no statistically significant differences were observed

Table 2. Post Hoc Comparison of Drivers' Experience Scores Under Different Spatial-temporal Frameworks

Multiple Comparisons							
Dependent Variable: LSD	Mean Score						
(I) Semantic	(J) Semantic	Mean Difference (I-J)	Standard Error	P	95% Confidence Interval		
					Lower Bound	Upper Bound	
Spatial-temporal framework	spatial framework	−0.097	0.258	0.708	−0.610	0.416	
	temporal framework	.970[a]	0.258	<0.001	0.457	1.483	
spatial framework	spatial-temporal framework	0.097	0.258	0.708	−0.416	0.610	
	temporal framework	1.067[a]	0.258	<0.001	0.554	1.580	
temporal framework	spatial-temporal framework	−.970[a]	0.258	<0.001	−1.483	−0.457	
	spatial framework	−1.067[a]	0.258	<0.001	−1.580	−0.554	

between the other comparisons. Therefore, the application of the spatial-temporal framework and the spatial framework seems to have a positive impact on improving drivers' experience scores, with no significant differences between the two.

Figure 2 presents box plots for each treatment group, allowing for a visual examination of each group's median, quartiles, and potential outliers. As can be seen in Fig. 2, Group 3's median is significantly lower than that of Groups 1 and 2. Under the spatial-temporal framework, the 75th percentile is 6.000, indicating that 25% of all drivers scored above 6.000. The median is 5.000, meaning that half of all driver experience scores are below or equal to 5.000, and the other half are above or equal to this value. The 25th percentile is 4.000, showing that 75% of drivers scored above 4.000. The lower bound is 1.000, revealing that low scores do indeed exist in the rating system. When considering the spatial framework alone, the box plot data for driver experience scores have a distribution similar to that of the spatial-temporal framework, with identical statistical values, suggesting that in our sample, the distribution of driver experience ratings when only spatial factors are considered is very similar to that when both time and space are considered. This finding may indicate that under certain conditions, spatial factors could be the primary influence on driver experience. Under the temporal framework, the 75th percentile decreases to 6.000, the median drops to 4.000, and the 25th percentile further declines to 3.000. These changes in the data suggest that when considering only the temporal framework, the overall distribution of driver experience scores is skewed towards lower values. This could mean that the time factors have a different impact on driver experience compared to spatial factors, or that in our sample, drivers generally have lower satisfaction with the temporal framework than with the spatial framework.

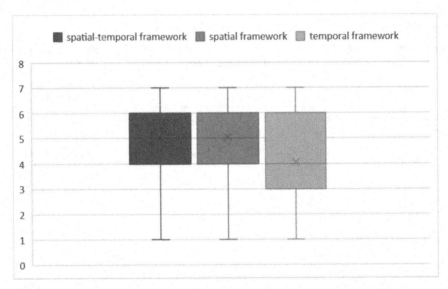

Fig. 2. Box Plots of Driver Experience Scores under Different Spatial-temporal Frameworks

By comparing the box plots under these three different frameworks, we find that the spatial framework may have a more significant impact on driver experience, whereas under the temporal framework, the scores for driver experience seem to be generally lower. Furthermore, the analysis of the box plots also indicates that variability in driver experience scores exists across the entire range of ratings.

5 Discussion

This study delves into the effects of various spatial-temporal frameworks on drivers' experience scores. Systematic experiments and data analysis revealed that the spatial-temporal framework and spatial framework were more effective in improving drivers' experience scores compared to the temporal framework alone. The results indicate that different spatial-temporal frameworks significantly influence drivers' experience scores. This discovery emphasizes the critical role of spatial-temporal framework in navigational information design, particularly regarding their impact on drivers' decision-making and actions.

From the depth interviews with participants, it emerged that the majority of drivers feel more reassured with clear spatial information rather than just temporal information. Nevertheless, some drivers provided feedback that "140 m" did not evoke a precise mental image, resulting in a vague spatial concept. "The message 'You will arrive at your destination in 140 m' feels robotic, though it offers a sense of security by accurately indicating the distance to the destination in a quantifiable way. However, the downside is my uncertainty about how far 140 m is. Commonly, time descriptions are used in daily life, like 'needing four to five minutes.' Such precision can lead to a somewhat negative experience for me; it doesn't feel personable," (participant14).

We also discovered that, in Chinese usage, the adverb "soon," as a time descriptor, can be colloquially softened to convey a concept of "approximately." Depending on different drivers' language habits, preferences for expressions within the spatial-temporal framework also vary. Some drivers believe that including the term "soon" allows for a margin of error in distance estimation. "In everyday life, we don't speak with high precision. For example, saying we're roughly 140 m from our destination gives a personified and warm feeling," said (participant14). Others, however, find "140 m later" and "soon" to be contradictory, affecting the driver's judgment of their proximity to the destination. "'140 m later' and 'soon' feel redundant, and upon closer examination, it's unclear whether it means one will arrive just after 140 m or if further driving is required," remarked (participant23).

In conclusion, although spatial framework and temporal-spatial framework scores are similar, related research [4] suggests that drivers better understand and execute simple auditory route information. This raises the question of whether, in practical applications, language information should be designed more succinctly.

6 Conclusion and Future Work

In our experiment, we investigated the effects of navigational announcements, representing different temporal-spatial frameworks, on drivers' experiences and choice preferences. The study found that the combined temporal-spatial framework and the spatial framework alone enhance drivers' experience scores more effectively than the temporal framework alone. This discovery emphasizes the importance of considering both temporal and spatial information in navigational information design, particularly when it involves route selection and decision-making processes. In navigation scenarios, drivers depend on quickly understanding and responding to verbal navigational cues, and therefore, the time–space framing effect significantly influences driving experience and stability.

Throughout the research process, we have identified questions that merit further exploration, such as whether the impact of temporal-spatial framework information on people's experiences and choice preferences remains consistent across different driving scenarios with variable distances. Additionally, we noted that many participants lacked a clear understanding of spatial distance, raising the question of whether the same type of temporal-spatial framework information should be used across various driving contexts.

We also acknowledge that despite the achievements of this study, there are limitations. The research was limited to a static temporal-spatial framework, while in real driving environments, temporal and spatial information is dynamic. To obtain more objective data, it would be necessary to include multiple physiological indicators as points of reference.

In summary, this study provides valuable insights for optimizing navigation information design and enhancing the driving experience. Future research could further expand

and deepen studies in this field to better meet drivers' needs and improve road traffic safety and efficiency.

Acknowledgements. This study was supported by the Natural Science Foundation of Hunan Province of China (No. 2023JJ30149).

References

1. Gonyn: 2022–2028 China mobile navigation industry panorama survey and market prospect forecast report (2022). https://bbs.csdn.net/topics/608363369
2. iiMedia: 2019 Q1 China mobile map market monitoring report (2019). https://www.iimedia.cn/c400/64147.html
3. Knapper, A., Nes, N.V., Christoph, M., et al.: The use of navigation systems in naturalistic driving. Traffic Inj. Prev. **17**(3), 264–270 (2016)
4. Walker, G.H., Stanton, N.A., Young, M.S.: Where is computing driving cars? Int. J. Hum. Comput. Interact. **13**(2), 203–229 (2001)
5. Kuang, Y., Huang, Y.N., Li, S.: A framing effect of intertemporal and spatial choice. Q. J. Exp. Psychol. **76**(6), 1298–1320 (2023)
6. Shi,Q., Yang, P., Chen, C.: Preference modeling of spatial description in human-robot interaction. In: 2020 IEEE International Conference on Networking, Sensing and Control (ICNSC), Nanjing, vol. 12, no. 2, pp. 1–7. IEEE (2020)
7. Simon, H.A.: The science of design: creating the artificial. Des. Issues **5**(3), 67–82 (1998)
8. Hao T., Yingli Z.: Safety-oriented intelligent vehicles information & interaction design research. In: 8th Art & Design, pp. 22–27. Tsinghua University Press, Beijing (2022). https://doi.org/10.16272/j.cnki.cn11-1392/j
9. General Administration of Quality Supervision, Inspection and Quarantine of the People's Republic of China & Standardization Administration of the People's Republic of China: Data classification and coding for navigation electronic map: GB/T 28442-2012[S], pp. 6–29 (2021)
10. State Administration for Market Regulation & Standardization Administration: Classification and codes for fundamental geographic information feature: GB/T 13923-2022[S], pp. 4–15 (2022)
11. Ministry of Natural Resources of the People's Republic of China: Data specification for road high definition navigation electronic map: CH/T 4026-2023[S], pp. 5–26 (2023)
12. Eikmeier, V., Schröter, H., Maienborn, C., Alex-Ruf, S., Ulrich, R.: Dimensional overlap between time and space. Psychon. Bull. Rev. **20**(6), 1120–1125 (2013)
13. Luca, R., Lotfi, B.M., Tomaso, V., Zaira, C.: The spatial representation of number, time, and serial order following sensory deprivation: a systematic review. Neurosci. Biobeh. Rev. **90**, 371–380 (2018)
14. Nelly, M., Jeffrey, R.S., Simon, M.R.: Spatial discounting of food and social rewards in guppies (Poecilia reticulata). Front. Psychol. **2**(9), 68 (2011)
15. Peters, E., Västfjäll, D., Slovic, P., et al.: Numeracy and decision making. Psychol. Sci. **17**(5), 407–413 (2006)
16. Ball, L., De Neys, W.: Dual Process Theory 2.0, vol. 9, no. 2, pp. 56–57 (2017)
17. Liping, Y., Yang, B., Xiaohua, Z., Yiping, W., Xiaoming, L.: Effects of navigation broadcast wording complexity on driving behaviors. J. South China Univ. Technol. (Nat. Sci. Edn.) (3), 139–148 (2021)

18. Laugwitz, B., Held, T., Schrepp, M.: Construction and evaluation of a user experience questionnaire. In: Holzinger, A. (ed.) USAB 2008. LNCS, vol. 5298, pp. 63–76. Springer, Heidelberg (2008). https://doi.org/10.1007/978-3-540-89350-9_6
19. Polkosky, M.D.: Toward a social-cognitive psychology of speech technology: affective responses to speech-based e-service (2005)
20. Hone, K.S., Graham, R.: Towards a tool for the subjective assessment of speech system interfaces (SASSI). Nat. Lang. Eng. **6**, 287–303 (2000)
21. Shi, X., Wang, Z., Li, X., et al.: The effect of ride experience on changing opinions toward autonomous vehicle safety. Commun. Transp. Res. **1**, 100003 (2021)

Investigating the Impact of Different Stressors on Trust in Intelligent Decision Support Systems

Xiangying Zou, Pei-Luen Patrick Rau$^{(\boxtimes)}$ (iD), and Yuehu Zhao

Department of Industrial Engineering, Tsinghua University, Beijing 100084, China
rpl@tsinghua.edu.cn

Abstract. AI-based intelligent decision support systems could enhance individuals' ability to handle emergencies, yet the impact of stressors arising from emergencies on human-AI trust remains inconclusive. This study aimed to investigate the impact of two stressors, time pressure and social pressure, on trust in Intelligent Decision Support Systems, taking into account the role of system reliability. The experimental task used the TNO trust task. Our findings indicated that neither time pressure nor social pressure significantly impacted individuals' trust in Intelligent Decision Support Systems, whether assessed subjectively or behaviorally. This finding was inconsistent with our hypothesis, and we discussed potential reasons for this unexpected result.

Keywords: Intelligent decision support system · Trust · Time pressure · Social pressure

1 Introduction

The advancements in artificial intelligence (AI) technology have endowed it with formidable capabilities in tasks such as recognition, search, and information organization. Effectively harnessing AI can enhance the productivity effect of human [1]. A study revealed that employees in the workplace express a desire for more AI, with data analysis and decision support being identified as the most beneficial tasks facilitated by AI [2]. In contrast to routine tasks, the appropriate application of AI-based intelligent decision support systems in a field with high risk and time pressure, such as emergency rescue, can yield greater assistance.

The utilization of AI by individuals is influenced by trust [3]. Research within AI-related domains indicates that trust affects both the reception of information provided by intelligent agencies and the willingness to adopt their recommendations [4]. Moreover, trust influences the usage frequency of automated systems [5]. This impact is not limited to general environments; in uncertain and risky contexts, trust similarly plays a crucial role. For instance, trust affects decision-making in uncertain environments [6], serving as the key determinant in whether or not to use intelligent assistive systems [7]. From a comprehensive perspective, trust governs the evolution of human-AI relationships [8]. Appropriate trust is crucial for enabling AI to effectively fulfill its role, as excessively

P.-L. P. Rau (Ed.): HCII 2024, LNCS 14700, pp. 308–320, 2024.
https://doi.org/10.1007/978-3-031-60901-5_22

high trust levels may result in overreliance, while excessively low trust levels may lead to abandonment [9].

Researchers have conducted extensive studies on the antecedents of trust in AI. They tend to categorize factors influencing trust into three dimensions: human-related factors, AI-related factors, and environment-related factors [3, 8, 10]. These dimensions further subdivide into numerous distinct factors, with reliability being identified as the most impactful factor, falling under the dimension of AI-related factors. Reliability serves as the foundation for trust formation and is the strongest predictor of trust [3, 11]. Generally, higher reliability corresponds to increased levels of trust in AI [10, 12, 13]. While environmental factors are acknowledged among the antecedents of trust, there is limited research on human-AI trust in emergencies.

In emergencies, rescue personnel commonly encounter high risks, time pressure, and uncertainty [14]. Individuals in such situations typically experience acute stress. During states of acute stress in humans, the hypothalamic-pituitary-adrenal (HPA) axis is activated in humans, leading to an increase in adrenal cortex hormone levels [15, 16]. Unlike normal states, the cognitive functions of individuals undergo alterations under stress, potentially altering the original state of human-AI trust. The cognitive impact of acute stress primarily manifests in memory and attention. Regarding attention, under acute stress conditions, individuals exhibit narrowed attention, focusing on stimuli perceived as most crucial or salient [17]. This state is accompanied by a reduction in attentional breadth [18], a decline in sustained attention [19], and the emergence of attentional bias [20]. In terms of memory, there is impaired retrieval of negative information from memory [21], a decrease in spatial working memory [19, 22], and diminished performance in working memory tasks requiring executive control [23]. The decrease in the amount of information individuals simultaneously consider during decision-making under acute stress [24] may be attributed to the decline in cognitive capabilities.

In addition to affecting cognitive functions, acute stress has been found to influence individuals' behavioral tendencies and patterns. For instance, in the Balloon Analogue Risk Task, acute stress induces a greater willingness in participants to take risks [25]. Moreover, stress not only diminishes individuals' goal-directed capabilities but also amplifies habitual behaviors, prompting a greater reliance on intuitive experiential systems and reinforcing existing cognitive biases [26]. The behavioral tendencies under acute stress manifest in interpersonal relationships as a bias in trust. Researchers have found that individuals exposed to stress exhibit reduced levels of trust [27], with stress levels showing a negative correlation with interpersonal trust [28]. However, conflicting results have also been reported [29]. The discrepancy in findings may be attributed to variations in the experimental tasks employed across studies. In the preceding two studies, experimental tasks were competitive, whereas, in the subsequent study, participants could gain more resources through cooperation. In emergencies, human-AI relationships tend to humans achieve better outcomes through AI assistance. From this perspective, trust in AI-based intelligent decision support systems is likely to increase under such circumstances.

While numerous studies on human-AI trust involve stressors, these studies either do not consider stressors as the primary factor or the stressors themselves are insufficient to induce physiological stress in individuals. Research examining risk as a stressor typically employs gambling as an experimental task [30], where the risk involved is usually associated with monetary loss. Even in cooperative tasks resembling urgent situations, the risk is framed as monetary loss [31]. Some studies also treat uncertainty as a form of risk [32]. However, the risks in these experiments lack genuine danger, and participants do not perceive a threat that would lead to physiological changes. Another stressor frequently explored in studies is time pressure. In these experiments, participants are usually tasked with completing specific assignments within a limited time frame. However, the allotted time under conditions of time pressure is often insufficient for task completion [33, 34]. The findings from these studies vary. In studies where risk is the stressor, trust in intelligent decision support systems generally decreases with increasing risk [32]. Conversely, in tasks with time pressure as the stressor, trust in intelligent decision support systems or robots tends to increase with rising time pressure [34, 35].

Interestingly, Robinette et al.'s emergency evacuation experiments yielded different results even under similar time pressure conditions [36, 37]. In their two experiments, participants were instructed by a robot to navigate to a meeting room in the first round. In the second round, a simulated fire occurred at the participant's location, requiring them to promptly locate an exit and evacuate the scene. These experiments aimed to assess participants' trust in the robot by evaluating whether they would follow the robot during evacuation. The procedures of the two experiments were generally similar, with the main distinction being that the first experiment was conducted using Virtual Reality (VR), while the second experiment took place in the physical environment using a real robot and introducing genuine smoke. Their findings revealed that in the VR experiment, if the robot led the participants astray in the first round, they were less likely to trust the robot in the second round [36]. In contrast, in real-world tasks, regardless of any prior instances of the robot leading participants off course, they tended to trust the robot [37]. The disparity in the results of these two experiments is likely attributable to differences in stress levels. The first experiment was conducted in a VR environment; participants were aware that the fire was simulated. Even though time constraints were imposed, the pressure generated by this time limitation may not have led to overt physiological changes due to the participant's awareness of the artificial nature of the stressor. Conversely, in the second experiment, participants believed the fire was real, and the sensation of confronting a genuine danger, coupled with uncertainty and time pressure, induced physiological changes, subjecting participants to an intense acute stress response.

In summary of the above research, it is found that various stressors lead to different trust. However, it remains unclear how distinct stressors influence trust. Despite variations in behavioral outcomes related to trust, physiological responses are similar among different stressors [16]. By exploring the impact of different stressors on trust, we aim to further understand the mechanisms underlying trust formation during acute stress.

In our study, we employed time pressure and social pressure as two stressors. On the one hand, time pressure is an unavoidable stressor in all emergencies, and it is easily manipulable in the experiment. On the other hand, though potentially less significant than factors like time pressure, uncertainty, and risk during emergencies, is inevitable for emergency responders who face societal expectations regarding successful rescue outcomes. Another reason for using social pressure is that the Trier Social Stress Test (TSST) is a very commonly used and mature technique for inducing acute stress in stress research, which can effectively induce stress response [38].

Prior research suggests that stressors tend to diminish cognitive abilities, potentially leading individuals to rely more on the recommendations of intelligent decision support systems when cognitive resources are insufficient [39]. From a cognitive bias perspective, acute stress in cooperative relationships between humans and AI may enhance prosocial tendencies, resulting in higher trust in intelligent decision support systems [29]. We hypothesize that acute stress, whether from time pressure or social pressure, will increase trust in intelligent decision systems.

Robinette et al.'s study found that stressors in VR conditions did not affect trust, whereas stressors in real environments influenced participants' final decisions [36, 37]. We speculate that the impact on trust becomes stronger with higher levels of acute stress, and the effects of different stressors may be cumulative. Therefore, we posit that under conditions involving two types of acute stress, trust in intelligent decision support systems will surpass all other conditions, while trust will be lowest in the without stressors.

We also considered the role of reliability, a critical factor influencing trust. Under acute stress conditions, cognitive abilities may decrease, potentially weakening the influence of reliability. We hypothesize that acute stress will reduce trust differences between high and low reliability.

In conclusion, our investigation delves into the impact of different stressors on trust in intelligent decision support systems, considering the role of reliability. We suggest that an increase in stressors enhances trust in intelligent assistance systems and attenuates trust differences arising from varying levels of reliability.

2 Methods

2.1 Participants

This study involved a total of 20 students from Tsinghua University, all of whom were informed about the experiment and consented to participate. Four participants were excluded from the data due to issues with the experimental procedures. Finally, data from 16 students were used in this study. There are 9 males and 7 females, with an average age of 24 (SD = 2.97).

2.2 Experiment Design

The study employed a $2 \times 2 \times 2$ mixed experimental design, with time pressure and social pressure serving as between-subject variables, and reliability as a within-subject variable. Time pressure had two conditions: with time pressure and without time pressure. Under the condition of time pressure, participants had only 3 s to make a choice; if no decision was made within this timeframe, the program would automatically proceed to the next step, and it was considered that the participant had not made a choice. Conversely, under the condition without time pressure, participants could deliberate extensively until confirming their choice. Reliability levels were determined based on previous research, with two levels: high (95%) and low (45%) [40]. It is crucial to note that, in this study, 95% reliability signifies that, out of 100 recommendations, the correct choice will be made 95 times. The order of reliability settings was balanced throughout the experiment. The dependent variables were subjective trust and behavioral trust. Subjective trust was participants' subjective evaluations of trust in the system after each trial, measured using a 9-point Likert scale. Participants were directly asked to what extent they trusted the recommendations of the system. Behavioral trust was the ratio of participants complying with the suggestions of the intelligent assistive system. Compliance is defined as when participants, faced with an inconsistency between their initial choice and the system's recommendation, alter their initial selection and adopt the advice of the intelligent assistive system.

2.3 Experimental Manipulation

TSST is a technology that creates acute stress. Participants who experience this situation not only show stress response in subjective assessment but also show significant physiological stress response [38]. Many studies have found that after TSST, the hypothalamic-pituitary-adrenal axis activities will change, and the hormone levels will change, such as the increase of cortisol in saliva [41].

We used a modified version of TSST, which includes 5 min of preparation time, 5 min of speech, and 5 min of mental arithmetic tasks. To assess the manipulation effect of TSST, we employed the Positive and Negative Affect Schedule (PANAS) scales [42]. The TSST process began with the participants arriving and being instructed to rest in room A. They were given 5 min to prepare a speech, defending themselves against an accusation of shoplifting, to be presented in front of the store manager and the police. After the preparation time, the experimenter escorted the participant to room B, where three experimenters in white coats were present. Upon arrival, one of the experimenters prompted the participants to start their speech, informed them of the 5-min time limit for the speech, and conveyed that recording was now to begin. If the participant completed the speech within 5 min, the experimenter reminded them, "You still have some time left. Please continue!" The speech had to last for the full 5 min. Following the speech, the participant engaged in a mental arithmetic task. This task required participants to start from 1022 and subtract 13 consecutively. If a participant made a mistake during the process, the experimenter would say, "Incorrect, start again from 1022." The mental arithmetic task had to last for 5 min. Throughout the entire process, the facial expressions of the three experimenters remained neutral [43].

2.4 Experimental Task

In our experiment, we utilized an adapted version of the TNO Trust Task [44]. This experimental paradigm had previously been employed to examine human reliance on intelligent decision support systems [40]. The task was a numerical sequence prediction task where participants were required to identify the pattern of the numerical sequence based on feedback. The numerical sequence employed in this task was a recurring 1-2-3-1-2, but to prevent participants from deducing the correct sequence, each digit in the sequence had a 20% chance of transforming into one of the other two digits. Each trial of the task asked participants to predict the next number in the sequence, choosing from 1, 2, or 3. After making their selection, participants received system advice. Subsequently, participants had to finalize their choice. Finally, participants were required to evaluate the level of trust in the system's recommendation using a single 9-point Likert scale. The process of a trial in the TNO Trust Task is illustrated in Fig. 1.

After every 5 trials, which constituted one block, participants received feedback on their performance in the preceding 5 trials. They were informed, "You have correctly predicted n times with the help of (the name of the intelligent system) in the previous five trials." It's important to note that participants only knew how many of their final choices were correct but were unaware of whether it was due to following or not following the system's recommendation.

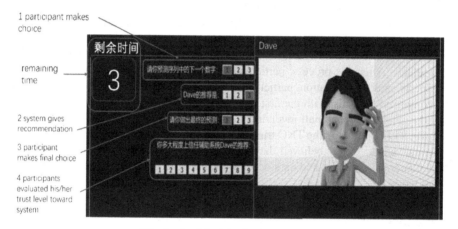

Fig. 1. A trial of the TNO Trust Task

In the experiment, there were a total of 80 trials, with 5 trials making up one block. Each reliability condition consisted of 8 blocks. After completing 8 blocks for one relia-bility condition, the experiment switched to another reliability condition. Each reliability condition was represented by a character with different appearances, as shown in Fig. 2. We did not disclose to participants the accuracy rate of the current intelligent deci-sion support system. Participants could only infer their perception of reliability through feedback given after every 5 trials. Subjective trust in the experiment was obtained by averaging subjective trust scores after each trial. Additionally, when participants faced time pressure, the top-left corner of the interface displayed the remaining time, while in the condition without time pressure, there was no content in the top-left corner of the interface.

2.5 Experimental Process

After the participants arrived at the laboratory, they initially read the experiment instruc-tions. In the absence of any questions, they proceeded to complete the informed consent

Fig. 2. The characters used in the experiment

form and furnish demographic information. Having signed the informed consent form, participants then proceeded to fill out the PANAS scale. Subsequently, they underwent experimental manipulation based on different groups. Participants in the social pressure group experienced the TSST, while those in the no social pressure group rested for five minutes. After this process, participants again filled out the PANAS scale. After the experimental manipulation, participants engaged in the TNO trust task. TNO Trust task comprised 80 trials, with the first half involving a system with, for example, 45% reliability, and the second half involving another system with a different reliability, for example, 95%. Following the TNO trust task, participants were asked to write down the numerical sequence they believed they encountered. They were then informed of the actual numerical sequence and their accuracy in the experiment. Participants received a reward based on their accuracy.

3   Results

3.1   Manipulation Check

We conducted a manipulation check on the TSST, and the results revealed that there was no significant difference in positive affect after experiencing the TSST ($M = 2.73$, $SD = 1.15$) compared to before the experience ($M = 2.89$, $SD = 0.94$), $t(7) = 1.03$, $p = 0.34$. However, negative affect after the TSST ($M = 2.44$, $SD = 0.79$) was significantly higher than before the experience ($M = 11.48$, $SD = 0.37$), $t(7) = 1.03$, $p = 0.006$. This outcome suggests that the manipulation in the experiment was successful.

3.2   Subjective Trust

The descriptive statistics for all independent variables regarding subjective trust are shown in Table 1.

We conducted a $2 \times 2 \times 2$ repeated measures analysis of variance (ANOVA) with subjective trust as the dependent variable, and the results are as follows:

Social Pressure. There was no significant main effect of social pressure, $F(1, 12) = 0.18$, $p = 0.68$, $\eta^2 = 0.02$.

Table 1. The descriptive statistics of subjective trust.

		social pressure		without social pressure	
		time pressure	without time pressure	time pressure	without time pressure
reliability	95%	5.31 (2.35)	6.33 (2.89)	6.48 (1.78)	6.58 (1.50)
	45%	5.31 (2.03)	3.89 (2.42)	4.44 (0.67)	4.78 (2.16)

n = 16, The values in parentheses are Mean (SD)

Time Pressure. There was no significant main effect of time pressure, $F(1, 12) = 0$, p $= 0.99$, $\eta^2 = 0$.

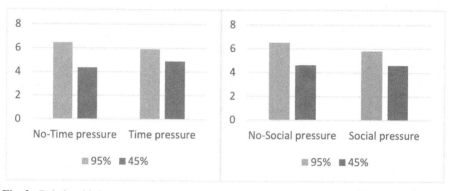

Fig. 3. Relationship between time pressure, social pressure, and system reliability, with subjective trust as the dependent variable

System Reliability. The main effect of system reliability was significant, $F(1, 12) = 6.92$, p $= 0.02$, $\eta^2 = 0.37$.

No significant 2-way or 3-way interactions were found.

Figure 3 illustrates the relationship between time pressure, social pressure, and system reliability.

3.3 Behavioral Trust

The descriptive statistics for all independent variables regarding behavioral trust are shown in Table 2.

We conducted a $2 \times 2 \times 2$ repeated measures analysis of variance (ANOVA) with behavioral trust as the dependent variable, and the results are as follows:

Social Pressure. There was no significant main effect of social pressure, $F(1, 12) = 0.16$, $p = 0.69$, $\eta^2 = 0.01$.

Time Pressure. There was no significant main effect of time pressure, $F(1, 12) = 0.43$, $p = 0.52$, $\eta^2 = 0.04$.

Table 2. The descriptive statistics of behavioral trust.

		social pressure		without social pressure	
		time pressure	without time pressure	time pressure	without time pressure
reliability	95%	0.59 (0.31)	0.73 (0.19)	0.88 (0.12)	0.75 (0.09)
	45%	0.51 (0.30)	0.36 (0.24)	0.43 (0.13)	0.41 (0.36)

n = 16, The values in parentheses are Mean (SD)

System Reliability. The main effect of system reliability was significant, $F (1, 12) = 32.23$, $p < 0.001$, $\eta^2 = 0.73$.

No significant 2-way or 3-way interactions were found. Figure 4 illustrates the relationship between time pressure, social pressure, and system reliability.

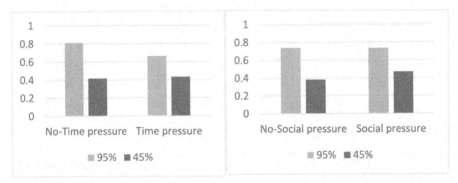

Fig. 4. Relationship between time pressure, social pressure, and system reliability, with behavioral trust as the dependent variable

4 Discussion

The purpose of this study is to explore the impact of different stressors on trust in intelligent decision support systems. Results of the manipulation check indicate the successful induction of acute stress through the TSST. However, our findings found that neither time pressure nor social pressure influences trust in intelligent decision support systems, whether in subjective or behavioral trust. We discuss the reasons for these results from various perspectives.

Firstly, in research examining the influence of time pressure on trust, many researchers have found that time pressure increases individuals' trust in decision support systems or automation [33–35]. However, in other studies, researchers did not observe the effect of time pressure [36]. The divergence may be attributed to differences in experimental paradigms. In the former studies, the experimental paradigm involved making choices within a short timeframe to determine whether to trust the recommendations of the decision support system. In contrast, the later experiments simulated scenarios where participants needed to find a safe exit from a burning room within a limited time. Although both scenarios involved time pressure, the latter was a single task with a longer time frame, allowing participants to think during the process of finding the exit without the need for immediate judgments. Thus, the impact of time pressure was relatively weaker compared to the former scenario.

The task in my experiment utilized the TNO Trust Task, which structurally resembled the former paradigm—making choices in a short timeframe. However, my results diverged from theirs. A significant reason for this discrepancy is that in tasks such as luggage inspection [34] or target diagnosis [35], participants could make correct judgments given sufficient time. In contrast, the TNO Trust Task involved random alterations to certain numbers to prevent participants from guessing the numerical sequences. Therefore, it is difficult for participants to make correct judgments, even if they have enough time. In situations where participants cannot make correct judgments independently, trust in intelligent decision support systems depends on their reliability. This also aligns with our finding that only the effect of system reliability is significant.

Secondly, in the examination of social pressure, prior research has indicated that tasks involving cooperation enhance trust [29], while tasks of a competitive nature diminish trust [27]. Our task aligns closely with cooperative tasks, yet the results diverge. The discrepancy may stem from the experimental setting, where the interactive agents are humans. In human-human interactions, prosocial behaviors tend to be more pronounced than in interactions between humans and robots [45]. One way to enhance people's prosocial behavior towards robots is to increase the anthropomorphism of the robot. However, the intelligent decision support systems used for interaction in our experiment did not exhibit strong anthropomorphic qualities, which could be a reason for the lack of impact from social pressure.

Both social pressure and time pressure independently failed to influence trust, and their combined impact did not yield higher trust. This suggests that the current experimental setup may not be suitable for studying human-AI trust mechanisms under acute stress. Future research needs to consider more details.

Thirdly, the main effect of system reliability is significant, consistent with previous research findings [11, 12]. Since the experimental paradigm used in this experiment is a task in which it is difficult for subjects to make correct judgments by themselves, and there is feedback on the results during the task, it is easy for subjects to perceive the differences in reliability and make judgments based on the differences in reliability. However, it's crucial to note that while stressors did not significantly narrow the trust gap caused by different reliabilities, there is an observable trend in the figure. With a relatively small number of participants in this study, this trend may become more pronounced with the inclusion of a larger sample.

Although this study does not obtain anticipated results, it lays the groundwork for future research. Through the observation of the experiment, we speculate that the trust of individuals under acute stress is probably the result of a rapid judgment of self and AI ability. Additionally, while the current results could be influenced by a limited number of participants, we also found some deficiencies in the experimental design and mechanism construction. In future research, we aim to enhance experimental design and propose potentially more comprehensive theories.

Disclosure of Interests. The authors have no competing interests to declare that are relevant to the content of this article.

References

1. Noy, S., Zhang, W.: Experimental evidence on the productivity effects of generative artificial intelligence. Science **381**, 187–192 (2023). https://doi.org/10.1126/science.adh2586
2. Employees Want More AI in the Workplace. https://www.snaplogic.com/resources/infograph ics/employees-want-more-ai-in-the-workplace. Accessed 30 Jan 2024
3. Kaplan, A.D., Kessler, T.T., Brill, J.C., Hancock, P.A.: Trust in artificial intelligence: meta-analytic findings. Hum. Factors **65**, 337–359 (2023). https://doi.org/10.1177/001872082110 13988
4. Freedy, A., DeVisser, E., Weltman, G., Coeyman, N.: Measurement of trust in human-robot collaboration. In: 2007 International Symposium on Collaborative Technologies and Systems, pp. 106–114 (2007). https://doi.org/10.1109/CTS.2007.4621745
5. Lee, J.D., See, K.A.: Trust in automation: designing for appropriate reliance. Hum. Factors **31** (2004)
6. Park, E., Jenkins, Q., Jiang, X.: Measuring trust of human operators in new generation rescue robots. In: Proceedings of the JFPS International Symposium on Fluid Power, pp. 489–492. The Japan Fluid Power System Society (2008)
7. Wang, M.E.: "We have to trust it, or else we can just throw it away": the use of decision support systems during extreme weather events (2018). https://www.duo.uio.no/handle/10852/63423
8. Hancock, P.A., Kessler, T.T., Kaplan, A.D., Brill, J.C., Szalma, J.L.: Evolving trust in robots: specification through sequential and comparative meta-analyses. Hum. Factors, 0018720820922080 (2020). https://doi.org/10.1177/0018720820922080
9. Parasuraman, R., Riley, V.: Humans and automation: use, misuse, disuse. Abuse Hum. Factors **39**, 230–253 (1997). https://doi.org/10.1518/001872097778543886
10. Schaefer, K.E., Chen, J.Y., Szalma, J.L., Hancock, P.A.: A meta-analysis of factors influencing the development of trust in automation: implications for understanding autonomy in future systems. Hum. Factors **58**, 377–400 (2016)
11. Hancock, P.A., Billings, D.R., Schaefer, K.E., Chen, J.Y., De Visser, E.J., Parasuraman, R.: A meta-analysis of factors affecting trust in human-robot interaction. Hum. Factors **53**, 517–527 (2011)
12. Chavaillaz, A., Wastell, D., Sauer, J.: System reliability, performance and trust in adaptable automation. Appl. Ergon. **52**, 333–342 (2016)
13. Ross, J.M., Szalma, J.L., Hancock, P.A., Barnett, J.S., Taylor, G.: The effect of automation reliability on user automation trust and reliance in a search-and-rescue scenario. In: Proceedings of the Human Factors and Ergonomics Society Annual Meeting, pp. 1340–1344. Sage Publications Sage CA, Los Angeles, CA (2008)
14. Klein, G.: Sources of Power: How People Make Decisions. MIT Press, Cambridge, MA (2017)
15. Ming-Ming, Q.I., Qing-Lin, Z., Li-Li, G., Juan, Y.: Neuroendocrine response and its mediators induced by acute psychosocial stress. Adv. Psychol. Sci. **19**, 1347 (2011)
16. Qun, Y., Yu, L.I., Sun, D., Lee, T.M.: The effects of stress on risky and social decision making. Adv. Psychol. Sci. **24**, 974 (2016). https://doi.org/10.3724/SP.J.1042.2016.00974

17. Staal, M.A.: Stress, Cognition, and Human Performance: A Literature Review and Conceptual Framework. Citeseer (2004)
18. Baddeley, A.D.: Selective attention and performance in dangerous environments*. Br. J. Psychol. **63**, 537–546 (1972). https://doi.org/10.1111/j.2044-8295.1972.tb01304.x
19. Olver, J.S., Pinney, M., Maruff, P., Norman, T.R.: Impairments of spatial working memory and attention following acute psychosocial stress. Stress. Health **31**, 115–123 (2015). https://doi.org/10.1002/smi.2533
20. Luo, Y., Gao, P., Zhao, S., Zhang, Y.: How acute stress affects attentional engagement and attentional disengagement towards threat: a neural mechanism study. Adv. Psychol. Sci. **25**, 381 (2017). https://doi.org/10.3724/SP.J.1042.2017.00381
21. Smeets, T.: Acute stress impairs memory retrieval independent of time of day. Psychoneuroendocrinology **36**, 495–501 (2011). https://doi.org/10.1016/j.psyneuen.2010.08.001
22. Bogdanov, M., Schwabe, L.: Transcranial stimulation of the dorsolateral prefrontal cortex prevents stress-induced working memory deficits. J. Neurosci. **36**, 1429–1437 (2016). https://doi.org/10.1523/JNEUROSCI.3687-15.2016
23. Schoofs, D., Wolf, O.T., Smeets, T.: Cold pressor stress impairs performance on working memory tasks requiring executive functions in healthy young men. Behav. Neurosci. **123**, 1066–1075 (2009). https://doi.org/10.1037/a0016980
24. Leder, J., Häusser, J.A., Mojzisch, A.: Stress and strategic decision-making in the beauty contest game. Psychoneuroendocrinology **38**, 1503–1511 (2013). https://doi.org/10.1016/j.psyneuen.2012.12.016
25. Reynolds, E.K., Schreiber, W.M., Geisel, K., MacPherson, L., Ernst, M., Lejuez, C.W.: Influence of social stress on risk-taking behavior in adolescents. J. Anxiety Disord. **27**, 272–277 (2013). https://doi.org/10.1016/j.janxdis.2013.02.010
26. Morgado, P., Sousa, N., Cerqueira, J.J.: The impact of stress in decision making in the context of uncertainty. J. Neurosci. Res. **93**, 839–847 (2015). https://doi.org/10.1002/jnr.23521
27. Steinbeis, N., Engert, V., Linz, R., Singer, T.: The effects of stress and affiliation on social decision-making: investigating the tend-and-befriend pattern. Psychoneuroendocrinology **62**, 138–148 (2015). https://doi.org/10.1016/j.psyneuen.2015.08.003
28. Takahashi, T.: Social memory, social stress, and economic behaviors. Brain Res. Bull. **67**, 398–402 (2005). https://doi.org/10.1016/j.brainresbull.2005.06.006
29. von Dawans, B., Fischbacher, U., Kirschbaum, C., Fehr, E., Heinrichs, M.: The social dimension of stress reactivity: acute stress increases prosocial behavior in humans. Psychol. Sci. **23**, 651–660 (2012). https://doi.org/10.1177/0956797611431576
30. Elder, H., Canfield, C., Shank, D.B., Rieger, T., Hines, C.: Knowing when to pass: the effect of AI reliability in risky decision contexts. Hum. Factors **66**, 348–362 (2024). https://doi.org/10.1177/00187208221100691
31. Satterfield, K., Baldwin, C., de Visser, E., Shaw, T.: The influence of risky conditions in trust in autonomous systems. Proc. Hum. Factors Ergon. Soc. Annu. Meet. **61**, 324–328 (2017). https://doi.org/10.1177/1541931213601562
32. Perkins, L., Miller, J.E., Hashemi, A., Burns, G.: Designing for human-centered systems: situational risk as a factor of trust in automation. Proc. Hum. Factors Ergon. Soc. Annu. Meet. **54**, 2130–2134 (2010). https://doi.org/10.1177/154193121005402502
33. Rieger, T., Manzey, D.: Understanding the impact of time pressure and automation support in a visual search task. Hum. Factors, 00187208221111236 (2022). https://doi.org/10.1177/00187208221111236
34. Rieger, T., Manzey, D.: Human performance consequences of automated decision aids: the impact of time pressure. Hum. Factors **64**, 617–634 (2022). https://doi.org/10.1177/0018720820965019
35. Rice, S., Keller, D.: Automation reliance under time pressure. Cogn. Technol. **14**, 36–44 (2009)

36. Robinette, P., Howard, A.M., Wagner, A.R.: Effect of robot performance on human–robot trust in time-critical situations. IEEE Trans. Hum.-Mach. Syst. **47**, 425–436 (2017). https://doi.org/10.1109/THMS.2017.2648849
37. Robinette, P., Li, W., Allen, R., Howard, A.M., Wagner, A.R.: Overtrust of robots in emergency evacuation scenarios. In: 2016 11th ACM/IEEE International Conference on Human-Robot Interaction (HRI), pp. 101–108 (2016). https://doi.org/10.1109/HRI.2016.7451740
38. Kirschbaum, C., Pirke, K.-M., Hellhammer, D.H.: The 'Trier Social Stress Test'–a tool for investigating psychobiological stress responses in a laboratory setting. Neuropsychobiology **28**, 76–81 (1993)
39. Sato, T., Yamani, Y., Liechty, M., Chancey, E.T.: Automation trust increases under high-workload multitasking scenarios involving risk. Cogn. Technol. Work **22**, 399–407 (2020). https://doi.org/10.1007/s10111-019-00580-5
40. Zou, X., Lv, C., Zhang, J.: The effect of group membership, system reliability and anthropomorphic appearance on user's trust in intelligent decision support system. In: Harris, D., Li, W.-C. (eds.) Engineering Psychology and Cognitive Ergonomics. Cognition and Design. LNCS (LNAI), vol. 12187, pp. 231–242. Springer, Cham (2020). https://doi.org/10.1007/978-3-030-49183-3_18
41. Yang, J., Zhang, Q.-L.: The introduction and the development of 'Trier Social Stress Test.' Adv. Psychol. Sci. **18**, 699–704 (2010)
42. Watson, D., Clark, L.A., Tellegen, A.: Development and validation of brief measures of positive and negative affect: the PANAS scales. J. Pers. Soc. Psychol. **54**, 1063–1070 (1988). https://doi.org/10.1037/0022-3514.54.6.1063
43. Lin, L., Wu, J., Yuan, Y., Sun, X., Zhang, L.: Working memory predicts hypothalamus-pituitary-adrenal axis response to psychosocial stress in males. Front. Psychiatry **11** (2020). https://doi.org/10.3389/fpsyt.2020.00142
44. de Visser, E.J., et al.: Almost human: anthropomorphism increases trust resilience in cognitive agents. J. Exp. Psychol. Appl. **22**, 331–349 (2016). https://doi.org/10.1037/xap0000092
45. Nijssen, S.R.R., Heyselaar, E., Müller, B.C.N., Bosse, T.: Do we take a robot's needs into account? The effect of humanization on prosocial considerations toward other human beings and robots. Cyberpsychology Behav. Soc. Netw. **24**, 332–336 (2021). https://doi.org/10.1089/cyber.2020.0035

Author Index

P.-L. P. Rau (Ed.): HCII 2024, LNCS 14700, pp. 321–322, 2024.
https://doi.org/10.1007/978-3-031-60901-5

Printed in the United States
by Baker & Taylor Publisher Services